CONFORMITY OF GOODS AND DOCUMENTS

This book provides a detailed examination of the issue of conformity of goods and documents under the United Nations Convention on Contracts for the International Sale of Goods 1980 (CISG). This issue lies at the heart of sales law and is one of the most frequently litigated. The book explores the Convention's requirements as to quality, quantity, description and packaging of the goods (conformity); the requirements flowing from the need for the goods to be free from rights or claims of third parties; and the questions of what documents the seller must deliver to the buyer and what constitutes a 'good' document under the CISG. The book engages extensively with a substantial body of cases decided under the CISG and academic commentary. It systematises the Convention's experience to date with a view to turning it into an integrated, comprehensive and distinctive CISG legal regime on conformity of goods and documents. The analysis is comparative and draws on the experience of some major domestic legal systems, such as English and US law. The focus is both analytical and practical. The book will be of interest to legal practitioners, academic lawyers and students with an interest in international and comparative sales, commercial and contract law.

Conformity of Goods and Documents

The Vienna Sales Convention

Djakhongir Saidov

·HART·
PUBLISHING
OXFORD AND PORTLAND, OREGON
2015

Published in the United Kingdom by Hart Publishing Ltd
16C Worcester Place, Oxford, OX1 2JW
Telephone: +44 (0)1865 517530
Fax: +44 (0)1865 510710
E-mail: mail@hartpub.co.uk
Website: http://www.hartpub.co.uk

Published in North America (US and Canada) by
Hart Publishing
c/o International Specialized Book Services
920 NE 58th Avenue, Suite 300
Portland, OR 97213-3786
USA
Tel: +1 503 287 3093 or toll-free: (1) 800 944 6190
Fax: +1 503 280 8832
E-mail: orders@isbs.com
Website: http://www.isbs.com

Hart Publishing is an imprint of Bloomsbury Publishing plc.

British Library Cataloguing in Publication Data
Data Available

ISBN: 978-1-84946-155-9

Typeset by Compuscript Ltd, Shannon

For Sanam and Anora,
Malika and Amina

Preface

The UN Convention on Contracts for the International Sale of Goods (also known as the Vienna Sales Convention or the CISG) is one of the most successful international commercial law instruments and represents a leading international sales law today. There is a substantial body of cases decided under the CISG and a great deal of scholarly commentary has been written on its various aspects. There is no doubt therefore that the law of the Vienna Sales Convention represents an area of commercial law and a legal discipline in its own right. Despite a considerable amount of academic writing on the CISG, much work is still to be done by the legal community to reflect on and strengthen the Convention's experience and to promote an understanding of its regime. The Convention faces a number of challenges which include its difficult path towards uniform application and numerous uncertainties surrounding the interpretation and application of its various provisions. This book seeks to contribute to meeting these challenges in the context of a specific issue of the seller's obligations in respect of conformity of goods and documents. The specific provisions of the CISG covered in this examination are primarily those relating to quality, quantity, description and packaging of the goods (Article 35) and those flowing from the need for the goods to be free from rights or claims of third parties (Articles 41 and 42). The book also explores the question of what documents the seller must deliver to the buyer and what constitutes a 'good' document.

These issues are important, both practically and in terms of the complexity of the required legal analysis. The book is based on the view that the Convention cannot be adequately understood if its experience is not brought out and analysed fully. This, in turn, requires a detailed focus and study of its key areas. This detailed study will help to understand the specific issues under consideration, but it will also reveal insights of broader significance to the Convention as a whole and possibly even to other sales laws. The book systematises and analyses the Convention's experience to date with a view to turning it into an integrated, comprehensive and distinctive legal regime on conformity of goods and documents. The goal is to construct a regime which rests on strong and sound analytical foundations and is practically relevant and effective.

I owe a debt of gratitude to many people who, in different ways, have helped me with this project. I wish to thank several generations of LLB and LLM students on the international sales law courses in the Birmingham Law School. It is the discussions with them that gave birth to this book and refined my understanding of the issues covered in it. I am very grateful to the following colleagues who have kindly commented on various draft chapters: Steven Hazelwood, Stephen Girvin, Nelson Enonchong, Martin Trybus, Sanam Saidova, Kim Barker and Tina Martin. Special thanks go to Linda Sellami, an LLM student, who has so helpfully translated a number of decisions on the CISG in German language. I am also very grateful to Hart Publishing for its support for this project. Finally, I must say thank you to my family for their never ending patience and support.

The book is based on the materials that were available to me as at 31st of August 2014.

Djakhongir Saidov
5 January 2015

Contents

Preface vii
Table of Cases xiii
Table of Legislation xxv

1. Introduction 1
I. A Brief Introduction to the CISG 1
II. The CISG Today and the Purpose and Scope of this Book 7
III. Rules on Conformity of the Goods: Underlying Considerations 10
IV. The Seller's Liability and the Buyer's Remedies 14
V. Conformity of Goods and Documents: Broader Insights into the CISG 17
A. General 17
B. Is the CISG a Well-Developed Sales Law? 17
C. Developing Substantive Content Within a 'Minimalist' Structure 19
D. Is the CISG the Best Law for International Sales? 20
E. Defining the Boundaries of the CISG 22
(i) General 22
(ii) Proof 22
(iii) Validity 25

2. Contractual Provisions on Conformity of the Goods 29
I. General 29
II. Pre-contractual Representations and Conduct 31
A. Puffery and Opinions 31
B. Public Statements 35
C. Direct Communications Between the Parties 37
D. Buyer's Knowledge 38
III. Post-contractual Statements and Conduct 41
IV. Description 43
V. Quality 49
A. Definition 49
B. Various Formulations of Quality Standards 50
C. Industry or Public Law Standards 52
D. Legislative Changes and/or Knowledge Acquired Subsequent to the Contract 57
E. Guarantee and Durability 59
F. Quantity and Packaging 64

3. Fitness for a Particular Purpose 68
I. Legal Nature of the Implied Rules on Conformity 68
II. Fitness for a Particular Purpose: General Considerations 70
III. Relationship with Article 35(1) CISG 72
IV. Defining a Particular Purpose 74
V. Conditions in a Specific Place 80
A. Public Law Regulations 80
B. Industry Standards and Standards Adopted by Private Entities and Trade Associations 86
C. Climatic and Other Conditions 89
VI. Durability 90
VII. Making Known 92
VIII. Reliance on the Seller's Skill and Judgement 96
IX. Proof 102
A. Burden of Proof 102
B. Standard of Proof 103
C. Admissibility of Evidence 105

4. Fitness for Ordinary Use 110
I. General 110
II. Does Article 35(2)(a) CISG Imply a Certain Level of Quality? 111
A. Does Article 35(2)(a) CISG Require an Inquiry into the Notion of Quality? 111
B. Different Quality Tests: The Debate 112
III. Ordinary use 119
IV. Description 125
V. Durability 126
VI. Health and Safety 128
VII. Instructions, Manuals and Labels 129
VIII. Servicing and Spare Parts 132
IX. Minor Defects, Appearance and Finish 132
X. Public Law Regulations 134
A. Informational Asymmetry and Guidelines in *New Zealand Mussels* 134
B. Imperative of a Case-by-Case Analysis 138
C. Changes to Public Law Regulations and Other Related Changes Subsequent to the Time of Assessing Conformity 140
D. Legal Nature of Public Law Regulations and the Reality of their Enforcement 142
E. Is Article 35(2)(b) CISG Better Suited than Article 35(2)(a) to Deal with the Case of Public Law Regulations? 144
XI. Proof 145

5. Conformity with a Sample or Model and Packaging; Exemptions from Liability 147
I. Conformity with a Sample or Model 147
A. General 147
B. How Far is a Sample or Model Allowed to 'Speak'? 153
C. Relationship with Contractual Provisions and Other Terms Implied under the Convention 155
D. Public Law Regulations 158
E. Proof 159
II. Packaging 160
A. General 160
B. Usual Manner 162
C. 'Adequate Manner' 164
D. Defective Packaging with Goods being Otherwise Conforming 167
E. Proof 168
III. Exemptions from Liability 170
A. Buyer's Knowledge 170
(i) General 170
(ii) Actual Knowledge 173
(iii) Implied Knowledge 174
B. Article 39 CISG 180
C. Disclaimers 181

6. Third Parties' Rights or Claims in Respect of the Goods (Article 41 CISG) 186
I. General 186
II. Third Parties' Rights 189
III. Third Parties' Claims 193
IV. Relevant Time 196
V. Freedom of the Goods from a Third Party's Right or Claim 198
VI. Seller's Rights or Claims 200
VII. Exemptions 202
A. Buyer's Agreement 202
B. Buyer's Notice 204
C. Exclusion Clause 205
VIII. Domestic Rules on Validity 206

7. Third Parties' Rights or Claims Arising from Intellectual Property (Article 42 CISG) 208
I. General 208
II. Industrial or Other Intellectual Property 210
III. Rights or Claims 213

A. General ... 213
B. Frivolous Claims ... 216
C. Relevant Time ... 218
D. Seller's Knowledge ... 218
IV. Territorial Restrictions ... 222
V. Exemptions from Liability ... 225
A. Buyer's Knowledge ... 225
B. Compliance with the Buyer's Specifications ... 228
C. Other Exemptions ... 231
VI. Burden of Proof ... 231
VII. Concluding Observations ... 232
VIII. Freedom from Third Parties' Rights or Claims: an Aspect of 'Conformity'? ... 234

8. Conformity of Documents ... 237
I. Introduction ... 237
II. Typical Documents: An Overview ... 238
A. Transport Documents ... 238
B. Other Documents ... 244
III. Conformity of Documents ... 247
A. Documentary and 'Physical' Obligations ... 247
B. What Documents Must the Seller Deliver? ... 248
C. Conformity of Documents ... 255
(i) Transport Documents: Contractual Requirements ... 255
(ii) Transport Documents: Contractual Silence ... 257
(iii) Other Documents ... 262
IV. Quality, Quantity, Origin and Other Certificates: Conformity and Beyond ... 263
A. General ... 263
B. Conformity ... 264
C. Finality Clause ... 268
D. Certificate as Extra-contractual Documentary Evidence ... 270
V. Emerging Themes ... 272
A. Is the CISG a Construction Site for Documentary Duties? ... 272
B. Assessing Conformity: Face of Documents versus Extrinsic Factual Inquiry ... 273
C. Attack on Party Autonomy and Legal Certainty ... 274
D. Documentary Performance and the Future of the CISG ... 274

Index ... 276

Table of Cases

National

Argentina

Appellate Court
31 October 1995 .... 63, 127
24 April 2000 .... 106, 109
21 July 2002 106
Commercial Appellate Court, 31 October 1995 250

Australia

Australian Knitting Mills Ltd v Grant(1933) 50 CLR 387 114
Castel Electronics Pty Ltd v Toshiba Singapore Pte Ltd [2011] FCAFC 55 .... 170, 174
Cortem SpA v Controlmatic Pty Ltd [2010] FCA 852 .... 53, 85
Fryer Holdings v Liaoning MEC Group [2012] NSWSC 18 .... 115, 121, 123
Ginza Pte Ltd v Vista Corporation Pty Ltd [2003] WASC 11 .... 52, 120
Healing (Sales) Pty Ltd v Inglis Electrix Pty [1969] ALR 533 201

Austria

Appellate Court Graz
6 R 194/95, 9 November 1995 .... 50, 152–3
5 R 62/13x, 19 June 2013 .... 94, 119
Appellate Court Linz, 1 R 206/11m, 8 February 2012 268
Supreme Court
10 Ob 518/95, 6 February 1996 193
2 Ob 191/98x, 15 October 1998 249
10 Ob 344/99g, 21 March 2000 249
2 Ob 100/00w, 13 April 2000 .... 81, 84, 134–6
2 Ob 48/02a, 27 February 2003 151
10 Ob 122/05x, 12 September 2006 .... 214, 226, 231
6 Ob 56/07i, 19 April 2007 92
Vienna Agricultural Exchange Arbitration Tribunal, 10 December 1997 269

Belgium

Appellate Court Antwerp
2001/AR/1737, 16 December 2002 .... 11, 145
AR 2006/AR/384, 22 January 2007 61
Appellate Court Ghent
2003/AR/2763, 4 October 2004 .... 131, 220
2006/AR/477, 16 April 2007 220

Commercial Court Hasselt
AR 05/4177
15 February 2006 79
19 April 2006 .... 79, 154
District Court Veurne, A/00/00665, 25 April 2001 .... 110, 121

Canada

Brown & Root Services Corp v Aerotech Herman Nelson Inc, 2002 MBQB 229, 2004 MBCA 63 36
Dunn Paving Ltd v Aerco Trading Inc [2001] OJ No 1736 151
La San Giuseppe v Forti Moulding Ltd [1999] OJ No 3352 133
Mansonville Plastics (BC) Ltd v Kurtz GmbH, 2003 BCSC 1298 .... 34, 133

China

Dalian Maritime Court, 29 June 2005 .... 256, 261, 265
Fujian High People's Court, Minjingzhongzi No 123, December 1994 104
Guangxi Beihai Maritime Court, (2001) Haishangchuzi No 119, 5 March 2002 189
New Pudong District People's Court of Shanghai, (2004) Pu Min Er (Shang) Chu Zi Di No 3221, 23 September 2005 261
Wuhan Economic and Technology Development Zone People's Court, Hubei Province, 30 June 2000 .... 162, 165
Wuhan Maritime Court, Hubei, (2000) Wu Hai Fa Shang Zi Di No 91, 10 September 2002 .... 250, 256
China International Economic and Trade Arbitration Commission (CIETAC)
23 February 1995 256
Agricultural Products, 18 September 1996 .... 65, 151, 160
Art Paper, 25 June 1997 263
Automobiles, 23 April 1997 47
Beech Log, 4 November 2002 .... 51, 266
BOPP Film, 8 September 1997 67
Broadcasting Equipment, 22 May 1996 .... 42, 73
Canned Asparagus, 8 November 2002 262
Channel Steel, 23 October 1996 73
Chemical Cleaning Product Equipment, 20 April 1999 42
Clothes, 3 June 2003 .... 115, 121
Coating Equipment, 15 July 2002 60
Cotton Bath Towel, 26 October 1996 .... 120, 271
Cow's Liver Fungus, 30 March 1994 167–70
Cysteine, 7 January 2000 271
Down Jacket and Winter Coat, 22 March 1995 .... 46–7, 121, 123
Engines, 6 September 1996 .... 46, 271
Fiberglass Mesh, 6 November 2003 150
Fishmeal, 1 April 1997 .... 258, 262
Flexo Label Printing Machine, 24 July 2007 .... 262, 265
Fluorite, February 2006 .... 256, 269–70

Gloves, 28 September 1996 .... 256, 260, 263, 267
Granite and Marble, July 2006 42
Health Supplement, 25 September 1998 .... 65, 162, 168
Heliotropin, 10 July 1993 .... 148, 154, 158, 160, 272
Hot-rolled Coils, 27 October 1997 .... 52, 184
Hot-rolled Steel Plates, 16 July 1996 .... 52, 65
Hydraulic Press, 20 January 1994 177
Hydraulic Press, 23 December 2002 .... 104, 145
Hydraulic Pressure Geologic Equipment, 12 September 2005 271
Industrial Raw Material, 4 June 1999 258
Isobutanol, 7 July 1997 262
Italian Textile Machine, June 2006 41
Leather Gloves, 26 November 1998 104
Linseed Cake, 9 January 1993 .... 42, 52, 184, 250, 271
Old Boxboard Corrugated Cartons, 8 March 1996 .... 47, 265
Old Paper, 11 April 1994 .... 250, 256
Piperonal Aldehyde, 1999 60
Polypropylene, 23 July 1997 267
Pork, 24 February 2005 257
PTA Powder, 18 April 2008 .... 62, 272
PVC Suspension Resin, 7 April 1999 .... 46, 66, 249
Raincoat, 10 August 1999 .... 249, 270
Rebar Coil, 20 November 1997 46
Shirt, 15 December 1998 270
Souvenir Coins, 2000 .... 48, 156
Spare Parts, September 2006 256
Steel Cylinders, 19 January 2000 .... 47, 265
Textile Manufacturing Equipment, 18 July 2002 .... 51, 97, 125
Water Pump, 3 August 2006 148
Wool, 27 February 1996 250

Czech Republic

Supreme Court, 32 Odo 725/2004, 29 March 2006 .... 61, 184

Denmark

Copenhagen Maritime Commercial Court, H-0126-98, 31 January 2002 47
District Court Copenhagen, 19 October 2007 40
Supreme Court, U.2006.2210H, 3 May 2006 183

Finland

Appellate Court Helsinki
S 96/1129, 29 January 1998 .... 41, 93
S 01/269, 31 May 2004 .... 62, 122
Appellate Court Turku
S 97/324, 12 November 1997 38
S 04/1600, 24 May 2005 56
Tampere Court of First Instance, 95/11193, 17 January 1997 38

France

Appellate Court Aix-en-Provence, 2005/377, 1 July 2005 121
Appellate Court Colmar, 1B 98/01776, 13 November 2002 227
Appellate Court Grenoble
93/4879, 26 April 1995 92
93/4126, 13 September 1995 .... 85, 164
Appellate Court Lyon, 01/02620, 18 December 2003 93
Appellate Court Paris, 95-018179, 13 December 1995 134
Appellate Court Rouen
1998/710, 17 February 2000 .... 213, 227
05/03275, 19 December 2006 121
Arbitration Chamber of Paris, Case No 9926, 2007 .... 95, 173, 176
District Court Besançon, 97 009265, 19 January 1998 126
District Court Versailles, 01/08276, 23 November 2004 .... 213, 225–6
Supreme Court
T 00-14.414, Arrêt no 526 F-P, 19 March 2002 .... 213, 227
1312 FS-P; 01-16107 D, 24 September 2003 .... 165, 169
07-11803, 16 September 2008 121

Germany

Appellate Court Celle, 10 March 2004 220
Appellate Court Dresden, 9 U 1218/06, 21 March 2007 .... 187, 189, 205
Appellate Court Düsseldorf, 17 U 110/02, 23 January 2004 220
Appellate Court Koblenz
2 U 923/06, 14 December 2006 .... 162, 169
1 U 486/07, 21 November 2007 121
2 U 1464/11, 19 December 2012 37
Appellate Court Köln
22 U 4/96, 21 May 1996 .... 179, 181
2 U 175/95, 9 July 1997 260
16 U 77/01, 14 October 2002 .... 121, 123
Appellate Court Munich
7 U 4419/93, 2 March 1994 46
27 U 346/02, 13 November 2002 263
Appellate Court Saarbrücken, 5 U 426/96-54,
17 January 2007 .... 89, 161–2, 164–5, 169, 177
Appellate Court Schleswig, 11 U 40/01, 22 August 2002 .... 123, 220
Appellate Court Zweibrücken, 7 U 4/03, 2 February 2004 .... 37, 42, 176
District Court Aschaffenburg, 1 HK O 89/03, 20 April 2006 153
District Court Baden-Baden, 4 O 113/90, 14 August 1991 124
District Court Berlin, 52 S 247/94, 15 September 1994 .... 116, 148, 155
District Court Coburg, 22 O 38/06, 12 December 2006 .... 76, 97, 121
District Court Darmstadt, 10 O 72/00, 9 May 2000 90
District Court Düsseldorf, 31 O 27/92, 25 August 1994 154
District Court Ellwangen, 1 KfH O 32/95, 21 August 1995 .... 72, 85
District Court Freiburg, 22 August 2002 .... 188–9, 197

District Court Hamburg
CISG/1998/12, 25 September 1998 65
419 O 218/03, 6 September 2004 .... 46, 120
District Court Köln
3 O 196/01, 25 March 2003 .... 110, 124
85 O 200/05, 5 December 2006 214
District Court Landshut, 54 O 644/94, 5 April 1995 .... 61, 126
District Court Munich
5 HKO 3936/00, 27 February 2002 .... 75, 91
5 HKO 10734/02, 29 November 2005 .... 121, 146
District Court Paderborn, 7 O 147/94, 25 June 1996 120
District Court Regensburg, 6 O 107/98, 24 September 1998 .... 119, 157
District Court Trier, 7 HO 78/95, 12 October 1995 105
Federal Supreme Court
VIII ZR 123/88, 5 July 1989 220
VIII ZR 159/94, 8 March 1995 ......18, 21, 56, 81, 83–5, 99, 134–9, 142–3, 221
VIII ZR 51/95, 3 April 1996 .... 15, 50, 253, 262, 265
VIII ZR 306/95, 4 December 1996 129
VIII ZR 121/98, 24 March 1999 .... 88, 122
VIII ZR 304/00, 9 January 2002 .... 23, 105, 145
VIII ZR 67/04, 2 March 2005 .... 11, 69, 120, 123, 140
VIII ZR 268/0411, January 2006 .... 189, 193–4
VIII ZR 100/11, 26 September 2012 .... 119, 121, 124, 128

Greece

Multi-Member Court of First Instance of Athens, 4505/2009, 2009 120

Israel

Supreme Court, 3912/90, 22 August 1993 .... 214, 227

Italy

Appellate Court Genova, 211, 24 March 1995 256
District Court, No 2280/2007, 11 December 2008 122–3
District Court Vigevano, 12 July 2000 .... 4, 23, 145–6

Mexico

Mexican Commission for the Protection of Foreign Trade (Compromex),
M/21/95, 29 April 1996 60
Mexican Commission for the Protection of Foreign Trade (Compromex),
30 November 1998 262

Netherlands

Appellate Court Arnhem
95/246 AL, 21 May 1996 213
97/700 and 98/046, 27 April 1999 .... 53, 69, 73, 81, 139

Appellate Court s-Gravenhage, 99/474, 23 April 2003 .... 11, 54, 57, 78, 143
District Court Arnhem, Rolnummer 82879/HA ZA
02-10528, June 2006 .... 119, 133
District Court Rotterdam
HA ZA 98-1405, 14 October 1999 .... 92, 157, 159
295401/HA ZA 07-2802, 15 October 2008 .... 73, 135
District Court s-Hertogenbosch, 9981/HAZA 95-2299,
2 October 1998 74
Netherlands Arbitration Institute, Case No 2319, 15 October 2002 113–14

New Zealand

International Housewares Ltd v SEB (2003), High Court
of Auckland, CP 395 SD 01 .... 115, 184
RJ & AM Smallmon v Transport Sales Ltd and Grant
Alan Miller [2011] NZ CA 340 .... 82, 84, 99–100, 134

Russia

International Commercial Arbitration Court at the Chamber of
Commerce and Industry of the Russian Federation (ICAC)
166/1995, 12 March 1996 .... 90, 145
155/1996, 22 January 1997 46
94/1996, 27 January 1997 184
99/1997, 21 January 1998 192
226/1999, 11 February 2000 266
168/2001, 17 February 2003 52
97/2002, 6 June 2003 41
56/2003, 2 February 2004 .... 65, 146, 244
39/2003, 21 December 2004 46
189/2003, 29 December 2004 105

Serbia

Foreign Trade Arbitration Court attached to the Yugoslav
Chamber of Commerce in Belgrade, Serbia, 25 May 2001 176
Foreign Trade Court of Arbitration, Serbian Chamber of
Commerce, 23 January 2008 263

Spain

Appellate Court Barcelona
340/1997, 4 February 1997 74
755/95-C, 20 June 1997 145
574/2003-A, 28 January 2004 95
862/2003-B, 28 April 2004 .... 37, 94
764/2006 357/2007, 3 July 2007 .... 11, 98
403/2008, 24 March 2009 .... 63, 127

Appellate Court Granada, 546/1999, 2 March 2000 173
Appellate Court Madrid, 683/2006, 20 February 2007 .... 52, 73, 263
Appellate Court Palencia, 227/2005, 26 September 2005 .... 94, 105
Supreme Court, 81/2001, 17 January 2008 .... 40, 178

Sweden

Stockholm Chamber of Commerce, Arbitration Award
5 April 2007 118
5 June 1998 129

Switzerland

Appellate Court Basel, 33/2002/SAS/so, 22 August 2003 .... 38, 57
Appellate Court Bern, 304/II/2003/wuda/scch, 11 February 2004 65
Appellate Court Geneva, ACJC/269/2010, 12 March 2010 117
Appellate Court Lugano, 12.97.00193, 15 January 1998 .... 266, 275
Appellate Court Valais
C1 97 167, 28 October 1997 173
C1 04 162, 21 February 2005 47
C1 06 95, 27 April 2007 102–3
Commercial Court Aargau, OR.2001.00029, 5 November 2002 .... 15, 75
Commercial Court Bern, 17 January 2002 220
Commercial Court St Gallen, HG.2010.421-HGK,
14 June 2012 .... 72, 80, 134, 150, 248, 263
Commercial Court Zürich
HG 930138.U/HG93, September 1993 .... 102, 104
HG 930634/O, 30 November 1998 .... 13, 43
HG 960527/O, 21 September 1998 133–4
District Court Lugano, OA.2000.459, 19 April 2007 .... 55, 75
District Court Schaffhausen, 11/1999/99, 27 January 2004 152
Supreme Court
4C.179/1998/odi, 28 October 1998 15
4C.296/2000/rnd, 22 December 2000 .... 40, 152, 156, 175, 269
4C.245/2003/ech, 13 January 2004 .... 76, 80
4A.617/2012, 26 March 2013 .... 248, 263, 275

United Kingdom

Air Transworld Ltd v Bomardier Inc [2012] EWHC 243 (Comm) 182, 184
Alfred C Toepfer v Continental Grain Co [1974] 1 Lloyd's Rep 11 247
Arcos Ltd v EA Ronaasen & Son [1933] AC 470 258
Arnold Karberg & Co v Blythe, Green Jourdain & Co
[1915] 2 KB 379 251
Ashington Piggeries Ltd v Christopher Hill Ltd; Christopher
Hill Ltd v Norsildmel [1972] AC 441 .... 35, 45, 52, 78
Berger & Co Inc v Gill & Duffus SA [1984] 1 AC 382 259
Bernstein v Pamsons Motors [1987] RTR 384 118–19

Bominflot Bunkergesellschaft fur Mineralole mbH & Co v Petroplus Marketing AG [2012] EWHC 3009 (Comm) 1145 268
Bramhill v Edwards [2004] EWCA Civ 403 142
Bristol Tramways, etc, Carriage Company v Fiat Motors Ltd [1910] 2 KB 831 118
Britvic Soft Drinks Ltd v Messer UK Ltd [2002] 2 Lloyd's Rep 368 35
Cammell Laird & Co v Manganese Bronze and Brass Co Ltd [1934] AC 402 .... 71, 102
Cehave NV v Bremer Handelsgesellschaft MBH ('The Hansa Nord') [1976] QB 44 52
Christopher Hill Ltd v Norsildmel [1972] AC 441 78
Colin & Shields v Weddel & Co Ltd [1952] 1 Lloyd's Rep 9 243
Comptoir d'Achat et de Vented u Boerenbond Belge SA v Luis de Ridder Lta (The Julia) [1949] AC 293 243
Cremer and others v General Carriers SA [1974] 1 WLR 341 .... 243, 245
Crooks v Allen (1879) 5 QBD 38 239
Dalmare SpA v Union Maritime Ltd, Valor Shipping Ltd (The Union Power) [2012] EWHC 3537 (Comm) 182, 184–5
David Agmashenebeli, The [2003] 1 Lloyd's Rep 92 261
Derry v Peek (1889) 14 App Cas 337 27
E Clemens Horst Co v Biddell Bros [1912] AC 18 246
Empresa Exportadora de Azucar v Industria Azucarera Nacional SA, (The Playa Larga and Marble Islands) [1983] 2 Lloyd's Rep 171 201
Enichem Anic SpA v Ampelos Shipping Co Ltd (The Delfini) [1990] 1 Lloyd's Rep 252 240
Erichsen v Barkworth (1858) 3 H & N 601, 157 ER 608 240
Esteve Trading Corp v Agropec International (The Golden Rio) [1990] 2 Lloyd's Rep 273 258
FE Hookway v Alfred Isaacs [1954] 1 Lloyd's Rep 491 155
Federal Commerce & Navigacion Co Ltd v Molena Alpha Inc (The Nanfri, The Benfri, The Lorfri) [1979] AC 757 241
Ficom SA v Sociedad Cadex Lda [1980] 2 Lloyd's Rep 118 254–5
Geddling v Marsh [1920] 1 KB 668 .... 160, 168
Glyn Mills Currie & Co v East & West India Dock Co (1882) 7 App Cas 591 .... 240, 256
Great Elephant Corp v Trafigura Beheer BV [2012] EWHC 1745 (Comm) 198–200
Hansson v Hamel & Horley [1922] 2 AC 36 .... 241, 259
Harlingdon & Leinster Enterprises Ltd v Christopher Hull Fine Art Ltd [1991] 1 QB 564 .... 49, 97
Hazlewood Grocery Ltd v Lion Foods Ltd [2007] EWHC 1887 (QB) 142
Henry Kendall & Sons v William Lillico & Sons Ltd [1969] 2 AC 31 .... 58, 75, 97, 99, 101, 141
Hindley & Co v East Indian Produce Co [1973] 2 Lloyd's Rep 515 259

Howard Marine and Dredging Co Ltd v A Ogden & Sons (Excavations) Ltd [1978] QB 574 35
James Drummond & Sons v EH Van Ingen & Co (1887) LR 12 App Cas 284 155
James Finlay & Co Ltd v NV Kwik Hoo Tong HM [1929] 1 KB 400 259
John Martin of London Ltd v AE Taylor & Co Ltd [1953] 2 Lloyd's Rep 589 245–6
Kingspan Environmental Ltd v Borealis A/S [2012] EWHC 1147 (Comm) 87–9
M Golodetz & Co Inc v Czarnikow-Rionda Co Inc (The Galatia) [1980] 1 WLR 495 241
Marimpex v Louis Dreyfus [1995] 1 Lloyd's Rep 167 48
Mash & Murrell Ltd v Joseph I Emanuel Ltd [1961] 1 WLR 862, [1961] 2 Lloyd's Rep 326 64
Medivance Instruments Ltd v Gaslane Pipework Services Ltd, Vulcana Gas Appliances Ltd [2002] EWCA Civ 500 86
Messer UK Ltd and another v Britvic Soft Drinks Ltd [2002] EWCA Civ 548 86
Microbeads AG and Alfred Ehrismann AG v Vinhurst Road Markings Ltd [1975] 1 Lloyd's Rep 375 198
Microbeads AG and another v Vinhurst Road Markings Ltd [1975] 1 WLR 218 214
Moore & Co Ltd and Landauer & Co Ltd, Re [1921] 2 KB 519 46
Moralice (London) v ED & F Man [1954] 2 Lloyd's Rep 526; *see* 258
Morelli v Fitch and Gibbons [1928] 2 KB 636 .... 160, 168
Niblett v Confectioners' Materials Co Ltd [1921] 3 KB 387 .... 208, 213
Norsk Bjergningskompagni A/s v Owners of the Pantanassa (The Pantanassa) [1970] 1 Lloyd's Rep 153 190–1
Novorossisk Shipping Co v Neopetro Co Ltd (The Ulyanovsk) [1990] 1 Lloyd's Rep 425 258
Oscar Chess Ltd v Williams [1957] 1 WLR 370 34
Phoenix Distributors Ltd v LB Clarke (London) Ltd [1967] 1 Lloyd's Rep 518 99
Procter & Gamble Philippine Mfg Corp v Becher [1988] 2 Lloyd's Rep 21 259
PT Putrabali Adyamulia v Société Est Epices (The Intan 6 v.360a SN); Same v Enrico Webb James SNC [2003] 2 Lloyd's Rep 700 259
R G Trading LLP v Feed Factors International Ltd [2011] 2 Lloyd's Rep 433 48
Reardon Smith Line Ltd v Yngvar Hansen-Tangen and Sanko Steamship Co Ltd ('The Diana Prosperity') [1976] 2 Lloyd's Rep 60 45
Robyn Rihanna Fenty and others v Arcadia Group Brands Ltd (t/a Topshop) and others [2013] EWHC 2310 (Ch) 212
Rubicon Computer Systems Ltd v United Paints Ltd (2000) 2 TCLR 453 200
Sanders Bros v Maclean & Co (1883) 11 QBD 327 .... 240, 256
Sea Success Maritime Inc v African Maritime Carriers Ltd [2005] 2 Lloyd's Rep 692 261

Sewell v Burdick (1884) 10 App Cas 74 239
SIAT di del Ferro v Tradax Overseas SA [1980] 1 Lloyd's Rep 53 258
Soules CAF v PT Transcap of Indonesia [1999] 1 Lloyd's Rep 917 190
SS Ardennes (Cargo Owners) v SS Ardennes (Owners) [1951] 1 QB 55 239
Steels & Busks v Bleecker Bik & Co Ltd [1956] Lloyd's
Rep 228 ....153, 155, 157
Stettin, The (1889) LR 14 PD 142 240
Teheran-Europe Co Ltd v ST Belton Ltd [1968] 2 QB 545 74
Toepfer v Continental Grain Co [1974] 1 Lloyd's Rep 11 50
Tradax Export SA v European Grain & Shipping Ltd [1983]
2 Lloyd's Rep 100 48
Tradax Int'l SA v Goldschmidt SA [1977] 2 Lloyd's Rep 604 264
Trafigura Beheer BV v Mediterranean Shipping Co SA
(The MSC Amsterdam) [2007] EWCA Civ 794 240
Webster Thompson Ltd v J G Pears (Newark) Ltd [2009]
2 Lloyd's Rep 339 35
WJ Alan & Co Ltd v El Nasr Export and Import Co [1972]
1 Lloyd's Rep 313 254

United States

BP Oil Int'l v Empresa Estatal Petroleos de Ecuador, 332 F
3d 333 (5th Cir 2003) 249
Cedar Petrochemicals, Inc v Dongbu Hannong Chemical
Co Ltd, F Supp 2d, 2011 WL 4494602 268
Chicago Prime Packers, Inc v Northam Food Trading Co,
2005 US App LEXIS 9355 239
China North Chemical Industries Corp v Beston Chemical Corp,
F Supp 2d, 2006 WL 295395 ....249, 261
Dingxi Longhai Dairy, Ltd v Becwood Technology Group, LLC,
F Supp 2d, 2008 WL 2690287 169
Jeanneret v Vichey 693 F2d 259 (2d Cir 1982) 187
MCC-Marble Ceramic Center v Ceramica Nuova D'Agostino,
144 F 3d 1384 (11th Cir 1998) 269
Medical Marketing v Internazionale Medico Scientifica,
F Supp 2d, 1999 WL 311945 ....84, 134
Miami Valley Paper, LLC v Lebbing Engineering & Consulting
GmbH, F Supp 2d, 2009 WL 818618 (SD Ohio) 33
Nat'l Transp, Inc v Inn Foods, Inc, 827 F2d 351, 354 (8th Cir 1997) 169
Norfolk Southern Railway Co v Power Source Supply, Inc,
66 UCC Rep Serv 2d 680 183
Schmitz-Werke GMBH & Co v Rockland Industries, Inc,
37 Fed Appx 687, 2002 WL 1357095 101
Siskiyou Evergreen, Inc, Debtor, Re, US Bankruptcy Court
for the District of Oregon, 29 March 2004 51
Supermicro Computer Inc v Digitechnic, SA, 145 F Supp 2d 1147 182
SV Braun, Inc v Alitalia-Linee Aeree Italiane, SpAF
Supp1994 WL 121680 260

Travelers Property Casualty Company of America and Hellmuth Obata & Kassabaum, Inc v Saint-Gobain Technical Fabrics Canada Ltd, 474 F Supp 2d 1075 115
Zapata Hermanos v Hearthside Baking, 313 F3d 385 (7th Cir 2002) 23

International

ICC Arbitration
Case No 7565, 1994 .... 46, 50, 73
Case No 7645, March 1995 .... 250, 255, 257–8, 263
Case No 8213, March 1995 .... 71, 95, 184
Case No 8247, June 1996 .... 46, 167
Case No 9187, June 1999 268
Case No 9773, 1999 154
Case No 10377, 2002 .... 128, 133, 146

Table of Legislation

As the entire work deals with the Convention on Contracts for the International Sale of Goods (CISG), only references to specific provisions of this instrument are included in the Table.

International

Berne Convention for the Protection of Literary and Artistic Works 210
Codex Alimentarius 54, 56–7
Commission Regulation (EC) 2439/1999 of 17 November 1999
on the conditions for the authorisation of additives belonging
to the group of 'binders, anti-caking agents and coagulants'
in feedingstuffs 124
Convention Establishing the World Intellectual Property
Organization (WIPO) 210–11
Art 2 210
Convention for the Unification of Certain Rules for International
Carriage by Air 1999 242
Arts 12.1–12.3 242
Convention on Contracts for the International Carriage of Goods
Wholly or Partly by Sea 2009 (Rotterdam Rules)
Art 1(10)(a)(ii) 240
Art 47(a)(i) 240
Convention on Contracts for the International
Sale of Goods (CISG)
preamble 1–2, 175, 188, 253
Art 1(1) 21
Art 1(2) 251
Art 2 2
Art 2(a) 23, 174, 251
Art 2(e) 185
Art 3(1) 2
Art 3(2) 2
Art 4 .... 2, 23, 183
Art 4(a) 2, 25, 181, 205–7
Art 4(b) 2, 189, 197
Art 5 2
Art 6 .... 2, 4, 66, 127, 149, 161, 171, 181, 205, 231
Art 7 .... 254, 259
Art 7(1) 4, 18, 28, 33, 163, 179, 207, 210, 236
Art 7(2) 4, 163, 201, 207, 212, 254
Art 8 .... 2, 26, 31, 36, 39, 72, 84, 93–4,114, 122, 132, 148–9,
171, 183, 203, 206, 245, 248, 254, 257, 264
Art 8(1) 2–3, 31, 251

Art 8(2) 3, 32, 176, 183, 250–1, 260–1
Art 8(2) and (3) 86
Art 8(3) 3, 27, 30, 32, 41, 49, 56, 64, 88, 107, 122, 127, 139, 143, 162–3, 165–6, 176, 223, 238, 255, 259, 261, 269
Art 9 .... 26, 31, 39, 64, 72, 84, 88, 93–4, 114, 122, 127, 132, 148–9, 151, 162, 165, 171, 183, 203, 206, 238, 245, 248, 257, 264, 268–9
Art 9 (former) 103
Art 9(1) 3, 88, 162, 165, 223
Art 9(2) 3, 174, 181, 250–1
Art 10(a) 251
Art 11 .... 105, 107–8
Art 12 204–5
Art 14 .... 2, 5, 31
Arts 14–24 .... 5, 27, 31, 183
Art 14(1) 5, 30
Art 16(2)(b) 5
Art 18 .... 2, 5, 203
Art 18(1) 252
Art 19 5
Art 23 .... 2, 5
Art 25 .... 5, 7, 15, 71, 103, 124, 127, 167, 195, 219, 251, 259
Art 29 .... 2, 41, 204, 254
Art 29(1) 191
Art 29(2) 5, 204
Art 30 .... 6, 10, 19, 186–7, 189, 192, 200–1, 205, 247, 251, 258
Art 31 .... 6, 192, 225, 260
Art 31(2) 173
Art 31(a) 196
Art 31(b) 43, 161, 251
Art 31(c) 161
Art 32 5
Art 32(1) 6, 173
Art 32(2) 6, 261
Art 32(3) 6
Art 33 6
Art 33(c) 258
Art 34 .... 5–6, 10, 19, 238, 247–8, 251, 258
Art 35 .... 6, 9, 19, 21–2, 25–7, 33, 46, 49, 71, 73, 102, 105, 110, 180–1, 186, 191–2, 202, 204, 234–6
Art 35(1) 9, 29–30, 39, 46, 51, 53, 64–7, 71, 72–4, 78, 87–8, 90–1, 126–7, 131, 137, 142, 153, 158, 160, 163, 171, 173
Art 35(2) 9, 11, 29, 38, 51, 60, 64, 68–70, 72, 106, 108, 118, 160, 170–1, 174, 178, 181, 184–5, 188, 202, 225, 235
Art 35(2)(a) 9, 45, 68, 70, 79–80, 87–8, 90, 110–19, 121–8, 132–3, 136–8, 140, 142, 144, 157–9, 163, 236
Art 35(2)(a) and (b) 51
Art 35(2)(b) 9, 23, 53, 68, 70–84, 87–92, 95–8, 104, 110, 121, 124–7, 132, 136–7, 142, 144, 153, 157–9, 163, 235–6

Art 35(2)(c) 9, 147–9, 151–3, 155–9, 178
Art 35(2)(d) 9, 160–3, 165, 167–8
Art 35(3) 9, 20, 38–9, 53, 170–6, 178–9, 202, 220, 225–6
Art 35(3)(c) 9
Art 35(3)(d) 9
Art 36(1) 58–60, 90, 127, 140, 145, 161, 166, 235
Art 36(2) 59–61, 64, 90–1, 127, 161
Art 37 5
Art 38 267–8
Arts 38–44 26
Art 38(2) and (3) 60
Art 38(3) 166, 174, 251, 267
Art 39 ....25, 27, 121, 180, 220, 234–5
Art 39(1) 44, 180
Art 39(2) 180
Art 40 ....27, 179–80, 220
Art 41 ....6, 9–10, 19, 21–2, 27, 186–208, 213–14, 216–17, 231, 234–6
Art 42 ....6, 9–10, 19, 21–2, 27, 82, 136, 204–5, 208–36
Art 42(1) 208–9, 217, 219–20, 251
Art 42(1)(a) 82, 209, 223, 232, 235–6
Art 42(1)(b) 136, 224, 232, 235–6
Art 42(2)(a) 220–1, 225, 227, 232–3
Art 42(2)(b) 228, 232
Art 43 ....204, 231, 235
Art 43(1) 174, 186, 205
Art 43(2) 205
Art 44 ....180, 205
Art 45 ....6, 187
Art 46 7
Art 46(1) 6
Art 46(2) 7, 15, 124, 167–8, 234
Art 46(3) 7, 15, 234
Art 47 ....5, 7
Art 48 ....5, 7, 15
Art 48(1) 15
Art 48(2) 6
Art 49 ....7, 15, 124, 168, 195, 259
Art 49(1)(a) 167
Art 49(1)(b) 167
Art 49(2) 5
Art 49(2)(b)(i) 174
Art 50 ....7, 16, 168, 234
Art 51 7
Art 52(1) 7
Art 52(2) 7, 64
Art 53 ....6, 192
Art 54 6
Art 55 5

Art 57 5–6
Art 57(1) 5
Art 58 .... 6, 10, 251–3, 264
Art 58(1) 252
Art 58(2) 252
Art 59 6
Art 60 .... 5–6, 192
Art 61 6
Art 62 6–7
Art 63 .... 5, 7
Art 64 .... 7, 21
Art 64(2)(b)(i) 174
Art 65 .... 7, 230
Arts 66–70 7
Art 67 .... 43, 260–1
Arts 67–69 60
Art 67(1) 59, 142, 161
Art 67(2) 173
Art 68 .... 59, 174
Art 69(1) 59
Art 69(2) 59
Art 69(3) 43, 173
Art 70 127
Art 71 7
Art 71(1) 215
Art 72 .... 7, 21
Art 72(1) 215
Art 73 21
Art 73(1) 7
Art 73(2) 7
Art 73(3) 7
Art 74 .... 5, 16, 71, 93, 105, 174, 195, 219, 251
Arts 74–77 .... 7, 259
Art 75 16
Art 76(1) 16
Art 76(2) 16
Art 77 .... 5, 16, 195
Art 78 7
Art 79 .... 23, 192
Arts 79–80 7
Art 79(1) 23
Art 79(4) 174
Art 80 .... 191, 229
Arts 81–84 7
Art 82 5
Art 85 5
Arts 85–88 7
Art 86 5

Arts 89–101 ... 7
Art 96 ... 204–5
Convention on International Multimodal Transport of Goods 1980 ... 244
Convention on the Contract for the International Carriage of Goods by Road (CMR) 1956 ... 242–3
Convention relating to a Uniform Law on the International Sale of Goods 1964 (ULIS) ... 28, 149, 160, 207–8, 214, 220, 228
Art 33(1)(c) ... 149
Art 53 ... 207
Art 89 ... 28
Draft Common Frame of Reference (DCFR) ... 8, 35, 150, 194, 202, 208
Art 2:302 ... 150
Art 2:303 ... 35
Art 2:305 ... 194
Art 2:306 ... 208
Art 2:307(1) ... 202
European Patent Convention, Art 64(1) ... 224
ICC Rules for the Use of Domestic and International Trade Terms ... 240
INCOTERMS 2010 ... 58, 190, 240–1, 249, 261
A1 CIF ... 249
A3 CIF ... 241, 246, 249
A8 CFR/CIF ... 256
A8 CIF ... 240–1, 248
B8 CIF/CFR ... 261
Madrid Agreement Concerning the International Registration of Marks, Art 4(1) ... 224
OHADA (Organisation for the Harmonisation of Business Law in Africa) Uniform Act Relating to General Commercial Law ... 8
Paris Convention for the Protection of Industrial Property
art 1(2) ... 210
art 1(3) ... 210
art 9(4) ... 225
Principles of European Contract Law (PECL) ... 8, 230
Art 1:302 ... 230
Treaty on Intellectual Property in respect of Integrated Circuits ... 210
UNIDROIT Principles of International Commercial Contracts 2010 ... 8
Uniform Customs and Practice for Documentary Credits (UCP) 600 ... 241, 245, 257, 260–1, 273
Art 2 ... 257
Art 14 ... 257
Art 14(d) ... 263
Art 15 ... 257
Art 18 ... 245
Art 18(c) ... 245
Art 20(a)(iv) ... 256

Art 20(ii) 256
Art 21 242
Art 21(a)(iv) 256
Art 22(a)(iv) 256
Art 23 256
Art 26(1) 256
Art 27 .... 241, 256
Art 28 246
Uniform Rules Concerning the Contract for International Carriage of Goods by Rail (CIM) 242–3
Universal Copyright Convention 210
WTO Agreement on Trade-related Aspects of Intellectual Property Rights (TRIPS) 210
Art 51 225

National

Argentina

Code of Civil Procedure 106
Commercial Code, art 476 106

Czech Republic

Commercial Code, art 433(2) 233

France

Civil Code 206
art 1599 206

Russian Federation

Customs Code, Art 68 193

United Kingdom

Carriage of Goods by Sea Act (COGSA) 1992 .... 239, 242
s 2(1)(c) 244
s 5(3) 244
Misrepresentation Act 1967, s 2(1) 26
Sale of Goods Act (SGA) 1979 .... 44, 71, 77, 111, 208
s 12(1) 208
s 12(2)(b) 198–9, 201, 208
s 13 44
s 14 185
s 14(2) 142
s 14(2)–(2B) 111
s 14(2B) 49
s 14(3) 71, 77

United States

Restatement (Second) of Conflict of Laws, § 138 .... 105, 108
Restatement (Second) of Torts (1977), § 552 28
Uniform Commercial Code (UCC) 13, 29, 32, 37, 77, 147, 163, 182–3, 206, 215
§ 2-312 .... 187, 205–6
§ 2-312(2) 206
§ 2-312(3) 208, 233
§ 2-313 .... 13, 32–3, 147, 150
§ 2-314 .... 52, 116, 125
§ 2-314(2)(c) 111
§ 2-314(f) 163
§ 2-315 .... 77, 100
§ 2-316(2) 181–3
§ 2-316(3)(a) 185
§ 2-316(3)(b) 177
§ 2-317 110

1

Introduction

I. A BRIEF INTRODUCTION TO THE CISG

EVERY COMMERCIAL AND contract lawyer today will be aware of the United Nations Convention on Contracts for the International Sale of Goods (hereafter referred to as the 'CISG' or the 'Convention'), an international instrument governing international sales transactions. The CISG was adopted in 1980 and has been in force for more than 25 years.[1] As at the time of writing, it has been ratified by 83 countries.[2] The Convention seeks to facilitate and promote international trade. It is based on the idea that the adoption of uniform rules governing contracts for the international sale of goods will contribute to the removal of barriers to trade,[3] which include transaction costs[4] and the need to resort to conflict of laws rules, that may give rise to opportunities for forum shopping.[5] The CISG is intended to be a neutral sales law, which creates a common legal language for those participating in international trade and makes it easier for them to enter into sales contracts. The Convention has been drafted bearing in mind 'the broad objectives in the resolutions adopted by the sixth special session of the General Assembly of the United Nations on the establishment of a New International Economic Order'.[6] These objectives include equality, fairness, economic advancement and social growth of all people and eliminating the gap between the developed and developing world.[7] The CISG is also based on the view that 'the development of

[1] The CISG entered into force on 1 January 1988 after 11 countries ratified the CISG in December 1986. See J Honnold (updated and revised by H Flechtner), *Uniform Law for International Sales under the 1980 United Nations Convention*, 4th edn (The Netherlands, Wolters Kluwer Law & Business, 2009) 3.

[2] See www.uncitral.org/uncitral/en/uncitral_texts/sale_goods/1980CISG_status.html.

[3] See the Preamble to the CISG.

[4] Costs are meant to be understood broadly and include costs in terms of time, effort and uncertainty as regards, for example, applicable law and its content.

[5] See, generally, L Mistelis, 'Is Harmonisation a Necessary Evil? The Future of Harmonisation and New Sources of International Trade Law' in I Fletcher, L Mistelis and M Cremona (eds), *Foundations and Perspectives of International Trade Law* (London, Sweet & Maxwell, 2001) 3–27.

[6] See the Preamble to the CISG.

[7] See United Nations General Assembly Resolution 3201 (S-VI): 'Declaration on the Establishment of a New International Economic Order', 1 May 1974, available at www.un-documents.net/s6r3201.htm.

international trade on the basis of equality and mutual benefit is an important element in promoting friendly relations among States'.[8]

Although imbued with high aspirations, the CISG is not exhaustive in its coverage of sales law. It governs only the formation of a sales contract and the rights and obligations of the buyer and seller arising from the contract.[9] Unless otherwise expressly provided for in the CISG, the validity of the contract, of any of its provisions or of any usage is not governed by the Convention.[10] The issue of the passage of property in the goods is also not covered by the CISG.[11] Certain types of transactions and goods are outside its scope.[12] The contracts which the Convention regards as those where the seller provides a service to the buyer also fall outside the CISG.[13] The Convention will not apply to the 'liability of the seller for death or personal injury caused by the goods to any person'.[14]

The CISG is rooted in the principle of party autonomy, reflected primarily in Article 6.[15] According to this provision, the parties 'may exclude the application of the Convention' or 'derogate from or vary the effect of any of its provisions'. The prevailing view today is that such an exclusion or derogation can be either express or implied.[16] Whether or not the parties intended to depart from a provision of the CISG, as well as any other inquiry into the parties' intentions, is to be resolved in accordance with Article 8. This provision sets out the rules for interpreting the parties' statements and conduct. Article 8(1) provides that 'statements made by and other conduct of a party are to be interpreted according to his intent where the other party knew or could not have been unaware what that intent was' (the so-called 'subjective' test). In practice, this test will often not be used.[17] One reason is that disputes tend to arise precisely because the parties had different expectations in respect of each other's rights and duties, which means that their intentions genuinely differed. That, in turn,

[8] See the Preamble to the CISG.

[9] See Art 4.

[10] See Art 4(a). For further discussion, see V below.

[11] See Art 4(b).

[12] See Art 2.

[13] These will be contracts where: (1) 'in a contract for the supply of goods to be manufactured or produced', 'the party who orders the goods undertakes to supply a substantial part of the materials necessary for manufacture or production' (Art 3(1)); or (2) 'the preponderant part of the obligations of the party who furnishes the goods consists in the supply of labour or other services' (Art 3(2)).

[14] Art 5.

[15] See also Arts 14, 18, 23 and 29.

[16] See I Schwenzer and P Hachem in I Schwenzer (ed), *Schlechtriem and Schwenzer, Commentary on the UN Convention on the International Sale of Goods (CISG)*, 3rd edn (Oxford, OUP, 2010) Art 6, paras 3, 25 (with further references); L Mistelis in S Kröll, L Mistelis and P Viscasillas (eds), *UN Convention on Contracts for the International Sale of Goods (CISG): Commentary* (Munich, CH Beck/Hart Publishing, 2011) Art 6, para. 16 (with further references).

[17] See, eg M Schmidt-Kessel in Schwenzer (n 16) Art 8, para 18.

means that the parties could not have known of each other's intentions. Another reason is that even if a party knew of the other party's intention, proving one's actual state of mind would be difficult. Consequently, Article 8(1) will often be invoked to establish a party's 'implied knowledge' of the other party's intention; that is to say, that the former party 'could not have been unaware' of the latter's intention. But then, this 'implied knowledge' test would largely overlap with the next, so-called 'objective', test in Article 8(2) which relies on an understanding of a reasonable person, unless the application of Article 8(1)[18] would reveal an understanding that is different to that which a reasonable person would have had.[19] More specifically, Article 8(2) stipulates that if Article 8(1) is not applicable, 'statements made by and other conduct of a party are to be interpreted according to the understanding that a reasonable person of the same kind as the other party would have had in the same circumstances'. It is this test that usually forms the basis for evaluating the parties' statements and conduct, which, in turn, are indicative of their intentions. For this reason, Article 8(2) is, in essence, a test for interpreting the parties' intentions.

Both paragraphs (1) and (2) of Article 8 need to be applied with due consideration to be given to ' all relevant circumstances of the case including the negotiations, any practices which the parties have established between themselves, usages and any subsequent conduct of the parties' (Article 8(3)). This provision shows that the CISG was not intended to provide hard and fast solutions. It is a flexible instrument seeking to achieve just, fair and reasonable outcomes in the particular circumstances of an individual case. As seen from Article 8(3), a practice that the parties may have established between themselves or a usage that may exist in a particular trade sector are part of the context against which contracts are interpreted. Whilst being presented in Article 8(3) as merely factors to be taken into account in interpreting the parties' intentions, a practice, if proved to exist, is binding on the parties; and so is a usage, if the parties have agreed to it.[20] If there is no express agreement between the parties as to the applicability of a usage, but a relevant usage does exist, the parties will be taken to have implicitly agreed to its applicability to their contract and its formation, unless there is an agreement to the contrary.[21] A usage is defined as one 'of which the parties knew or ought to have known and which in international trade is widely known to, and regularly observed by, parties to contracts of the type involved in the particular trade concerned'.[22]

[18] What a party in question 'could not have been unaware of' can be different to an understanding that a reasonable person would have had in the circumstances.

[19] See Schmidt-Kessel (n 17).

[20] See Art 9(1).

[21] See Art 9(2) (first sentence).

[22] Art 9(2) (second sentence).

In addition to these rules aimed at interpreting the *contract*, the CISG contains the provisions on how the Convention itself must be interpreted. Article 7(1) provides that the Convention must be interpreted having regard to 'its international character and to the need to promote uniformity in its application and the observance of good faith in international trade'. This provision reveals the Convention's nature as an international instrument and underscores its autonomy from domestic legal systems. The Convention must be interpreted solely with reference to *its own* rules, principles, concepts and terms. It invites an 'international' way of legal reasoning and, by enunciating the need to promote uniformity in its application, requires judges and arbitrators to take into account prior cases, decided under the CISG and involving issues similar to those that they face. This requirement falls short of creating a system of binding precedent, but the starting point is that prior cases are 'persuasive authority'.[23] Another way through which the CISG aims to develop an autonomous international sales law is through its rules on gap-filling in Article 7(2) which provide that:

> Questions concerning matters governed by this Convention which are not expressly settled in it are to be settled in conformity with the general principles on which it is based or, in the absence of such principles, in conformity with the law applicable by virtue of the rules of private international law.

When it comes to matters governed by it, the Convention's preference lies, therefore, with attempting to find solutions within its framework by means of identifying the relevant 'general principles'. This mechanism was intended to enable the CISG to grow in terms of its substantive content and autonomy from domestic legal systems. There are several ways in which such general principles can be developed. First, they can be derived from a particular provision.[24] These can be provisions of general applicability,[25] such as Article 6, reflecting the principle of party autonomy, or, more controversially, Article 7(1) referring to the notion of good faith.[26]

[23] See, eg District Court Vigevano, no 405, 12 July 2000 (Italy), available at http://cisgw3.law.pace.edu/cases/000712i3.html; PP Viscasillas in Kröll, Mistelis and Viscasillas (n 16) Art 7, para 41 (with further references); G Bell, 'Uniformity through Persuasive International Authorities: Does *Stare Decisis* Really Hinder Uniform Interpretation of the CISG?' in CB Andersen and UG Schroeter (eds), *Sharing International Commercial Law Across National Boundaries, Festschrift for Albert H Kritzer on the Occasion of his Eightieth Birthday* (London, Wildy, Simmonds & Hill Publishing, 2008) (advocating 'the civilian concept of "*jurisprudence constant*"—non-binding precedents which become even more persuasive if they are "*constants*" ie consistent over time'). For the discussion of related issues, see V below.

[24] See A Janssen and SC Kiene, 'The CISG and Its General Principles' in A Janssen and Meyer (eds), *CISG Methodology* (Munich, Sellier European Law Publishers 2009) 270–71.

[25] See ibid.

[26] The primary objection to treating good faith as a general principle is that doing so would contravene the compromise made by the drafters prior to the adoption of the Convention, whereby good faith was intended to be nothing more than a method of interpreting the Convention. This is confirmed by Art 7(1) where good faith is mentioned in the context of the interpretation of the Convention.

Alternatively, these can be non-generalist provisions concerned with a specific legal issue.[27] The relevant examples include: Article 57,[28] which can be used to construct a general principle as regards the place for the performance of monetary obligations; or Article 74,[29] from which the principle of full compensation can be derived. Secondly, a general principle can be inferred by drawing on a number of provisions, which, taken together, may reflect one common purpose.[30] The preservation of contracts,[31] a general duty to cooperate,[32] reasonableness,[33] protecting a party's reasonable reliance[34] are some examples of general principles that were developed through this method.[35]

Attention now needs to be turned briefly to the more specialist parts of the Convention. The Convention's approach to the formation of contracts is based on a traditional 'offer and a corresponding acceptance' model,[36] used by so many legal systems. The central idea underpinning the Convention's rules on the formation of contracts is the need for an agreement between the parties[37] in respect of the essential terms, such as the goods, the quantity and the price.[38] The CISG naturally differentiates between the obligations of the seller and the buyer. The key obligations of the seller are to 'deliver the goods, hand over any documents relating to

[27] See Janssen and Kiene (n 24) 271.

[28] Art 57(1): 'If the buyer is not bound to pay the price at any other particular place, he must pay it to the seller: (a) at the seller's place of business; or (b) if the payment is to be made against the handing over of the goods or of documents, at the place where the handing over takes place.'

[29] Art 74 (first sentence): 'Damages for breach of contract by one party consist of a sum equal to the loss, including loss of profit, suffered by the other party as a consequence of the breach'.

[30] See Janssen and Kiene (n 24) 271.

[31] See, eg Arts 25, 47, 63, 48, 49(2) and 82 CISG.

[32] 'This duty is deduced from the duties provided in the CISG in addition to the central performance obligations of the parties: from the duty to preserve goods to be returned which has just been explicated above (Art 85/86), the extensive duty to accept cure (Arts 34, 37, 48), the duty to avoid damages (Art 77), the numerous direct or indirect duties to notify the other party. These duties as well as Arts 32 and 60 CISG can be interpreted to express the general principle that every party is obligated to enable the other party to perform and not to jeopardize the contractual purpose' (U Magnus, 'General Principles of UN-Sales Law' (1995) *Rabels Zeitschrift für ausländisches und internationales Privatrecht* 469, also available at www.cisg.law.pace.edu/cisg/biblio/magnus.html).

[33] The idea of reasonableness is mentioned in more than 30 provisions of the CISG.

[34] See Arts 16(2)(b) and 29(2).

[35] For a much more detailed discussion of this issue, see, eg Schwenzer and Hachem (n 16) paras 31–41; Janssen and Kiene (n 24) 271–81; Magnus (n 32).

[36] See Arts 14–24.

[37] See Arts 14, 18, 19 and 23.

[38] See Art 14(1) ('A proposal for concluding a contract addressed to one or more specific persons constitutes an offer if it is sufficiently definite and indicates the intention of the offeror to be bound in case of acceptance. A proposal is sufficiently definite if it indicates the goods and expressly or implicitly fixes or makes provision for determining the quantity and the price'). But see Art 55 which allows for the possibility of a contract being validly concluded without fixing a price.

them and transfer the property in the goods, as required by the contract and this Convention'.[39] So far as the seller's duties in respect of the goods are concerned, there are rules providing for: what constitutes delivery;[40] the time for delivery;[41] giving notice of consignment to the buyer, specifying the goods, under certain circumstances;[42] the need to arrange carriage of the goods on specified terms, if the seller is bound to arrange for carriage;[43] the need to communicate, in certain cases, information to enable the buyer to effect insurance;[44] conformity of the goods;[45] freedom of the goods from third parties' rights or claims,[46] including those based on intellectual property.[47] As to the seller's obligations in respect of the documents, the CISG merely provides that '[i]f the seller is bound to hand over documents relating to the goods, he must hand them over at the time and place and in the form required by the contract'.[48] The main duties of the buyer are to 'pay the price for the goods and take delivery of them as required by the contract and this Convention'.[49] The remaining provisions concerned with the buyer's duties elaborate on the content of the obligations to pay the price[50] and to take delivery,[51] and provide for the time[52] and place of payment[53] of the price.

The CISG provides for an elaborate system of remedies for breach of contract and of the Convention. This system allows an innocent party to choose any remedy or remedies,[54] subject to them not being incompatible with each other.[55] The available remedies[56] are generally symmetrical as between the buyer and the seller. Both parties have the right to specific

[39] Art 30.

[40] Art 31: 'If the seller is not bound to deliver the goods at any other particular place, his obligation to deliver consists: (a) if the contract of sale involves carriage of the goods—in handing the goods over to the first carrier for transmission to the buyer; (b) if, in cases not within the preceding subparagraph, the contract relates to specific goods, or unidentified goods to be drawn from a specific stock or to be manufactured or produced, and at the time of the conclusion of the contract the parties knew that the goods were at, or were to be manufactured or produced at, a particular place—in placing the goods at the buyer's disposal at that place; (c) in other cases—in placing the goods at the buyer's disposal at the place where the seller had his place of business at the time of the conclusion of the contract'.

[41] Art 33.

[42] Art 32(1).

[43] Art 32(2).

[44] Art 32(3).

[45] Art 35.

[46] Art 41.

[47] Art 42.

[48] Art 34 (first sentence).

[49] Art 53.

[50] Art 54.

[51] Art 60.

[52] Arts 58 and 59.

[53] Art 57. See also n 28 above.

[54] See Arts 45 and 61.

[55] See, eg Arts 46(1), 48(2), 62.

[56] See also IV below.

performance;[57] to fix an additional time for performance of the other party's obligations;[58] to avoid the contract;[59] to exercise remedies for an anticipated non-performance[60] and for a breach of an instalment contract;[61] to claim damages;[62] and to claim interest on a 'sum that is in arrears'.[63] Some remedies are relevant only to one party. The remedies which are available only to the buyer are the right to reduce the price for the goods;[64] to demand replacement or repair of the goods;[65] the remedies for short delivery;[66] and the remedies available in cases where only part of the goods is in conformity with the contract,[67] where goods are delivered before the date fixed for delivery[68] and where the seller delivers quantity greater than that specified in the contract.[69] A breaching seller has the right to cure any failure to perform its obligations even after the due date for delivery.[70]

The remaining provisions of the CISG are concerned with the passage of risk of loss of or damage to the goods;[71] exemptions from liability;[72] consequences of avoidance of the contract;[73] preservation of the goods;[74] and the final provisions[75] that contain diplomatic clauses and deal with reservations, temporal aspects of the Convention and the relationship between the Convention and other instruments.

II. THE CISG TODAY AND THE PURPOSE AND SCOPE OF THIS BOOK

Thousands of cases have been decided under the Convention by courts and arbitration tribunals around the world. It is the subject of countless commentaries and continues to attract the interest of comparative contract and commercial law scholars worldwide. It has triggered and has been used as a model for law reforms in a number of countries, both developed and

[57] Arts 46 and 62.
[58] Arts 47 and 63.
[59] Arts 49, 64 and 25.
[60] Arts 71, 72 and 73(2).
[61] See Art 73(1) and (2). But see Art 73(3) which is applicable to the buyer.
[62] Arts 74–77.
[63] Art 78.
[64] Art 50.
[65] Art 46(2) and (3).
[66] Art 51.
[67] Ibid.
[68] Art 52(1).
[69] Art 52(2).
[70] Art 48. See also Art 65 which is applicable only to the seller.
[71] Arts 66–70.
[72] Arts 79–80.
[73] Arts 81–84.
[74] Arts 85–88.
[75] Arts 89–101.

developing.[76] It would seem that these facts would force even the greatest sceptic of international efforts to unify and harmonise commercial law to admit that overall the CISG has been a great success, which no other existing substantive commercial law instrument has been able to achieve. However, the value, viability of the CISG and the quality of its legal regime and its experience to date are sometimes criticised or even thrown into doubt.[77] The question of whether the CISG has proved to be a successful international sales law and has a future is therefore very much alive. In fact, this question seems more relevant than ever considering the increasingly complex commercial realities and a rapidly changing legal scene, with the apparently limitless imagination and energy of the legal community producing new global or regional initiatives and instruments, some of which can potentially rival the CISG.[78] This question requires a continuous assessment of the Convention and the dynamics of its development.

Much has been written about the CISG, but an in-depth examination of some of its core areas is still lacking. The strength of the Convention's regime, its ability to effectively govern and facilitate modern trade, with all its variety and complexity, cannot be adequately understood if its experience is not brought out and analysed fully. This book seeks to do just that by providing a detailed study of two areas of the CISG: the seller's obligations in respect of the goods and the documents. These areas lie at the very heart of sales law because it is the seller's duties that largely characterise the nature of a sales contract. Delivery of goods and documents relating

[76] See I Schwenzer and P Hachem, 'The CISG: Successes and Pitfalls' (2009) *American J Comparative L* 457, 461–62.

[77] See, eg CP Gillette and RE Scott, 'The Political Economy of International Sales Law' (2005) 25 *Int'l Rev L Economics* 226; G Cuniberti, 'Is the CISG Benefiting Anybody?' (2006) 39 *Vanderbilt J Transnational L* 1511; also M Bridge, 'A Law for International Sales' (2007) 37 *Hong Kong LJ* 17, arguing that the CISG is not as well suited to the trade in commodities as English law.

[78] See the UNIDROIT Principles of International Commercial Contracts 2010, available at www.unidroit.org/instruments/commercial-contracts/unidroit-principles-2010; European Commission, Proposal for a Regulation of the European Parliament and of the Council on a Common European Sales Law, COM(2011)635 final (11 October 2011), available at http://eur-lex.europa.eu/LexUriServ/LexUriServ.do?uri=COM:2011:0635:FIN:en:PDF; Draft Common Frame of Reference (DCFR) in C von Bar and E Clive (eds), *Principles, Definitions and Model Rules of European Private Law: Draft Common Frame of Reference (DCFR)* (Munich, Sellier European Law Publishers, 2009) vol II; The Principles of European Contract Law 2002 (PECL), available at www.jus.uio.no/lm/eu.contract.principles.parts.1.to.3.2002/portrait.pdf; OHADA (Organisation for the Harmonisation of Business Law in Africa) Uniform Act Relating to General Commercial Law, available at www.ohadalegis.com/anglais/audrtcomgb1.htm. For the discussion of regional harmonisation of contract law in Asia, see S Han, 'Principles of Asian Contract Law: An Endeavor of Regional Harmonization of Contract Law in East Asia' (2013) 4 *Villanova L Rev* 589. See also United Nations Commission on International Trade Law (UNCITRAL), Possible Future Work in the Area of International Contract Law; Proposal by Switzerland on Possible Future Work by UNCITRAL in the Area of International Contract Law (2012), available at http://daccess-dds-ny.un.org/doc/UNDOC/GEN/V12/534/54/PDF/V1253454.pdf?OpenElement.

to the goods are two modes of performance by the seller. The question of whether the seller has fulfilled its duties in relation to the goods and documents arises very frequently. The experience of the CISG and of domestic legal systems shows that the issue of whether conforming goods have been delivered is one of the most frequently litigated.[79] The seller's obligations in respect of goods and documents are, in short, of great practical significance to the contracting parties.

The book is concerned with *what* the seller has to deliver to the buyer. In respect of goods, there are two sets of requirements. One is what the Convention calls 'conformity' of the goods. These are the requirements that the goods must meet in relation to 'quality, quantity, description and packaging'.[80] The relevant provisions are contained in Article 35 which consists of three paragraphs. Article 35(1), examined in Chapter 2 of this book, reflects the primacy of party autonomy by providing that the goods must meet the contractual requirements as to their conformity. Article 35(2) provides for several implied terms as to conformity where the parties have not agreed otherwise. According to Article 35(2)(a), explored in Chapter 4, the goods are to be 'fit for the purposes for which goods of the same description would ordinarily be used'. Article 35(2)(b), discussed in Chapter 3, provides that the goods are to be 'fit for any particular purpose expressly or impliedly made known to the seller at the time of the conclusion of the contract'. Pursuant to Article 35(2)(c), the goods ought to 'possess the qualities ... which the seller has held out to the buyer as a sample or model'. Article 35(2)(d) requires the goods to be 'contained or packaged in the manner usual for such goods or, where there is no such manner, in a manner adequate to preserve and protect [them]'. Finally, Article 35(3) contains an exemption from liability of the seller under paragraph (2) in the case where, at the time of the conclusion of the contract, the buyer knew or could not have been unaware of a relevant lack of conformity. Article 35(3)(c) and (d) will be examined in Chapter 5.

The second set of requirements flows from the need for the goods to be free from rights or claims of third parties.[81] Article 41, discussed in Chapter 6, requires the seller to deliver goods 'which are free from any right or claim of a third party, unless the buyer agreed to take the goods subject to that right or claim'. This provision does not cover those rights or claims of third parties, which stem from intellectual property. The requirement that the goods be free from such rights or claims is contained in Article 42 which provides that the 'seller must deliver goods which are free from any right or claim of a third party based on industrial property or other intellectual property, of

[79] See, eg S Kröll, 'The Burden of Proof for the Non-Conformity of Goods under Art 35 CISG' (2011) 3 *Belgrade L Rev* 162; CJ Murrow, 'Warranty of Quality: A Comparative Survey' (1940) 14 *Tul L Rev* 327.

[80] See Art 35(1).

[81] See Arts 41 and 42.

which at the time of the conclusion of the contract the seller knew or could not have been unaware'.[82] Article 42 will be addressed in Chapter 7.

As to the seller's documentary duties, the provisions reproduced above (Articles 30 and 34)[83] show that the Convention is not nearly as elaborate as it is in the case of the goods. It largely contains a self-evident proposition that the seller's duties regarding documents must comply with the contract.[84] The questions that this book explores are these: What documents must the seller deliver and what constitutes a 'good' or 'conforming' document under the CISG? This discussion can be found in Chapter 8.

III. RULES ON CONFORMITY OF THE GOODS: UNDERLYING CONSIDERATIONS

Considering that a substantial part of this book is dedicated to conformity of the goods, it is helpful to explain, at the outset, the significance of the rules as to conformity of the goods not only with reference to their role in practice, but also on the basis of their underlying rationale and functions. The reasons for the existence of the seller's obligations as to conformity of the goods are many and of a different order. They are also tied to and reflect a broader economic, legal, intellectual and moral environment. For example, the well-known idea of *caveat emptor* ('let the buyer beware'), whereby the buyer is to bear the risks of any non-conformity in the goods, is often associated with rather primitive economies where trade occurred primarily at a market place where the buyer had an opportunity to examine a specific item.[85] *Caveat emptor* is also at times viewed as an ingredient in the individualistic philosophy and as being in harmony with the spirit of the *laissez-faire* economy:[86] with minimum state intervention and public control, individuals, left to their own devices, are expected to be self-reliant and stoic.[87] However, as the economy grew and commerce became more complex, sophisticated and important in terms of its role in a society, *caveat emptor* has lost much of its prominence as legal systems imposed conformity obligations on the seller,[88] expanding its liability. Whilst the ideals have not shifted to the opposite idea of *caveat venditor* ('let the seller beware'), in the modern world sellers are generally

[82] Arts 41 and 42 are not reproduced here in full. See Chs 6 and 7 for a complete and detailed discussion of these provisions.
[83] See nn 39 and 48 above and the accompanying main text.
[84] But see also Art 58.
[85] See M Bridge, *The Sale of Goods*, 3rd edn (Oxford, OUP, 2014) para 7.03.
[86] See E Zamir, 'Toward a General Concept of Conformity in the Performance of Contracts' (1991) 52 *La L Rev* 1, 12; Murrow (n 79) 330. Not all writers accept the link between *caveat emptor* and *laissez-faire* (see, eg K Llewelyn, 'On Warranty of Quality, and Society' (1936) 36 *Col L Rev* 699, 718).
[87] See WH Hamilton, 'The Ancient Maxim Caveat Emptor' (1931) 40 *Yale LJ* 1133, 1186.
[88] See Zamir (n 86) 23.

expected to bear a greater burden of ensuring a certain level of conformity of the goods than they have borne in the past.[89] In our largely consumerist age where the buyers' expectations are higher than ever before and where the goods traded are not just simple wares and natural products but also, among other things, mass produced goods, sales laws, even those not concerned with consumer transactions, cannot afford not having some kind of a minimum benchmark of quality and other aspects of conformity.[90] At this point, commercial sales law may become a conduit through which quality control in a society is promoted.[91] Some cases, discussed in this book,[92] demonstrate that sometimes a sales law may even be used as a vehicle through which some other broad societal and moral[93] considerations, such as equality of nations, are promoted.

The role of the rules on conformity in modern economies is therefore not insignificant and reaffirmed by a number of economic functions that these rules perform. First, by affording a level of protection (effectively a form of insurance) to the buyer, they provide the buyer with a certain level of confidence and security, thereby encouraging trade.[94] Secondly, by providing the rules on conformity, which are often said to mimic what the parties would have agreed to in the absence of transaction costs, the law saves the parties the costs of bargaining over the matters covered by these rules, again facilitating sales contracts.[95] Thirdly, the existence of these rules saves the buyer the costs of investigating conformity of the goods that it is

[89] See JJ White, 'Freeing the Tortious Soul of Express Warranty Law' (1998) 72 *Tul L Rev* 2089, 2102 ('the post-war academic literature has been much more sympathetic to the expansion of liability than to its restriction').

[90] '[T]he goods should conform to certain basic quality norms' (Appellate Court Antwerp, 2001/AR/1737, 16 December 2002 (Belgium), available at http://cisgw3.law.pace.edu/cases/021216b1.html). See also J Lookofsky, *Understanding the CISG*, 3rd Worldwide edn (The Netherlands, Kluwer Law International BV, 2008) 78 ('default rules in Article 35(2) affirm that today international buyer is entitled to expect goods which possess some basic qualities').

[91] In the context of English law, regulatory undertones were apparent as early as in the first half of the nineteenth century (see *Jones v Bright* (1829) 5 Bing 533). See further Bridge (n 85) paras 7.90, 7.96 and 7.107; JC Reitz, 'A History of Cutoff Rules as a Form of *Caveat Emptor:* Part I? The 1980 UN Convention on the International Sale of Goods' (1988) 36 *AJCL* 437, 438. For the discussion of this issue, see Chapters 2 and 3. For an emphatic view to the contrary, see HM Flechtner, 'Decisions on Conformity of Goods under Article 35 of the UN Sales Convention (CISG): The "*Mussels* Case", Evidentiary Standards for Lack of Conformity, and the "Default Rule" vs. "Cumulative View of Implied Conformity Obligations"' in I Schwenzer, Y Atamer and P Butler (eds), *Current Issues in the CISG and Arbitration* (The Hague, Eleven International Publishing 2014) 189.

[92] See the discussion of Appellate Court s-Gravenhage, 99/474, 23 April 2003 (The Netherlands), available at http://cisgw3.law.pace.edu/cases/030423n1.html in Chapter 2 and the discussion of Federal Supreme Court, VIII ZR 67/04, 2 March 2005 (Germany), available at http://cisgw3.law.pace.edu/cases/050302g1.html in Chapter 4.

[93] See also Appellate Court Barcelona, Recurso No. 764/2006; 357/20073, July 2007 (Spain), available at http://cisgw3.law.pace.edu/cases/070703s4.html, where the CISG was said to reflect 'a universally accepted sense of justice'.

[94] Reitz (n 91) 438.

[95] Ibid.

thinking of purchasing, since these rules either signal the quality and related aspects of the goods that the buyer can expect and/or induce the seller to share the information, directly or indirectly, with the buyer.[96] Fourthly, the existence of a standard against which the seller's performance can be measured reduces the risk of the so-called 'lemons problem', which refers to a situation where the sellers are not able to sell their products described as products of high quality.[97] Since buyers have no information regarding the products, they have no means of distinguishing between high and low quality products. In the absence of the rules on conformity, buyers have an incentive to treat all products as being of low quality,[98] which would result in high quality goods not being able to command appropriate prices[99] and ultimately being driven out of the market. This, in turn, results in the fall of quality of the goods, reduction[100] or even a total failure of the market.[101] The ability of the rules on conformity to perform all these functions is often thought to promote economic efficiency.

These rules are also necessary on practical and conceptual levels. Although there have been attempts to detach the seller's conformity obligations from the main sales contract,[102] from sales law[103] or even to give birth to them from outside contract law altogether,[104] it is clear that goods are the very subject matter of a sales contract and the rules on conformity are

[96] See CP Gillett and SD Walt, *Sales Law: Domestic and International*, 2nd edn (New York, Foundation Press/Thomson West, 2009) 317–21; F Parisi, 'The Harmonisation of Legal Warranties in European Sales Law: An Economic Analysis' (2004) 52 *AJCL* 403, 411.

[97] See GA Akerlof, 'The Market for "Lemons": Quality Uncertainty and the Market Mechanism' (1970) 84 *Quarterly J Economics* 488.

[98] C Gillette and F Ferrari, 'Warranties and "Lemons" under CISG Article 35(2)(a)' (2010) 1 *Internationales Handesrecht* 2, 3.

[99] All goods will be sold at the same price since the buyer has no means of distinguishing between the quality of the goods (see Akerlof (n 97) 490).

[100] Akerlof (n 97) 488.

[101] See TJ Holdych and BD Mann, 'The Basis of the Bargain Requirement: A Market and Economic Based Analysis of Express Warranties—Getting What You Pay for and Paying for What You Get' (1996) 45 *DePaul L Rev* 781, 795.

[102] By using, for example, the concept of a collateral contract (an agreement separate from the main sales contract) (see Zamir (n 86) 33; for the possibility of a collateral contract in English law, see *Benjamin's Sale of Goods*, 9th edn (London, Thompson-Sweet & Maxwell, 2014) paras 10-012–013); or, as was the case at some points in legal history (eg Roman law), where warranties of quality and title were created separately from the sales contract upon the seller making a solemn promise which was not included in the 'sale' itself (see E Rabel, 'The Nature of the Warranty of Quality' (1950) 24 *Tul L Rev* 273, 274; Murrow (n 79) 347).

[103] It has been reported that in some legal systems (eg France), an action for breach of an implied-in-law warranty is based on the law of mistake (see Murrow (n 79) 548; Rabel (n 102) 283). For a criticism of mistake being the conceptual basis for liability for non-conformity, see Zamir (n 86) 38–39.

[104] The tort origins of the warranty law in the United States are widely recognised (see, eg White (n 89) 2090 ('Warranty law started as tort but progressively, from sometime in the nineteenth century, has moved step-by-step from tort to contract'); Murrow (n 79) 331–32). For the explanation of the position in the United States that a breach of warranty and a breach of contract are distinct causes of action, see T Davis, 'UCC Breach of Warranty and Contract Claims' (2009) 61 *Baylor L Rev* 783.

what *defines* that subject matter:[105] 'a contract is normally a contract for a sale of something describable and described'.[106] Without these rules, it would be impossible to say what it is that the seller has agreed to deliver.[107] That is why they are not only an integral part of sales law, but they also lie at the core of the seller's primary obligations by being inextricably linked to its obligation to deliver the goods.[108]

The rules on conformity are also essential in terms of the function, performed by both a sales law and a sales contract, of allocating commercial risks between the parties. It is inevitable that buyers will complain about conformity of the goods, allege a breach and invoke remedies. It is essential therefore that there should be fairly clear legal rules, particularly those applicable by default, which are capable of allocating the risk between the parties, thereby producing legal certainty and reducing litigation.[109] Such allocation must also be guided by the right principles and one such principle is this: a party who is in the better position to reduce or to bear the risk of non-conformity or to insure against and/or to deal with the adverse consequences arising from non-conformity, should be the risk bearer. The conformity obligations are imposed on the seller because it often controls the manufacturing process or has the ability to bargain effectively with the manufacturer. In any case, often being better informed than the buyer, the seller can calculate the possible 'failure' rates.[110] This information, in turn, enables the seller to invest in product quality[111] and to set the price in a way that factors in the possible 'failure' rates and the resulting need to deal with the buyer's claim.

The idea that the risk should be placed on the party in the best position to reduce and to bear it has also been couched in terms of its fairness, which shows that the arguments used to justify the existence of the rules on conformity are not too far from the moral realm. In fact, the imposition of conformity obligations on the seller reflects, to a degree, some other moral considerations. It has been suggested that the move away from *caveat emptor*, a product of the age of individualism, is the move towards altruism.[112] The seller does not simply promise to deliver the goods, it also

[105] See point 6 of the Official Comment on § 2-313 of the Uniform Commercial Code (UCC) in *Uniform Commercial Code: 2009–2010 Edition* (West-Thomson Reuters, 2009) ('the whole purpose of the law of warranty is to determine what it is that the seller has in essence agreed to sell'); Bridge (n 85) para 7.11.

[106] Point 6 of the Official Comment on § 2-313 UCC (n 105).

[107] This statement is particularly true in respect of the notion of 'description', which is an aspect of conformity of goods under the CISG (see the main text accompanying n 80 above and Chapters 2 and 4).

[108] See Commercial Court Zürich, HG 930634/O, 30 November 1998 (Switzerland), available at http://cisgw3.law.pace.edu/cases/981130s1.html ('The seller's liability for the defect of goods follows from its primary obligations under the contract, ie delivery of the agreed goods').

[109] See, similarly, Bridge (n 85) para 7.02.

[110] See Gillett and Walt (n 96) 317–18.

[111] '[I]mposing on the seller an obligation to deliver the goods of a particular quality will induce the party in the best position to assure quality to achieve an optimal level of care' (ibid 318).

[112] See Zamir (n 86) 50.

promises, expressly or implicitly, to bear responsibility for a lack of conformity in the goods. Viewed in this way, the law can be said to make the seller have regard to the buyer's interests. A related point flows from the nature of promise keeping, another moral consideration. If the above point, that without the rules on conformity it is impossible to know what it is that the seller has agreed to sell, is accepted, it arguably follows that the promise to deliver the goods entails a promise that some standards of description and quality will be observed. Further, because these rules are able to encourage the sharing of information they promote communications between the parties and in this way facilitate trust.[113] Another point where morality is lurking behind the rules on conformity is when the 'lemons problem' is raised. This problem can be seen as one where the sellers of low quality products do not shy away from passing off their products as being of higher quality. Whilst economists view this as a problem because of the resulting 'major costs of dishonesty',[114] dishonesty can also be seen as a moral problem. From this point of view, the rules on conformity fight potential dishonest practices.

IV. THE SELLER'S LIABILITY AND THE BUYER'S REMEDIES

This book is concerned with the content of the seller's obligations in relation to goods and documents. It does not seek to examine remedies available to the buyer. Nevertheless, it is helpful to give a brief overview of the nature of the buyer's remedies for a lack of conformity because an understanding of remedies will at times influence the analysis of whether a seller has committed a breach in respect of goods or documents. If conforming goods and documents have been delivered, the seller has fulfilled its obligations in respect of them and the question of the seller's liability does not arise. If, however, the requirements as to conformity of goods or documents have not been met, the seller becomes liable and the buyer is entitled to invoke a number of remedies, set out earlier.

First, the buyer may be able to avoid the contract provided that a breach by the seller is 'fundamental'.[115] A breach is fundamental 'if it results in

[113] See Parisi (n 96) 412.

[114] Akerlof (n 97) 495 (the costs are the inability of high quality products to command adequate prices and the gradual driving out of these products, reduction of the market, and a general fall in product quality).

[115] See, generally, CISG Advisory Council Opinion No 5, 'The Buyer's Right to Avoid the Contract in Case of Non-Conforming Goods or Documents', available at www.cisg.law.pace.edu/cisg/CISG-AC-op5.html#iva; M Bridge, 'Avoidance for Fundamental Breach of Contract under the UN Convention on Contracts for the International Sale of Goods' (2010) 59 *ICLQ* 911; D Saidov, 'Remedies for a Documentary Breach: English Law and the CISG' in K Rowley, L DiMatteo, S Saintier and Q Zhou (eds), *Commercial Contract Law: Transatlantic Perspectives* (Cambridge, CUP, 2013) 434; BK Leisinger, *Fundamental Breach Considering Non-Conformity of the Goods* (Munich, Sellier European Law Publishers, 2007).

such detriment to the other party as substantially to deprive him of what he is entitled to expect under the contract, unless the party in breach did not foresee and a reasonable person of the same kind in the same circumstances would not have foreseen such a result'.[116] The threshold meeting this definition has been set at a high level by the courts. For example, they have held that there was no fundamental breach where the buyer could still use or resell non-conforming goods (even if at a discount)[117] or where the seller could repair the goods,[118] despite the Convention expressly subjecting the seller's right to cure any failure to perform its obligations to the buyer's right to avoid the contract.[119] In the case of a lack of conformity in the documents, some courts have gone as far as to hold that there was no fundamental breach if the *buyer* was in the position to cure a lack of conformity in the documents.[120] Whilst this approach arguably lacks a basis in the CISG and essentially rewrites the contract between the parties, shifting a burden of procuring a conforming document to the buyer, this decision, together with others, underscores the fact that the CISG is often interpreted as based on the idea of the preservation of contracts and that contracts should be kept alive as long as possible.[121] As a result, avoidance of the contract has often been seen by the courts as a remedy of last resort.

Secondly, the notion of a fundamental breach is also relevant if the buyer wishes to exercise its right to specific performance which can take the form of a right to demand 'delivery of substitute goods'[122] or that the seller 'remedy the lack of conformity'.[123] If the buyer wishes to demand that non-conforming goods be replaced with conforming ones, a lack of conformity must amount to a fundamental breach.[124] Otherwise, the buyer is confined to the right to require the seller to remedy the lack of conformity, 'unless this is unreasonable having regard to all the circumstances'.[125]

[116] Art 25.

[117] See, eg Supreme Court, 4C.179/1998/odi, 28 October 1998 (Switzerland), available at http://cisgw3.law.pace.edu/cases/981028s1.html.

[118] See, eg Commercial Court of the Canton of Aargau, OR.2001.00029, 5 November 2002 (Switzerland), available at http://cisgw3.law.pace.edu/cases/021105s1.html.

[119] See Art 48(1), stating that the seller's right to cure (provided for in Art 48) is subject to Art 49, which provides for the buyer's right to avoid the contract. This does not mean that this interpretation by the courts necessarily violates the wording of Art 48(1). It can be argued that, in these cases, the seller's ability to cure is used as a factor in determining whether a breach is fundamental under Art 25. Strictly speaking, the seller's right to cure is applied in the context of Art 25 and not Art 49.

[120] See Federal Supreme Court, VIII ZR 51/95, 3 April 1996 (Germany), available at http://cisgw3.law.pace.edu/cases/960403g1.html.

[121] See, eg Commercial Court of the Canton of Aargau (n 118). See also n 31 above.

[122] Art 46(2).

[123] Art 46(3).

[124] Art 46(2).

[125] Art 46(3).

Thirdly, the buyer has the right to reduce the price in the case of a lack of conformity. This remedy is exercisable whether or not the price has been paid,[126] but it is particularly valuable if the price has not been paid because then the buyer can exercise it unilaterally, by simply paying the seller the reduced price. The price can be reduced 'in the same proportion as the value that the goods actually delivered had at the time of the delivery bears to the value that conforming goods would have had at that time'.[127] It is evident from this formula that, in contrast with damages, whether the buyer has suffered any loss is irrelevant.

Fourthly, the buyer has the right to claim damages for all losses suffered as a consequences of the seller's breach.[128] The measure of damages is based on the principle of full compensation or the protection of the 'expectation' or 'performance' interest.[129] Simply put, damages are recoverable to the extent that they were foreseeable by the breaching party[130] and avoidable by the innocent party.[131] If the buyer avoids the contract, damages can be claimed for the difference between the contract price and the price in a substitute transaction provided that it was made within a reasonable time and in a reasonable manner.[132] If the contract is avoided, but a substitute transaction has not been made or it has not been made in a reasonable manner and within a reasonable time, damages can be claimed for the difference between the contract price and the current price at the time of avoidance.[133] The CISG is silent as to how damages are to be assessed if the contract has not been avoided, with the buyer having the goods on hand. In principle, there are a number of ways in which damages can be assessed in such cases.[134] If the buyer resells non-conforming goods at a reduced price, damages can be calculated as the amount by which the buyer's profit margin on a sub-sale has been reduced. Where the buyer cures a lack of conformity, the costs of cure can be a convenient and accurate measure of the buyer's loss. Damages can also be measured as the difference between the value of non-conforming goods actually delivered and the value of conforming goods that ought to have been delivered under contract.[135]

[126] See Art 50.
[127] Ibid.
[128] See Art 74.
[129] See ibid (first sentence).
[130] See ibid (second sentence).
[131] See Art 77.
[132] Art 75.
[133] Art 76(1) (first sentence). See also Art 76(2) (second sentence) ('If, however, the party claiming damages has avoided the contract after taking over the goods, the current price at the time of such taking over shall be applied instead of the current price at the time of avoidance').
[134] See D Saidov, 'Calculating Damages for Delivery of Non-Conforming Goods' in I Schwenzer, Y Atamer and P Butler, *Current Issues in the CISG and Arbitration* (The Hague, Eleven International Publishing 2014) 263.
[135] For further discussion, see ibid.

V. CONFORMITY OF GOODS AND DOCUMENTS: BROADER INSIGHTS INTO THE CISG

A. General

Any assessment of the Convention must draw on its experience in *all* of its key areas. Being confined to several specific questions, this book is not the place for a comprehensive evaluation of the CISG. An in-depth look into some specific issues nonetheless reveals much about the Convention's strengths and weaknesses, as well as throws up insights and questions whose significance goes beyond the issues at hand. What will the examination of conformity of goods and documents tell us about the Convention as a whole?

B. Is the CISG a Well-Developed Sales Law?

The discussion in this book will show that, particularly in the area of conformity of the goods, the Convention has grown into a well-developed legal regime. However, it can still be argued that the CISG cannot rival some major domestic legal systems. One reason for this argument is that the CISG has not been in existence as long as them and, therefore, cannot have the same richness of experience, and hence maturity, as they have. Another reason is that the CISG is interpreted and applied in numerous fora in different parts of the world. It is impossible to ensure consistency in its application and, as a result, the CISG can never provide a coherent and predictable body of sales law.

It is true that the CISG does not yet have the long history of some of its major domestic counterparts, but at the same time its reach is much wider and consequently it is used with much greater frequency. Time runs very differently in the world of the CISG, with each unit of time carrying greater weight and intensity than it does in the context of any domestic law. For example, as at the time of writing there were more than 450 cases reported just on the issue of conformity of the goods. Very few domestic legal systems would be able to generate such a substantial body of cases on such a specific sales law issue within the 25-year period. The strength and maturity of the law lies, of course, not only in the sheer number of cases, but in the quality of legal reasoning and substantive outcomes. The quality and rigour of legal reasoning in cases decided under the CISG vary greatly, but the discussion in this book will show that the outcomes reached in the vast majority of the decisions are generally fair, reasonable and in line with what traders would probably expect from a modern and developed sales law.

The argument that it is difficult to achieve uniform application of the CISG is more serious. Indeed, the long-term future and credibility of the

Convention is dependent on whether it is perceived by the business community as being a predictable and coherent sales law. The significance of this point is recognised by the CISG which requires that in its interpretation, 'regard is to be had to its international character and to the need to promote uniformity in its application'.[136] Absolute uniformity is not achievable in the absence of one centralised institution entrusted with ensuring consistency in the Convention's application, but there is room for moderate optimism. The Convention's experience in some areas such as the definition of a fundamental breach (a key concept in the Convention's remedial scheme)[137] has already been one where relatively uniform approaches have developed. The discussion in this book will reveal that the experience regarding conformity of the goods is similar. Considering the high number of cases on this issue, there are not that many instances where distinct non-uniform paths are identifiable. Moreover, conformity of goods is one of the few areas in the Convention which has given rise to the idea of a 'leading' case; that is to say, a case which has become well-known within the international legal community, far beyond its jurisdictional origin, and due to the persuasiveness of the decision in it has influenced the interpretation and application of the CISG in other jurisdictions and by arbitration tribunals. The case in point is what has become known as the *New Zealand Mussels* case, decided by the German Supreme Court.[138] This decision shows that despite all the challenges on the path to achieving uniformity, the CISG is capable of creating a global community which can ensure that sound and well-reasoned approaches to the interpretation of sales law are promoted internationally.

A few instances of this kind are unlikely to be sufficient to persuade sceptics about the viability and effectiveness of international instruments like the CISG. Therefore, much more work is needed to facilitate an understanding of the Convention and the continued growth of the international legal community around it. This resonates with what can be seen from the examination in this book. Only in very few cases, discussed here, have judges and arbitrators shown their awareness of or willingness to engage with prior decisions under the CISG addressing similar issues to those at hand. This shows that the international community (an essential condition for achieving a reasonable degree of uniformity in the Convention's application)[139] has not yet developed to include fully those who ultimately interpret and apply the Convention: judges, arbitrators and lawyers representing the parties in legal proceedings. With this in mind, this book consolidates and systematises the existing body of cases in order to bring all

[136] Art 7(1).

[137] See nn 115 and 122 above and the accompanying main text.

[138] Federal Supreme Court, 8 March 1995, VIII ZR 159/94 (Germany), available at http://cisgw3.law.pace.edu/cases/950308g3.html. See further Chapters 3 and 4.

[139] See, generally, C Andersen, 'The Global Jurisconsultorium of the CISG Revisited' (2009) 13 *Vindobona J Int'l Commercial L Arbitration* 43 (with further references).

these 'atomised' and apparently disconnected experiences of applying the CISG into an integrated, comprehensive and distinctive CISG legal regime on conformity of goods and documents.

Perfect uniformity is neither achievable nor desirable. Even within a domestic legal system, tensions within the law are not infrequently encountered. The law sometimes needs to accommodate various policies, which may all be valuable but conflicting at the same time. The ability of the law to absorb and balance between competing ideas or ideologies is probably an important characteristic of a mature and viable legal regime. This book will show a number of instances where the CISG is a battlefield of competing ideas[140] and that is a sign of a healthy instrument as long as it retains, as it does, its key characteristics, fulfils its overall objectives and provides a reasonable degree of legal certainty.

C. Developing Substantive Content Within a 'Minimalist' Structure

Many of the Convention's rules are not formulated with great detail and are open-ended and general. These features raise questions about how to turn the CISG into an instrument capable of governing wide-ranging sales transactions, with their multitude of factual scenarios, in a predictable manner. How can the minimalist and imprecise nature of the Convention's provisions be injected with meaning that does justice to each individual case *and* provides legal certainty? How creative must the legal community be in reading more detailed meaning into the CISG?

Beginning with the rules dealing with conformity of the goods,[141] it can be objected that, by the Convention's standards, they are one of the more elaborate provisions and therefore these questions are not applicable to them. However, it will be seen that these rules are just as incapable of having precise meaning in the abstract as many other parts of the CISG. In fact, what characterises the rules on conformity of the goods is that they are highly flexible and fact-sensitive. The challenge of injecting real meaning into them and providing guidance as to how they will be interpreted in a particular case is not easy to meet.

The same is true when it comes to the rules on the freedom of the goods from third parties' rights or claims[142] and, much more so, in the case of the seller's documentary obligations[143] on which the CISG says very little. Two conflicting considerations are at play. On the one hand, the Convention

[140] See, eg the debate about whether the CISG is based on an underlying quality standard and, if so, what it should be in Chapter 4.

[141] See Art 35 and the discussion in Chapters 2–5.

[142] See Art 41, which is exceptionally brief in its formulation, and Art 42. For the discussion of these provisions, see Chapters 6 and 7.

[143] See Arts 30 and 34 and the discussion in Chapter 8.

requires that every case be decided in its particular context. This openness to the particularities of the case is its strength because otherwise the Convention will not be able to achieve fairness in individual circumstances. On the other hand, certainty is part of justice and more specific meaning than that which is discernible from the text of the Convention has to be developed.

The approach that balances these considerations is, generally, twofold. First, where possible, as is the case in the context of the question of whether the seller must comply with the public law requirements in a place where the goods are intended to be used or sold,[144] guidelines, based on the Convention's policies and rationale underlying the relevant rule, are proposed. These guidelines are neither binding nor do they constitute a presumption to be rebutted by a party against whom they operate. They are, however, valuable in signalling a starting point for how risks should be allocated between the parties. Secondly, in many other cases, where no structured framework of guidelines can be given, the approach is to identify various factual patterns that arise in practice and to put forward relevant factors to be taken into account in allocating duties and risks between the parties in each of these cases.

Some questions that arise under the CISG simply require a 'yes' or 'no' answer. For example, should a seller be able to claim exemption from liability, as it is normally entitled to do,[145] where the buyer knew or could not have been unaware of a lack of conformity *if* the seller was fraudulent? Or should the seller who, as a result of complying with the buyer's drawings and specifications infringed a third party's intellectual property right and suffered harm, be able to claim that the buyer owed a duty to ensure that its specifications/drawings would not infringe a third party's intellectual property rights? These questions are not specifically addressed by the CISG, but courts and writers have developed specific solutions to them. To some extent, these are instances of legal creativity, where the CISG is injected with precise meaning developed in accordance with its underlying considerations and framework.

D. Is the CISG the Best Law for International Sales?

It is sometimes said that the CISG is superior to domestic sales laws because, in contrast with the latter, it has been specifically designed to address the needs of international trade. How accurate is this proposition in the context of conformity of goods and documents? It is true so far as the Convention's provision, requiring the goods to be free from intellectual

[144] See Chapters 2–4.
[145] See Art 35(3).

property rights or claims (Article 42), is concerned. This provision is unique to the CISG and it has been drafted with reference to the considerations which are specific to international transactions.[146] The proposition is more debatable in the context of other issues. There is nothing in the provisions, containing requirements as to freedom of goods from third parties' rights or claims (Article 41)[147] or as to the goods' quality, quantity, description and packaging (Article 35), that would reflect features or problems unique to international trade. These provisions are broadly similar to their counterpart provisions in some domestic legal systems.

The question then arises as to whether the Convention's legal regime should simply be viewed with reference to its text and framework or whether the cases in which it has been applied should also be regarded as its integral part. If the latter is the case, it is arguable that, notwithstanding any weaknesses that may be inherent in the Convention's experience to date, its legal regime is still more advanced and appropriate for international transactions. The cases decided under the CISG are, by definition, 'international'[148] and any problems peculiar to international sales are necessarily addressed in these cases. On this view, what really makes the CISG an effective global sales law is its *experience* of governing international transactions.

Adopting this view has its dangers. Some decisions made in cases governed by the CISG are not sound or well-reasoned, as will be seen, for example, in the context of the seller's documentary performance.[149] Treating such cases as part of the CISG will only undermine the strength and credibility of the Convention. Therefore, there must be a gradual process of 'natural selection'[150] where only the best reasoned cases, or those that identify valuable commercial or legal considerations or reveal unusual factual patterns, survive and represent the Convention's regime and evolution.[151] What ultimately predetermines the quality of decisions under the CISG is the level of expertise and professional experience of judges and arbitrators, as well as how internationally minded they are.

[146] See Chapter 6.

[147] Other than those stemming from intellectual property.

[148] As defined by the CISG; that is, that both parties have their places of business in different states (Art 1(1)).

[149] See Chapter 8.

[150] See MG Bridge, 'Issues Arising under Articles 64, 72 and 73 of the United Nations Convention on Contracts for the International Sale of Goods' (2005–2006) 25 *J L Commerce* 405, 406. The process is arguably taking place primarily through scholarly writings and private initiatives, such as the CISG Advisory Council (CISG AC) which seeks to promote uniform application of the CISG by preparing and promoting opinions on various topical issues under the CISG (see www.cisgac.com). See also the discussion of *New Zealand Mussels* in the main text above and in Chapters 3 and 4.

[151] See, similarly, Bridge (n 150) 406–7; also Viscasillas (n 23) ('a line needs to be drawn between "plainly wrong cases" on the CISG, as opposed to different legitimate views on the CISG').

In the area of conformity of goods (Article 35), the Convention's regime, based on many of its cases and scholarly commentary, is strong and well-developed. This makes the CISG a highly competitive legal instrument for governing international sales. The Convention's provisions on the goods' freedom from third parties' rights or claims (Articles 41 and 42) have so far generated a very small number of cases, compared to what has been reported under Article 35. Still, a considerable body of knowledge has been developed under these provisions thanks to scholarly writings. The Convention's experience in the area of documentary performance is, as will be demonstrated, in need of improvement. Otherwise, it will be difficult for the CISG to be an effective international sales law because documents are of special importance in *international* trade, particularly in such sectors as trade in commodities.

E. Defining the Boundaries of the CISG

(i) General

Despite the drafters' attempt to delimit the scope of the issues that are governed by the CISG, the boundaries beyond which the Convention does not extend are still very uncertain. This uncertainty regarding the Convention's scope remains a major obstacle to achieving uniformity in its application. There are not many provisions in the CISG that are as closely and extensively linked with the problem of defining the Convention's boundaries as are its provisions on conformity of the goods. The discussion in this section as well as in other chapters will identify at least two sets of issues in this regard. One relates to the questions flowing from the need to prove a claim. The other concerns the meaning of 'validity' of contract and of its provisions which, as explained,[152] is not intended to be governed by the CISG. The examination of these issues in the context of conformity of the goods will be valuable to a broader understanding of and debate about how far the Convention's reach should extend.

(ii) Proof

One controversial issue that arises in connection with the need to prove a claim is burden of proof. The Convention contains no express provisions as to how burden of proof is to be generally allocated and there is no agreement as to whether it is a matter governed by the CISG. That said, the view that is increasingly gaining recognition is that it is a matter governed by

[152] See n 10 above and the accompanying main text.

the CISG[153] and it is the view that is taken in this book, for two reasons. First, there are some specific provisions, such as most notably Article 79,[154] which seem to reveal the principle within the CISG as to the allocation of burden of proof. Secondly, the allocation of burden of proof will have a direct impact on the ways in which the rights *under the CISG* are exercised. If this issue is left to the applicable domestic rules, which vary significantly, the Convention's provisions will, in reality, be prevented from being applied in a uniform way. In contrast, developing and promoting an autonomous solution within the CISG will reduce the risk of the very same rights under the CISG not being exercised in the same way. An autonomous solution that flows from provisions such as Article 79 is that a party who asserts a right must prove the necessary preconditions for the existence of that right; whereas a party who invokes an exception to the other party's right must prove the necessary preconditions for the existence of that exception.

Similar considerations apply to a related issue of the standard of proof. The CISG is silent on the degree of precision with which the existence of a right must be established. In spite of the absence of an express legal basis, the position taken here is that the CISG should govern this issue for the same reason as has just been stated in respect of burden of proof. The standard of proof has a considerable impact on the exercise of rights under the CISG. Leaving this matter to domestic rules would lead to the very same rights being exercised in different ways depending on which rules are applicable.[155] This outcome would undermine the purpose of the CISG as an international uniform law instrument.

One objection to this position, both in respect of burden and standard of proof, is that these are usually treated as matters of procedural, rather than substantive law, whereas the CISG is about substance, not procedure.[156] A reply to this objection is that whilst this may be true in one legal system, the opposite may be the case in another. In other words, the distinction between procedural and substantive law matters is relative, as is widely

[153] See, eg Federal Supreme Court, VIII ZR 304/00, 9 January 2002 (Germany), available at http://cisgw3.law.pace.edu/cases/020109g1.html; District Court Vigevano, 12 July 2000 (n 23); Schwenzer and Hachem in Schwenzer (n 16) Art 4, para 25 (with a detailed list of further references).

[154] Art 79(1): 'A party is not liable for a failure to perform any of his obligations *if he proves* that the failure was due to an impediment beyond his control and that he could not reasonably be expected to have taken the impediment into account at the time of the conclusion of the contract or to have avoided or overcome it or its consequences' (emphasis added). See also Arts 2(a) and 35(2)(b).

[155] For further discussion, see Chapter 3.

[156] See, eg *Zapata Hermanos v Hearthside Baking,* 313 F3d 385 (7th Cir 2002) ('The Convention is about contracts, not about procedure'). See also H Flechtner and J Lookofsky, 'Viva Zapata! American Procedure and CISG Substance in a US Circuit Court of Appeal' (2003) 7 *Vindobona J Int'l Com L Arbitration* 93.

recognised.[157] Finding a solution within the CISG cannot depend on how domestic law categorises a given problem. Each issue needs to be resolved on a case-by-case basis having regard for the Convention's nature, purpose, framework and functions, on the one hand, and the interests and policies protected by the applicable domestic rules, on the other.

The discussion in this book will show that some cases involving a lack of conformity in the goods pose a unique challenge to the need to delimit the boundaries between the CISG and the applicable domestic rules. This challenge arises from domestic rules on the admissibility of evidence. This issue is probably treated as procedural by most legal systems,[158] in which case there is hardly any difficulty in the parties to a contract, governed by the CISG, being subject to these rules. After all, it is true that the CISG is an instrument of substantive law and the admissibility of evidence is widely perceived as a procedural law issue. Any non-uniformity in the exercise of rights under the CISG, arising from differences in the applicable rules as to the admissibility of evidence,[159] is therefore an inevitable result of the Convention being a substantive law instrument.

However, there are cases decided under the CISG that appear to suggest that in some systems the rules on the admissibility of evidence regarding a lack of conformity in the goods are rules of substantive law.[160] This situation, which again underscores the relativity of the substance-procedure distinction, poses a new challenge to defining the relationship between the CISG and domestic law. Should the CISG displace these domestic rules because, this time, they are substantive law rules? Or should these rules dictate what evidence the buyer must present to prove a lack of conformity under the CISG? As explained, a categorisation given by the applicable domestic law cannot be the basis for answering these questions. The function of these rules and the interests they protect need to be balanced against the Convention's aspiration of being an autonomous instrument which is applied uniformly. If the interests and policies that these domestic law rules protect are not those that the CISG is capable of protecting, these rules should apply. The CISG was never designed to protect and is incapable of protecting the policies and interests covered by the rules on the admissibility of evidence.[161]

[157] See, eg CG Orlandi, 'Procedural Law Issues and Law Conventions' (2000) 5 *Uniform L Rev* 23; I Schwenzer and P Hachem, 'The CISG: Successes and Pitfalls' (2009) *American J Comparative L* 457, 470–71.

[158] See Chapter 3.

[159] A buyer who seeks to prove its claim of a lack of conformity by means of evidence other than that stipulated in the applicable domestic law, will not be able to establish the seller's liability; whereas it would have been able to do so had a different domestic law, which admits the type of evidence presented by the buyer, been applicable.

[160] For a detailed discussion, see Chapter 3.

[161] See ibid.

(iii) Validity

The issues of the validity of the contract and of its provisions are excluded from the CISG.[162] Given that many legal issues can be categorised by domestic law as those of 'validity', the question is whether it is up to domestic law or up to the CISG to define the meaning of 'validity'.[163] This book takes the position that defining validity cannot be left to domestic legal systems because otherwise the Convention will not be capable of being applied uniformly. However, with the CISG not containing a definition of validity, how should its meaning be determined? It is argued that matters which are functionally dealt with by the CISG should not be treated as matters of 'validity', even if they are treated as such by the applicable domestic law. This competition between domestic rules on validity, on the one hand, and the CISG, on the other, will be evident in the context of clauses seeking to exclude or limit the rules implied under Articles 35,[164] 41 and 42, or in the case of domestic rules on validity treating the sale of goods that do not belong to the seller as being void.[165]

Another challenge to which a lack of conformity in the goods gives rise is the possibility of a buyer invoking, on the same set of facts, remedies under both the CISG and the applicable domestic law. One situation where the buyer may want to do so is where what the CISG conceptualises as a lack of conformity in the goods also gives rise to domestic law remedies for mistake. Even though in practice a buyer would normally prefer to invoke such CISG remedies for breach of contract as damages, in some cases, such as where the time limit for bringing a claim for a lack of conformity under the CISG has expired,[166] the buyer may want to escape from the contract by relying on the domestic law on mistake which may render the contract void. Should the buyer be allowed to do so? The question remains controversial,[167] but the majority and, it is submitted, a preferable view is that buyers should not be able to invoke domestic law remedies in respect of a mistake as to conformity of the goods.[168] Where the remedies under the CISG and under domestic law arise from substantially the same facts,[169] the remedies under the CISG

162 See Art 4(a).

163 See HE Hartnell, 'Rousing the Sleeping Dog: The Validity Exception to the Convention on Contracts for the International Sale of Goods' (1993) 18 *Yale J Int'l L* 1.

164 See Chapter 5.

165 See Chapters 6 and 7.

166 See Art 39 and the discussion of this provision in Chapter 5.

167 See, eg CR Heiz, 'Validity of Contracts under the United Nations Convention on Contracts for the International Sale of Goods, April 11, 1980, and Swiss Contract Law' (1987) 20 *Vanderbilt J Transnational L* 639.

168 Kröll in Kröll, Mistelis and Viscasillas (n 16) Art 35, para 204; I Schwenzer in Schwenzer (n 16) Art 35, para 47; Schwenzer and Hachem (n 76); PC Leyens, 'CISG and Mistake: Uniform Law vs Domestic Law, the Interpretative Challenge of Mistake and the Validity Loophole' available at www.cisg.law.pace.edu/cisg/biblio/leyens.html.

169 Honnold (n 1) 80.

should displace those available under the domestic law on mistake. This is essential to preserve the integrity of the Convention's legal regime and to protect its ability to unify the law of international sales. The CISG contains an exhaustive system of remedies for a lack of conformity and remedies under domestic law should not be allowed to disrupt and undermine this system.[170]

The possibility of a buyer invoking remedies for a seller's innocent[171] or negligent misrepresentation[172] is another instance where domestic law remedies can, in principle, be triggered by the same facts as those giving rise to the buyer's claim for a lack of conformity under the CISG.[173] The argument presented in the case of mistake is, to a considerable extent, relevant here; that is, the Convention's remedial scheme should not be undermined by domestic law remedies provided that the two sets of remedies arise from the same facts.[174] The Convention's rules are also functionally equivalent to the domestic law remedies for misrepresentation. In the case of innocent and negligent misrepresentation, these remedies are concerned with what the *buyer knew* about aspects of conformity of the goods at the time of the conclusion of the contract.[175] The Convention's rules have been designed to divide the risks between the parties with reference to their reasonable expectations, which, in turn, are derived from *their actual or implied knowledge*.[176] As one commentator has rightly observed, the CISG contains 'a delicate web of awareness-related rules which are based on a balanced distribution of informational risks' and '[t]his distribution should not be disturbed by the application of rules of domestic law which may (and often will) allocate these risks differently'.[177]

[170] See Schwenzer in Schwenzer (n 16) Art 35, para. 47.

[171] In the context of English law, see *Chitty on Contracts*, 31st edn (London, Sweet & Maxwell, 2014) para 6-005, defining 'innocent' misrepresentation as one which is neither fraudulent nor negligent.

[172] In English law, negligent misrepresentation is defined as one 'made carelessly and in breach of a duty owed by the representor to the representee to take reasonable care that the representation is accurate' (E Peel, *Treitel: The Law of Contract*, 13th edn (London, Sweet & Maxwell, 2011) 376). See also Misrepresentation Act 1967, s 2(1) (UK).

[173] Suppose that the seller makes a false statement about an aspect of conformity of the goods which induces the buyer to enter into the contract, with the seller's representation becoming a term of the contract. In this case, both domestic remedies for misrepresentation and the Convention's remedies for breach of contract can potentially be invoked.

[174] It has been noted, for example, that there is a high threshold to be met in order for the contract to be avoided under the CISG whereas rescinding the contract under domestic law for misrepresentation may be much easier (see, eg M Bridge, 'Uniform and Harmonized Sales Law: Choice of Law Issues' in JJ Fawcett, JM Harris and M Bridge, *International Sale of Goods in the Conflict of Laws* (Oxford, OUP, 2005) 947).

[175] See UG Schroeter, 'Defining the Borders of Uniform International Contract Law: The CISG and Remedies for Innocent, Negligent, or Fraudulent Misrepresentation' (2013) 58 *Villanova L Rev* 553, 572.

[176] See Arts 8, 9, 35, 38–44 and the relevant discussion in Chapters 2–6.

[177] Schroeter (n 175) 575.

This argument should apply regardless of whether a misrepresentation has become a term of the contract. To begin with, the CISG is not entirely unconcerned with a pre-contractual phase, as may appear to be the case.[178] It addresses the issue of the formation of contracts. In addition, pre-contractual circumstances are relevant as factors in interpreting the parties' intentions and their statements and conduct.[179] To that extent, it is arguable that the CISG has its own regime for governing the legal consequences flowing from pre-contractual representations. In any case, it is clear that the CISG was not intended to concede all legal issues at the pre-contractual stage to the applicable domestic law.[180] But these points are probably insufficient to prove that the CISG should pre-empt domestic law remedies for a misrepresentation, which has not become a term of the contract. What may point to this conclusion more strongly, apart from the above argument that the Convention's remedial scheme must not be undermined, is the fact that it is the CISG that decides whether a representation becomes a term of the contract.[181] This fact, in turn, can be seen as the Convention's implicit indication that the seller will not be subject to any remedies arising from pre-contractual circumstances.[182]

There is a general agreement[183] that the position should be different in the case of fraudulent misrepresentation,[184] even if the facts giving rise to domestic law remedies and to those under the CISG[185] are the same.[186] A duty not to defraud exists in domestic laws independently of the agreement between the parties[187] and may flow, for example, from

[178] *Cf* Bridge (n 174) 947–48.
[179] See Art 8(3).
[180] Schroeter (n 175) 570.
[181] Ibid 577.
[182] Ibid.
[183] See, eg Schroeter in Schwenzer (n 16) Arts 14–24, para. 59; Schwenzer in Schwenzer (n 16) Art 35, para. 49; Kröll (n 168) para. 205; P Schlechtriem, 'The Borderland of Tort and Contract: Opening a New Frontier?' (1988) 21 *Cornell Int'l LJ* 467.
[184] In English law, for example, a statement is fraudulent if made '(i) with knowledge of its falsity, or (ii) without belief in its truth, or (iii) recklessly, not caring whether it is true or false' (Peel (n 172) 374–75, discussing *Derry v Peek* (1889) 14 App Cas 337).
[185] The applicability of Arts 35, 41 and 42 does not depend on whether the seller had knowledge of a lack of conformity when making a representation about the goods. The seller's knowledge is only relevant to the seller's ability to rely on the buyer's failure to give notice of a lack of conformity under Art 39 (see Arts 39 and 40 and the discussion of these provisions in Chapter 5).
[186] There is a view that the facts giving rise to remedies under domestic law and the CISG are not the same (see Schroeter (n 183) para 59). However, this position does not seem to be correct. Suppose that the seller makes a representation as to conformity of the goods to the buyer, knowing that the representation is false, and the statement becomes a term of the contract. It is this very same scenario that can give rise to remedies under both domestic law on fraudulent misrepresentation and the Convention's provisions on a lack of conformity.
[187] Schlechtriem (n 183).

the extra-contractual[188] obligation of 'honesty'[189] or from pre-contractual 'fault'.[190] The CISG was not intended to displace the application of these areas of domestic law.[191] This should not mean, however, that domestic law remedies displace the remedies for a lack of conformity under the Convention. The preferable view is that both sets of remedies should be applicable concurrently and the buyer should have a choice as to which remedies to invoke. There is no reason why a buyer should be deprived of remedies for breach of contract under the CISG just because it can also invoke domestic law remedies for fraud.[192]

[188] 'Domestic rules granting remedies for fraudulent conduct often ... do so by way of an extra-contractual (tort) liability, and may also provide compensation for purely economic loss' (Schroeter (n 183) para 59).

[189] See, eg Comment (a) on § 552, Restatement (Second) of Torts (1977).

[190] See, eg *Chitty* (n 171) para 1-156 ('Some legal systems consider that cases of fraud or duress are merely examples of a wider category of "fault in the formation of contract", a category famously termed *culpa in contrahendo* by the German jurist, Ihering. In French law, despite its general rule against allowing delict to intrude between contractors (a rule known as *non-cumul*), pre-contractual fault can give rise to a claim for damages in delict, there being a very general principle of delictual liability based on fault').

[191] Art 89 of the Convention relating to a Uniform Law on the International Sale of Goods 1964 (ULIS), the predecessor of the CISG, expressly provided that '[i]n case of fraud, damages shall be determined by the rules applicable in respect of contracts of sale not governed by the present Law'. This provision was not included in the CISG, but this omission was not intended to indicate a different approach (see Schlechtriem (n 183)).

[192] See Schroeter (n 175) 585–86, advocating this position on the basis that depriving a buyer of remedies under the CISG would be 'irreconcilable with the promotion of good faith' under Art 7(1).

2

Contractual Provisions on Conformity of the Goods

I. GENERAL

AS IS THE case in most legal systems,[1] the CISG makes it clear that the first and primary source of what constitutes conforming goods is the sales contract. Article 35(1) states that the seller 'must deliver goods which are of the quantity, quality, and description required by the contract and which are contained or packaged in the manner required by the contract'. Thus, the parties always have the option of creating their own complete regime of conformity. Rooted in the principle of the primacy of the party autonomy,[2] this provision secures the effectiveness and integrity of the bargaining process[3] and enables the parties' intentions to be formulated and solidified, delimiting the boundaries of risk allocation in accordance with the parties' will.[4] The parties' ability to design their own regime compensates for the inherent limitations of the rules[5] on conformity implied under the CISG.[6] The seller's ability to offer goods said to comply with certain standards for sale also signals to the buyers that the seller

[1] See I Schwenzer, P Hachem and C Kee, *Global Sales and Contract Law* (Oxford, OUP, 2012) para 31.46.

[2] The advantages flowing from the protection of party autonomy, such as the freedom of contracting, supporting promise keeping and protecting reasonable expectations and reliance, seem self-evident.

[3] See VM Gonzales, 'The Buyer's Specifications Exception to the Implied Warranty of Fitness for a Particular Purpose: Design or Performance' (1987) 61 *S Cal L Rev* 237, 242.

[4] Party autonomy has been said to promote uniformity in the Convention's application because focusing on contract and not on the rules on conformity implied under the CISG, which may be difficult to disentangle from 'a millennial tradition of idiosyncratic interpretation', the Convention's international character is safeguarded (R Hyland, 'Conformity of Goods to the Contract under the United Nations Sales Convention and the Uniform Commercial Code' in P Schlechtriem (ed), *Einheitliches Kaufrecht und nationals Obligationenrecht* (Baden-Baden, Nomos, 1987) 329–30). Contract interpretation is certainly more detached from concepts and legal reasoning than the reliance on the Convention's implied terms, which may provoke parallels with similar domestic rules, but it is not immune from non-uniform interpretation. What is crucial is not the process of contract interpretation but whether courts and tribunals have due regard to prior decisions.

[5] See Art 35(2) CISG. See Chapters 3, 4 and 5 for discussion of these rules.

[6] Gonzales (n 3) 242.

possesses the necessary information which spares the buyers the costs of investigating the actual quality and condition of the product.[7] This may not only facilitate trade but may also promote efficiency, since without an ability to rely on the information in the seller's offer the buyer would have to incur, unnecessarily, the cost of finding out the information already possessed by the seller.[8] To secure these benefits, the seller must be held liable if the information proves inaccurate or the goods do not comply with the agreed standards[9]—a result which would be achieved under Article 35(1). Although being the ultimate risk bearer, the seller nevertheless also benefits because, with the law boosting the buyer's confidence, it may be able to market its products more effectively.[10]

Where the contract contains clear and comprehensive provisions regarding what constitutes conforming goods the main task is to determine whether the delivered goods in fact correspond to the contract. However, while it is common for contracts to have detailed specifications, those specifications are not always exhaustive, complete or sufficiently clear. This means that there is often a need for contract interpretation which, under the Convention's rules, requires an investigation of all relevant circumstances of the case, which include the parties' pre- and post-contractual statements and conduct, practices, trade usages and the surrounding commercial, economic, social and cultural environment.[11] The task of contract interpretation is to ascertain the meaning of the contract and, more specifically, what conformity obligations the seller has undertaken.

Contract interpretation is intimately linked with the application of the rules on the formation of contracts because the latter, by establishing whether the contract has been concluded, also determine the content of the contract. The Convention's rules on the formation of contract make it essential for the parties to agree on some aspects of conformity because a proposal can only constitute an 'offer' capable of acceptance if, among other things, it indicates the 'goods' (necessitating some bare bone description) and expressly or implicitly fixes or makes a provision for determining the quantity (an aspect of conformity)[12] and the price[13] (often

[7] CP Gillett and SD Walt, *Sales Law: Domestic and International*, 2nd edn (New York, Foundation Press and Thomson West, 2009) 321.

[8] One guideline for deciding whether a particular statement by the seller has become a term of the contract, which flows from this analysis, is that a statement should be a term if it reveals the information that can be reasonably regarded as being within the seller's knowledge or domain (see Gillett and Walt (n 7) 322). The 'best risk bearer' discussion in Chapter 1 also supports this guideline.

[9] See Gillett and Walt (n 7) 322.

[10] See Gonzales (n 3) 242; 'Special Project: Article Two Warranties in Commercial Transactions: An Update' (1987) 72 *Cornell L Rev* 1191.

[11] See Art 8(3).

[12] See Art 35(1).

[13] See Art 14(1).

a factor in evaluating conformity). In fact, it is possible to go further and to suggest that the rules on formation are themselves capable of determining the content of the contract. However, two points need to be borne in mind. First, contracts are sometimes concluded by means other than offer and acceptance and where this is the case, Part II of the Convention,[14] providing for the offer and acceptance model, is largely irrelevant.[15] More crucially, the rules on the formation of contracts are themselves dependent on the rules on the interpretation of the parties' intentions (Articles 8 and 9)[16] which are, ultimately, the central reference point in analysing the parties' agreement.

II. PRE-CONTRACTUAL REPRESENTATIONS AND CONDUCT

A. Puffery and Opinions

The conclusion of a contract is invariably preceded by discussions and negotiations between the parties or, at the very least, by some kind of representations made by the parties. Where the outcomes of negotiations are fully reflected in and consolidated into a detailed written agreement, there may be little need to investigate the content of the negotiations. In fact, the so-called 'entire agreement' or 'merger' clauses may evidence the parties' intention to disallow reliance on any representations made prior to the conclusion of the contract, with the written contract being the sole source of the agreement. But, in the absence of such an intention or due to the incompleteness or lack of clarity of the contract, the question of the nature and effect of pre-contractual statements and conduct will often be of some importance in interpreting the contract. Some of the central questions are: Did the seller's pre-contractual representations become part of the contract so that they now define its conformity obligations? If not, are they altogether irrelevant or do they still have a role to play in influencing the meaning of the contract? These and other related questions will now be addressed.

The Convention's rules on the interpretation of the parties' statements and conduct are very general. They recognise the legal significance of the party's actual intention only where the other party knew or could not have been unaware of the former's actual intention.[17] In other cases, a party's statement and conduct are to be interpreted in accordance with

[14] See Arts 14–24.

[15] But not wholly irrelevant, because Art 14 should arguably be used to infer the minimum content required for the contract to be concluded.

[16] Because it is these rules that determine: whether the offeror had an intention to be bound by its proposal for concluding a contract (offer) in case of acceptance; the content of the offer; and whether the offeree had an intention to assent to the offer.

[17] See Art 8(1).

an understanding and perception of a reasonable person.[18] Both tests, as noted,[19] are to be applied having regard to all relevant circumstances, including any practices established between the parties and trade usages. The general nature of these rules, and the Convention's language that only 'due consideration'[20] is required to be given to all relevant circumstances, has led to the view that the Convention's rules have not been designed to deal with the question of whether a representation has become part of the contract.[21] It is true that the Convention's rules are much more fluid and fuzzy than those of some of the developed legal systems, which either have more precise tests of what constitutes a contract term[22] or subsume pre-contractual representations into various categories,[23] each leading to a specific legal consequence. No such scheme is apparent on the face of the Convention, but that does not mean that the Convention is not capable of determining what amounts to a term of the contract. After all, where domestic laws rely on more elaborate criteria and classifications they do so largely to assist with contract interpretation by illustrating, for example, which representations are likely to carry enough weight in the eyes of the parties so as to amount to a contractual term. Therefore, the CISG is well capable of identifying a contract term,[24] but the challenge is to inject a reasonable degree of precision into its regime by identifying factual patterns and developing the corresponding guidelines which could help to interpret the myriad of scenarios in which pre-contractual representations are made in a principled and coherent way.

One guideline that has been proposed is to view a contract as a commercial relationship which, in turn, is a continuum not confined, by definition, to a precise moment. This continuum runs all the way from the pre-contractual discussions through to the post-contractual representations.[25] It has been further contended that if good faith is a relevant consideration, then it should demand honesty from the seller when it makes its representations.[26]

[18] See Art 8(2).

[19] See n 11 above.

[20] See Art 8(3).

[21] J Lookofsky, *Understanding the CISG*, 3rd Worldwide edn (The Netherlands, Kluwer Law International BV, 2008) 75.

[22] Such as the 'basis of the bargain' test in § 2-313 in the US Uniform Commercial Code (UCC) that provides that express warranties can only be created if an affirmation of fact, a promise, description or a sample or model become or are made part of the basis of the bargain (see § 2-313 in *Uniform Commercial Code: 2009–2010 Edition* (West-Thomson Reuters, 2009)).

[23] Such as, in the common law, puff, opinions, misrepresentations, contract term or collateral contract.

[24] Otherwise, it could not and would not be a functioning contract law instrument.

[25] See JE Murray, '"Basis of the Bargain": Transcending Classical Concepts' (1982) 66 *Minn L Rev* 283.

[26] Ibid 320.

Put differently, 'the seller's defense, in which he asserts an excuse based on the timing of his statement, would manifest obvious bad faith'.[27] A related argument is that if the buyer cannot trust the seller's statements, the buyer will be forced to be excessively cautious before entering into the contract of sale.[28]

If these were the only guidelines, pre- (as well as post-) contractual representations would generally be regarded as being the terms of the contract, in which case *sellers* would have to be extremely careful about what they say or do before and after the contract. Whilst promoting honesty and integrity is undoubtedly an aim of the CISG,[29] a contractual relationship is often preceded by a 'bargain' based on the pursuit of self-interest, which sometimes involves statements stretching the boundaries of what could otherwise be an entirely accurate and precise description of the goods. It is for this reason that legal systems often do not attach legal significance to 'puffing' which is simply intended to lure the buyer into the contract or to strike a better bargain. There is no doubt that the position is the same under the CISG.[30] Statements such as 'the machines just got out on to the market and ... are a very good deal',[31] for example, were rightly regarded as not intended to be part of the contract in one CISG case. As a general matter, to amount to a contract term a representation should be expected to convey something meaningful, and hence more or less concrete, about such matters as the goods' description and quality, which this statement does not do.[32] Otherwise, none of the considerations justifying the existence of the legal regime on conformity[33] (their ability to define the subject matter of the contract, to signal its characteristics and to divide the risks between the parties) could be promoted.

Other factors relevant in distinguishing 'puffs' from statements intended to become terms of the contract include:[34] time proximity to the conclusion of the contract;[35] the balance and level of the parties' expertise; whether the

[27] Ibid 321.

[28] Ibid 322–23.

[29] Art 7(1), for example, requires that in interpreting the Convention regard must be had to the observance of good faith in international trade.

[30] S Kröll in S Kröll, L Mistelis and P Viscasillas (eds), *UN Convention on Contracts for the International Sale of Goods (CISG): Commentary* (Munich, CH Beck/Hart Publishing, 2011) Art 35, para 40.

[31] *Miami Valley Paper, LLC v Lebbing Engineering & Consulting GmbH*, F Supp 2d, 2009 WL 818618 (SD Ohio).

[32] See also Gonzales (n 3) 241 (allowing puffs 'would permit commercial transactions to be executed on the basis of vague and imprecise statements').

[33] See Chapter 1.

[34] See, generally, M Bridge, *The Sale of Goods*, 3rd edn (Oxford, OUP, 2014) paras 8.10–8.15; also Official Comment on § 2-313 in Uniform Commercial Code (n 22) point 10.

[35] The statement is likely to carry greater weight if it is closer to the time when the contract is made than when it is more remote.

seller has assumed responsibility for its representation and/or invited the buyer to examine and check the accuracy of the representation; whether the statement is purely an informal remark;[36] whether it is important to the buyer; whether the untruthfulness of the statement is obvious;[37] whether the buyer relies on the representation; and the level of specificity of the statement. This latter factor was at play in a CISG case where the seller's statement that it produced 'high quality and state-of-the-art' equipment was not regarded as being part of the contract because 'it was too general and too difficult to measure in order to constitute a contractual warranty'.[38] However, it must not be assumed that statements such as this will always be regarded as mere puffs. It has been rightly observed that today when so much emphasis is placed on the continuously growing consumers' expectations, such a representation as to quality by a well-established manufacturer with a higher level of expertise than that of the buyer may well be regarded as sufficiently weighty so as to be treated as part of the contract.[39] In fact, the very same case supports this proposition because another representation by the seller, a well-known European manufacturer, that its equipment was 'easy to operate' was deemed to have been intended to be a term of the contract.[40] The question of whether a statement is a puff or a contractual term is thus not easily answered as the line between the two can be crossed very easily.[41]

A difficulty similar to that of identifying puffery also arises where the seller merely expresses an opinion relating to an aspect of conformity without intending it to be a contractual term. The factors set out in the previous paragraph are again relevant here. Taking the factor of the balance of the parties' expertise as an example, if the buyer possesses greater expertise than the seller and effective means of identifying the correctness of the seller's representation,[42] the seller's statements may well be treated as merely an expression of an opinion. The time when the statement was made, as well as other surrounding circumstances, may also prove relevant. Suppose that a seller makes a representation regarding a technical characteristic of the existing goods several months before the contract is made and before the time set for the mutually agreed inspection, which is intended to cover

36 If so, the statement is unlikely to have been intended to be a contractual term.

37 *Benjamin's Sale of Goods*, 9th edn (London, Thompson-Sweet & Maxwell, 2014) para 10-005.

38 See *Mansonville Plastics (BC) Ltd v Kurtz GmbH*, 2003 BCSC 1298, para 99. Another factor that was taken into account in this case was that the seller's representation did not necessarily relate to the goods intended to be sold to the buyer, but was applied to the seller's business generally.

39 See Bridge (n 34) paras 8.10–8.15.

40 See *Mansonville Plastics (BC) Ltd v Kurtz GmbH* (n 38) para 101.

41 *Benjamin's Sale of Goods* (n 37) para 10-005; Bridge (n 34) para 8.10 ('identifying puffery in the consumerist conditions of today is practically impossible').

42 See, eg *Oscar Chess Ltd v Williams* [1957] 1 WLR 370.

a characteristic referred to in the seller's representation. Suppose further that it is common in this trade sector to exchange drafts of the agreements with the detailed technical specifications.[43] It is arguable that because the buyer has an opportunity to inspect the goods and to set out its preferred specifications through draft agreements, an earlier statement was simply an opinion not intended to be binding on the seller. In addition, it may be helpful to pay attention to whether the goods are an established product or whether they are new and previously untested,[44] in which case it is likely that a reasonable person in the buyer's position will view the seller's remark as no more than an opinion.

B. Public Statements

Statements about the goods are often made in advertisements and other sources open to the public, such as suppliers' websites and brochures, and the question is whether the seller should be held liable where the goods do not answer those representations. It has been argued that the sellers should generally be held liable. First, even where the representations are not made by the seller, who is merely a trader in the chain, the seller should be liable[45] because there is a risk, particularly in the light of the strong consumer protection in some countries, that the buyer (or its sub-buyers) will be liable to the ultimate consumers relying on such representations.[46] It should be possible for the buyer to pass this liability to the seller as well as for the seller to pass the liability further up the chain since there is a need for consistency in legal treatment of all traders in the chain, coupled with an apparent policy in some jurisdictions of ensuring that the original suppliers be held responsible.[47] The second argument reinforces the first: considering that advertisements and similar public representations seek to induce the public as a whole, rather than a particular buyer, the seller should be held liable in order to protect the public and to encourage other sellers to stay true to their public statements.[48]

[43] See *Howard Marine and Dredging Co Ltd v A Ogden & Sons (Excavations) Ltd* [1978] QB 574.

[44] Gonzales (n 10) 1186.

[45] *Cf* Art 2:303 of Draft Common Frame of Reference (DCFR) in C von Bar and E Clive (eds), *Principles, Definitions and Model Rules of European Private Law: Draft Common Frame of Reference (DCFR)* (Munich, Sellier European Law Publishers, 2009) vol II.

[46] For a somewhat similar argument, reinforced by the reference to Consumer Sales Directive 1999/44/EC, see Schwenzer, Hachem and Kee (n 1) para 31.50.

[47] See, in English law, *Ashington Piggeries Ltd v Christopher Hill Ltd; Christopher Hill Ltd v Norsildmel* [1972] AC 441; *Webster Thompson Ltd v J G Pears (Newark) Ltd* [2009] 2 Lloyd's Rep 339; *Britvic Soft Drinks Ltd v Messer UK Ltd* [2002] 2 Lloyd's Rep 368.

[48] See Comment A on Art 2:303 DCFR (n 45) 1296.

These two points can also be looked at through the lenses of economic considerations. It is worth making the seller liable in order to facilitate the signalling function of the rules on conformity. If buyers feel secure in relying on public statements, they will be spared the costs of investigating the conformity of the goods, with greater efficiency being thereby promoted. Some have gone as far as to suggest that the seller makes a bargain with a 'market' as a whole, rather than with an individual buyer.[49] If so, whether a representation becomes a part of the contract should depend solely on whether the price of the product would be expected to include the advertised characteristics.[50] That expectation, in turn, is to be determined with reference to the market and market price.[51]

If these arguments are accepted in the context of the CISG, the focus will shift from the contracting parties to broader societal considerations, which are concerned with an impact of private contracts on a society and an economy. These arguments may well form part of the background against which contracts are interpreted, but ultimately it is the circumstances of an individual case that are decisive[52] and the crucial test is the view of a reasonable person in the buyer's shoes.[53] If the words, despite being a public statement, are in the nature of puffery, no liability should arise. Whilst not decisive, the price of the product is certainly a relevant factor. If, in the light of the current market, the advertised characteristics are expected to be part of the product given its price, the representation may have been intended to be binding on the seller. In one case, a representation in the seller's brochure that the goods would be a 'new product' was held to lead to the seller's obligation to deliver new goods, because the price asked for corresponded to the value of a new (that is, unused) product.[54] The time when a particular statement is made should also be taken into account. If, say, the advertisement precedes the contract by a lengthy period, the buyer's case may be weakened. The seller cannot be expected to be bound by its advertisement for an indefinite period as circumstances can change. This prolonged temporal distance may also be indicative of a lack of reliance by the buyer on the advertisement, which is likely to be relevant to whether a

[49] See Gillett and Walt (n 7) 330; TJ Holdych and BD Mann, 'The Basis of the Bargain Requirement: A Market and Economic Based Analysis of Express Warranties—Getting What You Pay for and Paying for What You Get' (1996) 45 *DePaul L Rev* 781, 800–3.

[50] Holdych and Mann (n 49) 802.

[51] 'Since the market price is an indicator of attribute existence, the market price reflects the value of all attributes purchased by a buyer, and it is inefficient for all buyers to engage in explicit negotiation and bargaining for warranty terms and other attributes' (ibid 800–1).

[52] See Art 8 CISG.

[53] See, similarly, Schwenzer, Hachem and Kee (n 1) para 31.51.

[54] *Brown & Root Services Corp v Aerotech Herman Nelson Inc*, 2002 MBQB 229, para 58; affirmed in Court of Appeal of Manitoba, 2004 MBCA 63.

statement was intended to be a contractual term.[55] Where a statement indicates a particular technical attribute in a highly specific and specialist manner, the buyer's reliance on it and/or the firmness of the parties' intentions to this effect can be inferred more readily.[56] This seems to have occurred in a case where the buyer, a public works contractor in Portugal, purchased metal covers for sewerage systems, and the Spanish seller was held liable for 'defects in resistance' of the covers because the delivered goods had resistance of 25 to 35 tons whilst the seller's catalogue clearly stated that resistance of the covers was to be up to 40 tons.[57]

C. Direct Communications Between the Parties

It is common for representations about the goods to be made in the course of direct communications and dealings between the parties before the contract is made. For example, an agreement, whereby a seller was to supply components originating from Germany to a milling facility in Iran, was inferred from the information to that effect in the pro-forma invoice, sent to the would-be buyer for presentation to its bank and to the Iranian authorities to arrange for permission to import the goods, and in the letter of credit, the opening of which was required for permission to import. The seller was thus held to be in breach of contract when components originating from Russia and Turkey had in fact been delivered.[58] An obligation to

[55] There has been much disagreement, in the context of US law, as to the precise status and function of reliance in establishing an express warranty (see sources referred to in this chapter; also S Kwestel, 'Freedom from Reliance: A Contract Approach to Express Warranty' (1992) 26 *Suffolk U L Rev* 959). The views range from advocating the reliance being a necessary precondition for finding an express warranty, to rejecting entirely the need for any reliance. The 'half way' approaches have also been taken contending that there should be presumptions of reliance which sellers can rebut (see, eg SZ Hodaszy, 'Express Warranties under the Uniform Commercial Code: Is there a Reliance Requirement?' (1991) 66 *NYU L Rev* 468). This disagreement, particularly when it comes to the positions at the opposite ends of the spectrum, illustrates how different approaches flow depending on what view of commercial and contract law is taken. If the focus is on societal concerns, an individual buyer's reliance on an advertisement (and other public representations) becomes irrelevant because the generally predicted economic and other kinds of impact on the public will dictate the need for holding the seller liable irrespective of the buyer's lack of reliance. If, in contrast, a traditional view of contract law, concerned with allocating risks in accordance with the parties' intentions, is taken, then reliance becomes a (powerful) factor in interpreting the contract. For discussion of the role of reliance in implying a contractual term under the CISG, see further nn 63 and 116 below and the accompanying main text.

[56] See Appellate Court Koblenz, 2 U 1464/11, 19 December 2012 (Germany), available at http://cisgw3.law.pace.edu/cases/121219g2.html.

[57] Appellate Court Barcelona, Rollo No 862/2003-B, 28 April 2004 (Spain), available at http://cisgw3.law.pace.edu/cases/040428s4.html.

[58] Appellate Court Zweibrücken, 7 U 4/03, 2 February 2004 (Germany), available at http://cisgw3.law.pace.edu/cases/040202g1.html.

deliver the goods of a very high quality may be established from the seller's representation that the goods would be better than 'Class I', particularly where the seller's brand is well known on the market.[59] In one such case involving the sale of canned food products, the seller was held to be in breach of contract in the absence of express quality provisions in the contract, where the cans contained foreign objects, fruits were dark in colour, soft and contained a high concentration of tin, resulting in a metallic taste and even making the content inedible.[60]

Where there are several not entirely consistent communications, the sequence in which they were sent is likely to be relevant. In one case,[61] the seller denied that it had agreed to deliver food products free from genetically modified organisms by referring to a letter it had sent to the buyer's (exclusive) customer, in which it stated that it had no practical means of identifying whether an ingredient had been genetically modified. The court rejected this argument relying on a subsequent letter, which the seller had sent to the buyer and which was attached to the contract, where the seller expressly certified that the goods would be free from genetically modified organisms. Although the decision does not elaborate on the reasoning, the reasons why the buyer prevailed seem clear. The subsequent letter was addressed directly to the buyer and that potentially carried greater weight than the letter to the buyer's customer since the contract was with the buyer. But what made the buyer's case compelling was that the letter to the buyer was sent after the first letter, which might have reflected subsequent negotiations changing the seller's original intentions, and that the second letter was attached to the contract, which pointed strongly to the parties' intention to avoid any misunderstanding as to what had been agreed.

D. Buyer's Knowledge

Article 35(3) CISG provides that the 'seller is not liable ... for any lack of conformity of the goods if at the time of the conclusion of the contract the buyer knew or could not have been unaware of such lack of conformity'. This provision, however, is expressly said to apply only to Article 35(2), which contains the Convention's implied terms of conformity of the goods and will be discussed in subsequent chapters.[62] The question that arises at

[59] Turku Court of Appeal, S 97/324, 12 November 1997 (Finland), available at http://cisgw3.law.pace.edu/cases/971112f5.html#cx, affirming Tampere Court of First Instance, 95/11193, 17 January 1997 (Finland). See also S Kuoppala, 'The Application and Interpretation of the CISG in Finnish Case Law 1997–2005', available at http://cisgw3.law.pace.edu/cisg/biblio/kuoppala2.html.

[60] See, particularly, Tampere Court of First Instance, 17 January 1997 (n 59).

[61] Canton Appellate Court Basel, 33/2002/SAS/so, 22 August 2003 (Switzerland), available at http://cisgw3.law.pace.edu/cases/030822s1.html.

[62] See Chapters 3–5.

this stage is whether it needs to be extended to Article 35(1) and, even if not, whether the buyer's knowledge, usually derived from having an opportunity of pre-contractual examination of the goods, should be relevant to deciding what conformity obligations were imposed on the seller by the contract.

There hardly seems to be any basis in the argument in favour of extending the application of Article 35(3) to paragraph (1). A specific statement of its applicability to paragraph (2) strongly points to the drafters' intention not to do so. But this does not mean that the buyer's knowledge of the actual state and condition of the goods prior to the conclusion of the contract is not relevant to interpreting the contract under Article 35(1). It is arguable that if the buyer, having seen the goods, knows that the seller's representation in respect of them is untrue, it can hardly have a reasonable expectation that the representation will form part of the seller's contractual obligations.[63] The buyer's reliance on the seller's representation is a powerful factor in favour of the parties' intention to treat that representation as binding on the seller, and no such reliance is present where the buyer knows the statement to be untrue. From a moral standpoint, it can be argued that ignoring the buyer's knowledge in interpreting the contract would be contrary to good faith. A view from an economic angle also supports this line of argument since the signalling and the risk allocation functions, based largely on the seller being the superior possessor of information, cease to be relevant.

These points are too obvious for the Convention's drafters not to have been aware of them and their answer is that Article 35(1) concerns not the terms implied under the CISG but what the contract itself provides for.[64] The buyer has the right to demand fully what the seller has agreed to do and the buyer's knowledge of the actual state of the goods cannot change the content of the seller's obligation. This argument is primarily targeted at the express provisions, which in commercial contracts are powerful evidence of the parties' intentions and agreement. It is much weaker when the terms are implied into the contract from the surrounding facts[65] since the buyer's knowledge is part of these facts and hence cannot be ignored.

The level of influence this factor will exert on contract interpretation will depend on the particular circumstances. At times, the fact of the buyer's inspection is hardly relevant, as was the case where the contract required a pony to be 'fully fit' and where the buyer had carried out a pre-sale veterinary examination, which, whilst adequate, revealed no signs of injury

[63] See JE Murray, '"Basis of the Bargain": Transcending Classical Concepts' (1982) 66 *Minn L Rev* 283, 294–95.

[64] CM Bianca in CM Bianca and J Bonell (eds), *Commentary on the International Sales Law* (Milan, Giuffrè, 1987) 273.

[65] See Arts 8 and 9 CISG.

or health problems.[66] The correctness of the decision holding the seller liable is evident from the express contractual stipulation, which was also preceded by the seller's representation of full fitness of the pony. In some other cases, in contrast, what has been fatal to the buyer's case is that it had actually seen the alleged lack of conformity and could be regarded as having given its unconditional consent to the receipt of those particular goods. This was the case where the buyer, before buying second-hand cars, inspected them and became aware of the defects,[67] which were apparently referred to in the contract along with the requirement that the vehicles were to be in 'good condition'. The latter was presumably not meant to indicate perfection but only a condition which could reasonably be expected from a second-hand car which had been previously subjected to normal use.[68]

A more complex case[69] involved the sale of a textile (rotary printing) machine. The contract referred to the 'rapport equipment length 641 mm, 1018 mm'. Before the contract was made, the buyer, a trader in textile machinery, had an opportunity to inspect the machine, which was not a new model (being 14 years' old) capable of operating at a full rapport length. Prior to the conclusion of the contract, the seller sent a fax to the buyer referring to the same rapport length as that included in the contract, stating that the machine was 'complete and operating as viewed'. After concluding the contract, the buyer also sent a purchase confirmation in which it declared that it would take over the machine 'complete and operating as viewed'. The buyer's breach of contract claim based on the fact that the stencil holders for a rapport length of 1018 mm were missing was dismissed on the ground that, being an expert, the buyer ought to have known that the machine would not conform to the latest technical specifications. Moreover, the seller 'was entitled to expect that the Buyer had concluded the contract in full knowledge of the technical possibilities of the machinery and its equipment'. In relation to contractual rapport length specification, the Supreme Court of Switzerland appears to have affirmed the decision of the Court of First Instance that 'rapport equipment was meant as technical information in respect to the possible rapport length, which could be printed if the necessary equipment was used'.

The court faced a difficult dilemma. On the one hand, the contract appears to have expressly required full rapport length. On the other hand, the surrounding factual evidence (an opportunity to inspect, the buyer's expertise, the seller's pre-contractual letter and the buyer's confirmation of purchase)

[66] District Court Copenhagen, 19 October 2007 (Denmark), available at http://cisgw3.law.pace.edu/cases/071019d1.html.

[67] Supreme Court, Recurso de Casación No 81/2001, 17 January 2008 (Spain), available at http://cisgw3.law.pace.edu/cases/080117s4.html.

[68] '[T]he particular [defects] known to the Buyer did not indicate any signs that the vehicles had been involved in accidents' (ibid).

[69] Supreme Court, 4C.296/2000/rnd, 22 December 2000 (Switzerland), available at http://cisgw3.law.pace.edu/cases/001222s1.html.

was overwhelmingly in the seller's favour. The court interpreted the contractual clause restrictively by assigning purely an informative function to it. Faced with an imperfect fit between the contract and the surrounding facts, the court seems to have done its best to achieve a fair result.

III. POST-CONTRACTUAL STATEMENTS AND CONDUCT

As noted, the parties' statements and conduct after the conclusion of the contract form part of the circumstances to be taken into account in interpreting the contract.[70] Their precise relevance lies at two points. First, they may prove useful in clarifying and establishing the parties' understanding and intentions prior to the conclusion of the contract, thereby helping establish the meaning of the contract. Secondly, they may evidence the parties' intention to modify, or the actual modification of, the terms of the contract.[71] Caution needs to be exercised before allowing the post-contractual conduct and/or statements to lead to either of these two outcomes. A party's possible incentive to attempt to manipulate the meaning of the contract by orchestrating its post-contractual conduct is well recognised.[72] Allowing post-contractual conduct to influence the meaning of a contract too readily may also undermine legal certainty, business planning and, ultimately, security in international trade. The conclusion of the contract is a point of fundamental commercial and legal significance for the parties and they should be able to rely on it. This means that only where tribunals are certain that post-contractual conduct/statements are, or are likely to be, a genuine reflection of the parties' intention should they be taken into consideration.

This may be the case where, after concluding the contract, the seller signs an agreement acknowledging the problems with the goods;[73] sends a message to the buyer setting out the specifications of the goods;[74] or signs certificates of quality and origin, which are then taken to reflect the seller's confirmation that the contract called for the goods of the quality and origin specified in the certificate.[75] The contract itself may require the seller to

[70] See Art 8(3) CISG.

[71] See Art 29 CISG.

[72] See, eg M Schmidt-Kessel in I Schwenzer (ed), *Schlechtriem and Schwenzer, Commentary on the UN Convention on the International Sale of Goods (CISG)*, 3rd edn (Oxford, OUP, 2010) Art 8, para 52.

[73] See *Italian Textile Machine*, CIETAC Arbitration, June 2006, available at http://cisgw3.law.pace.edu/cases/060600c2.html.

[74] See ICAC Arbitration, 97/2002, 6 June 2003, available at http://cisgw3.law.pace.edu/cases/030606r1.html.

[75] See Helsinki Court of Appeal, S 96/1129, 29 January 1998 (Finland), available at http://cisgw3.law.pace.edu/cases/980129f5.html; also Kuoppala (n 59).

send samples of the goods as a source of the goods' description or quality after the contract is made and where the buyer, having received the samples, does not raise any objections, the samples are likely to be an accurate representation of the parties' intention as to the conformity of the goods.[76] Where the contract does not provide for specifications or does not indicate the source from which such specifications can be derived, the seller's conformity obligations may be established with reference to a product manual, supplied after the contract is made, particularly where the dispute concerns complex machinery and technical characteristics.[77] In a case[78] involving the sale of 'two HVM-280 Horizontal Bag Packing/Sealing Machines' (amongst others), the seller's obligation as to the place of manufacture was defined with reference to the manual, despite the manual being 'a general document ... applicable to all HVM-280 equipment sold by product manufacturers worldwide'. Sellers should therefore bear in mind that their product manuals may entail legal consequences for their contractual obligations. If they wish to avoid this result, they are well advised to include specifications in the contract and to clarify the relationship between such specifications and their representations in the manuals.

A detailed assessment of the particular facts is similarly necessary to answer the question of whether the parties intended to modify the contract. As explained, a finding of such an intention requires strong supporting evidence. Such evidence was not present in a case[79] where the components for a milling facility were to be of German origin, but the seller argued that since the buyer inspected the goods prior to the shipment, it ought to have discovered that the components were actually of Russian and Turkish origin and, therefore, the buyer's non-objection indicated an implicit agreement to change the contract. This argument was rejected because the origin of the components was not discoverable upon that inspection, due to the lack of the buyer's technical expertise, and the seller failed to disclose the substitution of the components.

[76] See *Granite and Marble*, CIETAC Arbitration, July 2006, available at http://cisgw3.law.pace.edu/cases/060700c1.html. See also *Linseed Cake*, CIETAC Arbitration, 9 January 1993, available at http://cisgw3.law.pace.edu/cases/930109c1.html, where, similarly, the buyer did not object to the post-contractual sample and opened a letter of credit, but where the sending of a sample was not required by the contract and seems to have been simply sent at the buyer's request.

[77] See *Broadcasting Equipment*, CIETAC Arbitration, 22 May 1996, available at http://cisgw3.law.pace.edu/cases/960522c1.html, where the technical documentation provided with the delivery of the goods and during their testing was, along with attachments to the contract, used to establish the seller's conformity obligations.

[78] See *Chemical Cleaning Product Equipment*, CIETAC Arbitration, 20 April 1999, available at http://cisgw3.law.pace.edu/cases/990420c1.html.

[79] Appellate Court Zweibrücken, 7 U 4/03, 2 February 2004 (Germany), available at http://cisgw3.law.pace.edu/cases/040202g1.html.

In another case,[80] in contrast, even though the evidence did not arise from the dealings between the parties, it was nevertheless thought to be sufficiently clear to show that the contract had been modified. The buyer argued that the seller had breached the contract by delivering the lambskin coats bearing numbers different from those specified in the contract. The seller managed to prove that the buyer had implicitly consented to the modification of the contract, whereby the goods that would be delivered would have the same specifications but different numbers to those originally stipulated. It was shown that the contract goods had been resold to the buyer's customer who informed the buyer of its willingness to accept the goods with different article numbers and consented to the modification of their contract. Although the evidence did not relate directly to the contract between the parties, an inference in the seller's favour seems justifiable. The contract with the customer had been modified and the buyer's implicit consent to the parallel variation of its contract with the seller must be the necessary corollary to it. It was also clear that the buyer remained committed to the contract with its customer and, with the seller being the supplier, the buyer must have remained committed to the contract with the seller. With its customer having no objections in respect of different article numbers, the buyer had no business motive not to agree to the modification.

IV. DESCRIPTION

Contractual description serves a vital function of identifying, to a greater degree than other aspects of conformity, what it is that the seller has agreed to sell and deliver. This is particularly important where the contract is for unascertained goods, that is, those which have not been specifically identified by the parties.[81] In this case, the parties do not have any specific object in mind, and more detail and information than in the case of specific goods need to be included in the contract to clarify and delimit the content of the seller's obligation.[82] That is not to say that description is not needed in the case of specific goods, but there its target is not so much the identification of the goods but the attribution of further essential characteristics, additional to those whose existence the parties have already agreed upon or

[80] Commercial Court Zürich, HG 930634/O, 30 November 1998 (Switzerland), available at http://cisgw3.law.pace.edu/cases/981130s1.html.

[81] The clearest illustration of such unidentified goods relates to generic goods, such as rice, cotton, wheat or oil which, to be identifiable, need to be defined with reference to various characteristics (eg grade, weight, composition or admixture content).

[82] See Art 31(b), which evidences the Convention's recognition of the distinction between specific and unidentified goods. The importance of the identification of the goods can also be seen from the provisions on the passage of risk (see Arts 67 and 69(3)).

assumed.[83] For example, the parties may have agreed on a specific animal from the seller's farm that the buyer intends to buy, but further description may be included to define specific characteristics, such as precise age or level of fitness, which the buyer may not know.

In some legal regimes the concept of or the function performed by description is very important. Some civil law systems distinguish between the so-called *aliud* (delivery of the goods of a different nature to those agreed) and *peius* (defective goods). The former triggers the legal consequences flowing from non-delivery, which are very different to those attributed to the defective goods cases. Therefore, it becomes necessary to determine whether the seller's breach consisted of delivering something wholly different to what was stipulated in the contract or whether the seller has delivered the goods of the agreed *genus*, with the problem relating to them being defective. In English law, description has also traditionally played an important role, since the breach of a term of 'description' amounts to a breach of 'condition',[84] which, in turn, allows the buyer to reject the goods and terminate the contract.

The said civil law systems as well as English law have to battle with a difficult and, at times, a metaphysical question of whether a characteristic in question goes to the nature of the goods or whether it is a feature not going to their very essence. From this point of view, the CISG can be said to be superior to those legal systems as it avoids the need to ask such questions without any intellectual sacrifices. Whilst description under the Convention is an aspect of conformity, no distinct legal consequences follow depending on how an aspect at hand is characterised (eg whether it is a matter of quality or description). There have been suggestions that those exceptional cases involving the delivery of the goods wholly different from those contracted for should, under the CISG, be treated as cases of non-delivery.[85] If this position were accepted, one difference in practical and legal consequences would follow, namely, the inapplicability of the Article 39 notice requirement to non-delivery.[86] However, the prevailing and, it is submitted, the preferable view[87] does not accept this position because treating those exceptional cases as non-delivery would unnecessarily deprive the

[83] '[W]hat the description identifies is not the article which is *in fact* selected by the parties and earmarked to the contract but the essential characteristics which the article that has become so earmarked must possess if the seller is to fulfill his fundamental obligation' (E McKendrick, *Goode on Commercial Law*, 4th edn (London, Penguin Books, 2010) 321–22).

[84] Sale of Goods Act (SGA) 1979, s 13 (UK).

[85] Bianca (n 64) 272; Text of Secretariat Commentary on Article 29 of the 1978 Draft, para 3, available at www.cisg.law.pace.edu/cisg/text/secomm/secomm-31.html.

[86] Art 39(1) CISG: 'The buyer loses the right to rely on a *lack of conformity* of the goods if he does not give notice to the seller specifying the nature of the lack of conformity within a reasonable time after he has discovered it or ought to have discovered it' (emphasis added).

[87] Kröll (n 30) para 33 (with further references).

Convention of its advantage of largely dispensing with the need to engage in the discussion about what constitutes the essence of the goods, which, as the experience of domestic legal systems shows, only causes unnecessary complexity and a degree of uncertainty.[88] Except for the burden of the Article 39 requirement,[89] the level of legal protection afforded to the buyer in cases of a lack of conformity remains the same as that in cases of non-delivery.[90]

All this does not mean that the need to understand the meaning of 'description' under the CISG is solely a matter of theory. There are at least three sets of cases where characterising a term as falling within description will either trigger distinct legal consequences or will be needed to formulate the legal basis for a claim. Where the seller's liability is limited or excluded in relation to obligations of 'quality' or 'description', determining whether a term in question was a matter of 'quality' or 'description' is obviously essential.[91] Similarly, the contract may provide for some other special 'regime', such as the finality of a certificate clause[92] or a limited period within which the buyer can raise a claim, which applies only to matters of 'quality' or 'description', which again makes the characterisation necessary. Another situation is where no breach of a term as to quality, quantity or packaging is committed, but the buyer has still not received the goods it had contracted for.[93] The only remaining legal basis for the buyer's conformity claim will have to be a breach of description, and to formulate such a claim an understanding of this concept is needed. An understanding of this concept is also needed when applying Article 35(2)(a), which provides that conforming goods are those which 'are fit for the purposes for which goods of the *same description* would ordinarily be used'. To apply this provision, it may become important to identify the boundaries of what constitutes description.

As noted, the terms of description are those which, first and foremost, identify the goods, but arguably not in the sense of clarifying their location or enabling the parties to separate them from other goods, but in terms of revealing their nature and essential characteristics.[94] As a rule, description relates to the goods' physical attributes. The obvious cases of a breach of description are those where the seller delivers goods entirely different from

[88] In English law, see, eg *Ashington Piggeries Ltd v Christopher Hill Ltd* (n 47) 489; *Reardon Smith Line Ltd v Yngvar Hansen-Tangen and Sanko Steamship Co Ltd ('The Diana Prosperity')* [1976] 2 Lloyd's Rep 60.

[89] Which is not so heavy as to outweigh the Convention's advantage of being based on a relatively simple role allocated to the concept of 'description'.

[90] For further analysis of this point, see Kröll (n 30) para 33.

[91] See J Adams and H MacQueen, *Atiyah's Sale of Goods*, 12th edn (Harlow, Longman, 2010) 152.

[92] For the discussion of these clauses, see Chapter VIII.

[93] See Adams and MacQueen (n 91).

[94] For the distinction between identity and identification, see *The Diana Prosperity* (n 88).

those contracted for, such as where margarine is delivered instead of 'table butter'.[95] Occasionally, the delivered goods may not seem to be outside the contractually specified *genus*, but as a consequence of the high content of other components or admixtures may eventually be viewed as being entirely different goods. In a case of the sale of coke breeze, the tribunal found that the goods delivered by the seller, due to their 'intricate blend with substantial amounts of coal', could not be considered to be coke breeze.[96]

The finding that wholly different goods were delivered is not essential to find a breach of description as it covers other descriptive words or terms. In another case involving coke, the peculiarities of the composition did not turn the goods into goods of a different genus but the seller was still found to have been in breach of description.[97] It seems that it is such cases, where the question is whether certain potentially descriptive words or terms constitute description, that predominantly occupy judges and arbitrators when it comes to the issue of a breach of description. The range of items of description can potentially be extremely wide and may include colour,[98] weight,[99] place of origin, numerous technical attributes, age,[100] article numbers,[101] the manner of packaging[102] or a code to be indicated on packaging,[103] and

[95] See ICAC Arbitration, 155/1996, 22 January 1997, available at http://cisgw3.law.pace.edu/cases/970122r1.html.

[96] ICC Arbitration Case No 7565, 1994, available at http://cisgw3.law.pace.edu/cases/947565i1.html.

[97] Appellate Court Munich, 7 U 4419/93, 2 March 1994 (Germany), available at http://cisgw3.law.pace.edu/cases/940302g1.html. See also ICC Arbitration Case No 8247, June 1996, available at http://cisgw3.law.pace.edu/cases/968247i1.html, where the contract may have required the chemical compound to be supplied in the form of crystals and the tribunal held that even if that were the case, no breach had been committed because the delivered goods, which were 'stone hard', could be transformed into crystals. This decision is incorrect because a minor deviation from the specified conformity standards, including description, is regarded as a breach under the Convention. In the same vein, the ability of the goods to be cured is not relevant to the finding of a breach under Art 35, but may be relevant to the availability of the right to avoid the contract, demand specific performance and/or to the assessment of damages.

[98] *Down Jacket and Winter Coat*, CIETAC Arbitration, 22 March 1995, available at http://cisgw3.law.pace.edu/cases/950322c1.html; *Engines*, CIETAC Arbitration, 6 September 1996, available at http://cisgw3.law.pace.edu/cases/960906c1.html.

[99] *Rebar Coil*, CIETAC Arbitration, 20 November 1997, available at http://cisgw3.law.pace.edu/cases/971120c1.html.

[100] See ICAC, 39/2003, 21 December 2004, available at http://cisgw3.law.pace.edu/cases/041221r1.html (the seller's breach consisting in delivering a car manufactured in 1981 and not in 1988, as required by the contract); District Court Hamburg, 419 O 218/03, 6 September 2004 (Germany), available at http://cisgw3.law.pace.edu/cases/040906g1.html.

[101] CIETAC Arbitration, 6 September 1996 (n 98).

[102] *Re Moore & Co Ltd and Landauer & Co Ltd* [1921] 2 KB 519.

[103] See *PVC Suspension Resin*, CIETAC Arbitration, 7 April 1999, available at http://cisgw3.law.pace.edu/cases/990407c1.html, where a different code, 'H622' instead of 'F622' required by the contract, appeared on the packaging. Although the tribunal stated that the buyer had failed to prove that '"F622" and "H622" were different products', the seller was eventually held to be in breach under Art 35(1). The precise feature of conformity which the seller breached was not specified.

elements constituting the goods' content. It is submitted that the question of whether particular words or terms constitute description should ultimately be answered with reference to whether the parties intended them to be part of the description of the goods.

A practice between the parties and/or a relevant trade usage are clearly relevant. In one case,[104] the buyer's claim that the mackerel delivered by the seller was not of the type required by the contract was dismissed on the basis that the mackerel complied with the Latin designation in the seller's pre-contractual correspondence and that Latin specification was decisive because the parties traded in the past using Latin designations *and* because that practice was in accordance with the custom amongst fish merchants. Another factor in assessing the parties' intentions is the level of specificity of an alleged descriptive term. A term is unlikely to have been intended to describe the goods if the alleged description had no discernible meaning or content.[105] Thus, where the buyer relied on the alleged term that the jackets ought to be of 'European style', the tribunal rejected the claim on the basis that the buyer failed to prove 'the existence of an objective, internationally recognized definition of "European style"'.[106] An alleged term of description needs to be placed in the surrounding commercial context where it may have a fixed meaning. In one case,[107] while the term 'European Old Corrugated Cartons' (OCC) was found not to imply a particular level of quality, it seems to have been taken to have a clear meaning in the paper industry, as the tribunal held the seller in breach of contract for delivering goods with a lower level of OCC content than that specified in the contract. Contractual provisions requiring the goods to be 'new'[108] or 'as good as new'[109] have been regarded as sufficiently precise. Even such terms as 'normal Russian gasoil' may, in a given trading context, form part of the

[104] Copenhagen Maritime Commercial Court, H-0126-98, 31 January 2002 (Denmark), http://cisgw3.law.pace.edu/cases/020131d1.html.

[105] See *Automobiles*, CIETAC Arbitration, 23 April 1997, available athttp://cisgw3.law.pace.edu/cases/970423c2.html, where a tribunal held that the parties' failure to agree on certain attributes of the goods resulted in an 'indefinite description' and, as a result, the contract could not be performed and had to be terminated. This decision has no basis in the CISG where the contract can only be terminated by a party as a consequence of the other party's breach. If the goods are not 'sufficiently identified', that can lead to the conclusion that no contract has been made (see Art 14), but the decision makes clear that the tribunal regarded the goods as having been identified 'sufficiently definitely'. The tribunal ought to have applied Arts 8 and 35 to determine the seller's obligations.

[106] CIETAC Arbitration, 22 March 1995 (n 98).

[107] *Old Boxboard Corrugated Cartons*, CIETAC Arbitration, 8 March 1996, available at http://cisgw3.law.pace.edu/cases/960308c1.html.

[108] *Steel Cylinders*, CIETAC Arbitration, 19 January 2000, available athttp://cisgw3.law.pace.edu/cases/000119c1.html.

[109] Construed as meaning the second-hand CNC machine's ability to function, in Appellate Court Valais, C1 04 162, 21 February 2005 (Switzerland), available at http://cisgw3.law.pace.edu/cases/050221s1.html.

description.[110] To ascertain whether the parties intended the elements of content to be part of the description, it may be important to look at *where* in the contract the term is included. If, say, the 'fibre content' provision is located within the section titled 'description' this may be a factor in favour of finding an intention to treat fibre content as an item of description.[111] If the provision were to be outside this section under a different contractual category, that might well point to the contrary conclusion.[112]

In some cases, despite a contractual reference to description, it may still be unclear whether such a reference evidences an intention that the seller was to comply with that 'description'. In one case,[113] the seller agreed to sell souvenir coins, issued by the government of Macao to celebrate its return to China, and to deliver the 'descriptions and the certificates'. The contract, however, did not expressly require the seller to ensure the compliance with those descriptions and certificates, stating only that 'the subject matter and price includes coin sets, the descriptions and certificates'. The seller also agreed to provide samples of the coins, some of which were to be sealed and signed by the parties. The delivered coins complied with the samples, but not with the design in the certificate (the stars on the back of the coins were missing). The tribunal found the seller to be in breach of an 'implied duty' to ensure the compliance with the descriptions and the certificate on the ground that, otherwise, the contractual provision requiring the delivery of such descriptions and the certificate would be 'meaningless'. The seller had an obligation to comply both with the sample and the delivered descriptions and the certificate.

Whilst this interpretation seems correct, particularly considering that the contract stated that the goods and the price included descriptions and certificates, the decision leaves some questions unanswered. What was the relationship between the samples and description/certificates? Were the samples intended to be representative only of certain features of the coins?[114] If not and if the samples represented *all* features, the contract was internally contradictory because it could not require compliance with two incompatible sources of description, as follows from the fact that the coins did not meet the delivered descriptions and the design in the certificate.[115] The answer, implicit in the decision, then must be that the samples were intended to represent only some of the features of the goods.

[110] See *Marimpex v Louis Dreyfus* [1995] 1 Lloyd's Rep 167.

[111] See *Tradax Export SA v European Grain & Shipping Ltd* [1983] 2 Lloyd's Rep 100.

[112] See *R G Trading LLP v Feed Factors International Ltd* [2011] 2 Lloyd's Rep 433.

[113] *Souvenir Coins*, CIETAC Arbitration 2000, available at http://cisgw3.law.pace.edu/cases/000000c1.html.

[114] As noted, some of the samples were to be signed and sealed by the parties, which evidences an intention to treat the samples as a source of description of some significance.

[115] The inference is that the samples did not contain stars, whereas there should have been stars on the back of the coins, according to the design in the certificate.

In the absence of an express requirement, it seems that no showing of reliance by the buyer on a term is necessary to prove that that term is part of the description.[116] But where such reliance can be shown, it is likely to evidence the parties' intention to regard the term as being an item of description. The Convention relies on a general test of contract interpretation and avoids any detailed and firm scheme or classification of steps to be taken to prove the parties' intentions.[117] All potentially relevant circumstances are to be treated as factors[118] whose precise weight and relevance is to be determined in each individual case.

V. QUALITY

A. Definition

Quality is generally understood as referring to the physical features of the goods, such as their state or condition, safety, appearance and durability.[119] Quality also comprises 'all factual and legal circumstances concerning the relationship of the goods to their surroundings'.[120] Such surrounding circumstances include public law or industry standards, as well as features linked to public perception associated with a particular product, such as brand names and possibly even reputation.[121] Of increasing importance are various ethical considerations, such as those relating to human rights, child labour, other labour, health and safety, environmental and anti-corruption standards.[122] In the same vein, a place of origin may be part of quality either due to ethical considerations (where, for instance, the contract disallows goods from a particular country due to its political situation

[116] For the discussion of this issue in English law, see *Harlingdon & Leinster Enterprises Ltd v Christopher Hull Fine Art Ltd* [1991] 1 QB 564.

[117] See nn 20–24 above and the accompanying main text.

[118] See Art 8(3) CISG.

[119] *Cf* SGA 1979, s. 14(2B).

[120] I Schwenzer in Schwenzer (n 72) Art 35, para 9; see further Schwenzer, Hachem and Kee (n 1) para 31.70; Kröll (n 30) para 25.

[121] See K Maley, 'The Limits to the Conformity of Goods in the United Nations Convention on Contracts for the International Sale of Goods (CISG)' (2009) 12 *Int'l Trade Business L Rev* 82 (see in particular at 114 where the author suggests that 'negative reputation itself should be considered a fault rather than merely a consequence of a fault').

[122] For an example of a well-known international initiative in this respect, see United Nations Global Compact, www.unglobalcompact.org/. For a detailed discussion of these issues, see I Schwenzer, 'Ethical Values and International Sales' (2008) 47 *Norsk Jurisdisk Tidsskrift* 451; I Schwenzer, 'Conformity of the Goods: Physical Features on the Wane?' in I Schwenzer and L Spagnolo (eds), *State of Play: The Third Annual MAA Schlechtriem CISG Conference* (The Hague, Eleven International Publishing, 2012) 103.

and/or human rights record)[123] or because a place specified in the contract is associated with the goods of high quality.[124]

There is considerable overlap between quality and description and the same features often fall within the scope of both aspects of conformity. For example, the colour of marble, say whether 'gold yellow' or 'pink', is undoubtedly a matter of description, but it may also be a matter of quality if, as was argued in a CISG case,[125] pink marble is of inferior quality. An indication of a grade or class, age[126] or some other descriptive words, such as 'Hard Amber Durum Wheat',[127] are items of description but may also signify quality. The goods' composition may similarly be indicative of both quality and description.[128]

As seen from the above discussion, the circumstances where the potential difficulty of characterising a feature as one of quality or description or both will have to be grappled with are very limited. In the vast majority of cases no one, except for the perfectionist in matters of conceptual analyses, will be concerned about how exactly the seller's breach is described. Once the seller has not complied with its conformity obligation, whether it is one of quality or description (or relating to quantity or packaging), it is in *breach* of contract and the same legal consequences will follow. This relative simplicity, which eases the burden of drawing a sometimes shaky distinction between quality and description, is to be applauded, particularly on the international plane where coherence and consistency are so difficult to achieve.

B. Various Formulations of Quality Standards

The ways in which contracts specify quality standards vary greatly because of the differences in the type of markets, nature of the goods, the relevant regulatory and commercial environment, the parties' particular

[123] A CISG case that comes close to this scenario is Federal Supreme Court, VIII ZR 51/95, 3 April 1996 (Germany), available at http://cisgw3.law.pace.edu/cases/960403g1.html, where the buyer argued that it could not resell the goods originating in South Africa since such goods were subject to embargo in countries in which the buyer had been doing business. See also, eg Kimberly Process Certification Scheme, www.kimberleyprocess.com, a joint government, industry and civil society initiative, aiming to certify that the origin of rough diamonds is from sources free from conflicts funded by diamond production. See also Schwenzer, 'Conformity of the Goods' (n 122) 106, arguing that, in the diamond trade, this scheme amounts to a trade usage.

[124] See Schwenzer, Hachem and Kee (n 1) para 31.77.

[125] See Appellate Court Graz, 6 R 194/95, 9 November 1995 (Austria), available at http://cisgw3.law.pace.edu/cases/951109a3.html.

[126] Which may be regarded as indicating both description and quality (eg in the sale of cars).

[127] *Toepfer v Continental Grain Co* [1974] 1 Lloyd's Rep 11.

[128] See ICC Arbitration Case No 7565 (n 96); for a more detailed discussion, see *Benjamin's Sale of Goods* (n 37) para 11-020.

circumstances and bargain. The need to comply with a 'grade', for example, is quite common in the commodities trade,[129] but can also be found in other trade sectors. In one case,[130] the seller delivered Christmas trees of a different grade to that specified in the contract. Although the seller argued that quality of the delivered trees was even better than those of the contractually specified grade, the court rightly held that the seller was in breach of contract because the buyer was entitled to receive what it had contracted for. This decision was also made with reference to the benefits and functions of a grading system which 'assures the parties to a contract, and any subsequent buyers, of the nature and quality of the goods, without the need for elaborate or expensive reinspection', thereby facilitating further trade and reliance by sub-buyers on the quality of the goods.[131] The court further stated that not holding the seller liable would render the grading system 'meaningless'.

A contract may require compliance with a particular standard of quality, but even a detailed formulation of such a standard does not necessarily mean that issues of interpretation can be avoided. In one case,[132] the contract provided for the delivery of 'A-quality' beech logs which were to be 'clean outside' and to have no 'inner barks', and one question was whether the goods which were found to have 'scars' were conforming. The tribunal found that the term 'inner bark' referred to 'the calix formed during the growth of the trees' and the term employed in the timber industry to describe it was a 'scar', which meant that the goods were non-conforming. The tribunal also had to ascertain the meaning of such terms as 'gaps' and 'holes' and held that they also constituted non-conformity because that was not something that could be expected of 'A-quality' goods, which were to be 'clean outside', and because compared to other contractually prohibited features, such as twits, bents and knots, gaps and holes were much more severe defects.[133]

Highly detailed and elaborate specifications are common in the sale of complex technical equipment or machinery or even metal and steel products. In the case of commodities, chemical products or foodstuffs, a

[129] Bridge (n 34) para 7.136.

[130] *In Re Siskiyou Evergreen, Inc, Debtor*, US Bankruptcy Court for the District of Oregon, 29 March 2004, available at http://cisgw3.law.pace.edu/cases/040329u2.html.

[131] 'Without the assurance provided by the desired grade, the goods will not move through the marketplace, at least not without reinspection and regrading' (ibid).

[132] See *Beech Log*, CIETAC Arbitration, 4 November 2002, available at http://cisgw3.law.pace.edu/cases/021104c1.html.

[133] See also *Textile Manufacturing Equipment*, CIETAC Arbitration, 18 July 2002, available at http://cisgw3.law.pace.edu/cases/020718c1.html#iii, where the question of whether the contractual requirement that the 'speed of the machine should not be lower than 28 metres per minute for every 350 grams boarding machine for heavy chemical fabrics' applied to 'anti-pilling polar fleece' was extensively explored, primarily in the context of Art 35(2)(a) and (b). This question could also have been analysed under Art 35(1), which shows the sometimes inevitable overlap between paras (1) and (2) of Art 35.

detailed breakdown of the composition of the goods, including such matters as levels of admixtures or humidity, will often be found.[134] More vague formulations of quality such as 'fair and average quality' are also used at times, especially in the agricultural and foodstuffs trade,[135] and where so, it may not be easy to determine the precise content of this quality standard without investigating the surrounding market, implicit understandings and trade usages in the given sector and, of course, the correspondence of the quality to the price. In general, however, such clauses are likely to indicate 'the middle belt of quality, not least or worst that can be understood in the particular trade'.[136] The organic nature of foodstuffs is also indicative of the quality of the goods.

C. Industry or Public Law Standards

To alleviate the burden of drafting such elaborate contracts, the parties can agree upon established industry or governmental standards governing the goods at hand.[137] Some standards regulate the manufacturing process, setting out, for instance, benchmarks of safety, sustainability, duties of care or environmental protection. Where only such standards have been agreed upon, the seller's obligations will be assessed not with reference to the quality of the final product, but on the basis of whether the applicable manufacturing procedures have been observed. The focus of some standards is on the procedures and criteria to be followed during the inspection, and where the specified inspection methods are not observed, a buyer's allegation of a lack of conformity is likely to be rejected.[138] A reference to the applicable standards does not rule out further additional quality provisions in the contract and the question of the relationship between the two may arise. Thus, a contractual 'warranty clause' may contain a (not uncommon)

[134] See, eg CIETAC Arbitration, 9 January 1993 (n 76) ('The quality requirements are: PROFAT (ON DRY BASIS)—42% MIN, MOISTURE—12.5% MAX'); Appellate Court Madrid, Recurso No 683/2006, 20 February 2007 (Spain), available at http://cisgw3.law.pace.edu/cases/070220s4.html (humidity and impurities levels in olive stones specified).

[135] *Cehave NV v Bremer Handelsgesellschaft MBH ('The Hansa Nord')* [1976] QB 44; *Ashington Piggeries Ltd v Christopher Hill Ltd* (n 47).

[136] See Official Comment on § 2-314 in Uniform Commercial Code (n 22) point 9.

[137] See, eg ICAC Arbitration, 168/2001, 17 February 2003, available at http://cisgw3.law.pace.edu/cases/030217r1.html; *Hot-rolled Steel Plates*, CIETAC Arbitration, 16 July 1996, available at http://cisgw3.law.pace.edu/cases/960716c1.html; *Ginza Pte Ltd v Vista Corporation Pty Ltd* [2003] WASC 11.

[138] See *Hot-rolled Coils*, CIETAC Arbitration, 27 October 1997, available at http://cisgw3.law.pace.edu/cases/971027c1.html,where the standard (Russian GOST) applicable to hot-rolled steel coils required that surface defects be established by examining the entire consignment and that thickness be measured by taking samples 'at a distance of not less than 1.5 turns from the end of the rolled length'. The tribunal did not accept the results of the inspection, which did not meet these requirements.

warranty that the goods will be 'free from defects in material and workmanship' as well as conform to the rules and regulations in the buyer's country. Although the precise relationship between such stipulations is ultimately a matter of contract interpretation and of the regulations' essence and purpose, these contractual provisions may well target two distinct sets of quality aspects, as has been held in one such case, where the failure of the goods to pass the test required to obtain the certification under the regulations in the buyer's country was not deemed to constitute 'defects in material [or] workmanship'.[139]

The standards, particularly those emanating from the state, can be incorporated into contracts in different ways. Relevant regulations or statutes can be listed specifically in a contract. With this approach, the buyers may run the risk of the contractual list being incomplete[140] and that is why, as demonstrated by the previously mentioned case, some buyers prefer a broader clause referring to 'all relevant legislation or regulations'. Alternatively, a contract may explicitly allocate to the seller the risk of ensuring the goods' tradability or usability in the specified destination.[141] Where the contract appears to be silent on the applicability of some external standards, they must not be easily implied into the contract. First, if a party wants the standards to be applied, it is reasonable to expect it to bargain for it and include it in the contract. Secondly, the implication of a term into the contract under Article 35(1) cannot be done without regard for the rule in Article 35(2)(b), where the seller can be made liable if the goods do not comply with a particular purpose made known to it and which can easily cover the applicability of special standards. This rule is subject to two restrictions—that in Article 35(3)[142] and the seller's ability to eliminate the rule in Article 35(2)(b) if it can show that the buyer did not rely or it was unreasonable for the buyer to rely on the seller's skill and judgement—which are not mentioned in Article 35(1).[143] It is thus arguable that a buyer should not be able to avoid a relatively high threshold for the applicability of special standards in Article 35(2)(b) by relying on Article 35(1).[144]

This attitude has already manifested itself in a case[145] where the German buyer of mobile units argued that the seller had committed a breach of contract because they did not meet the construction standards in force in

[139] See *Cortem SpA v Controlmatic Pty Ltd* [2010] FCA 852, paras 83 and 84.
[140] See Schwenzer, Hachem and Kee (n 1) para 31.84.
[141] See ibid, also noting that it is a matter of the particular circumstances whether the buyer in such a case has a duty to cooperate with the seller.
[142] See II D above. For a detailed discussion of Art 35(3), see Chapter 5.
[143] See Kröll (n 30) para 48.
[144] For a detailed discussion of the relationship between Art 35(1) and Art 35(2)(b), see Chapter 3.
[145] Appellate Court Arnhem, 97/700 and 98/046, 27 April 1999 (The Netherlands), available at http://cisgw3.law.pace.edu/cases/990427n1.html.

Germany. Even a possible mention by the buyer to the seller of the existence of special requirements with respect to mobile units, together with the fact that the parties had a long-standing relationship and the seller's knowledge that the goods would be used in Germany, was deemed insufficient to imply an alleged term into the contract. The court took the view that the buyer was as much an expert in mobile units as the seller, and although the parties had had business dealings for a long time, the buyer never carried out sufficiently thorough investigations of whether the seller had been taking those special standards into account. On this basis, it was held that it was the buyer's responsibility to point out to the seller those specific governmental requirements which were applicable to mobile units.

In another case,[146] in contrast, domestic regulations in countries of both parties and international standards had a direct influence on how the contract was interpreted. The case concerned the sale, in August–September 1996, of 'EEC wheat flour type "Aigle du Nord"' by a Dutch seller to a Belgian buyer for further resale to Mozambique. The seller had added to the flour a bread enhancing substance containing potassium bromate, capable of causing cancer and damaging DNA structures, which upon delivery to Mozambique was confiscated by the authorities. The seller did not reveal the actual composition of the goods to the buyer, explaining its non-disclosure later in the proceedings on the ground that the composition of the goods was 'a company secret'. There was evidence that the import of flour enriched with potassium bromate was de facto permitted in Mozambique and that a company appointed by the Mozambican government had tested the batches of wheat before shipment and had issued a Clean Report for the purpose of an import licence.

These factors notwithstanding, the court emphatically held the seller liable. First, it was evident from the pre-contractual exchanges between the parties that the quality of the flour was very important to the buyer and that the seller declared the flour to be of very high quality. It was held that the buyer could reasonably interpret the seller's statement as warranting that the bread improvers would be of quality corresponding, at least, to international standards. The seller's statement as to the goods' fitness for human consumption could not have led to a different conclusion. If the seller did not have an intention to ensure compliance with international standards, it ought to have drawn the buyer's attention to the actual composition of the goods in accordance with the principle of good faith (Article 7 CISG). Secondly, for a number of years the use of potassium bromate had been banned in the Netherlands and in the European Union, of which the seller was aware. Thirdly, it was also prohibited by the Codex Alimentarius, a set of global and regional standards, which both the

[146] Appellate Court s-Gravenhage, 99/474, 23 April 2003 (The Netherlands), available at http://cisgw3.law.pace.edu/cases/030423n1.html.

Netherlands and Mozambique had agreed to use, and for this reason the court regarded the Codex as the 'appropriate general standard'. Fourthly, the court regarded the pre-shipment approval of the goods by a company appointed by the Mozambican government, and the question whether an import licence could be issued under the Mozambican law, as irrelevant to the construction of the contract. Finally, the court brushed aside the argument that the import of such goods to Mozambique was de facto permitted; accepting this argument would mean 'that products unfit for human consumption could be delivered without contractual sanction by a seller from a highly developed country to a purchaser from a less developed country, who, due to the contract, may rightfully expect to have delivered to him a product that is reliable according to international standards and fit for human consumption'.[147]

The decision suggests that courts are likely to take a strict view of the seller's obligations when the goods are potentially dangerous to human health and safety.[148] It also reflects the court's moral stance, which is evident in the implicit treatment of the seller's conduct as contrary to good faith and its outright dismissal of the argument that the import of products containing potassium bromate was de facto allowed in Mozambique essentially on the ground that less developed countries could not be used as a market for what is unacceptable in more developed countries. The court's commendable concern for equality and promotion of high standards throughout the world is in keeping with the Convention's ideals of, amongst others, promoting development, equality and fairness.[149] The CISG in this case appears to have been used not just as an instrument for allocating risks between the contracting parties but also as a vehicle for promoting quality standards internationally, as well as the said moral considerations and possibly even the rule of law.

The decision can, however, be criticised on more technical grounds. Whilst much weight appears to have been attached to Mozambican law since it had to be relied upon to arrive at *common* standards, some other aspects of Mozambican law,[150] or at least the way in which it is actually applied in practice,[151] were disregarded. The court stated that the 'question

[147] Ibid point 8.

[148] See also District Court Lugano, OA.2000.459, 19 April 2007 (Switzerland), available at http://cisgw3.law.pace.edu/cases/070419s1.html, where the seller was held to be in breach of contract when a children's play structure did not comply with legal and technical safety rules in Switzerland. The contract did not expressly set out any safety standards but the court stated that it was necessary to imply such an obligation because the play structure was intended to be used by the general public.

[149] The Convention is based on the idea that international trade promotes development and on the objectives and values underlying the 'New International Economic Order' (see the Preamble to the CISG and Chapter 1).

[150] Such as whether an import licence could be issued.

[151] De facto permission of import and the issuance of a pre-shipment approval certificate.

whether an import license, [could] be issued with regard to the content of Mozambican law' could not be relevant to contract interpretation and to determining the content of the seller's obligations. This does not sit easily with the parts of the decision recognising the relevance of Mozambican law, insofar as it reflected Mozambique's agreement to use the Codex Alimentarius. Those other aspects of Mozambican law ought not to have been simply dismissed as being wholly irrelevant because they are part of the surrounding factual background and the CISG requires that all relevant circumstances be taken into account in contract interpretation.[152] It would have been more accurate to recognise them as factors which are relevant but outweighed by more powerful factors in the buyer's favour.

In this case, potassium bromate was prohibited both in the seller's country and at the destination. It can be inferred from cases such as this[153] that the fact that the regulations in the seller's country and in the country where the goods are intended to be used or sold are the same, can point strongly to the parties' intention that the goods ought to comply with the *requirements* contained in both regulations. However, the mere fact of the regulations being the same in the two countries does not mean that the parties can be taken to have intended the seller to comply with the *regulations* in the country of use or sale. Such an intention can only be inferred if the seller was in the position to know about the destination *and* the regulations there. If that is not the case and in the absence of any other relevant circumstances, each party is likely to have intended that the goods ought to comply with the regulations in its own country. But since the regulations are the same, there happens to be a common intention that the goods ought to comply with the same set of requirements.

Where the regulations in the seller's country and the country where the goods are intended to be sold or used are different, there is no similar circumstance which self-evidently helps to ascertain the parties' intentions. In general, the seller will not have a duty to comply with the regulations in the country where the goods were intended to be used or sold.[154] Unless there

[152] See Art 8(3) CISG.

[153] See Appellate Court Turku, S 04/1600, 24 May 2005 (Finland), available at http://cisgw3.law.pace.edu/cases/050524f5.html#iii, where an EU Directive in force prior to the conclusion of the contract required the labelling of products subjected to radiation. The buyer's claim that the seller breached the contract by supplying radiated paprika powder was accepted, even though the contract did not refer to radiation and only required the steaming of the powder. Both parties were experts and therefore ought to have been aware of the Directive and must have intended that the goods would comply with it. The court also thought that the fact that the buyer's customers would not accept radiated products and the buyer's post-contractual demand for a certificate confirming that the powder was radiation free pointed to such an intention.

[154] See Federal Supreme Court, 8 March 1995, VIII ZR 159/94 (Germany), available at http://cisgw3.law.pace.edu/cases/950308g3.html and the discussion of the case in Chapters 3 and 4.

are good reasons why the seller should know about the regulations in that country, the buyer can reasonably be expected to inform the seller of such regulations or to include a contractual term to this effect.[155] Some circumstances such as pre-contractual communications evidencing the importance of quality to the buyer and the seller's declarations regarding high quality of its goods may be indicative of the parties' intention that the goods ought to comply with higher standards in the seller's country. If the seller's country and the country of use or sale, whilst having different regulations, have joined one and the same set of international standards,[156] that may also evidence the parties' intention that those *common* standards would govern the issue of the goods' conformity. If it is clear that the buyer has selected the seller precisely because it operated in a country well known for high quality standards, that is likely to be relevant in interpreting the contract as imposing an obligation on the seller to ensure compliance with regulations in the seller's country.[157]

D. Legislative Changes and/or Knowledge Acquired Subsequent to the Contract

Where the contract requires the goods to comply with certain public law requirements, the question may arise as to the point in time with reference to which such requirements are to be ascertained. The question becomes important where the relevant legislation changes subsequent to the conclusion of the contract. A CISG case that comes close to this situation[158] is a case[159] where food products were to be free from genetically modified organisms (GMOs). The seller argued that[160] a change in the regulations, made more than two years after the contract had been made (1999), meant that the amount of GMOs that were actually found in the delivered goods (between 0.1 and 1 per cent) was declared by the authorities in the buyer's country (Switzerland) as being 'GMO free'. The court rejected this argument, stating that 1997, the year when the goods seem to have been delivered and inspected and when no such change to the regulations was yet made, was decisive. The Convention's general rule is that the seller is liable for a lack of conformity which exists 'at the time when the risk passes to

155 See Chapters 3 and 4.

156 See Appellate Court s-Gravenhage (n 146), where the seller's country (the Netherlands) and the country of use (Mozambique) have both adopted the Codex Alimentarius, a set of global and regional standards, banning the use of products containing potassium bromate. That was one factor influencing the court in holding the seller liable.

157 See Kröll (n 30) para 95.

158 Although not fitting it exactly because no public regulations appear to have been specified in the contract.

159 Canton Appellate Court Basel, 22 August 2003 (n 61).

160 The contract seems to have been made at the end of 1997.

the buyer'.[161] The delivery terms being DDP,[162] the risk in all likelihood passed to the buyer some time in 1997 since this was when the goods were inspected by the buyer, which means that the decision was correct. Nevertheless, it must be borne in mind that the Convention's position is only applicable by default and an inquiry into the parties' intentions needs to be made to ensure that the parties did not intend to override it by allocating the risk of subsequent changes in the legislation to the buyer.

It also needs to be asked whether the result that the Convention produces in cases such as this is sound as a matter of principle and policy. On the one hand, not taking into account subsequent developments and knowledge about what constitutes 'GMO free' may seem artificial, since some part of that knowledge is excluded.[163] On the other hand, it can be contended that bringing such subsequent developments into assessing conformity would be contrary to the parties' bargain and unfair to a party, such as the buyer in this case. The bargain was made in the regulatory environment and market conditions as they existed in 1997 and the parties' reasonable expectations, against which quality is to be judged, were formed at that time.[164] Holding otherwise means that quality can never be tested with reference to a fixed point in time but is continuously subject to changes occurring until the time of legal proceedings in the regulations and in the relevant body of scientific knowledge.[165] Such a position destroys legal certainty because the parties are not able to assess their legal positions in respect of the conformity obligations. Similarly, neither the signalling nor the risk allocation functions of the conformity standards can sensibly be performed if a potential change to the parties' understanding and expectations is up in the air until the time of proceedings.

On balance, the arguments against taking into account the subsequent legislative changes and/or the after-acquired knowledge in assessing conformity seem considerably stronger and they point to the time when the contract is made, since this is when the bargain is finalised and the risks

[161] Art 36(1).

[162] '"Delivery Duty Paid" means that the seller delivers the goods when the goods are placed at the disposal of the buyer, cleared for import on the arriving means of transport ready for unloading at the named place of destination. The seller bears all the costs and risks involved in bringing the goods to the place of destination and has an obligation to clear the goods not only for export but also for import, to pay any duty for both export and import to carry out all customs formalities' (J Ramberg, *ICC Guide to Incoterms 2010: Understanding and Practical Use* (Paris, ICC Services Publication, 2011) 149). The risk under the DDP term passes after the goods have been delivered to the buyer (see ibid, A5, DDP), that is, after they have been placed 'at the disposal of the buyer on the arriving means of transport ready for unloading at the agreed point, if any, at the named place of destination on the agreed date or within the agreed period' (ibid, A4, DDP).

[163] See *Henry Kendall & Sons v William Lillico & Sons Ltd* [1962] 2 AC 31, 75 and 108–9 (per Lord Reid and Lord Guest).

[164] See ibid 119 (the dissenting view of Lord Pearce).

[165] McKendrick (n 83) 342.

are assumed. The Convention's provision, relying on the moment when the risk passes to the buyer, will often, but not always,[166] fix a later point in time,[167] and it will usually be the time of delivery.[168] The moment of delivery generally takes account of the arguments against having regard to subsequent developments because it is, as a rule, not removed too far in time from the conclusion of the contract. In some cases also, it may not be too unreasonable to expect the seller to bear the risks between the conclusion of the contract and delivery. Particularly where the contract goods are not specifically identified, the seller may have some choice of what goods to allocate to the contract with the buyer and to ensure their compliance with the quality standards which changed between the time when the contract is made and the time of delivery.

On the whole, the Convention's position is sound. It must not be forgotten that the situation being presently discussed will arise less frequently than a more typical case of some more straightforward defects found in the goods or of damage done to the goods. The Convention's rule is a general one, to be applied to *all* situations and, as such, it rightly relies (as do many legal systems)[169] on the time when the risk passes to the buyer. This is the time when the goods are generally thought to be outside the seller's sphere of control, which makes it appropriate to exclude any non-conformities arising after that time from the seller's responsibility, except for those which are due to any breach of its obligations or for which it has assumed responsibility.[170]

E. Guarantee and Durability

The seller is liable for any lack of conformity which exists at the time when the risk passes to the buyer.[171] This rule can be understood against the background of the rules on the passage of risk,[172] which are driven by the considerations of when the goods leave the seller's sphere of control and

[166] See Art 68 CISG where, in respect of goods sold in transit, the risk passes from the time when the contract is made.

[167] In the case of carriage of goods, the risk generally passes when the goods are handed over to the first carrier for transmission to the buyer (Art 67(1)). In other cases (also excluding the sale of goods in transit), the risk generally passes when the buyer takes over the goods and 'if he does not do so in due time, from the time when the goods are placed at his disposal and he commits a breach of contract by failing to take delivery' (Art 69(1)). Art 69(2) further provides that 'if the buyer is bound to take over the goods at a place other than a place of business of the seller, the risk passes when delivery is due and the buyer is aware of the fact that the goods are placed at his disposal at that place'.

[168] See Arts 67 and 69.

[169] Schwenzer (n 72), Art 36, para 2.

[170] See Art 36(2) CISG.

[171] Art 36(1).

[172] See Secretariat Commentary on Article 34 of the 1978 Draft.

when the buyer becomes in a better position to control, examine or salvage them, or whether the buyer is covered by insurance.[173] The seller will be held liable for a lack of conformity which exists at the time when the risk passes to the buyer 'even though the lack of conformity becomes apparent only after that time'.[174] The rationale for this provision is that a lack of conformity is not always identifiable at the time of the passage of risk, as is often the case with hidden defects or where there is no opportunity for the buyer to inspect the goods until they are carried to their destination.[175]

The seller may be liable for any lack of conformity which occurs after the time of the passage of risk, if it is due to 'a breach of any of his obligations, including a breach of any guarantee that for a period of time the goods will remain fit for their ordinary purpose or for some particular purpose or will retain specified qualities or characteristics'.[176] An 'ordinary' and a 'particular' purpose refer to the rules implied under Article 35(2), examined later,[177] while 'specified qualities and characteristics' are those provided for by the contract. This means that if non-compliance with the contractual provisions, arising after the passage of risk, is due to a breach of the seller, the latter will be liable. This may occur, for example, where: the goods are damaged in transit, but that damage results from the seller's failure to arrange a carriage contract in accordance with the sales contract (such as where non-stop carriage to destination and/or storage under specified temperature levels are required)[178] and/or the Convention; the seller did not comply with the contractual procedure in relation to assembling the goods after the risk has passed to the buyer; the seller breached its packaging obligations, resulting in damage to the goods;[179] damage or loss have occurred in the course of the seller's collection of its containers.[180]

The above quoted Article 36(2)[181] specifically states that the seller's liability for 'post-risk' non-conformities may also arise as a result of its breach of a guarantee of durability. Such guarantees may expressly specify a time period during which the goods will retain their contractual characteristics and/or functions.[182] But if the contract expressly provides for such an

[173] See Arts 67–69.

[174] Art 36(1).

[175] See Secretariat Commentary on Article 34 of the 1978 Draft; see also Art 38(2) and (3) CISG.

[176] Art 36(2).

[177] See Chapters 3–5.

[178] See *Piperonal Aldehyde*, CIETAC Arbitration, 1999, available at http://cisgw3.law.pace.edu/cases/990000c1.html.

[179] See Crompromex Arbitration, M/21/95, 29 April 1996, available at http://cisgw3.law.pace.edu/cases/960429m1.html.

[180] See Schwenzer (n 72) Art 36, para 5.

[181] See n 176 above and the accompanying main text.

[182] See *Coating Equipment*, CIETAC Arbitration, 15 July 2002, available at http://cisgw3.law.pace.edu/cases/020715c1.html.

express guarantee, what is the value and function of Article of 36(2) except for stating a self-evident position that flows from the contract in any case? Its value in this case does seem limited since it simply reaffirms the primacy of the contract.[183] It may be that Article 36(2) eases the buyer's burden of proof. The buyer needs to prove a lack of conformity, the existence of the guarantee[184] and that the former is covered by the latter,[185] but there is no need to establish when a lack of conformity occurred. The very fact of non-conformity makes the seller liable and the only way to avoid liability is for the seller to show that the non-conformity or factors causing it are outside the scope of the contractual guarantee.[186]

The value of Article 36(2) is perhaps greater when it comes to implicit guarantees of durability. The legislative history makes clear that the original draft, which had referred only to 'express' guarantees, was later amended when a proposal to delete the word 'express' had been accepted, indicating the drafters' intention to recognise implicit guarantees.[187] The recognition of the seller's implicit undertaking as to durability gives rise to the difficulty of identifying such an implicit intention. In some cases, of course, such an intention can be inferred quite easily. Clothes can reasonably be expected not to shrink by one or two sizes after the first washing[188] or where carpets are bought by a hotel, the parties cannot reasonably intend that those carpets will wear out quickly.[189] Many other cases will be more challenging and one such category of cases where this issue arises with some frequency is that of shipment contracts. One benefit of trade terms such as CIF,[190]

[183] J Honnold (updated and revised by H Flechtner), *Uniform Law for International Sales under the 1980 United Nations Convention,* 4th edn (The Netherlands, Wolters Kluwer Law & Business, 2009) 347.

[184] See Appellate Court Antwerp, AR 2006/AR/384, 22 January 2007 (Belgium), available at http://cisgw3.law.pace.edu/cases/070122b2.html (the buyer failed to prove that there was a guarantee that certain parts of the brushing carts would be replaced in the buyer's country); Appellate Court Innsbruck, 4 R161/94, 1 July 1994 (Austria), available at http://cisgw3.law.pace.edu/cases/940701a3.html (failure to prove a guarantee that flowers would bloom during summer).

[185] See, similarly S Kröll in Kröll, Mistelis and Viscasillas (n 30) Art 36, para 25.

[186] See, eg Schwenzer in Schwenzer (n 72) Art 36, para 7; P Schlechtriem and P Butler, *UN Law on International Sales* (Berlin/Heidelberg, Springer-Verlag, 2009) 122; Bianca (n 64) 285–86.

[187] For an outline of this aspect of legislative history see, eg Schwenzer (n 72) Art 36, para 1.

[188] District Court Landshut, 54 O 644/94, 5 April 1995 (Germany), available at http://cisgw3.law.pace.edu/cases/950405g1.html.

[189] Supreme Court, 32 Odo 725/2004, 29 March 2006 (Czech Republic), available at http://cisgw3.law.pace.edu/cases/060329cz.html.

[190] '"Cost, Insurance and Freight" means that the seller delivers the goods on board the vessel or procures the goods already so delivered. The risk of loss or of damage to the goods passes when the goods are on board the vessel. The seller must contract for and pay the costs and freight necessary to bring the goods to the named port of destination' (see Ramberg (n 162) 199).

CFR[191] or FOB[192] is that they clearly delimit the passage of risk of loss or damage between the parties, by shifting the risk from the seller to the buyer from the moment the goods are placed on board the vessel.[193] The buyer, as a rule, does not have the right to inspect the goods before loading under these trade terms but is provided with a degree of security through documents, including certificates relating to aspects of conformity.[194]

A situation which has caused some difficulty is where the goods are found to be non-conforming at destination. Where so and where their actual state and condition on shipment is not known with absolute certainty, three approaches to how this situation can be dealt with can be identified. First, it can be assumed that their non-conforming state at destination evidences their non-conformity on shipment. In this case, the seller becomes liable but not on the basis of its obligation to ensure the goods' durability but simply because the goods are assumed to be non-conforming before the risk has passed to the buyer. In a case of sale of 'colourless phenol' on FOB terms,[195] the phenol was found to have darkened when it arrived at its destination. The seller was found to be in breach of contract even though the inspection at loading showed that the phenol complied with the contract. It was found to be highly unlikely that the non-conformity had been caused by transportation, which was normal and usual, and it was extremely rare for phenol to change its colour under normal transportation conditions. The buyer also appears to have provided evidence which led the court to conclude that there must have been an unknown substance in the shore tank prior to shipment which had caused the phenol to darken and which the seller failed to disprove. Similarly, in a CIF case[196] the seller was held liable for the excessive amount of moisture in PTA powder (waste product) despite presenting a quality certificate issued on loading showing the contractually compliant level of moisture.

191 '"Cost and Freight" means that the seller delivers the goods on board the vessel or procures the goods already so delivered. The risk of loss of or damage to the goods passes when the goods are on board the vessel. The seller must contract for and pay the costs and freight necessary to bring the goods to the named port of destination' (ibid 183).

192 '"Free on Board" means that the seller delivers the goods on board the vessel nominated by the buyer at the named port of shipment or procures the goods already so delivered. The risk of loss of or damage to the goods passes when the goods are on board the vessel, and the buyer bears all costs from that moment onwards' (ibid 169).

193 See nn 190, 191 and 192 above.

194 See Chapter 8.

195 Appellate Court Helsinki, S 01/269, 31 May 2004 (Finland), available at http://cisgw3.law.pace.edu/cases/040531f5.html.

196 *PTA Powder*, CIETAC Arbitration, 18 April 2008, available at http://cisgw3.law.pace.edu/cases/080418c1.html.

This approach can be harsh on the sellers, particularly in CIF and FOB contracts, whose advantage is that the sellers, having shipped the goods (or appropriated those in transit) and supplied the necessary documents, evidencing the goods' compliance with the contract, can potentially consider themselves as having performed their obligations. This approach is not necessarily incorrect since the fundamental rule is that the seller should be liable for a lack of conformity existing prior to shipment. In these cases, the tribunals may merely have been trying to identify, in the conditions of imperfect knowledge, when the non-conformity occurred. But in doing so, the tribunals must not ignore the question of how the parties intended to deal with the difficulty of determining conformity of the goods and this is what these decisions fail to explore. In the case involving the sale of phenol, it was part of the seller's obligation to deliver a quality certificate, which attested to the goods' compliance. It is submitted that if the parties did intend this certificate to be conclusive and binding, the above decisions would be questionable because the central objective of such provisions is to allocate the risk of uncertainty between the parties. If there was no such intention, the decisions might well be correct since there was some evidence pointing to the defect occurring in the course of shipment. However, the question of the precise function of the contractual obligation to supply a quality certificate was unfortunately left unanswered.

The opposite approach is to assume that the goods were conforming before the risk passed to the buyer on the basis that a quality certificate showed compliance with the contract on shipment. It was held in a CFR case[197] that having delivered all the contractually stipulated documents, including a quality certificate, the seller did everything that a CFR seller could be required to do. In a C&F[198] case,[199] it was held that a quality certificate raised a *presumption* of compliance at the time of shipment which the buyer failed to rebut. This approach has due regard for the seller's documentary duties in shipment contracts, and particularly the latter case seems to offer a well-balanced solution to the question of the precise status and function of a quality certificate where it is not clear whether it was intended to be conclusive. On the one hand, the presumption of compliance was raised, recognising that the certificate was intended to be a document of some significance. On the other hand, in the absence of a 'finality' clause, the buyer could not have been left unprotected and was given a chance to rebut the presumption.

[197] Appellate Court Barcelona, Recurso de Apelación No 403/2008, 24 March 2009 (Spain), available at http://cisgw3.law.pace.edu/cases/090324s4.html.

[198] 'Cost and Freight' (see n 191 above).

[199] Appellate Court, 47.448, 31 October 1995 (Argentina), available at http://cisgw3.law.pace.edu/cases/951031a1.html, affirming the finding of the court of first instance.

It can be argued that these decisions do not take into account that it may have been an (actual or presumed) intention of the parties that, besides being conforming on shipment, the goods should also, as envisaged by Article 36(2) CISG, remain conforming for a certain period of time thereafter. It is this consideration that led courts in some domestic systems to hold that in shipment contracts the seller undertakes that the goods remain of the appropriate quality following a normal journey and a reasonable time thereafter.[200] In the context of Article 35(1), which rests on interpreting the parties' intentions in the particular circumstances, no general rule of this kind can exist.[201] More so, while an intention as to durability can be implied, such implication should be possible only where there is strong evidence to that effect, such as a practice or a trade usage,[202] generating an expectation of durability.[203] The buyers are thus well advised to include a specific provision as to durability in the contract, if they wish to shift the risk of the goods not retaining their contractual characteristics during a certain period to the seller. Where such an intention can be implied, the question arises as to the time period within which the goods are to retain their contractual characteristics. If there is no specific evidence to this effect, the Convention's general principle of reasonableness[204] can aid in interpreting durability with reference to a 'reasonable time', having regard to the nature of the goods and other relevant circumstances.[205]

F. Quantity and Packaging

Quantity is another feature of conformity. The delivery of a greater or lesser quantity[206] than required by the contract is a breach of the seller's obligations under Article 35(1). More often than not contracts will contain a provision on quantity of the goods, but the way in which quantity is fixed will vary from a precise indication (number of units or precise weight) to a more approximate formulation such as 'not less than', 'about', 'more or less', '+/-10%'.[207] It may even be that in the absence of such formulations,

[200] *Mash & Murrell Ltd v Joseph I Emanuel Ltd* [1961] 1 WLR 862 (C & F contract) (reversed on other grounds, [1961] 2 Lloyd's Rep 326).

[201] The situation may be different in the case of the rules implied under Art 35(2). See Chapter 3.

[202] See Arts 8(3) and 9 CISG.

[203] *Benjamin's Sale of Goods* (n 37) para 11-040.

[204] See, eg AH Kritzer, 'Reasonableness' www.cisg.law.pace.edu/cisg/text/reason.html#schl (with further references).

[205] See Schwenzer (n 72) Art 36, para 10.

[206] 'If the seller delivers a quantity of goods greater than that provided for in the contract, the buyer may take delivery or refuse to take delivery of the excess quantity. If the buyer takes delivery of all or part of the excess quantity, he must pay for it at the contract rate' (Art 52(2) CISG).

[207] See Schwenzer, Hachem and Kee (n 1) paras 31.57–31.69.

deviations from a specified quantity are acceptable in a given trade sector[208] or in the light of the practice established between the parties. It goes without saying that ultimately the parties' intentions are decisive in ascertaining the agreed quantity. Once it is determined what quantity has been agreed upon, the next question is whether the seller has complied with that obligation. Here, documents often play an important role as the contract may provide that a weight certificate or a bill of lading, for example, are conclusive as to weight and quantity of the goods delivered, helping to avoid further disputes about whether the seller has in fact complied with its obligation.[209] Even where there is no such a clause, transport documents and certificates, whether issued on delivery or after examination at destination, still play an important evidentiary function,[210] although they may not necessarily be regarded as conclusive.[211]

Packaging is a final aspect of conformity listed in Article 35(1). Where a contract contains specific provisions as to the type of packaging, the seller is in breach of Article 35(1) where the actual packaging does not meet the contractual requirements.[212] As with other aspects of conformity, the express provisions of the contract may not be exhaustive, causing the parties to dispute the content of the seller's packaging obligations, and, once again, some of the influential factors in interpreting the contract are the nature of the goods, the conditions of transportation, the goods' destination, the price,[213] practices and the expectations or usages in the given industry or trade. A number of these factors may be at play at the same time, with some possibly being in conflict. In one case,[214] where the contract provided for the delivery of food products in 'in neutral polyethylene bags' the buyer argued that the seller was in breach of contract by delivering goods in non-transparent

[208] See Schwenzer (n 120) para 8, n 30 (German cereals trade sector is referred to as an example).

[209] See Chapter 8.

[210] ICAC Arbitration, 56/2003, 2 February 2004, available at http://cisgw3.law.pace.edu/cases/040202r1.html (a mate's receipt accepted to prove quantity); *Hot-rolled Steel Plates*, CIETAC Arbitration, 16 July 1996, available at http://cisgw3.law.pace.edu/cases/960716c1.html (inspection reports accepted as proof of quantity).

[211] See Appellate Court Bern, 304/II/2003/wuda/scch, 11 February 2004 (Switzerland), available at http://cisgw3.law.pace.edu/cases/040211s1.html (a bill of lading does not seem to have been treated as conclusive and was rejected as evidence because the carrier had signed the bill without checking the quantity and because the entire consignment in relation to that one bill was missing).

[212] See *Agricultural Products*, CIETAC Arbitration, 18 September 1996, available at http://cisgw3.law.pace.edu/cases/960918c2.html (gunny sacks instead of paper boxes used to pack mushrooms).

[213] See *Health Supplement*, CIETAC Arbitration, 25 September 1998, available at http://cisgw3.law.pace.edu/cases/980925c1.html#ii, where the tribunal held that the fish oil had to be delivered in wide neck bottles because this packaging corresponded to the contract price, which was higher than what would be charged for more simple packaging.

[214] District Court Hamburg, CISG/1998/12, 25 September 1998 (Germany), available at http://cisgw3.law.pace.edu/cases/980925c1.html#ii.

bags because transparent bags had been used in previous deliveries. The argument was rejected for several reasons. First, the seller did provide 'neutral polyethylene bags', with 'neutral' having been interpreted as being as 'cheap as possible'. Secondly, it could not have been apparent to the seller that the buyer intended transparent bags for the purpose of the product being visible to its final customers. Faced with the contractual silence and considering that the buyer had to attach its own labels to the product, the seller bore no responsibility for ensuring that the goods were fully prepared for an eventual resale. In contrast with the present contract, the previous contracts to which the buyer referred had specifically required transparent bags. Thirdly, as followed from expert evidence, it was usual to market frozen products in non-transparent bags or foil. Finally, according to further amended expert evidence, frozen products were offered in retail stores in non-transparent colour-printed boards, which meant that both the packaging provided by the seller and the packaging demanded by the buyer were unusual in the trade.

The past dealings between the parties seem to have initially pointed to interpreting the contract in the buyer's favour, but were rightly dismissed as supporting the buyer's case since the fact that all past contracts had specifically required transparent bags was a more likely indication that that was a specially negotiated term and not an obligation which could be assumed to be present in future contracts. That conclusion was reinforced by a finding that transparent bags were not usual in that trade. The final finding that the usual packaging was non-transparent colour-printed *boards*, rather than *bags*, may not seem to sit well with the decision that the seller was not liable. While the buyer's demands were not controlling, it could be argued that the seller's obligation, having to be determined in the light of the expectations and standards in the relevant trade, was to supply non-transparent coloured boards and, if so, the seller was in breach. This view, however, loses sight of the contract requiring 'neutral polyethylene *bags*' which indicates the parties' implicit intention to depart from what was usual in the trade, insofar as the choice between bags and boards was concerned.[215]

It is sometimes argued that if the sole purpose of packaging is to ensure that the goods are transported without damage or deterioration and if the goods are so transported, but the packaging is not in accordance with the contract, the seller should not be liable on the basis of the good faith principle.[216] This view, however, has no support in the wording of Article 35(1) which treats the correspondence of packaging with the contract as an independent aspect of conformity. This means that non-compliance with

[215] See Art 6 CISG.

[216] See Kröll (n 30) para 35. This argument is relevant if good faith is regarded as a general principle of the CISG. See also CIETAC Arbitration, 7 April 1999 (n 103).

the packaging requirements is a breach of contract and of Article 35(1). It is true that the parties' intentions are ultimately decisive but, in the interests of certainty and clarity, it is argued that only where the contract is *explicit* about the mutual intention to treat the seller's packaging obligations as being of legal significance *solely* where the goods are damaged should the seller not be liable. But in this case, this result simply flows from the parties' intentions and there is no need to invoke good faith.[217] Invoking good faith in order to infer an *implicit* intention would unnecessarily create uncertainty and tension with Article 35(1) which, as noted, treats packaging as a seller's independent obligation. It is at the stage of analysing remedies, and not Article 35(1), that the concern for preventing the buyer invoking its technical rights, where no adverse consequences follow from non-compliance with the packaging requirements, is really relevant.[218]

[217] See *BOPP Film*, CIETAC Arbitration, 8 September 1997, available at http://cisgw3.law.pace.edu/cases/970908c1.html.

[218] For example, in assessing whether the breach is fundamental, for the purpose of specific performance or avoidance, or in ascertaining whether the buyer has suffered any loss, for the purpose of damages.

3

Fitness for a Particular Purpose

I. LEGAL NATURE OF THE IMPLIED RULES ON CONFORMITY

BESIDES REQUIRING THE seller to comply with the contractual provisions on conformity of the goods, the Convention provides, in its Article 35(2), for several implied rules which are intended to determine the content and parameters of the seller's obligations as to conformity of the goods. These implied rules are applicable along with the contractual provisions unless the parties have agreed otherwise.[1] Once it is established that there was no agreement to depart from these rules, the first question to be asked is whether the goods 'are fit for any particular purpose expressly or impliedly made known to the seller at the time of the conclusion of the contract'. Although this rule, contained in Article 35(2)(b), is preceded by another rule in subparagraph (a), Article 35(2)(b) has priority over subparagraph (a), because it is more specific in that it requires the determination of whether any *particular purpose* was made known to the seller.[2] Article 35(2)(a), in turn, is the ultimate fall-back rule according to which the goods are to be 'fit for the purposes for which goods of the same description would ordinarily be used'.[3] Article 35(2) contains two other requirements: according to subparagraph (c), the goods ought to 'possess the qualities ... which the seller has held out to the buyer as a sample or model'; subparagraph (d) requires the goods to be 'contained or packaged in the manner usual for such goods or, where there is no such manner, in a manner adequate to preserve and protect [them]'.

The rationale for the rules on conformity has already been explored.[4] A related question, which now needs to be addressed, concerns the legal nature of these provisions. One widely held view is that Article 35(2) constitutes a

[1] See Art 35(2).

[2] See I Schwenzer in I Schwenzer (ed), *Schlechtriem and Schwenzer, Commentary on the UN Convention on the International Sale of Goods (CISG)*, 3rd edn (Oxford, OUP, 2010) Art 35, para 12; P Huber and A Mullis, *The CISG: A New Textbook for Students and Practitioners* (Munich, Sellier European Law Publishers, 2007) 135; S Kröll in S Kröll, L Mistelis and P Viscasillas (eds), *UN Convention on Contracts for the International Sale of Goods (CISG), Commentary* (Munich, CH Beck/Hart Publishing, 2011) Art 35, para 61.

[3] Art 35(2)(a).

[4] See Chapter 1.

framework or an analytical tool of contract interpretation.[5] Article 35(2) is believed to provide for the rules to which most parties would have agreed if they had an opportunity, in the absence of time constrains and other transaction costs, to put their minds to the issues at hand. These provisions are thus often viewed as being based on the parties' 'presumed' intentions and as containing questions which need to be asked[6] in order for the parties' contractual expectations to be ascertained. On this view, the legal nature of Article 35(2) is largely rooted in the contract itself.

Whilst this is generally true, this rationale has its limitations and does not fully reveal the nature and functions of Article 35(2). The rules implied under the CISG cannot emanate solely from the contract because they are there precisely to fill gaps where the contract itself fails to provide answers. This leads to the second point that whilst the rules in Article 35(2) are highly dependent on the individual circumstances, they are nevertheless implied not by virtue of the contract (implication of terms in fact) but by virtue of the Convention, an international legislative instrument (implication in law). It has also been seen that the issue of conformity of the goods may sometimes be used to promote broad societal considerations, such as the promotion of minimum quality standards around the world and equality between the developed and developing countries.[7] In these and other instances, such as those involving health and safety concerns, courts may be prone to taking a rather prescriptive view as regards the seller's obligations.[8] Such an approach is a feature of the idea of *caveat venditor*.[9] In contrast, the view of the conformity rules as being rooted solely in the contractual sphere, which promotes the ideals of freedom of contract and of the parties' will, is more at home in the *laissez-faire* environment, which is usually associated with *caveat emptor*.[10] In practical terms, this proposition is unlikely to carry serious consequences because Article 35(2) will inevitably be applied in the context of the parties'

[5] In addition to the rules in Arts 8 and 9. See, eg P Schlechtriem and P Butler, *UN Law on International Sales* (Berlin/Heidelberg, Springer-Verlag, 2009) 115; J Honnold (updated and revised by H Flechtner), *Uniform Law for International Sales under the 1980 United Nations Convention,* 4th edn (The Netherlands, Wolters Kluwer Law & Business, 2009) 334.

[6] See R Hyland, 'Conformity of Goods to the Contract under the United Nations Sales Convention and the Uniform Commercial Code' in P Schlechtriem (ed), *Einheitliches Kaufrecht und nationals Obligationenrecht* (Baden-Baden, Nomos, 1987) 328.

[7] See the discussion of Appellate Court Arnhem, 97/700 and 98/046, 27 April 1999 (The Netherlands), available at http://cisgw3.law.pace.edu/cases/990427n1.html in Chapter 2.

[8] See the discussion of the Federal Supreme Court, VIII ZR 67/04, 2 March 2005 (Germany), available at http://cisgw3.law.pace.edu/cases/050302g1.html in Chapter 4. See also n 39 below and the accompanying main text.

[9] See Chapter 1.

[10] See Chapter 1; also E Zamir, 'Toward a General Concept of Conformity in the Performance of Contracts' (1991) 52 *La L Rev* 1, 12; C Murrow, 'Warranty of Quality: Comparative Survey' (1939–1940) 14 *Tul L Rev* 327, 330.

particular circumstances,[11] which include the contract.[12] But the point is that an occasional judicial impulse to treat the Convention as a vehicle for promoting broad societal objectives, external to the contract, shows that Article 35(2) should not be seen simply as a tool of contract interpretation.

II. FITNESS FOR A PARTICULAR PURPOSE: GENERAL CONSIDERATIONS

The two main implied rules require conformity to be assessed with reference to the goods' suitability for a purpose. A general rule in Article 35(2)(a) is based on the criterion of 'ordinary' purposes, while the rule in Article 35(2)(b) requires the goods to be fit for a particular purpose made known to the seller. As noted, because the latter is a more specific provision, it has priority over the former. For this reason, it will be considered first, reversing the order in which these rules are set out in the CISG.

The seller will be liable if the goods are not fit for a particular purpose made known to the seller, 'except where the circumstances show that the buyer did not rely, or that it was unreasonable for him to rely, on the seller's skill and judgement'.[13] This rule discourages the buyer from falling into a false sense of security because a mere communication of a particular purpose may not suffice to make the seller liable for the goods' unfitness for that purpose:[14] the seller may still be able to prove a lack of the buyer's reliance on the seller's skill and judgement. The rule further induces the seller who suspects that it is being relied upon to be clear about its expertise in order to preclude its liability if the goods do not meet the buyer's particular purpose. The rule also gives an incentive to the buyer to share the information with the seller about its particular purpose to ensure that the buyer gets what it wants, which may in turn save the seller potential costs of further inquiry into the buyer's circumstances.[15] Thus, with both parties being encouraged to share information with each other, the rule promotes efficiency since an efficient transaction is one where both parties have accurate information about the value of resources that constitute the subject matter of the contract.[16]

[11] This applies particularly strongly to Art 35(2)(b) since it requires the examination of the facts with a view to determining whether a particular purpose has been communicated and whether it was reasonable for the buyer to rely on the seller's skill and judgement.

[12] The real question, therefore, is one of the degree to which the contract and the contractual expectations should influence the meaning and scope of the rules implied under the CISG.

[13] Art 35(2)(b).

[14] CP Gillett and SD Walt, *Sales Law: Domestic and International*, 2nd edn (New York, Foundation Press and Thomson West, 2009) 331.

[15] VM Gonzales, 'The Buyer's Specifications Exception to the Implied Warranty of Fitness for a Particular Purpose: Design or Performance' (1987) 61 *S Cal L Rev* 237, 251.

[16] See Zamir (n 10) 43.

The rule has also been explained on two other bases. According to the 'assumption of risk' rationale, if the seller is informed or is in the position to know about a particular purpose, it has an opportunity to refuse to enter into the contract or to protect itself by other means such as including a limitation or exclusion of liability clause.[17] The seller's decision not to protect itself can then be taken to indicate its consent to this obligation. Another way of looking at the rule is to view the buyer's reliance on the seller as the basis of a contractual obligation.[18] By communicating a particular purpose for which it requires the goods, the buyer informs the seller that it is relying on the seller in 'such a way that the seller can be said to have contracted on that footing'.[19] Both the 'assumption of risk' and the 'reliance' bases of rationalising Article 35(2)(b) treat its legal nature as emanating from the parties' agreement.[20] This explanation is not free from difficulties. One difficulty is that it does not sit easily with the prevailing view that the parties' agreement is unnecessary for Article 35(2)(b) to apply.[21] It is also open to the above-mentioned criticism that the Convention's implied rules cannot be rationalised solely with reference to the contract. Finally, it is difficult to understand the difference between the purpose and scope of Article 35(1)[22] and Article 35(2)(b).

These difficulties notwithstanding, there is no doubt that the 'assumption of risk' and possibly the 'reliance' rationalisations capture the essence of the rule. But considering that Article 35(2)(b) contains a term 'implied by law', that the Convention's drafters rejected a proposal[23] to subject the fitness for a particular purpose rule to the parties' agreement and that Article 35 itself clearly differentiates paragraphs (1) and (2)(b), the

[17] Secretariat's Commentary on Article 33 of the 1978 Draft, para 7; Huber and Mullis (n 2) 138. Similar rationale has been used in relation to the foreseeability tests in the fundamental breach and damages provisions (Arts 25 and 74 CISG). The possibility of the Art 35(2)(b) obligation being imposed on the seller purely on the basis of an implicit communication of a particular purpose shows that it is not necessary for the buyer to show that the seller has accepted a duty to comply with that particular purpose, as some decisions appear to suggest (ICC Arbitration Case No 8213, March 1995, available at http://cisgw3.law.pace.edu/cases/958213i1.html).

[18] This rationale has been used in English law, which uses a similar test to that in Art 35(2)(b) (see Sale of Goods Act (SGA) 1979 (UK), s. 14(3)), but there is no reason in principle why it cannot be used under the CISG.

[19] *Cammell Laird & Co v Manganese Bronze and Brass Co Ltd* [1934] AC 402, 430 (in the context of the Sale of Goods Act 1893). See CM Bianca in CM Bianca and J Bonell (eds), *Commentary on the International Sales Law* (Milan, Giuffrè, 1987) 274, explaining the rule in the CISG in terms of its 'fairness'.

[20] See the view referred to in F Enderlein and D Maskow, *International Sales Law* (New York, Oceana Publications, 1992) 144 ('What matters here is that the purpose which is made known becomes a term of the contract by invoking the Convention').

[21] See Schwenzer (n 2) para 21; S Kruisinga, *(Non-)conformity in the 1980 UN Convention on Contracts for the International Sale of Goods: A Uniform Concept?* (Antwerp/Oxford/New York, Intersentia, 2004) 32; Kröll (n 2) para 109.

[22] See Chapter 2.

[23] By delegation of the Federal Republic of Germany.

conclusion must be that the 'seller's implied consent' under Article 35(2)(b) may well fall below the level required for the purpose of establishing the 'parties' agreement'. As to the buyer's reliance rationale, the fact of such reliance is taken to indicate the seller's agreement that fitness for a particular purpose constitutes a *contractual* obligation. However, proving reliance is not a precondition for an effective invocation of Article 35(2)(b), whereas it is arguable that if reliance had been the basis for implying a term into the contract, proving reliance would have been a necessary precondition for invoking a provision stipulating such an implied term. Once a particular purpose is communicated to the seller, reliance is presumed. The CISG does not place the burden of proving reliance on the buyer and it is only up to the seller to raise a lack of reliance (or of reasonable reliance) as a defence to the buyer's claim.

Two contrasting views can arise in this regard. On the one hand, this may indicate that to some extent the Convention de-emphasises the role of 'reliance' in explaining the *contractual* nature of the seller's obligation, even though the buyer's (reasonable) reliance is clearly seen by the CISG as a consideration worthy of protection. On the other hand, the fact that there is no need for the buyer to prove its reliance may mean exactly the opposite: reliance is given a pre-eminent position by virtue of it being presumed. In contrast with the first, this view does not stand in the way of reliance explaining the contractual nature of the seller's obligation.

III. RELATIONSHIP WITH ARTICLE 35(1) CISG

Whatever the correct theoretical explanation of Article 35(2)(b), it is evident that in many cases its overlap with Article 35(1) will be almost inevitable.[24] A particular purpose made known to the seller can often be easily classified as a term of the contract[25] implied from all relevant circumstances[26]

[24] Schlechtriem and Butler (n 5) 117; T Neumann, 'Features of Article 35 in the Vienna Convention: Equivalence, Burden of Proof and Awareness' (2007) 11 *Vindobona J Int'l Com L Arbitration* 81, para 20.

[25] See District Court Ellwangen, 1 KfH O 32/95, 21 August 1995 (Germany), available at http://cisgw3.law.pace.edu/cases/950821g2.html, where the Spanish seller was found to be aware of the goods' intended use in Germany and of the German Food Safety Laws. The decision was made under Art 35(1) but could have also been made on the basis that the seller was aware of the particular purpose that the goods were to be used in Germany and had to comply with the safety regulations in force in Germany. See also Commercial Court St Gallen, HG.2010.421-HGK, 14 June 2012 (Switzerland), available at http://cisgw3.law.pace.edu/cases/120614s1.html, where the contractual term that the goods had to be certified by Bio Suisse led to the implication of a particular purpose that the goods had to be fit for being used in the production of 'bio-' (organic) products.

[26] See Arts 8 and 9.

(implication in fact).[27] A close linkage between the two can also be seen in a reverse situation where a finding as to the absence of a contract term is followed by a finding of a lack of communication of a particular purpose. In one case,[28] what was apparently a contractual reference to the intended use of the mobile units in Germany was deemed insufficient to imply either a contractual obligation of compliance with special public law standards in Germany or, it seems, an obligation under Article 35(2)(b).[29] In some cases, a particular purpose may even be specified in a contract,[30] in which case the obligation of ensuring fitness for the specified purpose will flow from both the contract and the term implied under Article 35(2)(b).

At the same time, the circumstances envisaged by Article 35(2)(b) do not have to evidence the parties' agreement.[31] Considering that all that the buyer has to prove to invoke Article 35(2)(b) is that a particular purpose has been made known to the seller,[32] this provision can potentially be an effective way of bringing a claim against the seller since the preconditions for invoking this provision appear less stringent than what would be required to prove the parties' agreement. To prevent the use of Article 35(2)(b) as a means of bypassing an apparently more stringent test under Article 35(1) and the buyer's ability to 'unilaterally determine the contract by informing the seller of the particular purpose',[33] it has been argued that it has to be interpreted 'narrowly',[34] which presumably refers to a

[27] A substantial overlap may be responsible for some courts and tribunals referring to several paragraphs of Art 35 at the same time (see ICC Arbitration No 7565, 1994, available at http://cisgw3.law.pace.edu/cases/947565i1.html) or to Art 35 as a whole without specifying a precise basis for the decision (see District Court Rotterdam, 295401/HA ZA 07-2802, 15 October 2008 (The Netherlands), available at http://cisgw3.law.pace.edu/cases/081015n2.html).

[28] Appellate Court Arnhem, 97/700 and 98/046, 27 April 1999 (The Netherlands), available at http://cisgw3.law.pace.edu/cases/990427n1.html.

[29] There was no express reference to Art 35(2)(b), but the decision can be interpreted as alluding to this provision where it refers to the seller's knowledge of the export of the goods to Germany.

[30] See Appellate Court Madrid, No 683/2006, 20 February 2007 (Spain), available at http://cisgw3.law.pace.edu/cases/070220s4.html ('the olive stones shall be free of fruit flesh, pulp and other impurities since the goods would be used for energy production'); *Broadcasting Equipment*, CIETAC Arbitration, 22 May 1996, available at http://cisgw3.law.pace.edu/cases/960522c1.html (the purpose was specified in the contract, but the decision was made solely on the basis of the contract with no reference to Art 35(2)(b)); *Channel Steel*, CIETAC Arbitration, 23 October 1996, available at http://cisgw3.law.pace.edu/cases/961023c1.html (the purpose could be inferred from the contract, but the buyer chose to rely on Art 35(2)(b); the decision was made solely on the basis of the contract).

[31] See also n 23 above and the accompanying main text.

[32] Of course, that is so only until the seller invokes the lack of (reasonable) reliance defence.

[33] Kröll (n 2) para 108.

[34] Ibid paras 62, 108. It is interesting to contrast this proposition with the way the fitness for purpose test has developed in English law, where it has been given a wide interpretation, resulting in a paucity of decision on express warranties (see M Bridge, *The Sale of Goods*, 3rd edn (Oxford, OUP, 2014) para 7.89).

strict interpretation against the buyer. It may be debatable whether that is necessarily the right approach to Article 35(2)(b) since what matters is the underlying purpose and policy of this provision. The obligation prescribed in it is implied by the Convention and there is nothing inconceivable in an obligation implied by law containing a lower threshold for proving a lack of conformity than the one that would need to be met to prove a contractual term of conformity. However, considering an intensely close relationship and a substantial overlap between Article 35(2)(b) and Article 35(1), it may, as a matter of principle, be preferable to interpret the two provisions with a similar level of rigour.

Despite this close linkage between them, Article 35(2)(b) and Article 35(1) still constitute different legal bases and their application can lead to different results. In a case involving the supply of hot-melt glue,[35] it was held that while the product complied with the technical specifications set out in the contract, the seller was still liable because the glue was inadequate for the particular purpose of 'the permanent fixing of the cardboard boxes, filled with [their] product and piled up in times of extreme heat'. Thus, where the contractual provisions are not intended to displace the Convention's implied terms, Article 35(2)(b) can supplement the contract by imposing on the seller an obligation in addition to those flowing from the contractual specifications. In some such cases, a contractual term (Article 35(1)) can even help to define the particular purpose under Article 35(2)(b).[36] For example, where the seller knows the country where the goods will be used, the contractual specification of the maximum radiation level permitted in that country can lead to the conclusion that compliance with the public law regulations in that country was a particular purpose that the goods had to meet.[37]

IV. DEFINING A PARTICULAR PURPOSE

The goods must be fit for a 'particular purpose', made known to the seller. The words 'a particular purpose' give rise to some important and difficult interpretative questions. First, does the purpose have to be a specific purpose as opposed to a general or a broad purpose, or is it sufficient for *some* purpose, no matter how broadly formulated, simply to be specified or stated? For example, is stating that foodstuffs are needed to feed 'animals

[35] Appellate Court Barcelona, RA 340/1997, 4 February 1997 (Spain), available at http://cisgw3.law.pace.edu/cases/970204s4.html.

[36] This is true particularly of the goods' description. See *Teheran-Europe Co Ltd v ST Belton Ltd* [1968] 2 QB 545, 560.

[37] See District Court s-Hertogenbosch, 9981/HAZA 95-2299, 2 October 1998 (The Netherlands), available at http://cisgw3.law.pace.edu/cases/981002n1.html, where the court did not make any specific reference to Art 35. See also Kröll (n 2) para 115.

and poultry' a sufficiently 'particular' purpose, or is the buyer required to communicate its needs in more specific terms, by referring concretely to, say, pheasants or mink, some of which may be more sensitive to an ingredient in the foodstuffs than others?

On the one hand, whichever rationale of Article 35(2)(b) is taken—the assumption of risk or reliance—both require that a purpose be communicated with some degree of precision. The seller needs to know what obligation it is undertaking and/or in respect of what it is being relied upon. On the other hand, absolute precision can hardly be expected. If this were so, the threshold for invoking Article 35(2)(b) would be set too high, confining the application of this provision to relatively few cases and consequently depriving it of much of its practical value and substantially diminishing the level of the buyer's protection. The possibility of an implicit communication of a particular purpose, resulting in the seller not being required to have actual knowledge, indirectly signals the Convention's support of this view. Establishing an implicit communication requires an evaluation of the facts and drawing inferences from them, which means that it should be possible for a particular purpose to be formulated in relatively broad terms as long as it is possible to make more specific inferences from such a formulation.[38]

Where a children's play structure had been bought for 'commercial purposes and public use', an implicit requirement that the goods had to meet specific safety requirements in the country where the structure was to be used was readily inferred.[39] Similarly, where inflatable triumphal arches were bought as an 'advertising medium next to and across the racing track', it could reasonably be expected that the arches would be able to remain safely as an advertisement in the conditions surrounding the racing track.[40] Finally, where it was clear to the parties that expensive and sophisticated globes were bought in order to be displayed 'as respectable exhibits in the showrooms', the seller was found to be in breach of Article 35(2)(b) where the globes ceased to work (rotate) after only a few months.[41] Although no time-frame for the globes' durability was mentioned, the court held that their 'operational lifetime' should be three years on average, considering

[38] See, similarly, *Henry Kendall & Sons v William Lillico & Sons Ltd* [1969] 2 AC 31,114 ('Almost every purpose is capable of some sub-division, some further and better particulars It is not necessarily a narrow or closely particularised purpose').

[39] District Court Lugano, OA.2000.459, 19 April 2007 (Switzerland), available at http://cisgw3.law.pace.edu/cases/070419s1.html. The decision further explains that if there had been no requirement of compliance with safety regulations, 'the structure would not have been included in the risk covered by the insurance policy for enterprise and products civil liability'.

[40] See Commercial Court of the Canton of Aargau, OR.2001.00029, 5 November 2002 (Switzerland), available at http://cisgw3.law.pace.edu/cases/021105s1.html (the seller was held to have breached Art 35(2)(b) after the 'arch lost air and drifted with the wind towards the racing track').

[41] District Court Munich, 5 HKO 3936/00, 27 February 2002 (Germany), available at http://cisgw3.law.pace.edu/cases/020227g1.html.

that the parties contemplated a long-term relationship and high transportation costs[42] to the buyer's branches. Thus, a broadly stated particular purpose can lead to an inference of a more specific particular purpose and requirements.[43]

In some cases, the evidence will not support an inference of a particular purpose alleged by the buyer. This may be so where a broad description of the goods encompasses several normal purposes and the goods are fit for some but not all of these purposes. In one case,[44] the buyer argued that 'large' menthol crystals it had ordered from the seller did not correspond to the particular purpose for which it needed them because their size varied from '0.4 to 4 cms'. It was held that what the seller had supplied was *one* type of standard quality crystals which usually suited the seller's customers. There was no established meaning of the term 'large crystals' and because the buyer failed to specify what exactly it needed, no obligation under Article 35(2)(b) could be implied. It is submitted that this decision reflects a correct approach to this type of case. Whilst Article 35(2)(b) can in principle include normal purposes, it is applicable to those cases where *some* purpose is communicated. Where the goods can normally be used for a number of purposes, there is no way for the seller to know which of the normal purposes the goods need to meet. If the buyer wishes to benefit from Article 35(2)(b), it has to prove that the seller was informed, expressly or implicitly, of the normal purpose(s) for which the goods were needed.

A broadly stated particular purpose, whether normal or unusual, may have several sub-purposes within it.[45] The particular purpose of the goods being used as a children's play structure may have such sub-divisions as safety and functionality, as well as appropriate decoration. The purpose of globes to be used in respectable exhibitions and showrooms may include an ability to rotate and to glitter as some of its sub-divisions. Suppose that a children's play structure is safe and fully functional, but is painted in dark and scary images, or that globes are able to rotate but do not glitter. Is the seller required to ensure that the goods meet all possible sub-purposes or is the goods' ability to meet one or more but not all of them sufficient?

It can be argued that once a particular purpose has been established, the seller should be liable for all possible sub-purposes. This, it can be contended, is not only in line with the Convention's language requiring the

[42] '[T]he large Globes weighed almost 290 Kg including their wrapping' (ibid).

[43] See further District Court Coburg, 22 O 38/06, 12 December 2006 (Germany), available at http://cisgw3.law.pace.edu/cases/061212g1.html (a particular purpose was inferred, from the seller's knowledge of a specific location where the plants were intended to be grown, that the plants were to flourish in spring in the climatic conditions of that location; the obligation was, however, not implied due to the finding of a lack of the buyer's reliance on the seller's skill and judgement).

[44] Supreme Court, 4C.245/2003/ech, 13 January 2004 (Switzerland), available at http://cisgw3.law.pace.edu/cases/040113s1.html.

[45] See n 38 above.

suitability for a particular purpose (with, presumably, all that it covers) but also promotes certainty and settlement of disputes since under this position risks are clearly allocated. This view may also seem strengthened by the fact that some domestic sales laws, such as UK Sale of Goods Act (SGA) 1979, section 14(3), require the goods only to be 'reasonably' fit for a particular purpose, which can be seen as injecting flexibility into this test and softening the seller's position.[46] In contrast, the CISG appears to have no such flexibility and to expect the seller to be liable if the goods are not absolutely fit for a particular purpose. Whilst the Convention's general principle of reasonableness can conceivably be relied upon to interpret Article 35(2)(b) as meaning only 'reasonable fitness', that would probably result in an interpretation which is too invasive and contrary to the drafters' intention. Had the drafters wanted to introduce the 'reasonable fitness' test, surely they would have made that clear considering that SGA 1979, section 14(3) was used in the drafting of Article 35(2)(b).[47] At the same time, the prospect of the seller being liable for all possible sub-purposes is worrying because the seller can be held liable too easily. Once a broad particular purpose is established, there is no need to show that its sub-purpose was communicated and that may be harsh on the seller. At its core, the CISG is about openness to all factual peculiarities[48] and risks should be allocated on a case-by-case basis. No one generally applicable position can be taken.

It is arguable that if what initially appears to be a sub-purpose stretches the seller's liability too far, it may be possible to view it not as a sub-division of a particular purpose but as a different purpose altogether. But doing so may not always be possible or plausible. A better approach is to take the position stated at the beginning of the previous paragraph only as a starting point, in order to promote certainty and settlement of disputes. Referring to the above examples, the seller should be liable if a children's play structure is painted in inappropriate images and if globes are not able to glitter, since these sub-purposes are not outside the normal range of what a reasonable seller could expect in the light of the broadly stated particular purpose. At the same time, it is important to recognise that the CISG is against rigid and hard and fast solutions. This means that if a sub-division of a particular purpose is not one which the seller would normally contemplate and if the goods are fit for most other sub-divisions of which a reasonable person in the seller's position would be aware, no liability should attach as a result of the goods' unfitness for that improbable or rare sub-purpose.[49]

[46] See SGA 1979, s. 14(3).

[47] Art 35(2)(b) was modelled on SGA 1979, s. 14(3), as well as on § 2-315 Uniform Commercial Code (UCC) (see Schwenzer (n 2) para 19).

[48] See, eg Arts 8 and 9 CISG.

[49] For a similar position in the context of English law taken on the basis of the reasonable fitness for purpose provision in SGA 1979, s. 14(3), see J Adams and H MacQueen, *Atiyah's Sale of Goods*, 12th edn (Harlow, Longman 2010) 199–200.

The sellers ought to be aware of the dangers that allowing a broadly stated purpose may entail. In a leading English law case, *Ashington Piggeries*,[50] involving the sale of animal foodstuff, the buyer asked the seller to compound food according to the buyer's formula. The foodstuff caused thousands of mink to die because an ingredient, Norwegian herring meal, contained a toxic chemical (DMNA). The seller knew that the compound would be fed to mink, but the seller's Norwegian supplier, who sold the Norwegian herring meal, did not know that, although it knew that, in the past, herring meal had been fed to mink in Norway. Mink were more sensitive to DMNA than other animals. Both the seller and its supplier were held liable under the fitness for purpose test. The seller was held liable on the basis that once toxicity was proved, there was no need for the buyer to show that the foodstuff was dangerous to all animals other than mink. The presence of toxicity raised the presumption of the goods' unsuitability to all animals and the burden shifted to the seller to show that it was suitable to other species and that mink was merely an unusually sensitive species.[51] As to liability of the seller's supplier, the majority of the House of Lords took the view that the inclusion of the herring meal in feeding stuffs constituted a particular purpose that the herring meal had to be reasonably fit for use as food for animals, including mink.[52] This decision was made even though all that the Norwegian supplier could reasonably have known was that the goods *might*, and not *would*, be fed to mink. The reasoning was that the Norwegian supplier knew that herring meal was being fed to mink in Norway and therefore should have contemplated that it might be fed to mink.[53] The decision of the majority to interpret the fitness for purpose test in that way indicates the alleviation of the buyer's burden of proof and that, in turn, may well have been based on a drive to push 'liability up the distribution chain to the point where the defect was created'.[54]

Sellers in contracts governed by the CISG are not immune from being exposed to similar liability. The wording in Article 35(2)(b), referring to a 'particular purpose' which, at that, can be made known implicitly, leaves judges with much discretion allowing for various policies to be implemented.[55] As seen from *Ashington Piggeries*, some such policies have arguably resulted in the expansion of the sellers' liability under the

[50] *Ashington Piggeries Ltd v Christopher Hill Ltd; Christopher Hill Ltd v Norsildmel* [1972] AC 441.

[51] Ibid 492–93.

[52] Ibid 488, 496.

[53] Ibid 488.

[54] Bridge (n 34) para 7.107.

[55] The discussion of Appellate Court s-Gravenhage, 99/474, 23 April 2003 (The Netherlands), available at http://cisgw3.law.pace.edu/cases/030423n1.html in Chapter 2 has already illustrated this proposition in the context of Art 35(1).

fitness for a particular purpose test under English law, which bears much resemblance to its counterpart in Article 35(2)(b). With this in mind, the sellers, to whom a broadly stated purpose is communicated or who believe that the knowledge of such a purpose can be imputed to them in the circumstances, are well advised to clarify the buyer's specific needs to ensure that they are in the position to meet those needs, thereby reducing the risk of their potential liability.

It may be that a description which appears quite specific is still insufficient to support an inference of a particular purpose contended for by the buyer because that purpose is unusual and, in the light of the understandings common in a given trade sector, does not follow from the contractual description. In one case,[56] the buyer ordered doors made of Tulipwood described as 'blank permanently untreated'. The buyer rejected the goods on the ground that they showed differences in colour. The seller contended that Tulipwood was a kind of wood which contained differences in colour and had it known that the buyer wanted a uniform colour, it would have suggested a different kind of wood (Koto). The seller further contended that to make its needs clear the buyer, a specialist in the field, should have used a different description ('transparent treated').[57] The court appears to have broadly agreed with the seller's position. First, Tulipwood doors could be made in a uniform colour if they were painted, but it had not been proved that unpainted Tulipwood doors were unfit to be installed and used as doors.[58] Secondly, a particular purpose alleged by the buyer had not been communicated to the seller. Colour is a matter of preference and taste and in this case this was particularly so, considering that some doors were to be installed at the place of the buyer's customers. The description in the order did not convey the buyer's or its customers' preference for a uniform colour whereas that could reasonably be expected from the buyer who was said to be 'the biggest specialist shop in doors of the middle Netherlands'. Whilst the buyer had been provided with a sample of the wood, that sample was too small for the buyer to infer that 'there would be no difference in colour in the eventual delivery'.[59] This case sends a signal to buyers that they should be careful in formulating the description of the goods, because it can influence the finding of a particular purpose (or a lack thereof). They

[56] Commercial Court Hasselt, A.R. 05/4177, 19 April 2006 (Belgium), available at http://cisgw3.law.pace.edu/cases/060419b1.html.

[57] For a detailed exposition of these arguments, see an earlier decision in Commercial Court Hasselt, A.R. 05/4177, 15 February 2006 (Belgium), available at http://cisgw3.law.pace.edu/cases/060215b1.html.

[58] This point would be particularly relevant to Art 35(2)(a) (fitness for ordinary purposes), but in principle could also be relevant to Art 35(2)(b) if being used as doors is regarded as a particular purpose.

[59] 'It cannot be expected of the seller that it would deliver a complete door as a sample.'

should also communicate their needs with precision, especially where these needs are unusual or are not easily determinable, such as where they depend on individual tastes and preferences.[60]

The next question is whether a particular purpose necessarily refers to an abnormal, unusual or an idiosyncratic purpose, or whether normal and usual purposes are also covered. For example, most animals may be able to consume the foodstuffs supplied by the seller without any adverse effects, but mink to which the foodstuff was ultimately fed may die because of its unusual sensitivity to a particular ingredient. The 'methanol crystals' case, discussed above,[61] shows that Article 35(2)(b) has been interpreted as covering not only unusual and idiosyncratic purposes, but also normal purposes. In principle, this is the right approach because the buyers who want to use the goods for one or more but not all normal purpose(s) should be able to benefit from Article 35(2)(b), which is designed to protect those buyers who are communicating their specific needs to their sellers. In short, the buyer's needs vary and comprise ordinary and typical as well as unusual and idiosyncratic ones. All these can constitute a 'particular purpose' in a given transaction.[62] The necessary drawback of this approach is that it broadens the scope of Article 35(2)(b), creating an overlap with Article 35(2)(a)[63] which aims to govern the seller's obligations in cases of 'ordinary' purposes. That, in turn, may result in the duplication of the functions of the two provisions or, more importantly, in the diminishing of the role of Article 35(2)(a). The latter result is undesirable considering that Article 35(2)(a) is the ultimate fall-back rule of conformity.

V. CONDITIONS IN A SPECIFIC PLACE

A. Public Law Regulations

One problem peculiar to international transactions is whether the buyer's mere mention of a specific place, country or market where the goods are intended to be used or sold is sufficient to impose a duty on the seller to comply with the conditions peculiar to that place, country or market. These

[60] See Commercial Court St Gallen, 14 June 2012 (n 25), where the court took the position that the implication of a particular purpose that the goods were to be fit for being used in the production of organic/bio-products, was insufficient to lead to a further inference that the goods were to be accompanied by certain specifications. The information provided by the seller was sufficient for an inspection agency to issue the certificates required by the contract in order to confirm the organic nature of the goods, and it did not follow from this contractual requirement and from the stated particular purpose that the seller was to supply any further specifications.

[61] See Supreme Court, 13 January 2004 (Switzerland) (n 44).

[62] For a similar position, see Huber and Mullis (n 2) 138.

[63] See Chapter 4.

conditions can be of a different nature and include public law regulations, local industry standards, religious or cultural peculiarities or climatic conditions. A general principle, intended as guidance for dealing with this problem in the context of public law regulations has been pronounced in a leading CISG case, *New Zealand Mussels*,[64] where the mussels delivered by a Swiss seller to a German buyer did not comply with a recommendation of the German health authorities as to their cadmium content. It was held that the seller could not be expected to know about the regulations in the buyer's country unless: (1) the regulations were the same in the seller's country; (2) the buyer specifically drew the seller's attention to the regulations; or (3) the seller had a good reason to know about them, such as where the seller had a branch in the buyer's country, had a long established business relationship with the buyer, or had often previously exported the goods to or promoted them in that country. Since none of these circumstances were present, the seller was deemed not to have had a duty to ensure that the goods complied with the recommendation of the German authorities.

So far as Article 35(2)(b) is concerned, there is some disagreement about a precise legal basis for not holding the seller liable in cases such as *New Zealand Mussels*. One view is that a mere reference to a country where the goods will be used or sold simply lacks specificity and precision to communicate a particular purpose of compliance with public law regulations.[65] This position was taken even in a case (*G Mainzer Raumzellen v Van Keulen Mobielbouw Nijverdal BV*)[66] where the parties, both experts in the manufacture of mobile units, had had a long-standing business relationship and the seller had not only known that the goods would be used in Germany but had also been informed by the buyer that the German authorities had issued requirements in respect of such mobile units.

According to the other view, a reference to the country of use suffices to imply a duty on the seller to comply with the applicable regulations: since

[64] Federal Supreme Court, VIII ZR 159/94, 8 March 1995 (Germany), available at http://cisgw3.law.pace.edu/cases/950308g3.html. For the discussion of some of the reasons why it is regarded as a leading case, see HM Flechtner, 'Decisions on Conformity of Goods under Article 35 of the UN Sales Convention (CISG): The "*Mussels* Case", Evidentiary Standards for Lack of Conformity, and the "Default Rule" vs. "Cumulative View of Implied Conformity Obligations"' in I Schwenzer, Y Atamer and P Butler (eds), *Current Issues in the CISG and Arbitration* (The Hague, Eleven International Publishing, 2014) 180–82.

[65] This view also seems to be preferred in the *New Zealand Mussels* decision ('The agreement regarding the place of destination is in itself neither under subsection (a) nor under subsection (b) of CISG 35(2) sufficient to judge whether the mussels conform with the contract pursuant to certain cadmium standards used in Germany Decisive is that a foreign seller can simply not be required to know the not easily determinable public law provisions and/or administrative practices of the country to which he exports').

[66] Appellate Court Arnhem, 97/700 and 98/046, 27 April 1999 (The Netherlands), available at http://cisgw3.law.pace.edu/cases/990427n1.html (the case does not expressly refer to Art 35(2)(b)). See similarly, Supreme Court, 2 Ob 100/00w, 13 April 2000 (Austria), available at http://cisgw3.law.pace.edu/cases/000413a3.html.

the seller knows where the goods will be used or sold, the seller should be expected to investigate the regulations in that place.[67] This position is reinforced by drawing an analogy with Article 42 CISG,[68] which makes the seller liable for the existence of a third party's right or claim based on industrial or other intellectual property if such a right or claim arises 'under the law of the State where the goods will be resold or otherwise used, if it was contemplated by the parties at the time of the conclusion of the contract that the goods would be resold or otherwise used in that State'.[69] Those advocating this position acknowledge that not every seller can be expected to have the knowledge of the importing country's regulations, particularly where they are unusual,[70] or the resources to carry out such an investigation. However, they contend that such persons are not only free to define the goods' quality and characteristics in the contract, but are also adequately protected by the 'reliance on the seller's skill and judgement' provision[71] in Article 35(2)(b).[72]

The outcome of relying on either of these positions is likely to be the same in most cases. Whilst the second view is initially more demanding of the seller, it then seeks to protect it, by emphasising that the seller can contend that the buyer did not rely or that it was unreasonable for the buyer to rely on the seller's skill and judgement. Nevertheless, the second view may at times produce undesirable consequences. In contrast with the first view which gives sellers the peace of mind that mere knowledge of destination is not a communication of a particular purpose of compliance with public law regulations, it can still make sellers more cautious. It will alert them to the possibility that the provision on the reliance on their skill and judgement may not always offer them sufficient protection, especially because the burden of proving a lack of reliance lies with the seller, with the presumption of reliance raised as soon as the particular purpose is made known.[73] A cautious attitude is likely to induce some sellers to invest more time and

[67] See P Schlechtriem, 'Uniform Sales Law in the Decisions of the *Bundesgerichtshof*', http://cisgw3.law.pace.edu/cisg/biblio/schlechtriem3.html; Schwenzer (n 2) para 21; Kröll (n 2) para 121.

[68] See Kröll (n 2) para 121.

[69] Art 42(1)(a) CISG.

[70] See Schlechtriem and Butler (n 5) 119.

[71] Schlechtriem (n 67); Kröll (n 2) para 121. See *RJ & AM Smallmon v Transport Sales Ltd and Grant Alan Miller* [2011] NZ CA 340 (the seller's knowledge that trucks would be used in Australia was deemed to be a communication of a particular purpose, but it was held that it was not reasonable for the buyer to rely on the seller's skill and judgement).

[72] Where a business person, either due to the insufficient knowledge or a lack of resources available for the investigation, cannot be expected to know about the regulations in the importing country, it is unreasonable for the buyer to rely on the seller's skill and judgement.

[73] This follows from the principle that a party who invokes the exception to the other party's right must prove the necessary precondition for the existence of that exception. See VIII and IX A below.

resources into contract drafting to specify the goods' characteristics,[74] to subject the goods only to the requirements in the seller's country or to disclaim any potential liability for non-compliance with the regulations in the importing country.[75] The sellers will also be induced to invest additional resources into investigating the regulations in that country.[76] All these costs will not have to be incurred if the first view is adopted, since the seller knows that mere mention of a country of use will not suffice to infer a particular purpose. An economic rationale of the conformity rules seeks to reduce transaction costs whereas the second view risks doing the opposite. It also goes against the idea that a party who is better placed to reduce or avoid the risk of non-conformity or other adverse consequences, such as non-compliance with public law regulations, should be the risk bearer. Being generally in a better position to know the regulations in the importing country, the buyer should bear the adverse consequences of a lack of precision in communicating what is later alleged to be a particular purpose to the seller. Put differently, a less informed party should not bear any additional burden and costs where a better informed party can avoid them by communicating the information more clearly and fully. On balance, therefore, the first view is preferable.

This point regarding 'information asymmetry' between the parties demands taking a closer look at the 'special circumstances' in which, according to *New Zealand Mussels*, the seller will be responsible for non-compliance with public law regulations. In 'special circumstance' (2) (the buyer drawing the seller's attention to the regulations) and (3) (the seller having a good reason to know about the regulations), the buyer is not in a better position than the seller to know about the regulations at destination and it is for this reason that the seller has an obligation to comply with the regulations. However, 'special circumstance' (1) (where the regulations are the same in the seller's country and at destination) appears to be based on different considerations. If the seller knows about or cannot be unaware of both the country where the goods are intended to be sold or used and the regulations, the seller will be responsible for complying with them under 'special circumstance' (3) (or even (2) if the buyer drew the seller's attention to them), and the fact that the regulations are the same in the two countries is of no significance whatsoever. If the regulations are the same in the seller's country and at destination, but the seller is *not* in a position to know about the destination, then again the fact of the regulations being the same has no bearing on restoring the information asymmetry between the parties. Since the seller does not or cannot know the country where the goods are intended to be sold or used, the mere fact that the regulations are the same

74 See Schlechtriem (n 67).
75 See Schlechtriem and Butler (n 5) 119.
76 See, similarly, ibid.

in the two countries adds nothing to the seller's knowledge. Therefore, 'special circumstance' (1) is relevant only in respect of the communication of a particular purpose under Article 35(2)(b) if the seller knows about the destination *and* the regulations there. However, as noted, this scenario is already covered by 'special circumstance' (3), in which case (1) is redundant. The only other point where the fact of the regulations being the same is relevant in the context of Article 35(2)(b) is in relation to the 'reliance on the skill and judgement' provision.[77] The seller is unlikely to be able to invoke this provision and to argue that the buyer did not rely or that it was unreasonable for the buyer to rely on the seller's skill and judgement, because the very fact that the seller normally conducts its business activities in its own country, where the regulations are the same, demonstrates that it has the required skill and judgement to comply with the requirements embodied in such regulations.

While the approach taken in *New Zealand Mussels* has received a fair amount of support,[78] it can amount to no more than guidelines. Relying on the contextual rules of interpreting the parties' intentions,[79] the Convention requires every case to be decided in the light of its particular circumstances.[80] For example, whilst the decision in *New Zealand Mussels* explains that the seller can be held liable if it had a long-standing relationship with the buyer, in *G Mainzer Raumzellen v Van Keulen Mobielbouw Nijverdal BV*,[81] the seller was held not liable despite having a long-standing relationship with the buyer. This finding does not necessarily contravene *New Zealand Mussels*. It may simply be that a factual setting in this case contained other factors, such as the seller's contention that each German state imposed different construction requirements[82] or the regulations having been adopted recently,[83] which may have weakened the buyer's claim. If

[77] See Schlechtriem (n 67).

[78] See, eg *RJ & AM Smallmon v Transport Sales Ltd and Grant Alan Miller* (n 71); *Medical Marketing v Internazionale Medico Scientifica*, F Supp 2d, 1999 WL 311945 (ED La) (affirming a decision of an arbitration tribunal which accepted the approach in *New Zealand Mussels*, but held that a general rule did not apply due to the presence of one of the exceptions); Supreme Court, 2 Ob 100/00w, 13 April 2000 (Austria) (n 66) (not referring to *New Zealand Mussels*, but in essence taking a similar approach). Virtually every commentary on this issue under the CISG cites this case (see writings on the CISG referred to throughout this chapter; see also RF Henschel, 'Conformity of Goods in International Sales Governed by CISG Article 35: Caveat Venditor, Caveat Emptor and Contract Law as Background Law and as a Competing Set of Rules' (2004) 1 *Nordic J Commercial L*, www.cisg.law.pace.edu/cisg/biblio/henschel2.html, stating that 'the principles in the *Mussels* case now seem to have widespread acceptance').

[79] See Arts 8, 9 and 35(2)(b).

[80] See n 37 above and the accompanying main text.

[81] See n 66 above.

[82] This, in turn, shows the complexity of construction standards in Germany, which may be too difficult for the seller to grasp despite a long-standing business relationship with the buyer.

[83] This seems to have been the case considering that the buyer pointed out to the seller that the regulations had been issued in respect of mobile units (see n 66 above and the accompanying main text).

this is true, this case shows that a long-standing relationship with the buyer may not always be sufficient on its own to presume the seller's knowledge of the regulations in the country of destination.[84]

In contrast, a long-standing relationship may be supplemented by other factors, such as prior dealings where the buyer made it clear to the seller that the goods had to comply with the food safety regulations in its country and where the contract required the seller to deliver certificates showing compliance with such regulations.[85] Such circumstances leave little doubt that the buyer has sufficiently communicated a particular purpose of compliance with the regulations in its country.[86] The result in *G Mainzer Raumzellen v Van Keulen Mobielbouw Nijverdal BV* may also be explained, at least in part, by the fact that the buyer was, just like the seller, an expert in the manufacture of mobile units; with both parties having equal expertise, the buyer, with its superior access to the regulations in the importing country, is the more appropriate candidate to bear the adverse consequences of non-compliance with the regulations.

Besides being mere guidelines, the specific exceptions in *New Zealand Mussels* to a general proposition that mere knowledge of a place where the goods will be used or sold is insufficient to infer a particular purpose, are also non-exhaustive. For this reason, it is important to bear in mind the third *general* exception, which makes it clear that there may be other circumstances where the seller knew or was in the position to know about the regulations in the importing country. This exception is in line with the Convention's position that the facts of each case are decisive. One example of circumstances not specifically listed in *New Zealand Mussels* can be found in a case[87] which involved the sale of explosion-proof junction boxes between an Italian seller and an Australian distributor. Two categories of these products did not meet the requirements (TestSafe) of the Australian regulatory authority and the seller was held liable for non-compliance with these requirements in the light of the following facts, alleged by the buyer and not challenged by the seller. The goods were similar to those of the main international competitor and the seller assured the buyer that its goods were as good as those of their international competitors. Relying on such a representation, the buyer promoted the goods to the Australian

[84] But see Appellate Court Grenoble, 93/4126, 13 September 1995 (France), available at http://cisgw3.law.pace.edu/cases/950913f1.html, where the fact that the parties have had a business relationship for several months was deemed sufficient to hold the Italian seller liable to the French buyer for failing to label parmesan cheese in accordance with French law.

[85] District Court Ellwangen, 1 KfH O 32/95, 21 August 1995 (Germany), available at http://cisgw3.law.pace.edu/cases/950821g2.html (the amount of ethylene oxide in paprika exceeded the level permissible under the German Food Safety Laws whilst the contract required the seller to deliver the certificate of the absence of aflatoxins and salmonellae).

[86] See ibid.

[87] *Cortem SpA v Controlmatic Pty Ltd* [2010] FCA 852.

industry. The seller also stated that the products were fully compliant 'with all applicable Standards' and had been 'thoroughly tested and approved' by the Italian authorities. The buyer argued that these assurances generated an expectation that certification by the Australian authorities was to be achievable. The court accepted this argument, holding that the buyer 'had made known to [the seller] that his purpose was to sell these products into the Australian market by way of wholesale trade' and that 'the goods were not fit for that purpose, because they had not achieved TestSafe certification'.[88]

The result seems justifiable. The seller's reference to the goods being as good as those of the main competitors, which presumably had been subjected to TestSafe, can reasonably be interpreted as reflecting the seller's knowledge of TestSafe. A reference to the compliance with 'all applicable standards' reinforces this interpretation; although broad, this statement can be taken to acquire a specific meaning (of the need to comply with TestSafe), considering that the seller knew that the goods would be sold in Australia. What the seller can reasonably be taken to have said was 'all applicable standards in Australia'. Such an interpretation may be weakened by the seller's next statement referring to the certification and approval in Italy, but the seller referred to *all* applicable standards, which is likely to include the certification standards in Australia, Italy and possibly even some other standards well-known internationally. The reasonableness of the buyer's reliance on the seller's assurances, in the form of promoting the products to the Australian industry, was not challenged and therefore that conduct could also be taken to reaffirm the conclusion that a reasonable business person in the buyer's position[89] would have understood the seller's assurances as implicitly referring to the goods' ability to pass TestSafe.

B. Industry Standards and Standards Adopted by Private Entities and Trade Associations

The environment within which the goods are intended to be used or sold will often comprise not only public law regulations but also other features such as industry standards,[90] standards[91] and codes of conduct adopted by

[88] Ibid para 100.

[89] See Art 8(2) and (3) CISG.

[90] For examples of British standards in respect of heating appliances and carbon dioxide for industrial use, see *Medivance Instruments Ltd v Gaslane Pipework Services Ltd, Vulcana Gas Appliances Ltd* [2002] EWCA Civ 500 and *Messer UK Ltd and another v Britvic Soft Drinks Ltd* [2002] EWCA Civ 548, respectively.

[91] For a well-known global initiative, see the United Nations Global Compact, which is 'a strategic policy initiative for businesses that are committed to aligning their operations and strategies with ten universally accepted principles in the areas of human rights, labour, environment and anti-corruption', www.unglobalcompact.org/AboutTheGC/index.html.

private entities,[92] such as trade organisations and associations,[93] certain commercial, trading or manufacturing practices.[94] If any of these features is embodied in the law,[95] the question of whether the seller has an obligation to comply with them needs to be resolved on the basis of the approach set out above in respect of public law regulations. Even if they do not carry the force of law, the buyer may still argue that non-compliance with a feature of the environment makes the goods non-conforming because they cannot be sold or used in that environment. The reason is that these features are capable of generating a particular set of market and/or consumer expectations as regards the goods, and the buyer and/or its business partners cannot sell or use goods which do not comply with such standards or codes of conduct without damaging their reputations. For example, an industry standard, even if technically not binding, may be so well-known and widely used in the country where the goods are intended to be sold or used that any respectable business operating in that country is expected to follow it. The same may apply to a code of conduct, to which businesses may have publicly pledged to adhere.

As is the case with public law regulations, the question of whether the seller is liable where the goods do not comply with (strictly speaking) a non-binding industry standard or a standard issued by a private entity or a trade association, or a certain commercial or manufacturing practice, can fall within the scope of Article 35(2)(b), as well as within Article 35(1) and/or Article 35(2)(a), and is to be resolved on a case-by-case basis. That said, introducing general guidelines will alleviate the difficulty of determining the content of the seller's conformity obligations in individual cases and will promote legal certainty and consistency in the Convention's application. The starting point is that the seller should not be liable if the goods do not comply with a standard or practice adopted by an industry or a trade association at a place where the buyer intends to use or sell the goods. If the buyer wishes to ensure compliance with a particular industry standard

[92] See I Schwenzer and B Leisinger, 'Ethical Values and International Sales Contracts' in R Cranston, J Ramberg and J Ziegel (eds), *Commercial Law Challenges in the 21st Century, Jan Hellner in Memorium* (Stockholm Centre for Commercial Law Juridiska Institutionen, 2007) 249, 259 (referring to the following private initiatives: 'Examples are the "Equator Principles", "Fair Labor Association", the "Electronic Industry Code of Conduct", or the "Kimberley Process". The Electronic Industry Code of Conduct, for example, incorporates norms such as setting a maximum number of working hours at 60 per week, and prescribing human treatment or non-discrimination in supplier contracts, as, according to the introduction of this code, the participants are under an obligation to, at least, require their *next tier suppliers* to acknowledge and implement the code. Another example is the code of conduct implemented by "Yum!" [comprising] All American Food, KFC, Long John Silvers, Pizza Hut and Taco Bell and, thereby, represents nearly 34,000 restaurants in more than 100 countries and territories').

[93] See, eg *Kingspan Environmental Ltd v Borealis A/S* [2012] EWHC 1147 (Comm).

[94] On the interaction between ethical values and sales law, see Schwenzer and Leisinger (n 92).

[95] '[I]deological and other convictions are often converted into governmental rules and prohibitions' (Schlechtriem (n 67)).

or practice, it can do so by including a specific clause to this effect in the contract[96] or by communicating such a particular purpose to the seller.[97] The buyer is also generally in a better position than the seller to identify and investigate the particular industry, manufacturing or trading standards in the country of use or sale of the goods. It is therefore appropriate for the buyer to bear any adverse consequences flowing from non-compliance with such standards, without any liability on the seller's part.

This starting position may be displaced in circumstances broadly analogous to those set out in the case of non-compliance with public law regulations. Generally speaking, the seller should only be in breach of its conformity obligations where it knew or was in a position to know about the relevant standard and the need to comply with it due to market expectations at the place where the goods are intended to be used or sold. This precondition can exist where: (1) both the seller and the buyer are members of the industry, organisation or association which has issued the standard;[98] (2) the parties have complied with the standard in their past transaction(s);[99] (3) the need to comply with the standard was specifically communicated to the seller;[100] (4) there were other good reasons why the seller was in a position to know about the standard and the need to comply with it, such as where it constitutes a trade usage[101] or a practice between the contracting parties,[102] the seller had a branch in a country where the goods are intended to be used or sold, had a long-standing business relationship with the buyer, or often exported or promoted the goods in that country. These cases are

[96] Thereby creating a contractual obligation on the part of the seller (Art 35(1)).

[97] See Art 35(2)(b).

[98] But see *Kingspan Environmental Ltd v Borealis A/S* (n 93) paras 139–41, 641, where the fact that the contracting parties were both members of the same trade association did not appear to have been decisive in holding the seller in breach of Art 35(2)(b) as a result of the goods' non-compliance with the standard, adopted by that association.

[99] Federal Supreme Court, VIII ZR 121/98, 24 March 1999 (Germany), available at www.cisg.law.pace.edu/cases/990324g1.html (the seller 'was obligated, pursuant to CISG Art 35(2)(a), to deliver wax that is suitable for the treatment of vines, but that the black vine wax delivered by defendant in 1994 did not meet the industry standards, of which both parties were aware and which both parties applied, and that therefore the wax was not in conformity with the contract within the meaning of CISG Art 35'). Even if the parties' reliance on the standard in their past transactions does not amount to a practice within the meaning of Art 9(1), it may still be a *factor* in interpreting the parties' intentions (Art 8(3)), as opposed to a practice which is binding on the parties. See also n 102 below and the accompanying main text.

[100] See *Kingspan Environmental Ltd v Borealis A/S* (n 93), a case involving the sale of Borecene (used by the buyer to rotomould static tanks) where the court established that the seller had known that: the Borecene would be used by the buyers to manufacture rotomoulded tanks for the external storage of oil; the buyers wanted the tanks made by them from Borecene to last for up to 10 years outside in Europe; and the buyers wanted such tanks to comply with the standards of Oil Firing Technical Association for the Petroleum Industry(OFTEC) ('The OFTEC is a voluntary trade association consisting of tank manufacturers, installers, and material suppliers', ibid para 55).

[101] See Arts 8(3) and 9 CISG.

[102] See Arts 8(3) and 9(1).

not exhaustive and amount to no more than guidelines. The Convention's contextual rules of interpreting the parties' statements and conduct demand that every case be evaluated in accordance with its particular circumstances.

In a given case, the existence of one or more of the said situations may not be given sufficient weight to override a general position that a seller has no duty to ensure compliance with a particular standard. For example, it may be that the contracting parties are members of more than one trade association and each of these associations has adopted different (incompatible) standards. In the absence of sufficient evidence that a particular association's standard was intended to be followed, the seller should not be held liable for non-compliance with any of these standards.[103] Another example is where the parties' reliance on the standard in their past transaction(s) does not amount to a practice which is binding on them, and the past transaction(s) is merely a factor in interpreting the contract, which in a particular case does not reflect an intention to rely on the standard.[104]

C. Climatic and Other Conditions

A number of other conditions existing in a given country or place may give rise to the question of whether the seller is liable under Article 35(2)(b) because the goods are not suitable for or do not comply with the specific conditions in that place. It has been argued that there should be no difference in legal treatment between public law regulations and all other conditions in a particular country.[105] It is difficult to give a definitive evaluation of such a broad proposition because, ultimately, every case is to be decided on its own facts. What may be helpful to bear in mind is that public law regulations tend to be specialised and are not easily accessible, whereas some other conditions, such as climate or cultural or religious environment, may sometimes be matters of common knowledge. Where so, liability on the seller may be imposed more readily where the goods are not suitable to a particular environment than where they do not satisfy public law regulations. For example, one tribunal had no hesitation in imposing liability on a Russian seller, under Article 35(2)(b), for the failure of the equipment to operate in climatic conditions in Ecuador solely on the basis that it 'could not have been unaware of the climatic conditions of use of the goods when

[103] See *Kingspan Environmental Ltd v Borealis A/S* (n 93), where the buyer argued that the OFTEC Standard was the *only* polyethylene oil tank standard in force at the relevant time (para 632).

[104] See, eg Appellate Court Saarbrücken, 5 U 426/96-54, 17 January 2007 (Germany), available at http://cisgw3.law.pace.edu/cases/070117g1.html, where the fact that the same packaging was used by the seller in previous deliveries was not taken to reflect an implied agreement to use the same packaging in the present contract.

[105] Kröll (n 2) para 120.

he concluded the contract on delivery of the goods to Ecuador'.[106] At the same time, even if at first sight it may seem that the seller ought to have understood the peculiarities of a place where the goods were intended to be used or sold, the presence of some additional factors may not lead to the seller's liability. A German seller who knows that the goods will be sold in Switzerland may, at first, be expected to be aware that the instruction manuals will have to be delivered not only in German, but also in other languages spoken in Switzerland, such as French and Italian. However, where both parties knew that the contract goods would be delivered from the seller's existing stock which was prepared solely for the German market, it was held[107] that, in the absence of a specific agreement (or presumably at least some communication by the buyer) that translation into two other languages was expected, the seller could not be said to have a duty to supply the instruction manuals in French and Italian.

VI. DURABILITY

Just as the consideration of the goods' durability can arise in the context of Article 35(1), it can similarly arise under Article 35(2)(b). The question is this: where the goods are sold for a particular purpose, does the seller assume an obligation that they will be fit for a particular purpose not just at the time when the risk has passed to the buyer,[108] but also for a certain period thereafter? Article 36(2) contemplates such a possibility in respect of the seller's obligations under Article 35(2)(b), when it states that the seller may be liable for any lack of conformity after the risk has passed to the buyer, if a lack of conformity is due to 'a breach of any of his obligations, including a breach of any guarantee that for a period of time the goods *will remain fit ... for some particular purpose*'.[109] It has been suggested that such an approach may be particularly justifiable in relation to the fitness for a particular purpose test on the basis that in comparison with other tests of conformity,[110] it requires, more directly, an inquiry into the developments subsequent to the time of the passage of risk to ascertain whether the goods have in fact proved to be fit for the particular purpose.[111] For this reason

[106] ICAC Arbitration 166/1995, 12 March 1996, available at http://cisgw3.law.pace.edu/cases/960312r1.html.

[107] See District Court Darmstadt, 10 O 72/00, 9 May 2000 (Germany), available at http://cisgw3.law.pace.edu/cases/000509g1.html.

[108] Which is the time with reference to which conformity is to be assessed under the CISG (see Art 36(1)).

[109] See Art 36(2) (emphasis added).

[110] Such as contract interpretation under Art 35(1) or the fitness for the ordinary purposes test in Art 35(2)(a) (see Chapter 4).

[111] Bridge (n 34) para 7.116.

the fitness for purpose test is sometimes regarded as a 'more natural carrier for durability'[112] than other tests of conformity, with a consequence that no one time can be fixed for assessing the goods' fitness for a particular purpose.[113]

An argument to the contrary is that if the assumption of risk rationale of Article 35(2)(b) is accepted, the time of contract should be relevant for determining the seller's obligations because that is the only time when the seller can be said to have assumed the risk of non-compliance with a particular purpose.[114] This point, however, refers to a different time than the one fixed in Article 36(2) and therefore cannot be correct. In addition, even if the time of the contract were the relevant time, it would be possible for a seller, at that time, to assume an obligation that the goods would not only be fit for a particular purpose at the time of contract but also for a certain period thereafter. Put differently, even if the time of the conclusion of the contract were the time for applying the fitness for a particular purpose test, that would not necessarily exclude the need for the goods to be durable.

The real question under the CISG is whether an implicit guarantee that the goods will remain fit for a particular purpose can be inferred from the circumstances.[115] With a vast majority of cases on durability having been resolved in the context of Article 35(1),[116] there are currently very few examples in the CISG cases exploring durability as part of the fitness for a particular purpose test. One example can be found in an already mentioned case[117] which concerned the sale of large metallic cantilevers, known as globes, that were expected to be displayed and to rotate in the buyer's exhibition showrooms. The motor in the globes turned out to be incapable of making the globes rotate for a long period of time. It was held that, considering that the seller knew that the goods would be used in respectable exhibitions, and that the globes themselves were expensive and sophisticated items whose weight exceeded 200 kg, the seller ought to have understood that the buyer intended to use the globes as 'a permanent part of furniture for its offices'. That, in turn, meant that the goods could reasonably be expected to have a much longer operational life, which was deemed to be on average three years.

A typical situation in international trade is one involving the transportation of the goods. Where this is the case, with both parties contemplating a transport journey, the question arises as to whether knowledge of a

112 Ibid.

113 Ibid.

114 Kröll (n 2) para 113.

115 An explicit guarantee of durability will speak for itself, thereby expressly defining the seller's obligation as to the goods' durability.

116 See Chapter 2.

117 District Court Munich, 27 February 2002 (n 41).

particular purpose, that the goods ought to withstand a reasonable journey, can be imputed to the seller. If the contract goods are fragile or are known to be unable to withstand, or to be prone to high risk of deterioration due to, the rigours of transportation, there is little basis for inferring a duty on the seller to comply with the said particular purpose.[118] Where, however, the goods of the type specified in the contract are in principle able to withstand transportation, the seller' knowledge that the goods will be transported may be sufficient to imply such a particular purpose and the buyer in such circumstances may well be found to rely on the seller's skill and judgement to select the goods complying with this particular purpose.[119]

VII. MAKING KNOWN

For the seller to have a duty under Article 35(2)(b), a particular purpose must be 'made known' to the seller at the time of the conclusion of the contract.[120] The time of making the contract is particularly consonant with the assumption of risk rationale since it is by that stage that the seller has to decide whether to assume a particular obligation and/or to protect itself in respect of a possible breach of that obligation. This point in time also accords with the rationale of the buyer's reliance on the seller's ability to deliver the goods complying with a particular purpose: if by that time a particular purpose is communicated, the buyer can rely on the seller provided that the seller has not objected in some way to the undertaking of that obligation. The buyer, in other words, can regard the seller as having assumed that implied obligation. A particular purpose can be made known expressly or implicitly. Since the former mode of communication puts the seller in the position where it actually knew or could not have been unaware of that purpose, it raises no qualms about imposing on the seller an obligation under Article 35(2)(b). Such an express communication has taken place where: a particular purpose had been made known to,[121] or even accepted by,[122] the seller before the contract was made; the seller

[118] See *Benjamin's Sale of Goods*, 9th edn (London, Thompson-Sweet & Maxwell, 2014) para 11-067 (with further references).

[119] See ibid. See also Chapter 2 for a more detailed discussion of these issues in the context of Art 35(1).

[120] Art 35(2)(b).

[121] District Court Rotterdam, HA ZA 98-1405, 14 October 1999 (The Netherlands), available at http://cisgw3.law.pace.edu/cases/991014n1.html (the seller knew that the leather would be used to cover furniture and that the buyer's customers would dye the leather for this purpose). Appellate Court Grenoble, 93/4879, 26 April 1995 (France), available at http://cisgw3.law.pace.edu/cases/950426f2.html (the seller was told that a portable warehouse was to be capable of being reassembled in an identical manner).

[122] See Supreme Court, 6 Ob 56/07i, 19 April 2007 (Austria), available at http://cisgw3.law.pace.edu/cases/070419a3.html.

knew or could not have been unaware of the buyer's specifications, which revealed or embodied a particular purpose;[123] the need to comply with a public law standard was mentioned to and accepted by the seller during the precontractual negotiations.[124]

The case of an implicit communication needs to be treated with caution because imposing an obligation on the seller is a serious legal consequence and a court or tribunal needs to be certain that a particular purpose was indeed made known to the seller. This is especially so considering that a particular purpose does not need to be a term of the contract, which means that an obligation is imposed merely through the communication of a particular purpose. This potentially lower threshold for imposing an obligation on the seller has even been viewed as evidencing the buyer's 'right to unilaterally determine the content of the contract'.[125] The reasons for allowing an implicit communication and not requiring the seller's actual knowledge of a particular purpose are twofold. First, whilst the absence of a requirement of having actual knowledge of a particular purpose is sometimes viewed as being 'harsh' on the seller,[126] this reflects the Convention's commitment to a full factual inquiry and its openness to inferring legal consequences from the circumstances, which are evidenced by other provisions of the CISG based on the assumption of risk rationale.[127] Secondly, in practice the buyer will rarely be able to prove the seller's actual knowledge and it would be unjustifiable for the buyer to have to cross such a high threshold if the seller was in a position to know about a particular purpose.[128]

It appears that a particular purpose does not necessarily need to be communicated by the buyer.[129] A crucial question is whether the seller can reasonably be said to be in a position of being aware of a particular purpose.[130] Such knowledge can be inferred, for example, from the buyer's identity if the latter is closely associated with a particular activity, market

[123] See ibid; Appellate Court Lyon, 01/02620, 18 December 2003 (France), available at http://cisgw3.law.pace.edu/cases/031218f1.html.

[124] Ibid; Helsinki Court of Appeal, S 96/1129, 29 January 1998 (Finland), available at http://cisgw3.law.pace.edu/cases/980129f5.html; also S Kuoppala, 'The Application and Interpretation of the CISG in Finnish Case Law 1997–2005', http://cisgw3.law.pace.edu/cases/980129f5.html.

[125] Kröll (n 2) para 108.

[126] I Schwenzer, P Hachem and C Kee, *Global Sales and Contract Law* (Oxford, OUP, 2012) para 31.116.

[127] See, eg Art 74 CISG; also Arts 8 and 9. See also Kröll (n 2) para 111.

[128] Kröll (n 2) para 111; Schwenzer (n 2) para 22.

[129] BK Leisinger, *Fundamental Breach Considering Non-Conformity of the Goods* (Munich, Sellier European Law Publishers, 2007) 14.

[130] Other formulations refer to the seller's ability to 'take note' of a particular purpose (Enderlein and Maskow (n 20) 144) or to whether the information on a particular purpose has reached the seller's 'sphere of perception' (Leisinger (n 129) 14).

or ethical standards,[131] from the knowledge of the buyer's business,[132] or from the parties' past transactions and/or practices or possibly even a trade usage.[133] If the buyer sends a catalogue or specifications to the seller, the seller may be found to be in a position in which it cannot be unaware of a particular purpose stipulated in such a catalogue or specifications.[134]

In contrast, where it is the seller who sends a catalogue to the buyer and the catalogue makes clear that the goods are not suitable for the buyer's particular purpose,[135] an inference of a particular purpose becomes unlikely. In one such case,[136] the seller's catalogue referred to covers for sewerage systems which bore specifications different from those that the buyer needed and it was held that the buyer, an expert public works contractor, was in a position to recognise the differences in specifications. The court also pointed out that the fact that the seller had achieved a business quality accreditation (International Standard ISO 9001) did not mean that the seller should have been aware of the buyer's needs. The seller was thus found not to have been informed of the buyer's particular purpose, considering further that when, before the contract was made, the buyer had requested that the covers bore the inscription 'D400', the seller had replied that the request referred to a different model to those offered by the seller. This conclusion was reaffirmed by the parties' conduct subsequent to the conclusion of the contract whereby the seller sent to the buyer a sample of a model different from what the buyer needed and the buyer did not object to it. All this indicated the parties' understanding that the contract concerned the sale of a different model than the one that the buyer, as it turned out, actually needed.

131 See Schwenzer, Hachem and Kee (n 126) para 31.121.

132 See Appellate Court Palencia, 227/2005, 26 September 2005 (Spain), available at http://cisgw3.law.pace.edu/cases/050926s4.html. In this case, the seller was held liable for the printing machines' inability to print in accordance with the buyer's specifications. The seller argued that that was the result of other causes peculiar to the buyer's factory. Those alleged causes were, however, found not to be relevant to the alleged non-conformity. The decision suggests that the seller made 'a gigantic effort to document the factory's condition' and 'was aware of the necessary specifications for the production process of the buying entity'.

133 See Arts 8 and 9.

134 See n 123 above; also Kröll (n 2) para 114.

135 The nature of the documentation may be such that it cannot reasonably be expected to contain information as to the suitability of the goods to the buyer's particular purpose. For example, in one case, the seller sent a data sheet to the buyer who needed heavy oil of high viscosity. It was held to be unreasonable for the seller to include the relevant data about the maximum proportion of sediments in that document. First, this data sheet was a standard form. Secondly, extensive statistical evaluations would have been necessary to enable the seller to provide reliable data regarding the sediment content. Finally, this information was deemed to be irrelevant to the usual buyers of heavy oil (see Appellate Court Graz, 5 R 62/13x, 19 June 2013 (Austria), available at http://cisgw3.law.pace.edu/cases/130619a3.html, affirming the decision of the court of first instance).

136 See Appellate Court Barcelona, Rollo No 862/2003-B, 28 April 2004 (Spain), available at http://cisgw3.law.pace.edu/cases/040428s4.html.

The information concerning a particular purpose does not necessarily need to be communicated directly to the seller, and therefore some courts have sought to determine whether this information was made known through channels capable of transmitting specialist information in a complete and competent way. In one case[137] involving a dispute over the fitness of glue bought for sealing the boxes of foodstuffs, the parties disagreed as to whether discussing a particular purpose with a travelling salesperson of the seller's company sufficed to make a particular purpose known to the seller. It was held that bearing in mind that the buyer had a 'quality control department', it should have followed more rigorous internal procedures relating to communicating a particular purpose than merely discussing its needs with the seller's commercial traveller. Therefore, whether a particular purpose was made known to the seller depends on the extent to which the expertise of a party to whom information is communicated bears relevance to an alleged particular purpose. This is in line with the assumption of risk and reliance rationale: the seller can only be regarded as having assumed the risk of non-compliance with a particular purpose if it is in the position to fully grasp the nature of the buyer's needs and has an opportunity to refuse to enter into or to further negotiate a contract on such terms. Similarly, the buyer can hardly rely on the seller if, in the negotiations regarding a particular purpose, the latter is represented by a person lacking the relevant expertise. These two lines of rationalising Article 35(2)(b) also seem to demand that a person to whom the information is communicated ought to have authority to represent the seller or, at the very least, be someone who can reasonably be expected to pass the information, fully and competently, to the seller within the time enabling the seller to respond before the contract is made.

To conclude, a buyer, on the one hand, has an incentive to be as clear and precise in communicating a particular purpose as possible in order to ensure that the seller has an obligation to meet its particular needs. For example, the buyer cannot claim, as was done in one case,[138] that the steel billets delivered by the seller were unfit to be hot-rolled into the mill of the buyer's customer if the seller knew neither the features of that mill nor the identity of the buyer's customer.[139] On the other hand, a buyer may not always be willing to reveal its particular purpose because that may involve

[137] See Appellate Court Barcelona, Rollo No 574/2003-A, 28 January 2004 (Spain), available at http://cisgw3.law.pace.edu/cases/040128s4.html.

[138] See ICC Arbitration Case No 8213 (n 17).

[139] See, similarly, Arbitration Chamber of Paris, Case No 9926, 2007, available at http://cisgw3.law.pace.edu/cases/079926f1.html, where no obligation of fitness for purpose was implied on the basis that the buyer, who knew its customer's needs, did not stipulate them in the contract. Whilst the result is probably correct, the reasoning is questionable because the purpose of implied rules, such as the one in Art 35(2)(b), is precisely to supplement and to aid in contract interpretation in the case of contractual silence (for a detailed discussion, see I above).

divulging information regarding its business arrangements.[140] In the case just mentioned, it was found that the buyer 'intentionally kept' the identity of its customer from the seller for 'commercial reasons'. It is against this kind of commercial context that one commentator has aptly observed that a buyer's particular purpose 'somehow never gets revealed' until litigation.[141]

VIII. RELIANCE ON THE SELLER'S SKILL AND JUDGEMENT

Even if a particular purpose is made known to the seller, the seller may still be free from an obligation to comply with that particular purpose[142] if the 'the circumstances show that the buyer did not rely, or that it was unreasonable for him to rely, on the seller's skill and judgement'.[143] This provision seeks to redress an imbalance between the parties, which initially tilts in favour of the buyer considering that an obligation is imposed on the seller simply by virtue of the communication of a particular purpose.[144] The seller can raise a defence against this implied duty by showing that either the buyer did not rely *or* that it was unreasonable for the buyer to rely on the seller's skill and judgement. The former is a question of fact whereas the issue of reasonableness of reliance is largely a question of law but also necessarily of fact since the evaluation of reasonableness (a question of law) is to be carried out against the factual background. The Convention's reference to these defences as alternatives means that proving the existence of one of them is sufficient to exempt the seller from liability. For instance, even if the buyer did actually rely on the seller, no obligation would be implied if the seller shows that it was unreasonable for the buyer to do so. In practice, however, the issues of actual reliance and of its reasonableness tend to be closely linked and are often considered together. The factors taken into account in dealing with them are, on the whole, the same.

One such factor is the level and balance of the parties' expertise. If the buyer has greater expertise than the seller in relation to the goods and/or their suitability to the buyer's needs, it is likely that the buyer will not be found to have relied or that it is unreasonable for it to rely on the seller.

140 'How far had they a stake in keeping their clientele on either side from having information to diagnose the customer on the other side and to eliminate the intermediary's commission for the future' (K Llewelyn, 'On Warranty of Quality, and Society: II' (1937) 37 *Col L Rev* 314, 349).

141 Ibid.

142 On the rationalisation of this provision, see II above.

143 Art 35(2)(b).

144 See, similarly, Kröll (n 2) para 122, stating that this exception 'is the necessary limitation to the buyer's right to unilaterally determine the exact content of the contract'.

This was so held,[145] despite a long-standing business relationship, where the plants did not flourish in the climatic conditions of a specified location because the buyer, a specialist in gardening and landscaping, operated in that area and had better awareness of the peculiarities of that location than the seller.[146] The reliance defence may be available to the seller even where the buyer itself is not an expert, but is an agent for a party who has the relevant expertise. In one case[147] involving the sale of textile equipment, the buyer's principal was found to have made a decision on a specific model of the equipment on the basis of its prior knowledge of its special features and technical parameters. For this reason, the buyer's principal was found to have relied on its own, and not on the seller's, skill and judgement. It was further found that the equipment had a history of being imported into a country where the buyer's principal was based and the buyer's principal, having the relevant expertise and resources to investigate the machine's suitability for its needs, 'had complete capability to make the right judgment on the function and features of the machine before the conclusion of the contract'.[148] For this reason, it was also held to be unreasonable for it to rely on the seller's skill and judgement.

Where the parties have equal expertise, such as where they are both dealers intending to resell the goods, reliance is unlikely to be inferred because the buyer, whose expertise is as good as the seller's, is likely to rely on its own skill and judgement.[149] According to one CISG decision, Article 35(2)(b) 'is *only* to be applied where there is a "technological gap" between the parties'.[150] However, whilst this may be true in many cases, the balance of the parties' expertise is merely a factor to be taken into account and it is the overall evaluation of the circumstances that is ultimately decisive. To adopt one universally applicable position, as was done in this CISG case, is 'to convert a decision on fact into a rule of law and to ignore the fact that not all sales, even on a given market, not to mention sales on different markets, bear the same character, or involve the same incidents'.[151] Where the seller has greater expertise than the buyer, reliance can be expected to be easily inferred. That is why it is sometimes stated that where the seller is

[145] More precisely, it was held that it was unreasonable for the buyer to rely on the seller's skill and judgement.

[146] See District Court Coburg, 22 O 38/06, 12 December 2006 (Germany), available at http://cisgw3.law.pace.edu/cases/061212g1.html.

[147] *Textile Manufacturing Equipment*, CIETAC Arbitration, 18 July 2002, available at http://cisgw3.law.pace.edu/cases/020718c1.html.

[148] Ibid.

[149] See *Harlingdon & Leinster Enterprises Ltd v Christopher Hull Fine Art Ltd* [1991] 1 QB 564; also *Benjamin's Sale of Goods* (n 118) para 11-061.

[150] District Court Coburg, 12 December 2006 (n 146) (emphasis added).

[151] This well-known quotation from an English case is equally relevant in the context of the CISG (see *Henry Kendall & Sons v William Lillico & Sons Ltd* (n 38) 124 per Lord Wilberforce).

a manufacturer or where it presents itself as having the relevant expertise, reliance on its skill and judgement can be assumed.[152] Again, however, this cannot constitute a general position and there may be some other facts pointing to the contrary. The buyer may have insisted on the seller's compliance with the particular specifications and/or design, despite the seller pointing out that those specifications/design would not be well suited to the buyer's particular needs.[153] Clearly, in these circumstances, even if the seller has greater expertise, the buyer's insistence on its specifications/design shows that it is not relying on the seller's skill and judgement.[154]

On occasion, no obligation was imposed on the seller under Article 35(2)(b) where the seller resorted to a third party manufacturer to perform a contract with the buyer, who had the relevant expertise. In one such case[155] where the parties disputed the quality of the assembly diagram supplied by the seller, the court held that the buyer did not rely and that it was not reasonable for the buyer to rely on the seller's skill and judgement, partly because[156] the seller had communicated all the necessary information to its manufacturer and it was the latter who had prepared the assembly diagram. If taken as a general proposition outside these facts, this part of the decision may be questionable because, if followed, sellers will be easily absolved from liability merely by showing that they resorted to a specialist in order to perform the contract with the buyer. The buyer after all makes the contract with the seller and it is submitted that if a particular purpose has been duly communicated, the presumption of reliance or of reasonable

[152] See Leisinger (n 129) 16; Schwenzer (n 2) para 24.

[153] It has been suggested that where the seller is in a position to detect that the buyer's specifications or design are not fit for the buyer's particular purpose, the seller has a duty, stemming from the principle of good faith, to warn or advise the buyer (Secretariat Commentary on Article 33 of the 1978 Draft, para 7; Schwenzer (n 2) para 24; Kröll (n 2) para 127). The correctness of this argument depends, first of all, on whether there is a general principle of good faith under the CISG—a matter which has been the subject of a long-running debate. Secondly, even if there is no such general principle, a similar duty can arguably arise from some other alleged general principles, such as the duty to cooperate (see, eg U Magnus, 'General Principles of UN-Sales Law' (1995) 59 *Rabels Zeitschrift* para 11, also at www.cisg.law.pace.edu/cisg/biblio/magnus.html). Implying such a duty on the seller may be desirable because it may prevent the goods' non-compliance with the particular purpose (ie where the buyer accepts the seller's advice). Such an outcome may also promote economic objectives such as the reduction of costs and prevention of waste, both of which will occur if the buyer does not accept a (correct) advice from the seller. However, implying such a duty may have far-reaching consequences because once it is recognised, its breach can constitute a basis for the right to claim damages (see Kröll (n 2) para 127, with a further reference).

[154] See Secretariat Commentary on Article 33 of the 1978 Draft, para 7; Schwenzer (n 2) para 24; Enderlein and Maskow (n 20) 145.

[155] Appellate Court Barcelona, Recurso No. 764/2006; 357/2007, 3 July 2007 (Spain), available at http://cisgw3.law.pace.edu/cases/070703s4.html (only the abstract of the case is available in English).

[156] Another reason set out in the abstract of the decision, namely, that 'the buyer was imputing to the seller an error that bore no direct relation to what it had requested of the seller', does not seem to be sufficiently clear. Yet another factor that seems to have influenced the court is the fact that the buyer also possessed the relevant expertise.

reliance must not be displaced by showing that the services of a third party are used by the seller. Only clear and unequivocal evidence of a lack of such reliance, such as where the seller disclaims its liability for a failure to ensure fitness for a particular purpose, should preclude reliance.

Where the seller is merely a trader in a chain, such as where the goods are traded by means of the transfer of documents, it is unlikely that the seller is in a position to exercise its skill and judgement in relation to the conformity of the goods.[157] There may also be little room for the seller to exercise its skill and judgement if a state organisation in its country has a monopoly over the sale of the goods which are the subject matter of the contract. If all that the seller can do is to obtain the goods covered by a certificate issued by that state organisation confirming that the goods meet the requirements in the importing country, it may be that there is nothing else that the seller can do to ensure compliance with the requirements at destination.[158]

The balance of the parties' knowledge and expertise is also relevant in cases where the goods do not comply either with public law regulations in the importing country or with climatic conditions or religious or cultural peculiarities in that place. This issue has already been discussed in the context of whether the seller's mere knowledge of the place of destination suffices for imposing an obligation to comply with the regulations or other particular conditions in that place. However, even if such a particular purpose is deemed to be sufficiently communicated to the seller, the next question is that of reliance, actual or reasonable. The factors identified in the *New Zealand Mussels* case[159] are also relevant for deciding whether the buyer relied or whether it was reasonable for it to rely on the seller's skill and judgement.[160] But here these factors will be relevant not for determining whether the seller was in the position to know about the regulations, but for establishing whether there was reliance, actual or reasonable. The same set of facts can lead to the inference of the communication of a particular purpose of complying with the country's regulations, but fail to evidence the buyer's actual or reasonable reliance.

In a case[161] decided by the Court of Appeal of New Zealand, an Australian buyer, a transport operator with 20 years of experience in the road business in the Australian State of Queensland, was deemed to be the party which should bear the risk of the trucks' non-compliance with

[157] *Henry Kendall & Sons v William Lillico & Sons Ltd* (n 38) 84; see also Schwenzer (n 2) para 24; Leisinger (n 129) 17.

[158] See *Phoenix Distributors Ltd v LB Clarke (London) Ltd* [1967] 1 Lloyd's Rep 518.

[159] See n 64 above and the accompanying main text.

[160] 'Reliance of the buyer is ... almost always reasonable where identical public law requirements exist in the seller's own jurisdiction. Similarly where the seller has dealt previously in the foreign market in question, reliance by the buyer that the seller is familiar with the public law requirements will likely be reasonable' (Schwenzer, Hachem and Kee (n 126) para 31.126).

[161] *RJ & AM Smallmon v Transport Sales Ltd and Grant Alan Miller* (n 71).

registration requirements in Queensland, despite the fact that in the past the seller, an exporter from New Zealand, had exported trucks to Australia and advertised trucks in an Australian trade magazine. The seller had known that the trucks would be used in Australia and the Court of Appeal agreed with the judge that that particular purpose, which appears to have included the need to comply with the Australian Design Rules (ADR),[162] had been made known to the seller. At the same time, it was established that in the past no buyer to whom the seller had sold the goods had raised an issue of non-compliance with the registration requirements and the state authorities themselves had facilitated the registration process.[163] In its advertisements the seller made no promises regarding the registration process.[164] These two factors did not point in favour of imposing liability on the seller and the buyer's superior expertise became decisive. The Court of Appeal agreed[165] with the judge's conclusion that there was no actual or reasonable reliance by the buyer, which the judge had reached on the following basis:

> The [buyer]s were experienced transport operators. They were in a much better position to know the registration requirements of their own country than [seller]. The fact that the trucks did not have compliance plates was not hidden from them, but was there to be seen. As experienced transport operators, they could be expected to be able to identify a compliance plate. Further, [seller] recommended they engage specialist contractors, which they did. Significantly, [buyer] agreed with the proposition that the purpose of inspecting the vehicles was to see if they complied with ADRs and that at that stage they were acting on advice from Mr Walsh. In those circumstances, any reliance placed on [seller]'s expertise or knowledge or that of its company about the regulatory requirements in Australia would not in my view be reasonable.[166]

The mode by which the buyer orders the goods and its conduct as a whole may also provide much evidence about reliance or a lack thereof. If the buyer orders the goods with reference to a specific brand, trade mark, patent or model, it may be that there is not much room for the seller to exercise its skill and judgement,[167] unless the goods of the specified brand, trade mark, patent or model have also been recommended by the seller as meeting the buyer's needs.[168] The buyer's selection and even examination

[162] See the quotation from the judge's decision, reproduced below in the main text, which presupposes that the seller had some knowledge and expertise of the Australian regulatory requirements.

[163] *RJ & AM Smallmon v Transport Sales Ltd and Grant Alan Miller* (n 71) para 64.

[164] Ibid para 63.

[165] Ibid.

[166] Ibid paras 99–100.

[167] See, similarly, Schwenzer (n 2) para 24. This set of factors is well recognised by domestic legal systems using a similar test. See, eg *Benjamin's Sale of Goods* (n 118) para 11-065; Official Commentary on § 2-315 UCC in *Uniform Commercial Code: 2009-2010 Edition* (West-Thomson Reuters, 2009) point 5.

[168] See point 5 of Official Commentary on § 2-315 UCC (n 167).

of the goods before making the contract may also preclude any argument as to its actual or reasonable reliance.[169] The buyer's post-contractual queries addressed to the seller regarding the use of the goods for a particular purpose may reflect the parties' prior understanding that the buyer will be relying on the seller's expertise. In one case,[170] the fabric turned out to be unsuitable for the purpose of transfer printing[171] due to latent defects. After the contract had been made and the problems with the fabric had emerged, the buyer enquired from the seller about whether it should still continue with transfer printing and the seller expressly urged the buyer to continue. This factor seems to have influenced the court in deciding that the buyer had relied on the seller.

It is not entirely clear whether the buyer's reliance has to be total or whether partial reliance can also satisfy Article 35(2)(b). It is submitted that partial reliance is not excluded as long as a specific characteristic rendering the goods unfit for a particular purpose is one falling within the seller' skill and judgement. It is also arguable that if the reliance provision is justifiable on the ground that it underscores the largely *contractual* nature of the obligation to ensure fitness for a particular purpose, partial reliance should only be recognised if it *substantially* or *effectively* induced the buyer to enter into the contract with the seller.[172] Put differently, reliance cannot relate to a minor characteristic or a matter which in itself would not have induced the buyer to enter into the contract. Partial reliance can occur, for example, where the seller is to compound animal foodstuff for the buyer on the basis of the buyer's specifications but before doing so the seller is to supply and to include a particular ingredient. In this case, the buyer does not rely on the seller in respect of quality and condition of foodstuff insofar as they result from the execution of the instructions. But the buyer relies on the seller in relation to quality and condition of an ingredient supplied by the seller.[173] Where it is not clear whether non-conformity results from the drawings or from factors lying within the seller's sphere, the conclusion will have to be reached by drawing inferences from the circumstances. Suppose that the buyer, a manufacturer of ships, orders propellers from the seller, a specialist propellers manufacturer, to be made in accordance with the buyer's drawings and specifications. Two propellers, initially supplied, produce excessive noise, making them unfit for use as propellers in a vessel,

[169] Schwenzer (n 2) para 24; similarly in the context of English law, *Benjamin's Sale of Goods* (n 118) para 11-062.

[170] *Schmitz-Werke GMBH & Co v Rockland Industries, Inc,* 37 Fed Appx 687, 2002 WL 1357095 (CA 4 (Md)).

[171] 'Transfer printing is a process for imprinting the base fabric with dyes of particular colors or patterns' (ibid).

[172] See Adams and MacQueen (n 49) 194.

[173] See *Henry Kendall & Sons v William Lillico & Sons Ltd* (n 38).

and the cause of the noise cannot be established with absolute certainty. However, because the third propeller works satisfactorily, having been manufactured in accordance with the buyer's drawings just like the first two propellers, it may well be inferred that whatever the cause, it lies within the sphere involving the seller's choice about *how* to execute the buyer's design. It can thus be concluded that there was some room for the seller to exercise its skill and judgement and that the defect lay within the seller's sphere of responsibility.[174]

IX. PROOF

A. Burden of Proof

It is now increasingly recognised that the issue of burden of proof is a matter governed by the CISG.[175] One relevant general principle is that a party who asserts a right must prove the necessary preconditions for the existence of that right.[176] This means that the buyer bears the burden of proving that a particular purpose has been duly communicated to the seller.[177] In the same vein, a party who invokes an exception to the other party's right must prove the necessary preconditions for the existence of that exception. As discussed, the buyer's right to rely on the seller's obligation to ensure the goods' fitness for a particular purpose is available 'unless' there was no actual or reasonable reliance by the buyer. The reliance provision is, in other words, an exception to the buyer's entitlement to the goods being fit for a particular purpose and the burden of proof of the preconditions for that exception lies with the seller. If the buyer proves the goods to be unfit for a particular purpose and the seller does not raise the issue of reliance, the seller's liability will be presumed. The burden of proof includes the burden of adducing the relevant evidence and the burden of persuasion.[178]

The 'rule and exception' principle of the allocation of burden of proof, which has just been discussed, is not always applied strictly in practice because a burden of adducing evidence is sometimes placed on a party who has better access to evidence but who would not otherwise bear this burden

[174] See *Cammell Laird & Co v Manganese Bronze and Brass Co Ltd* (n 19).

[175] See, eg Commercial Court Zürich, HG930138.U/HG93, September 1993 (Swtizerland), available at http://cisgw3.law.pace.edu/cases/930909s1.html. See further Chapter 1.

[176] See, eg Canton Appellate Court Valais, C1 06 95, 27 April 2007 (Switzerland), available at http://cisgw3.law.pace.edu/cases/070427s1.html.

[177] See Commercial Court Zürich (n 175), taking this position in the context of Art 35 generally.

[178] See S Kröll, 'The Burden of Proof for the Non-Conformity of Goods under Art 35 CISG' (2011) 3 *Belgrade L Rev* 162, 165–66 (with further references).

on strict principles of the allocation of burden of proof.[179] This approach, known as 'proof proximity', is sometimes justified on the grounds of 'equity'.[180] Although those courts which have taken this approach may have done so on the basis of their domestic law, some commentators argue in favour of developing the general principle of proof proximity within the CISG,[181] drawing support from the drafting history of Article 25:

> Originally Art 25, which at the time was Art 9 provided that a breach was fundamental if 'it results in a substantial detriment to the other party *and* the party in breach foresaw or had reason to foresee such a result'. The 'and' was in the end replaced by the present 'unless' as it would be very difficult for the non-breaching party to prove that the breaching party did not foresee the result or could not have foreseen it. As the breaching party was much closer to the fact the burden of proof was imposed on it.[182]

There are undeniably differences in legal cultures, procedural environments and views of the purpose of judicial proceedings (that is, whether they are strictly adversarial or aim to establish the truth at all cost) which have a direct impact on the way evidence is taken. Therefore, a degree of non-uniformity can be expected in matters of taking evidence and, more broadly, of allocating burden of proof. It is suggested, however, that legal certainty should not be undermined any further by the introduction of the proof proximity principle into the CISG. As has already been alluded to, proof proximity can easily contravene the 'rule and exception' principle and its introduction necessitates a choice between the two which, in turn, gives rise to an additional layer of complexity and unpredictability. Reaching a substantial degree of international agreement on the 'rule and exception' principle is a hard-earned achievement, which has potential to promote legal certainty in all areas falling within the Convention's scope. From this standpoint, recognising proof proximity as a Convention's general principle would be an unwelcome development.

B. Standard of Proof

In contrast, using the Convention's general principles to develop a standard of proof does have the advantage of promoting uniformity in the Convention's application. The standard of proof concerns the amount of

[179] Canton Appellate Court Valais, 27 April 2007 (n 176) ('If the buyer rejects the goods by invoking their non-conformity the seller must prove that the goods are in conformity with the contract; if the buyer already accepted the goods the buyer would have to prove their non-conformity').

[180] Kröll (n 178) para 170.

[181] Ibid.

[182] Ibid 171.

evidence and the degree of precision flowing from it that are sufficient to prove the existence of a legal right.[183] There is a close connection between the burden and standard of proof[184] and having the former governed by the CISG and the latter by domestic law would make the Convention's scope piecemeal, inconsistent and incoherent. More importantly, a standard of proof has a direct impact on the *exercise* of the innocent party's rights. The Convention's goal of promoting uniformity in its application is hardly achievable if the rights established by the CISG cannot be exercised in the same way due to differences in standards of proof used by domestic legal systems. It is therefore submitted that a standard of proof should be regarded as a matter falling within the CISG and domestic legal systems should have no role to play in formulating the applicable standard.[185] In the light of the general principle of reasonableness[186] and of the fact that absolute precision in proving the preconditions of the existence of a legal right is not always achievable, it can be argued that under the CISG such preconditions only need to be proved with a reasonable degree of certainty.[187] Like all other issues falling within the CISG, the preconditions for the buyer's rights under Article 35 and for the exceptions to those rights, such as the provision on reliance on the seller's skill and judgement in Article 35(2)(b), need to be established with reasonable certainty.

In some cases, it may not be difficult to prove non-compliance with Article 35(2)(b). This may be so where the seller admits a lack of conformity expressly[188] or implicitly, such as where the seller does not object to the buyer's allegation of non-conformity[189] or agrees to carry out repair.[190] There will be more difficult cases of proving the seller's breach, such as those where it is not possible to establish with absolute certainty what caused an

[183] See, eg D Saidov, 'Standards of Proving Loss and Determining the Amount of Damages' (2006) 22 *JCL* 1, 5.

[184] Schwenzer (n 2) para 56.

[185] For a contrary position, see Flechtner (n 64) 182–87.

[186] See, eg AH Kritzer, 'Editorial Comments', available at www.cisg.law.pace.edu/cisg/text/reason.html#schl.

[187] For similar arguments in the context of damages, see, eg Saidov (n 183) 5–6, 56, 70; CISG Advisory Council Opinion No 6, 'Calculation of Damages under Article 74', available at www.cisg.law.pace.edu/cisg/CISG-AC-op6.html.

[188] See *Hydraulic Press*, CIETAC Arbitration, 23 December 2002, http://cisgw3.law.pace.edu/cases/021223c1.html, where the parties signed a joint memorandum setting out various defects in the goods.

[189] See Fujian High People's Court, Minjingzhongzi No 123, December 1994 (China), available at http://cisgw3.law.pace.edu/cases/941200c1.html.

[190] See *Leather Gloves*, CIETAC Arbitration, 26 November 1998, available at http://cisgw3.law.pace.edu/cases/981126c1.html. However, the seller's agreement to make improvements to the goods may not always evidence the seller's acceptance of non-conformity since it may be nothing more than a gesture of goodwill towards the buyer (see Commercial Court Zürich, September 1993 (n 175)).

alleged lack of conformity.[191] In such cases, the reasonable certainty standard, being a probability standard requiring the assessment of likelihood of the seller's conduct causing a lack of conformity, may still make it possible for the buyer to prove the seller's breach. For example, suppose that the printing machine delivered by the seller is unable to print in accordance with the buyer's specifications. Suppose also that the seller argues that this was the result of other causes peculiar to the buyer's factory, such as a lack of power and water supply. If these alleged causes are found to bear little relevance to the alleged non-conformity and if there is evidence that the seller had good knowledge of the buyer's factory and of the necessary specifications, it is likely that it is the structural design of the machine, for which the seller was responsible, that caused its malfunction.[192] Similarly, if the seller delivered wine which contained water, prohibited under the regulations at destination for which the seller assumed the risk, the seller might argue that it was the buyer who added the water. However, if the wine was examined the day after the buyer had taken delivery, the buyer would have little time to add water, making it highly likely that it was the seller who had done so.[193]

C. Admissibility of Evidence

The evaluation and admissibility of evidence are often treated as falling into the procedural law realm,[194] which is outside the scope of the CISG,[195] a substantive law instrument. In contrast with a standard of proof, which may be classed as an issue of substantive or procedural law depending on the applicable legal regime, the admissibility of evidence appears, at first sight, to fall more clearly into the procedural law realm. Therefore, it would seem that the applicable procedural law should govern

[191] See ICAC Case No 189/2003, 29 December 2004, available at http://cisgw3.law.pace.edu/cases/041229r1.html (where it could not be established whether it was the seller's conduct or the buyer's failure to follow the instructions that caused the breakdown of the equipment); Federal Supreme Court, VIII ZR 304/00, 9 January 2002 (Germany), available at http://cisgw3.law.pace.edu/cases/020109g1.html ('the Court of Appeals explained that, according to the expert report of Prof Dr F, the result of the analysis of IS, which was based on a spot check analysis of the powdered milk upon arrival in Antwerp, did not permit a definitive statement about the "sole decisive question" whether the powder was infested by inactive lipase at the time of the transfer of the risk').

[192] See Appellate Court Palencia, 26 September 2005 (n 132).

[193] See District Court Trier, 7 HO 78/95, 12 October 1995 (Germany), available at http://cisgw3.law.pace.edu/cases/951012g1.html.

[194] It seems to be treated as a procedural law issue in most jurisdictions (see, eg § 138 of Restatement (Second) of Conflict of Laws (1971); P Schlechtriem and M Schmidt-Kessel in Schwenzer (n 2) Art 11, para 4 (with further references).

[195] See, similarly, Schwenzer (n 2) Art 35, para 50 and Art 74, para 60.

this matter. However, in some domestic systems an issue may possibly be regarded as a matter of substantive law. In one case,[196] the buyer's evidence, based on testimony of a German inspection company to support its claim that charcoal was non-conforming under Article 35(2) CISG, was held inadmissible. It was so held because the buyer did not follow a procedure fixed under article 476 of the Argentine Commercial Code according to which in order to contest the quality of the goods the buyer ought to appeal to expert arbitration.[197] The Argentine Appellate Court reasoned that the CISG did not 'contain any rule, [or] general [principle], concerning the procedure to follow in order to determine the quality of goods' and ruled that since 'the buyer did not determine the quality of the charcoal in accordance with the expert arbitration procedures required by article 476 of the Argentine Commercial Code, his evidence consisting of a testimony of a German witness, the quality of the charcoal could not be determined'.[198] A similar decision was subsequently reached in another Argentine case.[199]

Whilst the requirement regarding the referral of a matter of a lack of conformity to expert arbitration may seem to be procedural in nature,[200] some writers point out that the fact that this requirement is contained in the Argentine Commercial Code, as opposed to the Code of Civil Procedure, suggests the possibility that the admissibility of evidence was treated as a matter of substantive law.[201] If so, does the fact that the admissibility of evidence may be regarded as a substantive law issue in some domestic systems mean that the Convention should now be regarded as governing this issue, for the same reasons as those advanced in respect of the standard of proof? These cases reaffirm the point that the distinction between the procedural

[196] Appellate Court, 24 April 2000 (Argentina), available at http://cisgw3.law.pace.edu/cases/000424a1.html#ii.

[197] For a detailed explanation of the nature and purpose of an expert arbitration under art 476 of the Commercial Code of Argentina, see AJ McMahon, 'Differentiating between Internal and External Gaps in the UN Convention on Contracts for the International Sale of Goods: A Proposed Method for Determining "Governed by" in the Context of Article 7(2)' (2006) 44 *Colum J Transnat'l L* 992, 1020–23.

[198] Ibid.

[199] Appellate Court, 21 July 2002 (Argentina), available at http://cisgw3.law.pace.edu/cases/020721a1.html ('the [buyer]'s demand has ignored the procedure fixed imperatively by article 476 of the Commercial Code, according to which the buyer who refutes the quality of the goods should appeal to the know-how by arbitration.... [E]xpert arbitration is the road legally contemplated to settle this type of controversy as regards commercial sales of goods ... [The analysis by a German laboratory] does not replace the trial of expert arbitrators, without which [buyer]'s allegations are not proven').

[200] This view is taken in McMahon (n 197) 1028–29.

[201] See JB Lopez, 'Cámara Nacional en lo Comercial 24 April 2000', http://cisgw3.law.pace.edu/cases/000424a1.html#ii.

and substantive law issues is relative[202] and in itself it cannot constitute an appropriate basis for deciding what falls within or outside the Convention's scope. This does not necessarily mean that the admissibility of evidence can be regarded as a matter governed by the CISG. The issue requires careful consideration going beyond the scope of this book. Therefore, only some tentative and general observations will be made.

As illustrated by the Argentine cases, the admissibility of evidence does endanger a uniform application of the Convention's conformity provisions since in a number of other jurisdictions the expert witness' report may well be admissible. A universally agreed approach to the question of the admissibility of evidence would certainly be a significant step in promoting the Convention's uniform application. There are provisions which can, conceivably, be used to develop a relevant general principle to the effect that the CISG takes a liberal approach to taking evidence and all relevant evidence must be admitted. Article 11 CISG provides that a contract 'need not be ... evidenced by writing', 'is not subject to any other requirement as to form' and 'may be proved by any means, including witnesses'. Article 8(3) requires that in interpreting the parties' statement and conduct, all relevant circumstances need to be taken into consideration and can therefore be seen as 'based on the principle of the admissibility of all evidentiary materials for the interpretation of the parties' declarations'.[203]

That said, there is still a strong sense that for the CISG to deal with the admissibility of evidence outside the parameters of Articles 11 and 8 is to stretch its scope beyond that intended by the drafters. It has been suggested that these two provisions were included to make it clear that there was no place in the CISG for the common law doctrines of 'parol evidence' and 'statute of frauds'.[204] Had the drafters intended the CISG to embrace fully an issue as broad in its reach as the admissibility of evidence, they would, surely, have indicated that with much greater clarity. More so, because the admissibility of evidence is *usually* regarded as a procedural matter, many countries will be surprised, if the Convention is held to deal with it, to discover that the CISG displaces their procedural law regimes. It is highly likely that this was not the understanding the countries had in deciding to ratify it.[205] Considering that any general principle which can be potentially developed will be inherently general and incapable of matching the level of detail of domestic rules on evidence, such an approach may also deter ratification by other countries.

[202] See, eg CG Orlandi, 'Procedural Law Issues and Law Conventions' (2000) 5 *Uniform L Rev* 23, quoting V Denti in n 29 ('there exists no systematic abstract criterion that would enable a given case to be classified unequivocally and rationally as being either of a "procedural" or a "substantive" nature'); I Schwenzer and P Hachem, 'The CISG: A Story of Worldwide Success' (2009) 57 *AJCL* 119, 133–34.

[203] Schlechtriem and Schmidt-Kessel (n 194) para 13.

[204] McMahon (n 197) 1026.

[205] See, similarly, McMahon (n 197) 1026–28.

It is also doubtful whether the CISG is capable of governing and embracing this matter in all its complexity. The relevant domestic law rules on the admissibility of evidence are based on a variety of policies and protect various interests,[206] many of which are outside a contract law instrument like the CISG. Many such policies will undoubtedly be worthy of legal protection whilst the CISG will be incapable of catering for them. Finally, it can also be argued that it is best to leave the admissibility of evidence to domestic legal systems for the reasons of efficiency, speed and practical convenience. As explained in commentary on § 138 of the US Restatement (Second) of Conflict of Laws, the 'trial judge must make most evidentiary decisions with dispatch if the trial is to proceed with celerity. The judge should therefore, as a general rule, apply the local law of his own state'.[207] All these arguments point in favour of the admissibility of evidence being entirely outside the CISG and the outcomes in the Argentine cases would then be correct.

These arguments notwithstanding, uncertainty as regards the Convention's relationship with the domestic rules on the admissibility of evidence has led to the emergence of more flexible approaches. In the context of Article 11, it has been contended that what is decisive is not how a rule is characterised in a given domestic jurisdiction, but its function. If a domestic law rule substantially undermines a party's evidentiary position, the rule should be classed as a rule of substantive law and therefore displaced by Article 11. If the evidence in question 'merely makes it easier to prove matters', the domestic law rule on the admissibility of evidence, being usually classified as a procedural rule, should apply as such.[208] By analogy, it can be argued that what is decisive in cases such as the Argentine cases above is whether the buyer's evidentiary position, and consequently its ability to establish its rights under Article 35(2) CISG, would be substantially undermined by the domestic rules on the admissibility of evidence. If so, the admissibility of evidence should be treated as part of the substantive law regime which ought to be displaced by Article 35(2). Underlying this position is the view

[206] The common law of evidence, for example, includes rules against hearsay evidence; on expert witnesses (who can only give opinion on matters requiring their expertise without expressing views on the ultimate issues of the case); against evidence of bad character; on protecting confidential communications between lawyer and client; against evidence which might be injurious to public interest (the public interest immunity doctrine). Each of these rules is based on its particular rationale (see I Dennis, *The Law of Evidence,* 4th edn (London, Sweet & Maxwell/Thomson Reuters, 2010) 86–87). Perhaps, what all different types of rationale may have in common is that they 'will represent a judgment that the "costs" of the type of evidence in question are sufficiently great to justify a general rule of restriction' (ibid 87). Some of these types of rationale may also be based on the 'need to protect certain rights of parties to litigation or the need to ensure legitimacy of decision in the adjudication' (ibid 87). Apart from these, every rule pursues different objectives and policies.

[207] Restatement (Second) of Conflict of Laws (1971) § 138, comment a.

[208] Schlechtriem and Schmidt-Kessel (n 194) para 13.

that the recourse to domestic evidence rules 'must be the exception, not the rule'[209] in order not to undermine the Convention's uniform application. If this standpoint were taken, the above discussed Argentine case[210] would be wrongly decided because the buyer was deprived of an opportunity to rely on the inspection company's report to prove a lack of conformity—a piece of evidence which would probably be acceptable in many other jurisdictions.

209 See Orlandi (n 202).
210 Appellate Court, 24 April 2000 (n 196).

4

Fitness for Ordinary Use

I. GENERAL

THIS CHAPTER WILL explore the general fall-back rule of conformity, provided for in Article 35(2)(a). This rule requires the goods to be 'fit for the purposes for which goods of the same description are ordinarily used'[1] (hereinafter referred to as fitness for the 'ordinary use' or 'ordinary purpose(s)'). Before examining the meaning of this provision, it may be helpful to address the question of its relationship with subparagraph (b) discussed in the previous chapter. It has already been explained that because Article 35(2)(b) concerns a more specific scenario, it has priority over subparagraph (a). This, however, does not answer the question of whether the two provisions are mutually exclusive or whether they can apply cumulatively, as is the case in some domestic legal systems.[2] In principle, they can be applied cumulatively.[3] They will also produce the same result where a particular purpose is interpreted as having the same meaning as ordinary use. For instance, the ordinary use of racing carts is to be driven in a race and where the carts are delivered unassembled and hence incapable of being driven, the seller was held to be in breach of both Article 35(2)(a) and (b).[4] Similarly, where a small diesel tram was bought for promotional purposes it was held that the 'speed of 25 km per hour [was] not incompatible with the "ordinary use" and/or the "particular purpose" mentioned in Articles 35(2)(a) and (b) CISG'.[5]

Where the buyer communicates a particular purpose which is unusual or idiosyncratic, such a communication should not necessarily mean that the buyer is not entitled to expect the goods to be fit for their ordinary use,

[1] See Chapter 1.

[2] See § 2-317 of the US Uniform Commercial Code (UCC).

[3] See S Kröll in S Kröll, L Mistelis and P Viscasillas (eds), *UN Convention on Contracts for the International Sale of Goods (CISG), Commentary* (Munich, CH Beck/Hart Publishing 2011) Art 35, para 61.

[4] See District Court Köln, 3 O 196/01, 25 March 2003 (Germany), available at http://cisgw3.law.pace.edu/cases/030325g1.html.

[5] See District Court Veurne, A/00/00665, 25 April 2001 (Belgium), available at http://cisgw3.law.pace.edu/cases/010425b1.html.

unless the circumstances clearly indicate the parties' intention to derogate from Article 35(2)(a). Suppose, however, that the buyer makes known to the seller that it needs the goods for only one particular purpose, which is one of several *normal* or *ordinary* purposes for which the goods can be used. If there is no evidence of the seller's readiness to undertake a more extensive obligation of complying with more than that one normal purpose, there is little justification for affording the buyer a more extensive protection by applying Article 35(2)(b) and (a) cumulatively. It is suggested that only subparagraph (b) is applicable and the parties should be regarded as having implicitly derogated from subparagraph (a).

II. DOES ARTICLE 35(2)(A) CISG IMPLY A CERTAIN LEVEL OF QUALITY?

A. Does Article 35(2)(a) CISG Require an Inquiry into the Notion of Quality?

In fixing the ultimate implied rule of conformity of the goods, many domestic legal systems rely on some notion of quality, such as 'average', 'merchantable', 'satisfactory' or 'acceptable' quality, which is intended to indicate the level of quality that the buyer can expect. In some of these systems, 'fitness for an ordinary or a common purpose' is merely one of the components that make up the notion of 'quality' or one of the questions to be asked in determining whether the goods meet the required standard of quality.[6] Against this background, the Convention's rule in Article 35(2)(a) appears narrow and limited in its content and scope. On its face, this provision does not rely on any notion of quality,[7] with the only relevant question seemingly being whether the goods are fit for 'the purposes for which goods of the same description would ordinarily be used'. In other words, the Convention only seems concerned with whether the goods are fit for their ordinary purposes and not with quality. Quality is a broader notion that may include not only fitness for ordinary purposes but a number of other aspects, such as the goods' physical state and condition, intrinsic qualities and features, safety, durability, appearance, finish and freedom from minor defects.[8] However, fitness for purpose will often depend on quality[9] and this means that there is a close link between them.[10] Does this mean that there are cases where an inquiry into the level of quality is necessary?

[6] See, eg Sale of Goods Act (SGA) 1979 (UK), s 14(2)–(2B); § 2-314(2)(c) UCC.
[7] See F Enderlein and D Maskow, *International Sales Law* (New York, Oceana Publications, 1992) 143.
[8] See, eg SGA 1979, s 14(2)–(2B).
[9] Kröll (n 3) para 73.
[10] Ibid.

It is difficult to conceive of a scenario where the fitness for ordinary purposes will be totally incapable of resolving a situation. However, some circumstances will require this test to embrace fully the particular facts. The type of case that is likely to pose challenges to this test is that involving goods of varying grades (eg different grades or classes of wheat) or levels of performance (eg the amount of fruits a juice-making machine can process within a certain time period). The delivered wheat may be capable of being processed into flour or the juice-making machine may be more than suitable for making a fruit juice, but the buyer may contend that to be 'fit for the ordinary purpose(s)', the wheat had to be of a higher grade or the machine ought to be capable of processing more fruits per hour than it actually does. Such a contention will not be justifiable if the ordinary purpose is construed in very simple and abstract terms, that is, whether the wheat can be processed or whether the machine is capable of making a fruit juice.

The test is only workable if the ordinary purpose(s) is (are) interpreted in light of the surrounding facts, such as where they point to a highly sophisticated nature of the buyer's business and its strong reputation for high-end products, in which case the buyer may be entitled to demand goods of a higher grade or level of performance. To be workable, the ordinary purpose has to be interpreted not with reference to what are *generally* common or ordinary purposes, but to what can reasonably be regarded as ordinary in the *particular* circumstances of the buyer and the seller. That said, if the Convention specified some general level of quality that buyers could normally expect, it could possibly provide greater clarity as to the content of the seller's duty.[11] If so, an inquiry into the notion of quality can supplement and facilitate the test of fitness for ordinary purposes, but it does not seem essential.[12]

B. Different Quality Tests: The Debate

Much of the discussion in cases and writings on the CISG seems to reflect a view different from that taken in the previous section, implying that the inquiry into the notion of quality is necessary. This discussion, in turn, makes it necessary to choose between various quality tests. In one

[11] For a further discussion of the meaning of various quality tests, see below.

[12] Some writers suggest that such an inquiry is needed even where the goods *are* fit for the ordinary purpose(s). See Kröll (n 3) para 74; CP Gillette and F Ferrari, 'Warranties and "Lemons" under CISG Article 35(2)(a)' (2010) 1 *Internationales Handesrecht* 2, 7. However, it is argued that a quality standard, in addition to the fitness for purpose test, is unnecessary because, as explained, Art 35(2)(a) is not concerned with quality as such, but with fitness for purpose. The suggestion that a further inquiry into quality is necessary even if the fitness for purpose has been established unjustifiably extends the scope of Art 35(2)(a), and transforms it into a test of quality, which it is not.

well-known case,[13] the buyer alleged non-conformity in oil condensate, known as Rijn Blend, due to a high level of mercury. The buyer, a major player in the oil and gas business, contended that the levels of mercury made Rijn Blend unacceptable for further processing and sale. The arbitration tribunal, applying Article 35(2)(a), identified three main approaches to quality.

One, derived from the English common law, is the merchantable quality test which, in the tribunal's words, raises the question of whether 'a reasonable buyer would have concluded contracts for Rijn Blend at similar prices if such a buyer had been aware of the mercury concentrations'.[14] Relying on the evidence of the seller's resale of the condensate at reduced prices after the buyer's non-acceptance, the tribunal held that, if this standard were applied, there would be a breach by the seller because 'other buyers in the market for Rijn Blend were ... unwilling to pay the price [sellers] had agreed with [buyer]'.[15] Considering the second test of 'average quality' used in some civil law jurisdictions, the tribunal held that the buyer had failed to meet its burden of proof as regards the issue of 'whether there [was] a common understanding in the refining industry what average quality for blended condensates (such as Rijn Blend) should have been and what levels of mercury [were] tolerable'.[16] The buyer would thus not be liable if that test were applied. Having found no overwhelming support in case law or academic writing for either of these two approaches, and noting their domestic law origins and the fact that the Convention's legislative history indicated the rejection of both standards, the tribunal held them not to be applicable.

Instead, the standard of 'reasonable quality' was applied. In the tribunal's view, the standard was more in line with the Convention's international character and the need to promote uniformity in its application, as well as based on its general principle of reasonableness. It was held that the seller was in breach of the reasonable quality standard for two reasons. First, the tribunal once again noted that the contract price could not, in all likelihood, have been obtained from selling Rijn Blend if other buyers were informed about the levels of mercury. The Rijn Blend with low level of mercury was apparently valued more highly than that with increased mercury content.[17] Secondly, the parties had had a long-term business relationship and the buyer sufficiently established that when delivered under the previous contracts, the condensate had not contained the increased level of mercury found in the delivery

[13] Netherlands Arbitration Institute, Case No 2319, 15 October 2002, available at http://cisgw3.law.pace.edu/cases/021015n1.html.
[14] Ibid para 89.
[15] Ibid para 90.
[16] Ibid para 100.
[17] Ibid para 120.

under the contested contract. Therefore, '[the buyer] was entitled under the contracts to a constant quality level of the Rijn Blend corresponding to the quality levels that had been obtained during the ... initial period of the Contracts and on which [buyer] and its customers could reasonably rely'.[18]

The reasoning and the choice of a legal basis for the decision are far from flawless. The reasonable quality test was applied along the same lines as the merchantability test would have been, had it been used:[19] that is, a critical point was the evidence that the Rijn Blend with a higher level of mercury could not have been sold to any other buyer aware of the true level of mercury at the same price as that fixed in the contract with the buyer. Not only does this create confusion as to whether there are any differences between the two tests, but it also weakens the tribunal's case for the rejection of the merchantability test. Looking at the tribunal's reasoning, the relevance of Article 35(2)(a) also becomes doubtful. The possibility of selling the goods only at a reduced price and the delivery of the condensate with a low level of mercury under the previous contracts were the decisive factors leading to the seller's liability. However, these factors have little to do with the ordinary purposes test in Article 35(2)(a) and are primarily relevant for the purpose of contract interpretation under Article 35(1).[20]

Despite these shortcomings, the decision is helpful in several respects. It highlights several quality tests that can potentially be relevant to the application of Article 35(2)(a). It also demonstrates that although these tests are inherently vague, they may not be entirely devoid of distinct content and consequences, contrary to the view of some writers.[21] In fact, the decision illustrates how the tests, namely the merchantability and the average quality tests, can produce different results, which shows the possible significance of choosing between them.

Choosing between these tests is difficult. The merchantable quality standard does entail the danger of its strong association with some common law systems,[22] but it has the advantage of being based on a clear and workable test: if the goods can be resold on a market without the abatement of the price,[23] the goods are of merchantable quality and the seller

[18] Ibid para 121.

[19] See Arts 8 and 9 CISG. See, similarly, Gillette and Ferrari (n 12) 8.

[20] See, similarly, ibid 9.

[21] See J Adams and H MacQueen, *Atiyah's Sale of Goods*, 12th edn (Harlow, Longman 2010) 166.

[22] For discussion of the development of this test in English law, which saw it as comprising more than just saleability on the same terms as those in the parties' contract (with description, fitness for purpose and acceptance being other relevant aspects of merchantability), see M Bridge, *The Sale of Goods*, 3rd edn (Oxford, OUP, 2014) paras 7.46–7.55.

[23] A classic formulation of this version of the test was made in *Australian Knitting Mills Ltd v Grant* (1933) 50 CLR 387, 413 ('[the goods] should be in such an actual state that a buyer fully acquainted with the facts and, therefore, knowing what hidden defects exist and not being limited to their apparent condition would buy them without abatement of the price obtainable for such goods if in reasonable sound order and condition and without special terms').

is not liable.[24] From the standpoint of economic considerations, the test has received some support[25] on the basis that, in contrast with the other two tests, it does not give rise to any undesirable incentives for the seller because it refers to a measurable benchmark: a market price.[26] It also deals with the problem of informational asymmetry by signalling the quality and other features of the goods as well as the seller's investment in the product:

> Assuming relatively competitive markets, price should reflect the inputs that the seller invests in product quality, and thus it is likely to incorporate the seller's information concerning defect rates. Price also is likely to incorporate information that buyers have about the good. Buyers are unlikely to purchase a good that carries a price in excess of the buyer's expected value for it. When buyers agree to pay a particular price for a good, therefore, they have a set of expectations about the good's characteristics. Sellers who have superior information about the qualitative characteristics of the good reveal those features through the pricing mechanism. Price, in effect, serves as a substitute for a more detailed description of the goods that would constitute an express warranty of quality.[27]

The proponents of this position, resting on the supremacy of economic considerations, recognise some of the drawbacks of the merchantability test. One is its ability to distort the parties' negotiations by virtue of implicitly setting the price limit that the seller can charge: '[i]n effect, this test can be interpreted to transform price, standing alone, into a warranty'.[28] Another is that the price may accommodate factors other than those relating to quality (for example, luxury goods, oligopolistic markets or markets where the seller occupies a dominant market position), and this means that the goods' ability, or lack thereof, to command certain prices may be due not only to quality but to those other factors. That, in turn, means that in such cases the merchantability test is not fully determinative of the quality of the goods. For this reason, those favouring this test have not advocated a firm application of the merchantable quality test but have argued in favour of its presumption, which can be displaced upon demonstrating that the price was not fully reflective of quality.[29]

[24] There are cases on the CISG which have explicitly interpreted Art 35(2)(a) as based on the merchantability test: see *Clothes*, CIETAC Arbitration, 3 June 2003, available at http://cisgw3.law.pace.edu/cases/030603c1.html (expressly stating that Art 35(2)(a) means that the goods must be merchantable; 'the goods delivered by the [seller] were [of] poor quality and ... could not be resold even at a discounted price. Therefore, the goods delivered by the [seller] were not resalable'). See also the following cases decided in the common law jurisdictions where the courts simply read the merchantability test into the CISG with no attempt to explain the reasons for doing so: *Fryer Holdings v Liaoning MEC Group* [2012] NSWSC 18; *International Housewares v SEB* (2003), High Court of Auckland, CP 395 SD 01, para 59; *Travelers Property Casualty Company of America and Hellmuth Obata & Kassabaum, Inc v Saint-Gobain Technical Fabrics Canada Ltd*, 474 F Supp 2d 1075. This approach clearly violates the Convention's international character.

[25] Gillette and Ferrari (n 12) 12.

[26] See below.

[27] Gillette and Ferrari (n 12) 12–13.

[28] Ibid 14.

[29] Ibid 15.

The average quality test has also found some support.[30] This test can be viewed as almost a mathematical test as it implies a 'middle belt of quality'.[31] This shows that it also has a discernible content and should therefore be workable. It may also point to a balanced standard, particularly for the goods of variable quality, by being set in the middle between high and low quality levels. The test has, however, been criticised on the ground that it has the effect of making products that are below average quality drop out of the market. That, in turn, will push the average quality upwards because the disappearance of quality below average changes the meaning of 'average quality' since what was the middle of the range becomes the bottom end of the range. As a result, average quality 'becomes meaningless because of the constant change in the standard'.[32] Whilst this outcome may well logically follow as a matter of theory, it may be questioned whether there is evidence of this test actually producing such results in practice, considering that this test has been used in many domestic legal systems, some of which govern quality in highly developed markets and economic systems.[33]

Some have favoured the reasonable quality standard due to its relative neutrality. It is not associated with the well-known quality tests in domestic legal systems, which can make it more conducive to promoting uniformity and the Convention's international character. Similar to what has been stated in the arbitration decision discussed above,[34] the standard has been praised for its flexibility and its consonance with the idea of reasonableness underlying the CISG. Flexibility is highly desirable, in some commentators' view, because fitness for the ordinary purposes may require a level of quality which is higher or lower than average quality.[35]

Still, the standard has been criticised for creating the 'lemons problem'.[36] Assume that there is a range of products, from low to high quality, all of which are fit for their respective ordinary purposes. Since reasonable quality does not fix and signal a level of quality with any precision, the buyers, who have no means of investigating the goods' quality before taking delivery, will fear that what is presented to them as high quality goods are in fact goods of low quality. If it turns out that the goods are of low quality, the seller will not be held liable because those goods are still fit for

[30] See, eg District Court Berlin, 52 S 247/94, 15 September 1994 (Germany), available at http://cisgw3.law.pace.edu/cases/940915g1.html ('The goods must be of average quality, and it does not suffice that they can only just be traded').

[31] Comment 7 of the Official Comment on § 2-314 UCC in *Uniform Commercial Code: 2009–2010 Edition* (West-Thomson Reuters, 2009).

[32] Gillette and Ferrari (n 12) 11.

[33] See, eg I Schwenzer, P Hachem and C Kee, *Global Sales and Contract Law* (Oxford, OUP, 2012) paras 31.127–31.128.

[34] See n 13 above and the accompanying main text.

[35] Kröll (n 3) para 79.

[36] See Chapter I.

the ordinary purpose. Faced with this prospect, buyers will treat all goods as being of low quality and refuse to pay a higher price for higher quality goods. That will result in the high quality sellers being gradually driven out of the market.[37]

None of these standards emerges as a clear winner and this aspect of Article 35(2)(a) is likely to remain controversial in the foreseeable future. If the CISG is ever to be revised or if a new international sales law is ever adopted, some thought will need to be given to whether there is a need for an underlying quality standard. This is a question of policy. There have been instances where the CISG has been seen as a vehicle for promoting quality standards around the world[38] and, if there is some truth in this position, it would point strongly to the need to articulate an underlying quality standard. In that case, what minimum level of quality can reasonably be expected in international trade? At one end of the spectrum, there is a view that the lowest grade within the range of contractual description is sufficient,[39] whilst at the other end, some may believe that even such standards as 'average' or 'satisfactory' quality, which tend to be associated with 'mediocrity',[40] are not good enough in the modern day of increasing consumers' expectations.

The merchantability standard is helpful in that the price will often be a powerful signal of a benchmark of quality, and consequently of fitness for the ordinary purposes, which the buyer can reasonably expect. The goods' ability or inability to be resold on a market at the same price as that in the parties' contract is a practically useful test. However, the suggestion that it should operate as a presumption seems to overstate its utility for several reasons. To begin with, there may not be a market for the goods to provide a reference point.[41] What constitutes a market can also be a tricky question, as markets can be defined broadly or narrowly.[42] There are many variables affecting a market price in the particular circumstances (the need to transport the goods, location of a market, seasonal nature of the goods, time-frames) and direct price comparability between the contract price and the price obtainable on a 'market' may not always be possible or fully reflective of quality.

In addition, the test's reference to a sale on a market may be more suitable for some goods than for others. For example, a market can be found

[37] See Gillette and Ferrari (n 12) 9–10.
[38] See Chapter 2.
[39] P Huber and A Mullis, *The CISG: A New Textbook for Students and Practitioners* (Munich, Sellier European Law Publishers, 2007) 135.
[40] Adams and MacQueen (n 21) 159.
[41] See Appellate Court Geneva, ACJC/269/2010, 12 March 2010 (Switzerland), available at http://cisgw3.law.pace.edu/cases/100312s1.html.
[42] See, e.g D Saidov, 'The Present State of Damages under the CISG: A Critical Assessment' (2009) 13 *Vindobona J Int'l Commercial L Arbitration* 197, 209–14.

more easily in respect of commodities than in the case of heavy and highly specialist machinery.[43] It has also been suggested that the use of this test is more relevant where the goods are bought for resale, rather than use.[44] Yet another reason against the presumption relates to its likely consequence of interfering with the parties' bargain. The seller may have managed to bargain for a better price, which would not normally be obtainable for the goods at hand. Later holding this seller liable on the basis that it should have delivered goods of higher quality fails to respect and uphold the bargain that the parties struck. If the CISG is interpreted in this way, it will undermine the freedom of contract and place the Convention's regime too close to the extreme point of *caveat venditor.* Sellers would undoubtedly be discouraged by such a position and that, in turn, would hamper trade and induce parties to exclude or derogate from the CISG. Neither of these outcomes is in line with the Convention's aims of encouraging participation in international trade and being an effective international uniform law.

Thus, if a choice had to be made, a flexible standard of reasonable quality may be the right way to move forward. To inject greater certainty into the standard, a key consideration should be that found in the merchantability test, that is, reliance on a market price and focus on whether the goods can be resold to a buyer with full knowledge of the goods' actual state and condition without any reduction in the price. Such a test would be both sufficiently flexible and certain. Without creating any presumption, it draws on the practicality and good sense underlying the merchantability test, while at the same time avoiding not only domestic law associations but, more importantly, the limitations of merchantability. For example, if there is no market to provide a reference price, or if a market price is not fully reflective of quality, the reasonable quality standard is flexible and broad enough to take account of other relevant considerations. It also does not presuppose a fixed benchmark, as is the case under the average quality test. The lack of a fixed benchmark under the reasonable quality standard is more in line with the ordinary purposes requirement: this requirement may refer, depending on the circumstances, to quality which is lower or higher than average.

With quality having to be reasonable, perfection, in the sense that the goods have to be flawless, would not, as a rule, be required.[45] However, in the case of mass-produced and manufactured goods there may justifiably be an expectation of a higher level of quality, not far from perfection, because

[43] See *Bristol Tramways, etc, Carriage Company v Fiat Motors Ltd* [1910] 2 KB 831, 840.

[44] See *Bernstein v Pamsons Motors* [1987] RTR 384, 387.

[45] There is support for this view in the context of Art 35(2) even without any reference to the reasonable quality test. See *Pressure Sensors*, Stockholm Chamber of Commerce Arbitration Award, 5 April 2007, para 144, available at http://cisgw3.law.pace.edu/cases/070405s5.html (the seller commits no breach if defects are minor and can easily be avoided by the buyer or an end user).

'modern manufactured goods are marketed and sold against a background of high expectations and quality control procedures'.[46] In this context, even minor defects may not be tolerated. The same may be the case if the goods are described in the contract as 'new', which almost naturally signals a greater expectation of high quality, bordering on perfection. That said, even a new product, such as a car, complex machinery or software,[47] will sometimes need a 'teething'[48] or adjustment period. In this case, a minor defect, if it is normal or common for the goods in the initial stages of their operation, is unlikely to amount to a breach of reasonable quality and, consequently, of the fitness for ordinary purposes test.

III. ORDINARY USE

'Ordinary use' has been understood to refer to 'normal'[49] purposes.[50] For example, a normal use of fabric by a knitwear factory is to be used in making clothing and, in the absence of any special evidence, their ability to be cut economically is more than what the ordinary purpose requires.[51] Similarly, in one case,[52] the finding that 'heavy oil ZR' was usually used by cement mills and similar plants without restrictions led to the conclusion that the unsuitability of this oil to a bricks manufacturing business did not mean that the goods were not fit for their ordinary purpose. It is

[46] Bridge (n 22) para 7.69.

[47] District Court Arnhem, Rolnummer 82879/HA ZA 02-10528, June 2006, available at http://cisgw3.law.pace.edu/cases/060628n1.html ('Although the Court finds that it has to be tolerated that new developed software may have "teething troubles" or "start-up problems" in the beginning—this is how the Court interprets Art 7.1 of the contract which reads "Supplier does not warrant that operation of the Products will be error free or uninterrupted, or that all non-conformities can be corrected"—it must be possible to use the software in a normal way from the beginning on. The testimonies proved that this was not the case, as there were frequent interferences and as data could not be found or loaded without consulting a technical clerk'). See also *Benjamin's Sale of Goods*, 9th edn (London, Thompson-Sweet & Maxwell, 2014) para 11-069, referring to the view, in the context of the fitness for purpose test in English law, that there should be no strict liability for non-conformities in software.

[48] *Bernstein v Pamsons Motors* (n 44) 390 ('minor teething troubles could be expected in any new motor car').

[49] I Schwenzer in I Schwenzer (ed), *Schlechtriem and Schwenzer, Commentary on the UN Convention on the International Sale of Goods (CISG)*, 3rd edn (Oxford, OUP, 2010) Art 35, para 13.

[50] See Federal Supreme Court, VIII ZR 100/11, 26 September 2012 (Germany), available at http://cisgw3.law.pace.edu/cases/120926g1.html (the goods 'do not have to be fit for all theoretically perceivable forms and possibilities of use, but only for such uses that suggest themselves in light of the material and technical specificities of the goods and *reasonable market expectation* based thereon' (emphasis added)).

[51] See District Court Regensburg, 6 O 107/98, 24 September 1998 (Germany), available at http://cisgw3.law.pace.edu/cases/980924g1.html.

[52] See Appellate Court Graz, 5 R 62/13x, 19 June 2013 (Austria), available at http://cisgw3.law.pace.edu/cases/130619a3.html.

also often said that ordinary use means that the goods have to be 'honestly resaleable'[53] because resale is the main purpose for which the goods are normally bought in international trade.[54] This view, of course, recognises that the goods cannot be infinitely resold and will eventually be used or consumed and for this reason 'resaleability' is viewed broadly to include, for example, in the case of food products, their ability to be fit for consumption.[55] Even then, however, it seems that the interpretation of the 'ordinary use' or 'ordinary purpose(s)' cannot proceed only from the premise that they have to be resaleable because the use or consumption of the goods may be just as ordinary a purpose. Custom-made software or machinery specifically designed for the particular buyer's needs are not products bought for resale. In such cases, resaleability, even if it is capable of being interpreted broadly, unduly narrows down a range of possible ordinary purposes.[56] Therefore, normal or typical purposes are to include not only resale but also a typical use of the goods,[57] with both of them capable of accommodating consumption of the goods.[58]

In many cases, the ordinary purpose is self-evident and in such cases the seller will be liable if the goods are not fit for that purpose. This will be so, for example, where: there are oily stains, dirt and broken lines on towels;[59] the granules used in the manufacture of rods for roll-down shutters have a low titanium dioxide content which prevents the shutters from blocking the light;[60] contact lenses are not sterile;[61] bullet proof vests can be penetrated by bullets;[62] there are problems with stability and carrying capacity of containers, caused by the seller's modifications to the bottom-struttings;[63]

[53] Secretariat Commentary on Article 33 of the 1978 Draft, para 5.

[54] J Lookofsky, *Understanding the CISG*, 3rd (Worldwide) edn (The Netherlands, Kluwer Law International BV, 2008) 79.

[55] See Federal Supreme Court, VIII ZR 67/04, 2 March 2005 (Germany), available at http://cisgw3.law.pace.edu/cases/050302g1.html.

[56] See, similarly, S Kruisinga, *(Non-)conformity in the 1980 UN Convention on Contracts for the International Sale of Goods: A Uniform Concept?* (Antwerp/Oxford/New York, Intersentia, 2004) 31 ('It is doubtful that saleability is sufficient').

[57] 'As the term 'ordinary use' suggests, the goods must be usable under such circumstances as are typical for that kind of goods' (Schwenzer, Hachem and Kee (n 33) para 31.127).

[58] For example, if foodstuffs are bought for the initial purpose of being used as ingredients in a compound meal which will eventually be sold for consumption, it is arguable that those foodstuffs ought to be suitable for use in a compound meal and ought not to make the meal unfit for consumption.

[59] *Cotton Bath Towel*, CIETAC Arbitration, 26 October 1996, available at http://cisgw3.law.pace.edu/cases/961026c1.html.

[60] District Court Paderborn, 7 O 147/94, 25 June 1996 (Germany), available at http://cisgw3.law.pace.edu/cases/960625g1.html.

[61] *Ginza Pte Ltd v Vista Corporation Pty Ltd* [2003] WASC 11.

[62] Multi-Member Court of First Instance of Athens, 4505/2009, 2009 (Greece), available at http://cisgw3.law.pace.edu/cases/094505gr.html.

[63] District Court Hamburg, 419 O 218/03, 6 September 2004 (Germany), available at http://cisgw3.law.pace.edu/cases/040906g1.html.

jackets allow leakage resulting from poor workmanship,[64] a coat's arm-holes are so tight that a customer will have to force him/herself into them, or trousers are so tightly cut that they cannot be pulled up;[65] shoes fall apart because of defects in leather, dissolution of the glue or loose soles and seams;[66] potato seeds are contaminated with a quarantinable disease, such as Brown Rot;[67] or fragments of glass are found in soft drink bottles.[68]

These simple examples highlight some of the main factors that are relevant in identifying the ordinary purpose(s), that is, the nature of the goods and the normal expectations of the general public,[69] market,[70] or of an average user:[71] shoes and clothes are there to be worn; health- (contact lenses) and hygiene-related products (towels) are, by definition, expected to be sterile, safe and clean; a small diesel tourist train used for promotion purposes does not necessarily need to achieve a speed of 40 km/h;[72] food and related products are to be safe for consumption. Determining the products' fitness for consumption is not always a straightforward process. The frozen sliced peppers may, as a result of being broken and sticky, be unsuitable either for sale for direct consumption or for further processing (due to the impossibility of separating the slices). They may, however, be suitable for the use in ready-made meals or soups. With the meals and soups destined for consumption, can the goods be said to be fit for their ordinary use of being consumed if there is no evidence of what consumption means in the given context? In one such case,[73] the court had no hesitation in ruling that the goods were not fit for their ordinary purposes. Assuming that

[64] *Down Jacket and Winter Coat*, CIETAC Arbitration, 22 March 1995, available at http://cisgw3.law.pace.edu/cases/950322c1.html (the seller was held liable notwithstanding a low price the buyer had to pay).

[65] Appellate Court Köln, 16 U 77/01, 14 October 2002 (Germany), available at http://cisgw3.law.pace.edu/cases/021014g1.html; for further examples of defects in clothing, see *Clothes*, CIETAC Arbitration, 3 June 2003, available at http://cisgw3.law.pace.edu/cases/030603c1.html.

[66] Appellate Court Koblenz, 1 U 486/07, 21 November 2007 (Germany), available at http://cisgw3.law.pace.edu/cases/071121g1.html; Appellate Court Aix-en-Provence, 2005/377, 1 July 2005 (France), available at http://cisgw3.law.pace.edu/cases/050701f1.html (however, the buyer failed to prove the seller's breach and, in any event, lost the right to rely on this lack of conformity by virtue of Art 39).

[67] Appellate Court Rouen, 05/03275, 19 December 2006 (France), available at http://cisgw3.law.pace.edu/cases/061219f1.html, affirmed by Supreme Court, 07-11803, 16 September 2008 (France), available at http://cisgw3.law.pace.edu/cases/080916f1.html.

[68] See *Fryer Holdings v Liaoning MEC Group* (n 24). For the criticism of the decision, see n 24 above.

[69] See Kröll (n 3) para 71.

[70] Federal Supreme Court, 26 September 2012 (Germany) (n 50).

[71] See ibid; District Court Coburg, 22 O 38/06, 12 December 2006 (Germany), available at http://cisgw3.law.pace.edu/cases/061212g1.html.

[72] '[A] speed of 25 km per hour is not incompatible with the "ordinary use" and/or the "particular purpose" mentioned in Articles 35(2)(a) and (b) CISG' (see District Court Veurne, 25 April 2001 (n 5)).

[73] District Court Munich, 5 HKO 10734/02, 29 November 2005 (Germany), available at http://cisgw3.law.pace.edu/cases/051129g1.html.

all three possible uses of these goods—sale for direct consumption, their ability to be processed, and to be used in ready-made meals and soups—constitute ordinary purposes for which frozen sliced peppers are ordinarily used, the decision raises the question of whether the goods are required to be fit for *all* ordinary purposes or whether their fitness at least for one purpose is sufficient. The decision appears to take the former position and this is also the prevailing view today.[74] With Article 35(2)(a) providing for the seller's basic obligation, the buyer should be able to expect that all ordinary purposes, and not just some of them, are met. The purposes are, after all, only required to be normal or typical and allowing the seller not to meet all of them would set a basic threshold at too low a level considering that consumers' expectations are continuously on the rise. The burden should thus be on the seller to warn the buyer that the goods will not or may not meet all normal purposes.

Apart from the nature of the goods, many other factors can be relevant in determining what constitutes an ordinary use. Public representations by the seller or the manufacturer or advertisements highlighting certain qualities or features of the goods can shed light on the meaning of the goods' ordinary use.[75] The parties' past practices, trade usages,[76] industry standards,[77] and even the nature of the parties' business and commercial standing can either help to identify the purpose(s) for which the goods are ordinarily used or set the context for doing so.[78] Where the seller, a trader in shoes, knows that the buyer has a similar business and understands the buyer's market, the ordinary use would mean possessing those characteristics which make them saleable in the buyer's market.[79] If the seller is known to be a supplier of luxury cars, it may be more readily inferred that an ordinary use includes not only a car's ability to be driven safely and lawfully on the road, but also its ability to be presented as a luxury item,[80] containing the most advanced and fashionable features.[81]

[74] See, eg Secretariat Commentary (n 53) para 5; Schwenzer (n 49) para 13 (with further references); Kröll (n 3) para 69. See also Appellate Court Helsinki, S 01/269, 31 May 2004 (Finland) and the discussion of the case in S Kuoppala, 'The Application and Interpretation of the CISG in Finnish Case Law 1997–2005' http://cisgw3.law.pace.edu/cases/040531f5.html ('only colourless phenol could be used for all the purposes phenol was normally used. The purpose of use of the coloured phenol was more limited than that of the colourless phenol').

[75] Kröll (n 3) para 71.

[76] See Arts 8 and 9.

[77] See Federal Supreme Court, VIII ZR 121/98, 24 March 1999 (Germany), available at www.cisg.law.pace.edu/cases/990324g1.html, where the black vine wax was found not to comply with Art 35(2)(a) because it did not meet the relevant industry standards.

[78] See Art 8(3).

[79] See District Court, No 2280/2007, 11 December 2008 (Italy), available at http://cisgw3.law.pace.edu/cases/081211i3.html.

[80] See a similar example in Kröll (n 3) para 71.

[81] The reliance on a quality standard, such as reasonable quality, may be particularly appropriate and helpful in such circumstances.

The nature of the buyer's business may also be influential in ascertaining an ordinary use. To use again an example of a car, the type, model and technical characteristics of a car which the seller can be required to deliver under Article 35(2)(a) is likely to depend on: whether the buyer is a transport company,[82] in which case cars would ordinarily be expected to be used frequently and to transport certain types of products; or whether the buyer operates a non-transport business. In the latter situation, a car may ordinarily be expected to support its office operations and it may not be necessary for the car to be able to carry products and to be used as intensively as in the former case.[83] The contract price of the goods will often be highly indicative of an ordinary use and, consequently, of the quality to be expected of the goods.[84] As noted, resaleability will often be an ordinary purpose for which the goods are bought. Where it is clear that the goods are not resaleable at all, such as where food products are contaminated and dangerous to human health and safety,[85] or the goods contain obvious defects clearly making them incapable of being resold in a particular market,[86] there is usually little doubt that the seller is in breach of Article 35(2)(a). In other cases, the goods may be resaleable, but the question is whether they can be sold at the same price as that at which the buyer bought them.[87] This test may be particularly suitable for commodities where, for example, the buyer argues that the goods are of a different grade to the one that a trader in its position would ordinarily expect. There is usually a market for commodities and the existence of a market and of a market price is indicative of what can ordinarily be expected for the price paid by the buyer, a commodities trader, usually buying the goods for further resale.[88]

Finally, does the fact that the buyer is able to cure the goods and make them fit for their ordinary use, especially at a trifling cost, exempt the seller from liability for the initial non-conformity? It is submitted that the answer should be 'no'. The question of whether the goods can be cured and of

[82] And if so, what is the scale of its operations and what are the types of products it transports?

[83] See, similarly, Kröll (n 3) para 72.

[84] '[Because] the [contract] price is much lower than market price for goods of the same quality, the Tribunal finds that [buyer]'s expectations in terms of the quality of the down jackets was unreasonably high' (CIETAC Arbitration, 22 March 1995 (n 64)). See also Appellate Court Schleswig, 11 U 40/01, 22 August 2002 (Germany), available at http://cisgw3.law.pace.edu/cases/020822g2.html ('If the [seller] delivered stock-to-be-fattened, instead of sheep for slaughter, there was a discrepancy in quality of the livestock, since sheep, mature to be slaughtered immediately qualify as livestock of a higher quality and hence for a higher price').

[85] See Federal Supreme Court, 2 March 2005 (Germany) (n 55).

[86] District Court, 11 December 2008 (Italy) (n 79). See also Appellate Court Köln (n 65) ('all this is about fashion products for the summer season in the high price segment and that, in this market segment, the sale already starts at the beginning of May, when even faultless goods are only saleable with a discount').

[87] See *Fryer Holdings v Liaoning MEC Group* (n 24).

[88] See also the discussion at II above.

how difficult or easy it is for the buyer to do so may be relevant to whether the breach is fundamental.[89] The buyer's ability to cure cannot, however, diminish the seller's basic obligations in respect of conformity of the goods. Otherwise, the burden of ensuring conformity would be partly shifted to the buyer. As explained below,[90] sellers are already sufficiently protected by the position that the goods are unlikely to be required to be flawless and minor 'defects' are sometimes tolerated. There are indications that courts will be unwilling to let the seller's burden of ensuring conformity be shared by the buyer. In one case,[91] although the seller delivered defective tiles, the seller also delivered a greater number of tiles than that ordered by the buyer. It was probably the case that because of the greater quantity, a sufficient number of conforming tiles could have been selected. Nonetheless, the court held the seller liable stating that '[it could not] be expected or required of the buyer to open all packages, to sort out the tiles, to test to see if enough of one sort were delivered and then to pack them again'.[92]

In another case,[93] the seller's delivery of racing carts which were not fully assembled was also regarded as a breach of Article 35(2)(a).[94] Although it was possible for the buyer to assemble the carts,[95] the ordinary purpose was held to mean that the carts were to be in a 'functioning and 'ready-for-race condition'. It may be still be asked whether the buyer's ability to prevent the cause of non-conformity may, in some cases, be seen as part of the goods' 'ordinary use'. In one case,[96] the seller delivered dioxin-contaminated clay which was to be used as a separator of potatoes with high and low starch content. The buyer's ability to easily wash and clean the separated potatoes from dioxin residues could not override the fact that the seller delivered dioxin-contaminated clay, because cleaning would have constituted an 'extra effort' by the buyer. Nevertheless, in making this decision the court pointed out that the applicable regulations relating to feedingstuffs[97] contained no additional cleaning requirement and for this reason were not 'characteristic for the intended use'. This suggests the possibility that had the food and animal feed regulations, which seem to have been taken into account in interpreting the ordinary use, required potatoes to be cleaned,

[89] If a breach is fundamental (see Art 25), the buyer will be able to avoid the contract (Art 49) or to demand the delivery of substitute goods (Art 46(2)).

[90] See at IX below; also nn 47 and 48 above and the accompanying text.

[91] District Court Baden-Baden, 4 O 113/90, 14 August 1991 (Germany), available at http://cisgw3.law.pace.edu/cases/910814g1.html.

[92] Ibid.

[93] District Court Köln, 25 March 2003 (n 4).

[94] As well as of Art 35(2)(b).

[95] '[S]ignificant assembly and modification works' were required.

[96] Federal Supreme Court, 26 September 2012 (Germany) (n 50).

[97] Commission Regulation (EC) 2439/1999 of 17 November 1999 on the conditions for the authorisation of additives belonging to the group of 'binders, anti-caking agents and coagulants' in feedingstuffs.

the ordinary use would have been seen as including cleaning by the buyer, in which case dioxin residues would have been washed off. The seller's argument that the clay was fit for the ordinary use might well succeed in such a scenario. The very requirement that the goods need to be cleaned (as part of their ordinary use) presupposes that the goods may contain impurities or be contaminated; and if the required cleaning process is sufficient to remove dioxin contamination, the argument that the presence of dioxin does not render the goods unfit for the ordinary use may not be easy to refute.

IV. DESCRIPTION

The Convention underscores the importance of the goods' description in defining the purpose for which they are ordinarily used.[98] In one case,[99] the buyer argued that the infra-red radiation heating and shaping machine delivered by the seller was non-conforming because it was not able to shape anti-pilling polar fleece at the speed of 28 metres per minute. It was established that only a 'heated-air shaping machine' would have been able to do so. The buyer further argued that since the seller had won the bid which had borne the title 'Production Line of Anti-Pilling Polar Fleece', the seller ought to have known that the machine was intended to be used to shape anti-pilling polar fleece. The tribunal held that Article 35(2)(b) was not applicable due to the lack of the buyer's reliance on the seller's skill and judgement. There was no other evidence in the tribunal's view showing that the seller contractually undertook to deliver the machine for shaping anti-pilling polar fleece at the speed of 28 metres per minute. At that speed, the infra-red radiation heating machine was only able to shape regular '350 grams chemical heavy fabric'. With no clear contractual undertaking by the seller and with Article 35(2)(b) held inapplicable, the tribunal had to decide whether the machine complied with Article 35(2)(a). Although cited, this provision was not duly evaluated. But it seems implicit in the decision that there was no breach of this provision. First, the tribunal relied on an expert's report stating that 'the shaping of anti-pilling polar fleece does not fall into the scope of the ordinary purpose of the machine'. Secondly, the machine had no defects and did what an infra-red radiation heating machine was expected to do. Finally, the machine *was* in fact capable of shaping anti-pilling polar fleece, albeit at the speed of below 28 metres a minute.

[98] The goods are to be 'fit for the purposes for which goods of the *same description* would ordinarily be used' (Art 35(2)(a) (emphasis added)). Similarly, see Official Comment on § 2-314 UCC (n 31) point 1; C Ervine, 'Satisfactory Quality: What Does it Mean?' [2004] *JBL* 684, 688.

[99] *Textile Manufacturing Equipment*, CIETAC Arbitration, 18 July 2002, available at http://cisgw3.law.pace.edu/cases/020718c1.html.

It can probably be inferred from this decision that the tribunal did not deem the title of the seller's bid to be sufficient to incorporate the description into the contract. It is arguable that had it been otherwise, the seller's obligation under Article 35(2)(a) would have been to deliver a machine capable of shaping 'anti-pilling polar fleece' and, possibly, of doing so at the speed of 28 metres a minute, considering that this was the speed specified in the contract. If this proposition is true, it is evident that the goods' descriptions can exert much influence on the meaning of an 'ordinary use' and consequently on the allocation of duties and risks between the parties. This decision also signals that buyers should clearly formulate the description of the goods and incorporate it into the contract to alleviate any doubt as to what should be seen as the goods' ordinary use. But, of course, a more effective way of ensuring that the seller has a duty to deliver goods which are fit for a particular purpose is to fix the relevant requirements in the contract (Article 35(1))[100] or, at least, to communicate that purpose to the seller (Article 35(2)(b)).[101]

V. DURABILITY

The issue of the goods' fitness for their ordinary use will involve the assessment of many other aspects and features of conformity. There is little doubt that an ordinary use implies their ability to be used for a certain period of time which can be considered as normal or reasonable having regard to the nature of the goods and to the way(s) in which they are typically used.[102] For example, clothes can certainly be expected not to shrink by one or two sizes after their first washing.[103] Some shrinkage may be expected and that is why the parties will sometimes dispute the amount of shrinkage that is normal. In one such case,[104] the court rejected the manufacturer's contention that 5 to 7 per cent shrinkage after washing was normal for judo clothing and upheld the buyer's position that customary shrinkage could not exceed 3 per cent. Even where the goods are expected to be durable, regard also needs to be had to the way in which the buyer has used them. The buyer who exposed the goods to excessive 'wear and tear' may not be in the position to complain about their lack of durability.[105]

[100] See Chapter 2.

[101] See Chapter 3.

[102] CM Bianca in CM Bianca and J Bonell (eds), *Commentary on the International Sales Law* (Milan, Giuffrè, 1987) 273.

[103] District Court Landshut, 54 O 644/94, 5 April 1995 (Germany), available at http://cisgw3.law.pace.edu/cases/950405g1.html.

[104] District Court Besançon, 97 009265, 19 January 1998 (France), available at http://cisgw3.law.pace.edu/cases/980119f1.html.

[105] See Schwenzer, Hachem and Kee (n 33) para 31.134.

If the goods are normally expected to be transported to a particular destination, their ordinary use is likely to include their ability to withstand the rigours of a normal journey to that destination. If the risk of loss of or damage to the goods has passed to the buyer and the goods are found to have been damaged or deteriorated in the course of a normal journey, the very fact of deterioration or damage during the journey is in itself unlikely to constitute a breach of Article 35(2)(a). Rather, it is a powerful indication that the goods did not prove to be durable and consequently were not fit for their ordinary use at the time when risk passed to the buyer, which is the time with reference to which conformity is to be assessed.[106] Article 36(2) CISG also provides that the seller is liable for any lack of conformity which occurs after that time if the non-conformity is due to a breach of any of the seller's obligations. This provision extends the seller's liability further by stretching its obligations, in appropriate cases, beyond the point of the passage of risk. Therefore, it is also open to the buyer to argue that although a lack of conformity arose after the risk had passed to it, non-conformity was due to the seller's breach of its obligation to ensure durability under Article 35(2)(a). Article 36(2) is thus another basis of establishing the seller's liability in such cases. Finally, if the seller's failure to ensure durability is treated as a fundamental breach,[107] the rules on the passage of risk 'do not impair the remedies available to the buyer on account of the breach'.[108]

In case of doubt about whether the goods can ordinarily be expected to be durable or about the extent of their durability, such factors as contract description, price, the parties' past dealings, expectations or usages in a given trade may help to determine whether durability can be expected in the circumstances.[109] That said, if buyers want to ensure that goods are able to withstand a transport journey, they are strongly advised to include a relevant provision in the contract (Article 35(1)) or at least to communicate the need for durability to the seller (Article 35(2)(b)). A lack of a contractual reference to durability may conceivably encourage courts and tribunals to hold that durability is 'ordinarily' not expected of such goods or to imply an implicit intention to derogate[110] from durability that might otherwise have been implied as part of the ordinary use test under Article 35(2)(a).[111]

[106] See Art 36(1). See also *Benjamin's Sale of Goods* (n 47) para 11-040.

[107] See Art 25.

[108] See Art 70.

[109] See Arts 8(3) and 9.

[110] See Art 6.

[111] See *Benjamin's Sale of Goods* (n 47) para 11-040. See also cases involving C&F and CFR terms, discussed in Chapter 2 (Appellate Court Barcelona, Recurso de Apelación No 403/2008, 24 March 2009, available at http://cisgw3.law.pace.edu/cases/090324s4.html; Appellate Court, 47.448, 31 October 1995 (Argentina), available at http://cisgw3.law.pace.edu/cases/951031a1.html) where the consideration of durability was disregarded.

VI. HEALTH AND SAFETY

The health and safety considerations are likely to exert much influence on defining the ordinary purpose(s). The goods can ordinarily be expected not to pose a danger to human life or health and therefore a lack of safety will usually put the seller in breach of Article 35(2)(a). In a case involving the sale of a household textile-producing machine,[112] it was established, on the basis of an expert's report, that the hands of the workers who operated the machine could be injured by the cutting cylinder. Relying on this finding, the tribunal held the seller liable:

> Machines of the same description like the one in question are regularly fit to produce the product without injuring or endangering workers. As the Expert states, due to the lack of safety measures, the Machine does not meet this standard. The Machine is not fit for the purposes for which machines of the same description would ordinarily be used and, therefore defective since it is not fitted with the required safety measures in order to protect the workers who operate the Machine.[113]

However, a commercial buyer may well want to purchase goods which are potentially dangerous to human life and health.[114] Therefore, a mere fact of a sale of dangerous goods does not make the seller liable. In such cases, the allocation of risks will rest not on the dangerous nature of the goods but on whether adequate instructions and warnings have been provided by the seller to enable the buyer to use the goods safely. If not, the goods cannot be regarded as fit for their ordinary use which implies their ability to be used in a manner that is free from danger to human life and health.[115] Viewed this way, the ordinary use requirement probably gives rise to the seller's (implied) duty to warn the buyer of the dangers associated with the goods in a case where the buyer is not aware of them.[116] A failure to do so is also likely to make the seller liable.

A similar approach should probably apply when it comes to animal safety, as is illustrated by the earlier mentioned case,[117] where the seller delivered dioxin-contaminated clay used to separate potatoes with high and low starch content. The potatoes with low starch content together with the waste peels from potatoes with high starch content were used in animal feed processing. The court in that case held that the seller, who was

[112] ICC Arbitration Case No 10377, 2002, available at http://cisgw3.law.pace.edu/cases/020377i1.html.

[113] Ibid para 22.

[114] See *Benjamin's Sale of Goods* (n 47) para 11-039.

[115] For a similar position, see ibid.

[116] Similarly, see ibid.

[117] See Federal Supreme Court, 26 September 2012 (Germany) (n 50) and the main text accompanying n 96 above.

aware of considerable dioxin contamination, 'should have disclosed this circumstance to [buyer], giving [buyer], if it had nevertheless accepted the clay, the possibility to take appropriate safety measures like washing of the separated potatoes after passing through the clay-water bath to avoid a contamination of the derivative products by the dioxin'. This was held to be so even though the seller was not aware of the process that the buyer followed in grading potatoes.[118] The court took the view that this lack of knowledge should have caused the seller to be extra cautious.[119]

VII. INSTRUCTIONS, MANUALS AND LABELS

The question of whether the seller is required to provide warnings, instructions or manuals also arises in a less drastic situation where a danger to human life and health is not an issue, but where the buyer contends that, due to a lack of information, the goods could not be used at all[120] or broke down after a certain time. Whether such a claim is justified will depend on the circumstances and, particularly, on the level of the buyer's expertise, which will be determinative of what the buyer can be expected to know. In one case,[121] the manufacturer of a large and a highly complex press[122] substituted a different lockplate to the one described in the design documents provided to the buyer. Because the buyer installed the lockplate improperly when assembling the press, it collapsed after having been used without incident for almost three years. It was common ground that the seller was entitled to make a replacement as long as it was as secure and suitable as the original arrangement.[123] The lockplate used by the seller was also not found

118 'During the grading process the potatoes transit through a clay-water bath'.

119 Ibid.

120 See Federal Supreme Court, VIII ZR 306/95, 4 December 1996 (Germany), available at http://cisgw3.law.pace.edu/cases/961204g1.html, where the Court of Appeal held that a failure to deliver documentation containing instructions on how to operate a computer printing system was a breach of Art 35. The decision was reversed by the Supreme Court (on other grounds) and remanded to the Court of Appeal for further determination of facts.

121 Stockholm Chamber of Commerce Arbitration Award, 5 June 1998, available at http://cisgw3.law.pace.edu/cases/980605s5.html.

122 '[O]ver 50 feet (16 metres) high, over 44 feet (13 metres) wide and about 28 feet (6 metres) deep, weighed one million eight hundred and fifty thousand pounds, and consisted of tens of thousands of individual parts.'

123 '[I]t is clear—and undisputed—that the A-5750 key retainer is not specified in the contractual documents proper (but only in the service manual accompanying the Press at delivery; see further below). It is also undisputed by [buyer] that [seller] was entitled to replace the A-5750 key retainer with another part or arrangement, provided that this was equally secure and suitable as the A-5750 key retainer arrangement. Consequently, and though the use of the P-52 in fact did not "conform" to [seller's] intended design or the assembly diagram included in the service manual, the replacement of A-5750 does not amount to a non-conformity in itself' (para 6.3(a)).

to depart from industry practices, but the way in which the lockplate was to be installed was not self-evident. The contractual and technical documentation given to the buyer did not contain any details of how it was to be installed. The seller explained that it did not provide its customers with detailed descriptions of all the details for 'proprietary reasons' and instead provided supervisory services to ensure proper installation. There was some dispute between the parties as to whether the supervision could detect an improper installation of the lockplate, but the tribunal found that 'it [was] clear from [seller's] own position that it would have been possible by using the micro-inching function to inspect the installation of the lock-nut and the lockplate if this had been considered important'.[124] The conclusion on this point was that there was nothing to 'indicate anything but that [buyer] was entitled to assume that [seller] did not consider it important to inspect or supervise [buyer's] installation of the P-52 lockplate in the holes prepared by [seller]'.[125] On these facts, the tribunal held the seller liable:

> [with regard to] the absence of any information on the installation or follow-up by [seller], and the circumstances related to [buyer's] installation, the Tribunal is of the opinion that the Press in respect of this item falls short of what [buyer] was entitled to expect under the provisions of CISG. The Tribunal considers the P-52 part of the Press, in view of the possibility of improper installation and the resulting possible or even probable ultimate failure of the lockplate, not to be fit for the long, continuous operation of the Press without serious failure that unquestionably was [buyer's] reasonable expectancy and the purpose of its investment.[126]

It is submitted that this decision is correct. The lockplate may have been, as the buyer put it, a 'tiny' part of the press, but it and its proper installation were vital to a successful operation of the press, as demonstrated by the facts. The buyer was not in the position to know about the substitution and, consequently, about the proper methods of installing the lockplate.[127] Had it been correctly installed, the press would have operated for much longer than three years[128] and, as explained earlier, durability is part of goods' ordinary use. Therefore, without the seller providing the relevant information, whether in the manuals, other documentation or during supervision, the press could not be regarded as fit for its ordinary use.

In this case, when it came to the intricacies of the press's constitution and assembly the balance of the parties' expertise was unequal, with the seller being a specialist manufacturer. Where, however, the buyer has equal

124 Ibid.

125 Ibid.

126 Ibid.

127 As the tribunal explained, 'It is difficult to see why [buyer] should be in a position to question the location of the lockplate that the designer and manufacturer of the Press had itself apparently determined when assembling the Press in its own factory' (ibid).

128 The buyer argued that its normal working life was 30 years.

expertise with the seller in respect of the contract goods, much less is likely to be expected of the seller. In one case,[129] the buyer, who purchased plates for greenhouses, argued that the seller had a duty to inform the buyer that using the plates in a non-vertical position would create the risk of spots and mould appearing on the plates. The court rejected this contention, pointing out that the buyer was a specialist in the placement of greenhouses and therefore might be 'considered to know what it ordered and whether it was completely appropriate for what the plates were aimed for'. The court then explained that the seller's duty to provide information is much less stringent towards a specialist than it would be if the buyer had no expertise:

> It is clear that the plates can also be used in other ways. It is not up to the seller to list these uses and to state each time that that way of using the plates is less appropriate. To the contrary, it is up to the buyer to request necessary technical information on the basis of the given concrete information about the application.[130]

The seller in the 'lockplate' case also appears to have alluded to the position that it could not be expected to provide complete information in respect of every detail of the press. The danger of this position is that it can encourage sellers not to provide information regarding the goods merely by virtue of the fact that the buyer is also a specialist. The approach which truly strikes a fair balance between the parties is one which takes account of all relevant circumstances. The 'plates' case may seem to support the view that if the parties have equal expertise the seller should have no duty to provide information regarding the use of the goods. But a closer look at the decision shows that there may be other factors contributing to such an allocation of risks. The court doubted whether mould and spots could really be described as 'defects' and was inclined to view them merely as a matter of the plates' 'appearance', which was incapable of either affecting the life-span of the plates or causing their 'disintegration or rotting'. Thus, the plates could be viewed as fit for their ordinary purpose, unless there was strong evidence that their appearance also had a role to play in fulfilling that purpose.[131] The decision also pointed out that, in the past, the buyer had ordered plates which were coated with a coating intended to prevent the formation of mould, as the buyer knew or ought to have known. A failure to order coated plates could be treated as the buyer's implicit acceptance of the risk of mould formation. As a matter of legal analysis, this latter point could have been treated in different ways. It could have been regarded as: an issue of contract interpretation under Article 35(1) based on the buyer's implicit

[129] Appellate Court Ghent, 2003/AR/2763, 4 October 2004 (Belgium), available at http://cisgw3.law.pace.edu/cases/041004b1.html.

[130] Ibid.

[131] Generally, minor defects are unlikely to make the goods unfit for their ordinary use (see IX below).

acceptance of the risk of mould formation; an implicit derogation from Article 35(2)(a) in the unlikely case that mould formation would render the plates unfit for their ordinary purpose; a communication of a particular purpose under Article 35(2)(b) which *included* the risk of mould formation; or signalling to a reasonable person in the seller's position that the purpose for which non-coated plates, as opposed to coated plates, would ordinarily be used (Article 35(2)(a)) would *include* the risk of mould formation. It is only the latter interpretation that brings this factor within the ambit of Article 35(2)(a). To conclude, this case does not support the proposition that mere equality of the parties' expertise exempts the seller from the need to supply information since the outcome is also likely to have been influenced by two other factors.

VIII. SERVICING AND SPARE PARTS

There is some disagreement as to whether the seller is under a duty to provide services, such as installation, maintenance and repair, and spare parts.[132] These differing views may well reflect different ideological positions in respect of where the parties should be positioned on the spectrum between *caveat venditor* and *caveat emptor.* The view favouring the implication of such a duty has a much greater expectation of what constitutes the goods' fitness for their ordinary use than the view opposing such a duty. A broad formulation of Article 35(2)(a) and the Convention's openness to the surrounding context, however, militate against the adoption of one uniform approach. As in other respects, the precise content of the seller's duties will crystallise after the evaluation of all relevant circumstances. The standards and expectations in the given industry or commercial sector, a trade usage or the parties' prior course of dealing[133] may give an indication as to whether the goods are ordinarily expected to be accompanied by an undertaking of servicing or providing spare parts. The contract price may also carry much influence in determining what the buyer can reasonably expect.

IX. MINOR DEFECTS, APPEARANCE AND FINISH

It has already been noted that minor defects or flaws will often be regarded as insufficient to make the goods unfit for their ordinary use, particularly if

[132] Compare E McKendrick, *Goode on Commercial Law*, 4th edn (London, Penguin Books, 2010) 361 (advocating an additional implied term providing for the seller's duty of servicing and providing spare parts) with Adams and MacQueen (n 21) 191 (arguing against any servicing and maintenance obligations by the seller).

[133] See Arts 8 and 9 CISG.

this test is interpreted as being based on the 'reasonable' quality standard. There is ample support for this position in cases. Where machinery, cars[134] or software[135] are involved, so-called 'teething' problems can reasonably be expected. The seller may therefore not be in breach of Article 35(2)(a) if the goods cannot be put to immediate use.[136] The goods supplied in large quantities may often contain some minor defects. In one case,[137] involving the supply of picture frame mouldings, the court accepted that defects which appeared to be minor,[138] in the range between 5 to 8 per cent, could be expected from any supplier.[139] A similar approach can be expected where a 'defect' has negligible negative impact on the use of the goods. For instance, the delivery of catalogues in which one line on one page was misplaced was held not to amount to a breach because the text's readability was not affected.[140]

This may be taken to mean that the problems with aesthetic features of the goods, such as their design, appearance and finish, are of no legal significance. That would not be true. To begin with, the problems with, say, the goods' design may have a direct impact on their functionality and performance, as happened in a case where a faulty design of a textile machine led to frequent interruptions in the product process requiring a high level of maintenance and cleaning.[141] Such consequences of the faulty design have rightly been regarded as making the machine unfit for its ordinary use.[142] But even where there is no direct or obvious impact on the functionality of the goods, it is submitted that problems with appearance and finish can make the seller liable under Article 35(2)(a). The description of the goods, the contract price, the parties' business reputation and prior course of dealing will be some of the relevant factors. If the goods are described as 'new', 'luxury' or 'premium' and are priced in accordance with the value that the goods so described have on a market, even scratches and other minor faults

[134] See n 48 above.

[135] See District Court Arnhem, June 2006 (n 47).

[136] *Mansonville Plastics (BC) Ltd v Kurtz GmbH* [2003] BCSC 1298.

[137] *La San Giuseppe v Forti Moulding Ltd* [1999] OJ No 3352.

[138] 'The exhibits filed were mostly small lengths of moulding, often with small defects' (ibid para 37).

[139] Ibid.

[140] Commercial Court Zürich, HG 960527/O, 21 September 1998 (Switzerland), available at http://cisgw3.law.pace.edu/cases/980921s1.html. The position that minor faults do not generally amount to a breach on the seller's part will necessitate an examination of whether a fault at hand can be regarded as 'minor'. In one case, it was accepted that a certain amount of breakages of bricks was normal in the use of a machine for rectification of bricks. However, the machine could not be regarded as fit for its ordinary use if the breakage was as high as 75–84 per cent (see Court of First Instance of Tudela, 29 March 2005 (Spain), available at http://cisgw3.law.pace.edu/cases/050329s4.html; the decision does not appear to have been over-turned in this respect in further instances).

[141] See ICC Arbitration Case No 10377 (n 112) paras 24–25.

[142] Ibid.

in their appearance are likely to render them unfit for the purpose for which the goods of this description are ordinarily used. Higher demands will also be imposed on the seller trading in manufactured goods, which, due to stringent manufacturing controls and modern advancement in technology, can achieve 'something like technical perfection'.[143] If there is evidence showing the difference in value between the goods with and without the faults in their appearance, finish or design, then that is likely to be a strong indication that the goods are not fit for the purpose for which the goods of *that* description are ordinarily used.[144]

X. PUBLIC LAW REGULATIONS

A. Informational Asymmetry and Guidelines in *New Zealand Mussels*

What is an ordinary use may depend on a place and context in which the goods are intended to be used. Where there are public law regulations in a country where the goods will be sold or used, the question arises whether an ordinary use is to be defined with reference to the regulatory requirements in that country or according to the standards and expectations in the seller's country. Different answers are found in cases and academic writings, with either the reliance on the standards in the seller's country[145] *or* the standards in the importing country[146] being seen as controlling. Nevertheless, a position which has been gaining wide acceptance[147] is the

[143] Bridge (n 22) para 7.72.

[144] Whether or not there was a drop in the value of the catalogues as a result of one line of the text being misplaced was a factor taken into consideration in Commercial Court Zürich (n 140) ('[Buyer] thus cannot seriously claim that, due to this minor flaw, the products had been devalued').

[145] Commercial Court St Gallen, HG.2010.421-HGK, 14 June 2012 (Switzerland), available at http://cisgw3.law.pace.edu/cases/120614s1.html; Bianca (n 102) 273; Enderlein and Maskow (n 7) 143.

[146] See P Schlechtriem, 'The Seller's Obligations under the United Nations Convention on Contracts for the International Sale of Goods' in N Galston and H Smit (eds), *International Sales: The United Nations Convention on Contracts for the International Sale of Goods* (New York, Matthew Bender 1984) para 6-20. Possibly, Appellate Court Paris, 95-018179, 13 December 1995 (France), available at http://cisgw3.law.pace.edu/cases/951213f1.html.

[147] See Supreme Court, 2 Ob 100/00w, 13 April 2000 (Austria), available at http://cisgw3.law.pace.edu/cases/000413a3.html (not referring to *New Zealand Mussels*, but in essence taking a similar approach); *RJ & AM Smallmon v Transport Sales Ltd and Grant Alan Miller* [2011] NZ CA 340; *Medical Marketing v Internazionale Medico Scientifica*, F Supp 2d, 1999 WL 311945 (ED La) (affirming a decision of an arbitration tribunal which accepted the approach in *New Zealand Mussels*, but held that a general rule did not apply due to the presence of one of the exceptions). Virtually every commentary on this issue under the CISG cites this case (see, eg RF Henschel, 'Conformity of Goods in International Sales Governed by CISG Article 35: Caveat Venditor, Caveat Emptor and Contract Law as Background Law and as a Competing Set of Rules' (2004) 1 *Nordic J Commercial L*, www.cisg.law.pace.edu/cisg/biblio/henschel2.html ('the principles in the *Mussels* case now seems to have widespread acceptance').

one set out in the *New Zealand Mussels* case,[148] discussed in the previous chapter.[149] In general, the seller is not expected to know of and to comply with the public law regulations in the importing country, even if the seller is aware of the ultimate destination.[150] However, the seller may be held liable for non-compliance with the regulations in the importing country if: (1) the regulations in the country of use are the same as those in the seller's country; (2) the buyer specifically drew the seller's attention to the regulations; (3) the seller has a branch in the buyer's country, has a long-established business relationship with the buyer, or has often exported the goods to or promoted them in the country of use in the past.[151]

The issue of (non-)compliance with public law regulations highlights a major dilemma in the application of the implied rules on conformity. On the one hand, their broad formulation, flexibility and need to be defined with reference to the surrounding context unequivocally dictate that they must be applied on a case-by-case basis. On the other hand, a lack of any general guidelines would create uncertainty in this important area of sales law and give rise to an argument that they lack content and meaning. This is undesirable since an effective sales law is one which promotes a reasonable degree of predictability, as well as signals and enhances a coherent set of objectives, values and policies. A balance thus needs to be struck between formulating a meaningful guideline, based on the Convention's policies and on the rationale of the implied terms, and responding to the particular circumstances of the case.

The approach in *New Zealand Mussels* strikes this balance. Taking, as a starting point, a clear position as to whether or not the seller has a duty to deliver goods which comply with public law regulations promotes legal certainty. This is neither a fixed rule nor a presumption, and is merely a general guideline.[152] Providing for 'special circumstances' is a way of ensuring that the Convention is fully responsive to the particular circumstances and that the seller will have such a duty where there are good reasons for doing so. The next question is whether the starting position of not requiring the seller to comply with regulations is right as a matter of principle. One main argument against it is based on drawing an analogy with

[148] Federal Supreme Court, 8 March 1995, VIII ZR 159/94 (Germany), available at http://cisgw3.law.pace.edu/cases/950308g3.html.

[149] See Chapter 3.

[150] See Supreme Court, 13 April 2000 (Austria) (n 147); District Court Rotterdam, 295401/HA ZA 07-2802, 15 October 2008 (The Netherlands), available at www.cisg.law.pace.edu/cisg/wais/db/cases2/081015n2.html.

[151] Federal Supreme Court, 8 March 1995 (Germany) (n 148).

[152] *Cf* J Honnold (updated and revised by H Flechtner), *Uniform Law for International Sales under the 1980 United Nations Convention*, 4th edn (The Netherlands, Wolters Kluwer Law & Business, 2009) 335, suggesting that no starting point should be adopted.

Article 42(1)(b),[153] whose final default position is that the seller has an obligation to deliver goods which are free from third parties' rights or claims based on intellectual property, if such rights or claims flow from intellectual property under the law where the buyer has its place of business.

Drawing this analogy may not be entirely appropriate. First, one condition for making the seller liable under Article 42 is that the seller knew or ought to have known of the existence of intellectual property rights, whereas, here, it is providing for 'special circumstances' (namely, exceptions (2) and (3)) that caters for the situation where the seller knows or is in the position to know about the regulations. The very question is whether *in the absence* of such special circumstances, the seller should be liable. The premise of the problem discussed here is therefore different from that underlying Article 42. Secondly, it has been argued that having the goods free from third parties' claims or rights based on intellectual property is what the buyer is entitled to expect under the contract and the CISG.[154] In contrast, the need to comply with public law regulations in the country where the goods will be sold or used may not be seen necessarily as a basic obligation which self-evidently should be imposed on the seller.[155] Another point against allocating the risk to the seller arises in connection with the argument that the risk should be on the seller *if* it is aware of the goods' destination. This point has already been addressed in the context of Article 35(2)(b), where it was shown that, on balance, there are doubts as to whether this approach is entirely justifiable. It is even less satisfactory in the context of Article 35(2)(a). The said position can, in principle, be validly taken under Article 35(2)(b) because the provision on the reliance on the seller's skill and judgement will usually protect the seller where it is unfair or unreasonable to hold it liable merely by virtue of its knowledge of destination. There is, however, no such provision in Article 35(2)(a) and taking that view would weaken the seller's position and disturb a fair balance between the parties.

It is both fair and efficient to allocate the risk to the party who is in a better position to access the relevant information, to insure against the risk of non-compliance with the relevant regulations or to avoid it. Subject to the special circumstances listed in *New Zealand Mussels*, the buyer is generally in a better position than the seller to know about the regulations in the importing country. The buyer can reduce the risk of non-compliance by drawing those regulations to the seller's attention or providing for the need to comply with them in the contract. It is also, as a rule, cheaper for the

[153] See Kröll (n 3) para 87, making a similar point.

[154] Bianca (n 102) para 3.2.

[155] See, similarly, Kröll (n 3) para 88; Supreme Court, 13 April 2000 (Austria) (n 147) ('It cannot be derived from the information of the country of destination that the seller is bound to observe the public law provisions of this country').

buyer to carry out the necessary investigations.[156] Making the buyer bear the burden of doing so avoids the higher cost which would otherwise have to be incurred if this burden were borne by the seller. If sellers were put in the position of being compelled to investigate the relevant regulations, in order to alleviate the risk of being held liable in the future, the prices for the goods would also have to rise because they would have to spread that additional cost and/or risk of liability to buyers. That would only hinder commerce by making trade more expensive. In short, allocating this risk to the buyer promotes economic efficiency.

In the context of Article 35(2)(b), it has been explained that in contrast to 'special circumstances' (2) and (3) set out in *New Zealand Mussels*, 'special circumstance' (1) does not seek to resolve the information asymmetry between the parties and consequently has little relevance under subparagraph (b). However, this exception may have greater relevance in the context of Article 35(2)(a) which is not concerned, as is subparagraph (b), with communicating a purpose to the buyer, but is based on the 'purposes for which the goods would ordinarily be used'. Since the regulations are the same in the seller's country and at destination, there is no other set of regulations in any other country that would be relevant to defining the 'ordinary purpose(s)'. With regulations being the same, the requirements contained in them are likely to determine the meaning of the 'ordinary purpose(s)'. But if the seller knows about or cannot be unaware of the destination of the goods and the regulations there, 'special circumstance' (1) is redundant since 'special circumstance' (3) already covers this scenario. This leaves cases where the seller does not know or cannot know about the destination or the regulations there.

Where the seller knows about or cannot be unaware of the destination, but not the regulations there, it has been held that the seller cannot be held liable for non-compliance with regulations at destination.[157] Should the fact that the regulations are the same in both countries change this position? The answer is 'yes'. If the 'ordinary use' is interpreted on the basis of what the parties could reasonably have intended, then, as stated in the context of Article 35(1), each party, in the absence of any relevant circumstances, is likely to have expected the 'ordinary use' to be defined with reference to the regulations in its own country. Because the requirements in the regulations in both countries are the same, there emerges a common intention that the 'ordinary use' means that the goods ought to comply with the *requirements* contained in the two regulations. The result will be the same even if the 'ordinary use' is interpreted in a way which is detached from the parties' intentions or state of mind (actual or presumed). It can be argued that since it is only these two countries that are relevant to the parties' contract, the goods will ordinarily be used in such circumstances in a way which is

[156] See Gillette and Ferrari (n 12) 8; CP Gillett and SD Walt, *Sales Law: Domestic and International*, 2nd edn (New York, Foundation Press and Thomson West, 2009) 364.

[157] See n 150 above.

compliant with the (same) requirements in both regulations. Thus, the value of 'special circumstance' (1) lies in its ability to help to define the 'ordinary use' of the goods where the seller is not in the position to know about the regulations at destination or even the destination itself.

B. Imperative of a Case-by-Case Analysis

The propositions in *New Zealand Mussels* being merely guidelines, the circumstances of each case are decisive. The special circumstances mentioned in this case cover a wide range of scenarios where it may be more appropriate for the responsibility to be allocated to the seller. For example, where the public law requirements are the same in the country of the seller and in the importing country, such as where these countries are Member States of the European Union, there will usually be little doubt that a reasonable person in the seller's position will regard the ordinary use of the goods as including compliance with what are the same regulations in both EU Member States.[158] However, there may be many other factors, such as the price, the parties' prior course of dealing, trade usages or industry standards, the parties' identities or business standing,[159] which can also be relevant in assessing whether the ordinary use includes compliance with the regulations in the country of destination.[160] These other factors, on the one hand, and the presence of the special circumstances mentioned in *New Zealand Mussels*, on the other, may point to different conclusions.

Suppose that prior to the conclusion of the contract a new standard is adopted in the industry to which both parties belong, and that standard is based on different requirements to those in the regulations in the country of use. Suppose also the parties have had a long-standing business relationship (mentioned in *New Zealand Mussels* as a special circumstance) and that the seller supplied the goods in the past complying with the public law regulations in the country of use, which were the same as the previous industry standard. But on this occasion, the seller chose to comply with the new industry standard and not with the regulations in the country of use. The seller may or may not be in breach of Article 35(2)(a),[161] but

[158] See Schwenzer, Hachem and Kee (n 33) para 16.

[159] See ibid para 31.138 (arguing that much greater knowledge of the regulations in the country of use can be expected of a multinational company than of a small business which exports the goods to that country for the first time).

[160] See, similarly, Kröll (n 3) para 93.

[161] The seller may argue that because the regulations and the previous industry standard were the same, it did not need to differentiate between the two but that the parties' intention was to follow the industry standard because both parties were part of the industry. The seller may also argue that it would not be reasonable for the buyer to expect the seller not to follow the industry standard since doing so might negatively affect its business reputation and standing. Such considerations may be taken into account in evaluating what constitutes the goods' ordinary use in those circumstances.

what the example shows is that the mere presence of one of the 'special circumstances' is not necessarily sufficient to hold the seller liable since that circumstance will have to be evaluated against other relevant factors.[162] This example requires the evaluation of whether, in the eyes of a reasonable person, the ordinary use should be defined with reference to a newly adopted industry standard or public law regulations.

The buyer may bring a claim not only in connection with non-compliance with the regulations in the country of use, but also because the goods do not meet the requirements in the seller's country. This may be so where the requirements in the seller's country are higher and more demanding than those in the country of use. In such a case, the reasoning seeking to deal with the asymmetry of information, such as that found in *New Zealand Mussels*, loses much of its relevance. Claims of this kind are to be resolved on a case-by-case basis, with a number of factors being potentially relevant.[163] The fact that the contract price[164] corresponds to the market value of high quality goods, based on standards such as those in the seller's country, may indicate the parties' intention that the regulations in the seller's country were to define the goods' ordinary use. The same may be the case if there is evidence showing that the buyer has selected this seller as a result of a competitive bidding process and the selection was likely to be due to the seller being based in a country known for high quality standards.[165] In principle, a communication by the buyer, particularly prior to making the contract, noting the importance of quality[166] may also be a factor pointing in favour of the intention to link the goods with the higher standards.[167] In the absence of any of these factors and where the goods meet the requirements in the country of use, there can be strong arguments to the contrary. It can be contended that the buyer's failure to specify the applicable standards or to communicate them as a particular purpose, and the very fact that the goods do not meet the requirements of the seller's country and are sold to another country, meeting the latter's standards, show a lack of any intention to subject the goods to the regulations in the seller's country.[168]

[162] See the discussion of Appellate Court Arnhem, 97/700 and 98/046, 27 April 1999 (The Netherlands), available at http://cisgw3.law.pace.edu/cases/990427n1.html in Chapter 3 illustrating the same point.

[163] Schwenzer (n 49) para 16.

[164] See, similarly, ibid.

[165] Kröll (n 3) para 95.

[166] Even if it falls short of communicating a particular purpose or being a contractual term.

[167] See Art 8(3); also Kröll (n 3) para 95.

[168] See Schwenzer (n 49) para 16; Kröll (n 3) para 94.

C. Changes to Public Law Regulations and Other Related Changes Subsequent to the Time of Assessing Conformity

Assuming that the goods *are* subject to public law regulations, whether in the seller's country or in the country of use, the next question is whether changes to those public law regulations or other changes (such as newly emerging scientific evidence or suspicions about the goods being unsafe), which happen after the time when the contract was made and after the time with reference to which conformity is to be assessed (time of the passage of risk),[169] are to be taken into account in evaluating conformity. In *Frozen Pork*,[170] a Belgian seller sold, in April 1999, to a German buyer frozen pork which was eventually delivered to the buyer's clients in Bosnia-Herzegovina. The risk had passed to the buyer in April, but in June suspicions had arisen that the meat originating in Belgium contained dioxin which led, between June and July 1999, to the adoption of regulations in Germany, the European Union and Belgium declaring the meat unmarketable unless accompanied by a certificate declaring it as 'dioxin free'. On 1 July, the authorities in Bosnia-Herzegovina also prohibited the sale of the delivered goods without a certificate and, after the seller failed to provide one after repeated requests by the buyer, the goods were destroyed. The German Federal Supreme Court held the seller liable for breach of its obligation to deliver goods fit for their ordinary use,[171] which was interpreted as meaning that the goods ought to be marketable and resalable. The subsequent suspicions of contamination[172] which arose and were followed by the regulations throughout Europe led the Court to draw an inference that at the time the risk had passed the goods had already been contaminated.

The CISG recognises that a lack of conformity may exist at the time of the passage of risk, but may become apparent only after that time, in which case the seller is still liable.[173] In this respect, the decision may be justifiable. But it is the Court's explanation for drawing the said inference that is less convincing, demonstrating a strong drive to ensure that the seller is held liable. The decision states that '[w]hether and to what extent the meat delivered to [the buyer] was actually contaminated with dioxin is irrelevant because the suspicion alone, which excluded the marketability, which became apparent later and which was not invalidated by the Seller, has a bearing on the resaleability and tradeability'. Seemingly wary that such a statement could open doors to numerous weak or even frivolous claims,

[169] Art 36(1).

[170] Federal Supreme Court, VIII ZR 67/04, 2 March 2005 (Germany), available at http://cisgw3.law.pace.edu/cases/050302g1.html.

[171] See Art 35(2)(a).

[172] See, generally, I Schwenzer and D Tebel, 'Suspicions, Mere Suspicions: Non-Conformity of the Goods?' (2014) 19 *Unif L Rev* 152.

[173] See Art 36(1).

based on alleged subsequent suspicions, the Court somewhat qualified its stance by stating that it did not need to 'decide whether the suspicion that certain goods may be harmful to health always represent[ed] a breach of contract with regard to foodstuffs' and that '[a]t least if the suspicion, as in this case, has led to public measures that preclude the goods' tradeability, the goods must be viewed as not conforming with the contract for the area of wholesale and intermediate trade'.

The decision has been criticised on the ground that it ignores the Convention's requirement as to the time with reference to which conformity is to be assessed, since both the suspicions of contamination and the ensuing regulations arose after the relevant time.[174] At the relevant time, in April 1999, when the risk passed to the buyer, there were neither suspicions of contamination nor regulations in respect of these goods. But the issue is probably more subtle than that because the real question is whether subsequent developments (whether public law regulations, suspicions and/or after-acquired knowledge) should, as a matter of principle, be taken into account when assessing conformity of the goods *at an earlier time*, when the risk passed to the buyer. The decision seems to have been driven by an impulse, only strengthened by the existence of public law regulations, to hold the seller liable because the goods were potentially dangerous to human life and health. However, that impulse, or arguably even a drive to ensure that dangerous goods are not traded and to send a strong signal that high safety standards are expected of sellers, appears to have led the Court not to engage sufficiently rigorously with the requirement as to the time with reference to which conformity is to be assessed.

Two sets of views can arise in this regard. On the one hand, it can be argued that this decision is correct because subsequent developments were *evidence* of a lack of conformity at the time of the passage of risk. As a matter of policy, it can be stated that whilst neither party may be blamed for the after-acquired knowledge or subsequent suspicions and regulations, the buyer is the 'least blameworthy' party[175] and should therefore be protected. It is also arguable that ignoring subsequent developments would simply be 'artificial'.[176] On the other hand, such decisions create much uncertainty for sellers who will not be able to predict whether their conformity obligations have been complied with. Having regard to subsequent developments interferes with and limits the parties' ability to divide responsibilities between themselves at the time when the contract is made. Whilst the Convention's rule on the time with reference to which conformity is to be assessed is not always based on the time when the contract is made, it is based on that

[174] See H Nakamura, 'Conformity of Goods with Regulatory Restrictions: BGH Decisions in the Mussels and the Pork Case' (2011) 15 *Vindobona J Int'l Commercial L Arbitration* 53.

[175] Schwenzer, Hachem and Kee (n 33) para 31.142, in the context of the issue of whether suspicions alone can affect the evaluation of conformity of the goods.

[176] *Henry Kendall & Sons v William Lillico & Sons Ltd* [1969] 2 AC 31.

time in some cases.[177] Legal risks, flowing from the approach in *Frozen Pork*, may induce sellers to exclude the Convention or to incur additional costs in drafting contracts in a way preventing such an approach. Neither of these outcomes is in line with the Convention's aspirations of becoming a uniform law and facilitating trade, by promoting economically efficient outcomes.

Both views highlight valuable considerations and a balanced solution is called for. One solution could be a guideline that courts and tribunals should exercise much caution before deciding to take subsequent developments into account in order not to generate uncertainty in the international legal environment. Subsequent developments must clearly evidence the existence of a lack of conformity at the time of the passage of risk if they are to be taken into consideration. Another solution is to establish a rebuttable presumption that subsequent developments are not taken into account and leave it to a party with an interest in proving otherwise to bear the burden of doing so. The latter solution accommodates well the concerns for legal certainty, but it is difficult to ensure its uniform implementation. Therefore, at least, the former solution needs to be promoted.

D. Legal Nature of Public Law Regulations and the Reality of their Enforcement

In *New Zealand Mussels*, the regulations issued by the relevant authorities in the buyer's country were not binding and were in the nature of a recommendation. It was not necessary to decide whether that would have had any bearing on allocating the responsibilities between the parties because the seller was found not to have had a duty to comply with those regulations. Nevertheless, the question, which is relevant not only under Article 35(2)(a) but also under Article 35(2)(b) and Article 35(1) is this: if the regulations in the country of use are in principle found to be applicable, should their legal nature and the question of how rigorously they are in fact enforced have any bearing on determining the content of the seller's conformity obligations? Some domestic legal systems, for example, are sensitive to these matters and would give an affirmative answer.[178] The Convention's

[177] A general rule is that 'in respect of goods sold in transit', the risk 'passes to the buyer from the time of the conclusion of the contract' (Art 67(1), first sentence).

[178] In the English case *Hazlewood Grocery Ltd v Lion Foods Ltd* [2007] EWHC 1887 (QB), the position of the Food Standards Agency was initially in the nature of an *advice*, which did not compel a recall of the chilli powder containing Para Red, but the court nevertheless interpreted the satisfactory quality test with reference to that advice because the recall of the products was 'the inevitable and foreseeable consequence of the FSA advice'. In another English case, *Bramhill v Edwards* [2004] EWCA Civ 403, non-compliance of a vehicle with the requirements as to width under the applicable Regulations was not held to be a breach of SGA 1979, s 14(2) because in practice such vehicles were still able to be insured and the authorities did not enforce the regulations strictly, which meant that there was no real risk of prosecution.

experience thus far is tentatively pointing in the opposite direction. Although the issue did not arise directly in *New Zealand Mussels*, this decision may be seen as implying that had the regulations been applicable, the seller would have been deemed to be liable notwithstanding their recommendatory nature. This issue arose more directly in another case (*Rynpoort Trading*)[179] where the Dutch seller of flour containing potassium bromate, which was banned in the European Union and under the international standards adopted by both the Netherlands and the importing country, Mozambique, pointed to the fact that the import of the banned potassium bromate was de facto permitted by the authorities in Mozambique. This point was reinforced by the approval of the goods by a government appointed company after its pre-shipment inspection. That argument was dismissed, with the reality surrounding the application of the formal laws ignored for the purpose of a legal analysis.

The case where formal law is not strictly enforced is analogous to that where the regulations are recommendatory, since in both cases there may be a reasonable expectation that the relevant standards do not always have to materialise. A preferable view is that neither the regulations' legal nature nor how they are actually applied in practice can be ignored in defining the seller's obligations. The broad nature of the Convention's rules on conformity and the Convention's demand for identifying the parties' reasonable expectations in the light of the circumstances dictate that these factors be taken into account.[180] The nature of the regulations and how they are enforced in reality are part of the background against which parties operate and against which reasonable expectations should be inferred. That does not mean that a mere fact that regulations are advisory in nature will necessarily absolve the seller from what would otherwise be its duty to comply with those regulations. The issue depends on the circumstances. If, for example, it can be demonstrated that all respectable traders in the industry are expected to comply even with those regulations which are only recommendatory, and that their business reputations would otherwise suffer, it may well be reasonable to treat such regulations on a par with those of a mandatory nature. In contrast, their formal status of being mandatory should not necessarily be decisive, if there is strong evidence that in reality the authorities routinely turn a blind eye on them.

[179] Appellate Court s-Gravenhage, 99/474, 23 April 2003 (The Netherlands), available at http://cisgw3.law.pace.edu/cases/030423n1.html. See also Chapter 2 for the discussion of this case.

[180] See Art 8(3).

E. Is Article 35(2)(b) CISG Better Suited than Article 35(2)(a) to Deal with the Case of Public Law Regulations?

Article 35(2)(b) has been seen by some commentators as being better suited than Art 35(2)(a) to deal with the allocation of responsibilities in the case of the goods' non-compliance with the public law regulations in the country of use.[181] It has been suggested that subparagraph (b) provides a more just solution[182] by affording greater flexibility and better accommodating the individual circumstances than subparagraph (a).[183] The notion of an *ordinary* use arguably implies a use or a purpose which has gained a degree of *common* recognition. That may not sit too comfortably with the infinity of factual scenarios, which include countless and differing public law regulations across the world, as well as a variety of different circumstances in which the parties find themselves. Compliance with the regulations seems more consonant with being a special or a particular purpose. Therefore, it may be preferable for Article 35(2)(b), rather than (2)(a), to be the primary vehicle and legal basis for allocating responsibilities for non-compliance with regulations in the country of use. If so, the finding that the buyer has not made known to the seller a particular purpose of complying with such regulations, or that there was no actual or reasonable reliance on the seller's skill and judgement, should, in most cases, provide the final and definitive resolution of the issue of the seller's liability. Only in rare cases where no communication of a particular purpose can be inferred but where it is still arguable that the seller can be reasonably expected to comply with regulations in the country of use[184] can Article 35(2)(a) prove to be of value. However, subparagraphs (a) and (b) are not presented in the Convention as mutually exclusive, with the result that they can be applied cumulatively and/or successively. Courts and tribunals have also routinely used Article 35(2)(a) to allocate responsibilities for non-compliance with public law regulations. In the light of this, the suggestion that (2)(b) should be the primary legal framework for dealing with public law regulations may be too difficult to implement. It may also disrupt the existing body of cases, which have relied on Article 35(2)(a), and, bearing in mind the Convention's aspirations of uniform application, it may not be worthwhile for this suggestion to be pursued too rigorously.

[181] See P Schlechtriem, 'Uniform Sales Law in the Decisions of the *Bundesgerichtshof*' http://cisgw3.law.pace.edu/cisg/biblio/schlechtriem3.html; Schwenzer (n 49) para 18.

[182] Schelchtriem (n 181).

[183] Schwenzer, Hachem and Kee (n 33) para 31.139.

[184] For example, if there is a trade usage in a particular sector that suppliers, as a matter of course, are expected to comply with public law regulations in a country to which the goods are exported.

XI. PROOF

The principle that the party who asserts a right must prove the preconditions for the existence of that right means that the buyer bears the burden of proving that the goods are not fit for their ordinary purposes.[185] In some cases, the discharge of this burden may not pose any particular difficulties for the buyer. The seller may accept that it has committed a breach,[186] or its conduct, such as where it has agreed to replace the goods, may be taken to mean that the seller has admitted a breach.[187] In some other cases, the difficulties of proof are not as easy to overcome. It may simply be impossible to establish whether a lack of conformity arose before or after the risk of loss of or damage to the goods has passed to the buyer.[188] In a case where the buyer brought a claim in respect of contaminated milk powder, it was held that a spot check analysis of the powder 'did not permit a definitive statement about the "sole decisive question" whether the powder was infested by inactive lipase at the time of the transfer of the risk'.[189] That meant that the evidence based on such an analysis was incapable of proving that contamination had occurred prior to the passage of risk. The buyer may also be prevented from furnishing sufficient evidence of a lack of conformity if the goods have already been consumed or used as a component in the production process. In one case[190] involving the sale of dye for clothes, the court dismissed the buyer's claim of defects in the goods on the basis that there could have been a number of factors, other than those within the seller's sphere of influence, which could have caused the defects in clothes produced with the use of the dye:

> The merchandise supplied by [seller] only constitutes part of [buyer's] production process. That merchandise is the ink that, with heat, is printed on the fabric supplied by other parties. The final product depends on the fabric base, the atmospheric and conservation conditions, the printing temperature, etc. It is, therefore,

[185] See Appellate Court Antwerp, 2001/AR/1737, 16 December 2002 (Belgium), available at http://cisgw3.law.pace.edu/cases/021216b1.html; District Court Vigevano, 12 July 2000, available at http://cisgw3.law.pace.edu/cases/000712i3.html. See Chapter 3 for a detailed discussion of the issues of proof.

[186] See *Hydraulic Press*, CIETAC Arbitration, 23 December 2002, available at http://cisgw3.law.pace.edu/cases/021223c1.html, where the seller signed a joint memorandum acknowledging various defects.

[187] ICAC Arbitration No 166/1995, 12 March 1996, available at http://cisgw3.law.pace.edu/cases/960312r1.html.

[188] Which is the relevant time for assessing conformity (see Art 36(1)). See Appellate Court Antwerp, 16 December 2002 (n 185) ('In the current state of the procedure ... it is impossible to determine when the defect has arisen').

[189] Federal Supreme Court, VIII ZR 304/00, 9 January 2002 (Germany), available at http://cisgw3.law.pace.edu/cases/020109g1.html.

[190] Appellate Court Barcelona, 755/95-C, 20 June 1997 (Spain), available at http://cisgw3.law.pace.edu/cases/970620s4.html.

difficult to see how any examination of the resulting fabric, could show the origin of the defect.[191]

A lack of conformity can, in principle, be established by different types of evidence, including witnesses,[192] testimony of experts[193] and documents.[194] But, as explained earlier, the buyer's right to adduce evidence may be restricted by domestic rules on the admissibility of evidence.[195] In one case, the evidence produced by the buyer's expert was rejected by a court in Italy on the basis that 'under Italian procedure, [a technical] opinion can be rendered only by an expert witness appointed by the court'.[196]

[191] Ibid.

[192] See District Court Munich, 29 November 2005 (n 73).

[193] See ICC Arbitration Case No 10377 (n 112).

[194] Such as a bill of lading, a mate's receipt and a certificate of quality. See, eg ICAC No 56/2003, 2 February 2004 ('the materials of the case contain certificates of cargo quality inspection ... confirming the conformity of the goods with the quality requirements of the contract, as well as the mate's receipt ... confirming the conformity of the quantity of the goods and their description with the requirements of the contract'). For a detailed discussion, see Chapter 8.

[195] For a detailed discussion of this issue, see Chapter 3.

[196] District Court Vigevano, 12 July 2000 (n 185).

5

Conformity with a Sample or Model and Packaging; Exemptions from Liability

I. CONFORMITY WITH A SAMPLE OR MODEL

A. General

IN SOME CASES, the seller may provide the buyer with a sample or model of the goods before a contract is made and the question then arises as to whether the seller is bound by the qualities and characteristics of that sample or model. The Convention's rule in Article 35(2)(c) provides in this respect that if the parties have not agreed otherwise, the goods are non-conforming unless they 'possess the qualities of goods which the seller has held out to the buyer as a sample or model'. Giving out a sample[1] or model[2] will often seek to provide a tangible and concrete demonstration of description and quality of the goods,[3] as well as of some other features of conformity, such as packaging. In fact, in some cases a sample may be the only way for the parties to agree on characteristics of the goods, such as where a particular characteristic is incapable of being described in a contract or expressed sufficiently precisely in a language, through formulae or technical specifications. For example, if the contract is for the sale of a chemical used to make perfumery, it is only the use of a sample that can make it possible for the parties to determine and agree on a flavour of the

[1] A sample is drawn from the bulk of the goods.

[2] A model is provided where the goods themselves are not available and, in contrast with a sample, is not drawn from the bulk of the goods (see, eg Comment 8 on § 2-313 of the Uniform Commercial Code (UCC) in *Uniform Commercial Code: 2009–2010 Edition* (West-Thomson Reuters, 2009)).

[3] See CM Bianca in CM Bianca and J Bonell (eds), *Commentary on the International Sales Law* (Milan, Giuffrè, 1987) 275.

chemical.[4] Normally, once the buyer obtains access to a sample or model, it is then expected to examine it, and if no objection is raised, the sample/model becomes the basis for the parties' bargain. Consequently, if the goods do not conform with the sample/model, the seller is in breach of both the contract and Article 35(2)(c).

This is an idyllic picture, which does not reveal the difficulties inherent in this provision. There may be, first of all, some disagreement as to its legal nature. On the one hand, there is a view that this provision can only be triggered if the parties have intended that the sample or model would represent a benchmark against which conformity of the goods is to be evaluated. The proof of such an intention or lack thereof may benefit or disadvantage either of the two parties, since in different cases each of them may want to treat the sample/model as the basis of the contract. The seller may argue that the goods are conforming because an alleged lack of conformity was present in the sample shown to the buyer. In one such case, the seller's claim was rejected. The court stated that a 'sample only has binding effect where the parties actually agreed so' and held that the seller had failed to prove such an agreement, as well as to show 'specifically that the sample also had the same defects as [those] alleged by the buyer'.[5] The buyer, in turn, may contend that a lack of conformity was not present in the sample and therefore the goods' non-compliance with the sample makes the seller liable. In one case, where the sample had been shown to the buyer before the conclusion of the contract, such a claim by the buyer was dismissed because 'neither in the Contract nor in the communications between the two parties was there [an] agreement indicating that [the seller] should deliver goods in conformity with the samples'.[6]

On the other hand, it has been suggested that the mere act of 'holding out'[7] of a sample or model is in itself sufficient to make it compulsory for the seller to comply with the sample/model.[8] On this view, no finding of any implicit agreement or intentions to this effect is necessary[9] because,

[4] See *Heliotropin*, CIETAC Arbitration, 10 July 1993, available at http://cisgw3.law.pace.edu/cases/930710c1.html ('under the current scientific and technical position, the comparison [with the sample] method is the only feasible one; that the sample is the basis to inspect color and flavor'). So central was a sample in this case that the approval of the sample by the buyer was the condition of the contract coming into force.

[5] District Court Berlin, 52 S 247/94, 15 September 1994 (Germany), available at http://cisgw3.law.pace.edu/cases/940915g1.html.

[6] *Water Pump*, CIETAC Arbitration, 3 August 2006, available at http://cisgw3.law.pace.edu/cases/060803c1.html. The original quotation referred to an 'express agreement'. Even if the view that there must be an agreement for a sample to be binding on the seller is adopted, there is little justification in requiring an express agreement. Arts 8 and 9 make it clear that an agreement does not need to be express and may be implied.

[7] As provided for in Art 35(2)(c).

[8] I Schwenzer in I Schwenzer (ed), *Schlechtriem and Schwenzer, Commentary on the UN Convention on the International Sale of Goods (CISG)*, 3rd edn (Oxford, OUP, 2010) Art 35, para 25.

[9] Ibid.

generally, a sample/model is supplied for the purpose of describing the goods and demonstrating their various characteristics.[10] The proponents of this view suggest[11] that it is for this reason that the CISG, in contrast with its 1964 predecessor, the Convention relating to a Uniform Law on the International Sale of Goods (ULIS), does not require a seller's express or implicit undertaking of conformity with a sample/model.[12]

At first sight, there is a considerable difference between the two positions. The first view looks at the provision as entirely dependent on the parties' intentions, as they are *actually* interpreted in the light of the facts. The seller's obligation is implied *in fact*. The second view may seem to detach Article 35(2)(c) from the particular facts and to imbue it with an autonomous meaning: whenever a sample/model is held out, the obligation to ensure conformity with it is implied. If so, the obligation is implied *in law*. The latter view has the advantage of providing certainty, but appears to be blind to the particular circumstances and may therefore produce injustice in individual cases. This, however, may not be an entirely accurate representation of the second view. The words 'holding out' in Article 35(2)(c) can be interpreted not just as giving or handing over a sample/model, as was the case in the ULIS, but also as proffering it as something that a seller is willing and able to supply.[13] Viewed this way, 'holding out' would imply that the mere giving of a sample/model is not sufficient for Article 35(2)(c) to be triggered. A seller's intention to present it as what will be supplied under a contract would seem to be a prerequisite. If this is true, there is not much difference between the two views, since the second view would also require the seller's intention to be bound by the sample/model to be proved.

This is in line with the Convention's position which, through its contextual rules of interpretation of the parties' statements and conduct,[14] makes clear that the parties' intentions in the particular circumstances are decisive. In any case, even if Article 35(2)(c) had a fixed meaning whereby a mere handing over of a sample/model led to the implication of an obligation of compliance with it, Article 6 would still allow parties to derogate from it, expressly or implicitly. Therefore, there is no doubt that every case has to be decided on the basis of its facts. At the same time, there is much to be said for giving buyers and sellers some general guidance about the premise

[10] S Kröll in S Kröll, L Mistelis and P Viscasillas (eds), *UN Convention on Contracts for the International Sale of Goods (CISG): Commentary* (Munich, CH Beck/Hart Publishing, 2011) Art. 35, para 129.

[11] Ibid.

[12] 'The seller shall not have fulfilled his obligation to deliver the goods where he has handed over: (c) goods which lack the qualities of a sample or model which the seller has handed over or sent to the buyer, unless the seller has submitted it without any express or implied undertaking that the goods would conform therewith' (Art 33(1)(c) ULIS).

[13] See Bianca (n 3) 275.

[14] See Arts 8 and 9.

from which the allocation of risks will proceed. A sample/model is usually provided to demonstrate the goods' description and characteristics with a view to contract on this basis,[15] and that should give rise to a reasonable expectation on the part of the buyer that the goods will correspond with the sample/model.[16] For this reason, sellers ought to be aware that even mere sending or handing over of a sample/model may be treated as implying an obligation of compliance with it. If that is not their intention, sellers are well advised to make their intentions clear when supplying a sample/model. In any event, it would seem that a party who wishes to contend that the sample/model was not intended to be the basis of a contract has, on balance, a somewhat greater burden of presenting evidence and persuasion than that borne by the party relying on the sample.[17]

As explained, however, whether conformity with a sample or model is required is, ultimately, a matter of interpreting the parties' intentions. It may be helpful, therefore, to identify some common scenarios which highlight certain patterns in how the parties' intentions are likely to be interpreted. For example, the buyer's rejection of the sample/model or its delivery by the seller 'without any obligation'[18] will usually evidence that there was no intention for the sample/model to be binding on the seller. If in its complaint to the seller the buyer refers to a particular defect in the goods but raises no objections as to any inconsistency between the goods and an earlier provided sample, that may be taken as evidencing the parties' intention not to treat the sample as binding on the seller. In a case where it was so decided, the tribunal held that by sending a sample to the buyer, the seller was merely trying to promote its products.[19] Where the buyer of scrap metal inspects the seller's facilities, there may be insufficient evidence

[15] See Comment IV on Art 2:302 of the Draft Common Frame of Reference (DCFR) in C von Bar and E Clive (eds), *Principles, Definitions and Model Rules of European Private Law: Draft Common Frame of Reference (DCFR)* (Munich, Sellier European Law Publishers, 2009) vol II, 1290 ('As a rule, the goods sold must conform to the sample given prior to the purchase').

[16] Kröll (n 10) para 129.

[17] For a somewhat similar position, see Comment 8 on § 2-313 UCC (n 2) ('In general, the presumption is that any sample or model, just as any affirmation of fact, is intended to become a basis of the bargain. But there is no escape from the question of fact').

[18] See P Schlechtriem and P Butler, *UN Law on International Sales* (Berlin, Heidelberg/Springer-Verlag, 2009) 120.

[19] *Fiberglass Mesh*, CIETAC Arbitration, 6 November 2003, available at http://cisgw3.law.pace.edu/cases/031106c1.html. The tribunal also based its decision on a position that for a sample to be binding, 'the parties [ought to] seal up the samples and stipulate [their binding character] definitely in the contract'. There is no basis in either of these two requirements in the CISG. If these requirements (or at least the one concerning the 'sealing up' of the samples) were derived from contract interpretation, there is no explanation of why the contract should be interpreted in that way. See also Commercial Court St Gallen, HG.2010.421-HGK, 14 June 2012 (Switzerland), available at http://cisgw3.law.pace.edu/cases/120614s1.html, where the specific qualities relied upon by the buyer were not apparent from the sample and the court held that the sample was used to give the buyer a general impression of the product, its taste and texture.

as to the binding character of a sample even if the buyer takes the samples of the goods. In a case[20] based on these facts, it was held that, having toured the seller's facilities, the buyer knew what it was buying, which must have meant that no reliance had been placed on the sample. Several price allowances were also given by the seller in this case because of excessive sand contamination and the court appeared to rely on this fact in rejecting the argument that the contract was 'a sale by sample'. However, subsequent price allowances do not necessarily point to any lack of intention to contract on the basis of a sample. What they may be taken to show is an intention to vary the original agreement that the goods were to be free from sand, only confirmed by the sample if it were sand free, and/or to waive the right to demand that the goods were free from sand contamination.[21]

Where the seller stated that the goods would be of better quality than the samples delivered to the buyer, the sample had been taken to represent the minimum benchmark of quality and description that the buyer was entitled to expect.[22] At the same time, such statements by the seller may show that the sample was given only for guidance, with the parties' intention being that the seller would deliver the goods of better quality than that represented by the sample. In such a case, Article 35(2)(c) is unlikely to be applicable. A trade usage[23] may also have something to say on what can be used as a sample.[24] In one case,[25] the court was inclined to accept that there was a trade usage that a sample of fish ought to come from the current year's catch: 'If the seller, knowing the international trade custom that fish must be from the current catch-quota, nonetheless delivers [old] fish as a sample without disclosing that fact, then the lack of conformity with the contract in this shipment [of the sample] is not a characteristic within the meaning of CISG Art 35(2)(c)'. Even if common understandings in a particular trade sector do not amount to a trade usage, they can still be relevant in explaining a commercial context against which the parties' intentions are interpreted. Thus, insights from a particular commercial sector may shed light as to how frequently sales occur with reference to a sample or model or even as to the procedure of tendering samples/models. For example, in the modern trade in commodities, 'goods are more likely to

[20] *Dunn Paving Ltd v Aerco Trading Inc* [2001] OJ No 1736 (Canada).

[21] '[E]ven if this was a sale by sample, over the term of the contract, Aerco acquiesced in the method of adjustment and cannot now be said to complain and ask the court to go back to day one and revise the course of business dealings between the two companies between April of 1995 and May of 1997' (ibid para 11).

[22] *Agricultural Products*, CIETAC Arbitration, 18 September 1996, available at http://cisgw3.law.pace.edu/cases/960918c2.html.

[23] See Art 9 CISG.

[24] See, similarly, *Benjamin's Sale of Goods*, 9th edn (London, Thompson-Sweet & Maxwell, 2014) para 11-074.

[25] Supreme Court, 2 Ob 48/02a, 27 February 2003 (Austria), available at http://cisgw3.law.pace.edu/cases/030227a3.html.

be sold according to grades based on analysis and protein content, and laid down by inspection agencies, than by sample',[26] but if samples *are* used in the commodities trade there will often be a machinery for tendering them.[27]

As noted, a typical scenario of a sale 'by sample or model' is where one is provided before the contract is made. What if a sample is given after that time? Whilst this is not a 'paradigm sale by sample',[28] it is submitted that Article 35(2)(c) can in principle be triggered in such a scenario. If the contract itself states that the goods are to correspond to the sample or model which the seller will provide, that is a clear indication of the parties' intentions that a sample/model will be the source of the goods' description, quality and possibly some other characteristics. If the seller has a choice as to whether to tender a sample/model,[29] the question of whether a sample/model, when tendered, is intended to be binding depends on the parties' intentions and the guidelines above are relevant here. If the contract already contains some description or quality provisions, the first question is whether the sample/model is used to define some other characteristics, which are not covered by the contract. If so, there is a clear division of functions between the contract and the sample/model, with each of them defining different aspects of conformity. If not, the next question is whether it is the contract or the sample/model which is intended to define the relevant aspects of conformity. Once again, the answer depends on the parties' intentions. If the contractual provisions on quality and description are very detailed, they may well have been intended to govern conformity of the goods, as in one such case[30] where a 'sample model' was deemed to be given only for the purpose of 'orientation'. But where they are not as detailed, a sample/model may be viewed as a more appropriate source of defining conformity. In such a case, the sample/model may be held to be intended as the sole source of description and quality, with the contract provisions merely intended to give general information on the kind of goods with which the contract is concerned.[31]

There will be situations where it is the buyer and not the seller who provides a sample/model. On one occasion, the court was prepared to treat such a case as falling within Article 35(2)(c). The fact that the sample had been held out by the buyer was seen as 'insignificant'.[32] There is some

[26] M Bridge, *The Sale of Goods*, 3rd edn (Oxford, OUP, 2014) para 7.136.

[27] E McKendrick, *Goode on Commercial Law*, 4th edn (London, Penguin Books, 2010) 354.

[28] See *Benjamin's Sale of Goods* (n 24) para 11-077.

[29] See ibid.

[30] District Court Schaffhausen, 11/1999/99, 27 January 2004 (Switzerland), available at http://cisgw3.law.pace.edu/cases/040127s1.html.

[31] See ibid. See also the discussion of Federal Supreme Court, 4C.296/2000/rnd, 22 December 2000 (Switzerland), available at http://cisgw3.law.pace.edu/cases/001222s1.html in Chapter 2.

[32] Appellate Court Graz, 6 R 194/95, 9 November 1995 (Austria), available at http://cisgw3.law.pace.edu/cases/951109a3.html.

strength in this position because arguably what matters is whether or not the parties have agreed that a particular sample/model would be the basis of their bargain and not which of the two parties has 'held it out'. However, legal certainty demands adherence to the text of Article 35(2)(c) which leaves no doubt that it applies where the seller holds out a sample/model to the buyer. For this reason, the prevailing view in literature which regards such cases as not falling within Article 35(2)(c)[33] is preferable. This means that where a buyer holds out a sample/model, the question of whether the seller is bound to comply with such a sample/model will be resolved on the basis of Article 35(1).[34]

It may be that by delivering a sample/model the buyer communicated a particular purpose to the seller within the meaning of Article 35(2)(b). In a case involving the sale of cotton twilled fabric,[35] the buyer's supply of a sample was deemed to constitute an implicit communication of a particular purpose, which related to the fabric's seam slippage strength required for manufacturing mattresses. This decision was made in light of the fact that both parties operated in the mattresses production industry and were in the position to know about the purpose for which the fabric had been ordered. The contract was also silent on the seam slippage strength which, the court found, was 'highly unusual'. This factor could only strengthen the conclusion that the sample was indeed meant to communicate a particular purpose.[36]

B. How Far is a Sample or Model Allowed to 'Speak'?[37]

The next question is whether any kind of non-compliance with a sample or model constitutes a breach of Article 35(2)(c) or whether in every case it needs to be determined what characteristics a sample/model represents. The former position has little regard for the particular circumstances. If it were adopted, a party contending that a sample/model was not intended to be binding in respect of a particular characteristic would, in many cases, be unjustifiably disadvantaged. A better way is to interpret Article 35(2)(c) as being fully responsive to the surrounding circumstances. There are two

33 Schwenzer (n 8) para 28; Kröll (n 10) para 136; Schlechtriem and Butler (n 18) 141.

34 See Appellate Court Graz (n 32) ('Even if one assumed that Art 35(2)(c) CISG was not applicable to such a case, an agreement of the parties that the stone was to correspond to the color sample would constitute an agreement on a specific quality under Art 35(1) CISG ').

35 District Court Aschaffenburg, 1 HK O 89/03, 20 April 2006 (Germany), available at http://cisgw3.law.pace.edu/cases/060420g1.html.

36 '[T]he Court holds that in providing this sample, which had been produced by another manufacturer, [the Buyer] still had implicitly specified its order concerning the required slippage strength, respectively, seam slippage strength'.

37 The phrase is borrowed from *Steels & Busks v Bleecker Bik & Co Ltd* [1956] Lloyd's Rep 228, 239.

basic interrelated scenarios which show why it would be unfair to interpret it otherwise. The first is where the parties' intention is that a sample/model will be used as the source that will define and describe *some* characteristics of the goods. In other words, not every feature to be found in a sample/ model may be intended to be used for defining and describing the goods. For example, a sample of clothing may be supplied only for the purpose of indicating the measurements and sizes of clothes that the seller is able or willing to supply.[38] Some other samples may be intended to show to the buyer only the colours and/or flavours available.[39] In some trade sectors, there may be a common understanding as to what the samples can represent. In one case,[40] it was held that the 'buyer could not argue that infected buckwheat delivered from China did not conform to the sample, as in the cereal business samples had a limited aim, being intended to define such type-specific characteristics as the kind of buckwheat and the colour and size of the kernel; they were irrelevant to phytosanitary purposes'. In all these cases, holding the seller liable for the goods' non-compliance with the features of a sample/model, which were not expected to define the goods, would contravene the parties' intentions. It may not always be easy to determine what the parties' intentions were and, of course, in such cases they need to be inferred from the circumstances. In one case,[41] for instance, the buyer's claim that the colour of the Tulipwood doors did not correspond to an earlier sample was rejected on the ground that the sample was 'too small for the buyer to be entitled to derive from it that there would be no difference in color in the eventual delivery'.[42]

The second scenario is where a characteristic contained in a sample/ model may not be discoverable upon an ordinary and reasonable examination of it. Taking a stance on how this situation is to be resolved is important in two cases. One is where a sample/model contains some additional characteristics not found in the goods, but which are discoverable upon an unusually rigorous examination. In this case, the *buyer* may want to argue that the goods ought to have contained those additional characteristics. The second case is where a defect in the goods of which the buyer complains was similarly present in a sample/model and not discoverable upon a reasonable examination. In this scenario, the *seller* may want to argue that it

[38] See District Court Düsseldorf, 31 O 27/92, 25 August 1994 (Germany), available at http://cisgw3.law.pace.edu/cases/940825g1.html, where there was a discrepancy between the size of the goods and the sample.

[39] See CIETAC Arbitration, 10 July 1993 (n 4).

[40] ICC Arbitration Case No 9773, 1999 (an excerpt of this case is available at http://cisgw3.law.pace.edu/cases/999773i1.html).

[41] Commercial Court Hasselt, AR 05/4177, 19 April 2006 (Belgium), available at http://cisgw3.law.pace.edu/cases/060419b1.html. The decision states that the seller could not be expected to deliver a whole door as a sample. This raises the question of whether the court regarded this as a 'sale by sample' at all.

[42] Ibid.

has fulfilled its obligations under Article 35(2)(c) because the defect was present in the sample/model, which the buyer examined without raising objections, and because the goods conformed to the sample/model.[43]

It is suggested that the very purpose of using a sample/model would be considerably undermined if a party were allowed to invoke its characteristics not identifiable under a normal examination since the parties' normal intention would be that only a reasonable examination would be carried out. In the first case, the seller would be disadvantaged if it were held liable for non-compliance with the sample/model in those respects which were not identifiable under a normal inspection:

> Pulled to pieces and examined by unusual tests which curiosity or suspicion might suggest, it would doubtless reveal every secret of its construction. But that is not the way in which business is done ... Some confidence there must be between merchant and manufacturer.[44]

Made cautious, sellers would be reluctant to provide a sample/model or would have to invest extra time, effort and funds into a detailed inspection of samples/models prior to delivering them to their buyers. Such costs will not have to be incurred if a sample/model is relied upon only in respect of reasonably discoverable characteristics. As alluded to in the above quotation, there is also a risk that such interpretation would create an environment of mistrust between buyers and sellers. Similarly, in the second case, the buyer would be penalised for merely doing what is reasonable. It would be compelled to carry out (expensive) investigations of a sample/model, which go beyond what traders are normally expected to do, or to face the adverse consequences of not proceeding with such investigations. All this goes against the Convention's objectives and principles, which seek to promote a fair balance between the parties, reasonable conduct and to advance trade by reducing costs for the parties. It is thus submitted that a sample/model should only bind the seller in respect of the characteristics discoverable upon a reasonable examination. Therefore, the extent to which a sample is allowed 'to speak'[45] depends on what constitutes a reasonable or normal examination in the circumstances.[46]

C. Relationship with Contractual Provisions and Other Terms Implied under the Convention

As explained, a sample or model will, in many cases, be a visual demonstration of the goods' description and/or quality. However, there may be

[43] District Court Berlin, 15 September 1994 (n 5).

[44] *James Drummond & Sons v EH Van Ingen & Co* (1887) LR 12 App Cas 284, 297.

[45] See n 37 above.

[46] For example, in certain trade sectors only a visual examination may be expected. See *FE Hookway v Alfred Isaacs* [1954] 1 Lloyd's Rep 491 (shellac); *Steels & Busks v Bleecker Bik & Co Ltd* (n37) (rubber).

express contractual stipulations as to description or quality referring to features or characteristics which are different to those in a sample/model or which contain more or fewer features than those found in a sample/model. Is it with reference to the contract or to the sample/model that the seller's conformity obligations are to be defined? The answer depends on the construction of the contract and, more specifically, on which of the two were intended to take priority.[47] Some examples have been given above where the parties intended a sample/model to represent only certain characteristics. In such cases, *other* characteristics will be governed by the relevant contractual stipulations. Where there is evidence of the parties' intention that the sample/model is the sole source of description and quality, the contractual provisions to the contrary can be interpreted as being no more than a 'label for designation of the subject matter'[48] or a source of general information about the goods of a similar kind to those in the contract.[49]

Some cases have given rise to the question of whether certain representations and sources outside a written contract were intended to be part of it. In one case,[50] the seller agreed to sell souvenir coins and to deliver the 'descriptions and the certificates'. The contract did not expressly require compliance with those descriptions and certificates, stating only that 'the subject matter and price [include] coin sets, the descriptions and certificates'. The delivered coins complied with the samples, but not with the design in the certificate. The tribunal found the seller in breach of an 'implied duty' to ensure compliance with the descriptions and the certificate on the ground that, otherwise, the contractual provision requiring the delivery of such descriptions and the certificate would be 'meaningless'. The implication is that the samples were not intended to be the sole description of the goods.[51]

There is also some uncertainty concerning the relationship of Article 35(2)(c) with subparagraphs (a) and (b). There is a view that, being 'a factual description and ... a contractual way to determine the kind and quality of the goods'[52] the application of Article 35(2)(c) excludes the applicability of subparagraphs (a) and (b).[53] It is submitted, however, that there can be no fixed position and every case requires an individual evaluation of whether the use of a sample/model was intended to exclude other implied terms. When there is no evidence of such an intention, there is no doubt

[47] Schwenzer (n 8) para 26; Kröll (n 10) para 132.
[48] *Benjamin's Sale of Goods* (n 24) para 11-086.
[49] See Federal Supreme Court, 22 December 2000 (Switzerland) (n 31).
[50] *Souvenir Coins*, CIETAC Arbitration, 2000, available at http://cisgw3.law.pace.edu/cases/000000c1.html.
[51] See also Chapter 2 for further discussion of this case.
[52] Bianca (n 3) 275.
[53] Ibid.

that Article 35(2)(a) and/or (b)[54] *and* (c) will apply cumulatively.[55] That said, in many cases, the use of a sample/model will lead to the inapplicability of Article 35(2)(b). With a sample/model on hand, a buyer is often in the position to determine the goods' suitability for its particular purpose. That, in turn, will often make it unnecessary for the buyer to communicate its particular purpose and/or indicate reliance on its own, rather than the seller's skill and judgement.[56]

Still, cases where a particular purpose has been communicated and the buyer, despite having a sample/model, has relied on the seller's skill and judgement cannot be ruled out.[57] This may happen, for example, where the buyer does not have expertise or equipment to identify the characteristics in a sample which are relevant to the goods' ability to meet a particular purpose.[58] The seller may also have confirmed its understanding of a particular purpose and given assurances about its ability to comply with that purpose, leaving little doubt that Article 35(2)(b) would apply. The provision of a sample/model in such a case may well be construed as merely seeking to promote a product or to provide some general information. Finally, it may be worth repeating that a sample/model may only be intended to demonstrate certain features of the goods and these features may not cover an entire range of characteristics necessary for the goods to be able to fulfil a particular purpose.

There is less clarity about the relationship of Article 35(2)(c) with the fall-back rule in (2)(a). It can be argued that being a more specific rule, subparagraph (c) should displace the general 'fitness for the ordinary purposes' test.[59] But courts and tribunals, it is submitted, should be slow to infer an intention to displace Article 35(2)(a). Being the fall-back rule containing a seller's basic obligation, it provides the minimum level of protection to

[54] On the relationship between Art 35(2)(a) and (b), see Chapter 4.

[55] See District Court Regensburg, 6 O 107/98, 24 September 1998 (Germany), available at http://cisgw3.law.pace.edu/cases/980924g1.html, where the buyer alleged that the seller was liable on the basis that the textile fabrics could not be cut economically. The court assessed the seller's obligations applying Art 35(2)(a), (b) and (c), and found the seller not to be in breach of these provisions. See also District Court Rotterdam, HA ZA 98-1405, 14 October 1999 (Netherlands), available at http://cisgw3.law.pace.edu/cases/991014n1.html ('If the [seller] fails to [prove that the goods complied with the sample], it will have to be examined whether the delivered leather indeed cannot be used for the particular purpose, as meant in Art 35(2)(b) CISG').

[56] Schwenzer (n 8) para 26; Kröll (n 10) para 135. See also *Steels & Busks v Bleecker Bik & Co Ltd* (n 37) ('The manner in which goods are bought, including the request for a sample, may well in the circumstances negative reliance on the seller').

[57] Schwenzer (n 8) para 26; Kröll (n 10) para 135.

[58] It is, however, arguable that if, as argued above, a sample is binding only with respect to those characteristics which are reasonably discoverable, a sale would not be 'by sample' in this case if a reasonable person in the buyer's position could not be expected to examine the characteristics pertaining to the particular purpose. Therefore, this may not be an example of the divergence of outcomes flowing from Art 35(2)(c), on the one hand, and (b), on the other.

[59] See Kröll (n 10) para 134.

the buyer. There are two other reasons showing an important role of subparagraph (a). The first reason is, once again, based on the possibility of a sample/model covering only some characteristics. The fitness for ordinary purposes, being a broad test, may encompass some other characteristics not intended to be covered by a sample. Article 35(2)(a) is necessary to protect the buyer in respect of those other characteristics. If there is a discrepancy between the outcomes produced by (2)(a) and (c) in respect of the features which *are* intended to be covered by the sample/model, then those features should not be governed by (2)(a). That would go against (2)(c) being a more specific rule than (2)(a), as well as against the parties' intentions. Secondly, a case of a latent defect in a sample/model which is not discoverable upon a reasonable examination needs to be borne in mind. If the argument that a sample is only binding in respect of its features which are discoverable upon a reasonable examination is adopted, such a sample/model would not trigger Article 35(2)(c). Article 35(2)(a) would then apply normally as the final implied term. If, contrary to the position taken in this book, such a sample is nonetheless regarded as triggering (2)(c), subparagraph (a) is all the more necessary to protect the buyer from latent defects.[60] Doing otherwise would probably be contrary to the consensual nature of the contract since it cannot be presumed that the buyer, if it knew of the hidden defect, would agree to enter into the contract solely on the basis of the sample to the exclusion of (2)(a).[61] It then falls to (2)(a) to determine whether the goods with those defects are 'fit for the ordinary purposes'.

D. Public Law Regulations

It has been seen above that the existence of public law regulations governing various aspects of conformity of the goods may have implications for the seller's obligations under Article 35,[62] which include those governed by Article 35(2)(c). If regulations are held to dictate the content of the seller's obligations,[63] their impact, in the context of this provision, can conceivably manifest itself in at least three ways. First, the regulations can themselves stipulate that a sample or a model ought to be used as a source defining conformity of the goods. Secondly, they can specify the particular features that a sample/model is required to represent.[64] Thirdly, they can provide for how a sample/model must be examined.[65] Therefore, the question of

[60] See, similarly, ibid.
[61] Ibid.
[62] See Chapters 2, 3 and 4.
[63] Whether by virtue of Art 35(1), (2)(a) and/or (b).
[64] See CIETAC Arbitration, 10 July 1993 (n 4).
[65] See ibid.

which country's public law regulations or some other standards, such as industry standards, are relevant for determining the seller's obligations also arises under Article 35(2)(c). One tribunal held in this regard that the seller was required to comply with the regulations or industry standards in the country of 'origin of the goods',[66] which would often be the country of the seller. It is submitted, however, that no general rule can be laid down since it is the parties' intentions in a particular case that are decisive. The general guidelines for interpreting the parties' intentions in such cases have been explored in previous chapters.[67]

E. Proof

Both the buyer and the seller may want to invoke Article 35(2)(c). The buyer will want to do so to establish that the goods were non-conforming due to their non-compliance with a sample or model. The seller will want to invoke this provision to defend itself against the buyer's claim of non-conformity, based on some other provision(s) of Article 35. For example, if the buyer alleges that the goods do not comply with the contract or with the terms implied under Article 35(2)(a) or (b), the seller may want to establish that the parties' intention was to sell and purchase the goods solely with reference to the sample/model, with which the goods fully complied and which may even have contained the alleged lack of conformity.[68] Whichever of the two parties seeks to rely on Article 35(2)(c), the preconditions for establishing its applicability are as follows. The party relying on it will have to prove that the 'seller has held out a sample or a model to the buyer'. As explained, this will primarily necessitate proving that conformity of the goods or a particular aspect thereof was intended to be defined with reference to the sample/model and that the sample/model was provided by the seller. However, where the seller relies on this provision, it will often have an incentive to prove that the parties' intention was not merely to sell and purchase the goods with reference to a sample/model (leaving out the possibility of other provisions of Article 35 affording the buyer additional protection), but to do so *exclusively* with reference to the sample/model. Further, where the buyer invokes Article 35(2)(c), it will need to prove that the goods did not conform to the sample/model, whereas the seller, invoking Article 35(2)(c), will need to prove the opposite.[69] Conformity with a

[66] Ibid.
[67] See Chapters 2, 3 and 4.
[68] See District Court Rotterdam, 14 October 1999 (n 55).
[69] 'In stating now that the leather delivered at the end of July 1997 showed defects, the [seller] will have to prove that the leather delivered to the [buyer] around 31 July 1997, was of the same quality as the sample' (District Court Rotterdam, 14 October 1999 (n 55)).

sample/model (or lack of it) can be proved by a variety of means, including witnesses, expert evidence, photographs or inspection certificates.[70] The parties' conduct may also be relevant in assessing the strength of the evidence and of a party's case. For instance, the seller's failure to object to statements in, and to an inspection organisation which issued, a certificate showing non-compliance with a sample, which was sent by the buyer to the seller, may be taken as proof of the seller's acceptance that the goods did not comply with the sample.[71]

II. PACKAGING

A. General

Legal systems take different approaches to dealing with legal issues arising from packaging. Some expressly provide for requirements concerning packaging,[72] whereas in some other systems the seller's obligation as to packaging may be implied by virtue of general principles of law, a contract or a trade usage.[73] In the second category of cases, the seller's obligation is viewed as separate from its obligations as to conformity of the goods.[74] In some of these systems, packaging is regarded as part of the goods.[75] The approach of the CISG is to treat packaging as part of conformity of the goods,[76] as has been seen from the earlier discussion.[77] This approach is further evident from the Convention's rules in Article 35(2), one of which (Article 35(2)(d)) is directly concerned with packaging and provides that where the parties have not agreed otherwise, the goods are non-conforming unless they 'are contained or packaged in the manner usual for such goods or, where there is no such manner, in a manner adequate to preserve and protect the goods'.[78] In general, the primary purpose of packaging is to preserve and to protect the goods so that they are delivered to the buyer in a state and condition which meets other requirements of conformity of the goods.[79] It acquires particular significance where, as is often the case

[70] See, eg CIETAC Arbitration, 18 September 1996 (n 22).

[71] See CIETAC Arbitration, 10 July 1993 (n 4).

[72] See detailed references to various legal systems in von Bar and Clive (n 15) 1291; I Schwenzer, P Hachem and C Kee, *Global Sales and Contract Law* (Oxford, OUP, 2012) para 31.146.

[73] Schwenzer, Hachem and Kee (n 72); von Bar and Clive (n 15).

[74] Schwenzer, Hachem and Kee (n 72).

[75] See *Geddling v Marsh* [1920] 1 KB 668; *Morelli v Fitch and Gibbons* [1928] 2 KB 636 (in the context of English law).

[76] See Art 35(1).

[77] See Chapter 2.

[78] There was no such requirement in the ULIS, the predecessor of the CISG.

[79] See, similarly, Kröll (n 10) para 137.

in international transactions, the goods need to be transported, but it is equally applicable where the seller's duty to deliver consists of merely placing the goods at the buyer's disposal at a particular place[80] or at its own place of business.[81]

The implied terms on packaging provide the minimum level of protection to the buyer,[82] which means that the parties' agreement to displace them will not be easily inferred, particularly if the alleged agreement is said to provide for packaging falling below the standard in Article 35(2)(d). Thus, in one case,[83] marble panels were damaged during transportation due to inadequate packaging and the panels not having been fastened to the pallets. The court held that the fact that the same packaging was used by the seller in previous deliveries could not have been seen as reflecting an implied agreement to use the same packaging in this contract. The decisive factor appears to have been the fact that the packaging did not meet the requirement of Article 35(2)(d), but two other considerations were also taken into account. First, the court noted that because the previously delivered goods were not damaged, the buyer had no reason to raise the issue of packaging. Secondly, not all of the previously delivered goods were marble panels of the same type that were the subject matter of this contract. The decision is correct since, whilst the parties do have a right to derogate from Article 35(2)(d),[84] much stronger evidence will be needed to prove an agreement to lower the level of legal protection afforded to the buyer in respect of packaging.

The seller's duty as to packaging is linked to Article 36(2) more closely, perhaps, than any other obligation under the CISG in the sense that it provides a paradigmatic illustration of the application of this provision. Article 36(2) provides that the seller is liable for any lack of conformity which occurs after the risk has passed to the buyer (which is the time with reference to which conformity of the goods is to be assessed)[85] and 'which is due to a breach of any of his obligations'. The seller's packaging duty will usually be such an obligation. Damage to the goods will often occur during carriage after the risk has passed to the buyer,[86] but if such a damage is due

[80] See Art 31(b).

[81] See Art 31(c). See also Kröll (n 10) para 137; Schwenzer (n 8) para 31 (pointing out that in such a case it may follow from the parties' agreement that the buyer who is collecting the goods may have a duty to provide receptacles).

[82] See F Enderlein and D Maskow, *International Sales Law* (New York, Oceana Publications, 1992) 146.

[83] See Appellate Court Saarbrücken, 5 U 426/96-54, 17 January 2007 (Germany), available at http://cisgw3.law.pace.edu/cases/070117g1.html.

[84] See Art 6.

[85] See Art 36(1).

[86] See Art 67(1) CISG: 'If the contract of sale involves carriage of the goods and the seller is not bound to hand them over at a particular place, the risk passes to the buyer when the goods are handed over to the first carrier for transmission to the buyer in accordance with the contract of sale.'

to inappropriate packaging, the seller will be liable not only for its breach of Article 35(2)(d), but also for any other lack of conformity that arose as a consequence of defective packaging.[87]

B. Usual Manner

As Article 35(2)(d) makes clear, the starting point for assessing the seller's obligations as to packaging is to determine whether there is a 'usual manner' in which the contract goods are 'contained or packaged'. Generally speaking, this question needs to be answered with reference to common understandings and expectations in a particular trade. In other words, what packaging would be regarded as usual and customary by a reasonable trader? A usual manner is unlikely to be capable of being defined in abstract. Regard needs to be had to all the relevant circumstances,[88] which include: any trade usages[89] or standards in the particular commercial sector or industry;[90] any relevant practices the parties may have established between themselves or any prior dealings they may have had;[91] the purpose of packaging,[92] such as whether the goods are required to withstand transportation, and the intended mode of transport,[93] unless the seller is not in the position to know about how the goods will be transported;[94] the nature and value of the goods;[95] the environment, climatic or other conditions, to which the goods will be exposed and which can have an impact on their state and condition.

[87] See Wuhan Economic and Technology Development Zone People's Court, Hubei Province, 30 June 2000 (China), available at http://cisgw3.law.pace.edu/cases/000630c1.html, where the seller packaged knives without effective 'damp-proof measures', as a result of which knives arrived rusted. With the contract being on CIF terms, damage occurred after the risk has passed to the buyer (that is, when the goods were placed on board), but the seller was still in breach of Art 35(2)(d). See also Appellate Court Koblenz, 2 U 923/06, 14 December 2006 (Germany), available at http://cisgw3.law.pace.edu/cases/061214g1.html.

[88] See P Huber and A Mullis, *The CISG: A New Textbook for Students and Practitioners* (Munich, Sellier European Law Publishers, 2007) 141; Enderlein and Maskow (n 82).

[89] See Art 9 CISG.

[90] See Kröll (n 10) para 139.

[91] See Arts 8(3) and 9(1). But see Appellate Court Saarbrücken, 17 January 2007 (n 83).

[92] See Schwenzer (n 8) para 30.

[93] '[The seller] admitted that it fell within its own sphere of responsibility to provide for packaging that allowed for a safe and secure carriage by truck to their final destination as defined under the contract' (Appellate Court Koblenz, 14 December 2006 (n 87), where the seller was in breach of Art 35(2)(d) because of the 'improper packaging [of bottles] with a particular porous and unsuitable foil').

[94] This may be the case where the seller's duty to deliver is merely to place the goods at a particular place (see Kröll (n 10) para 139).

[95] *Health Supplement*, CIETAC Arbitration, 25 September 1998, available at http://cisgw3.law.pace.edu/cases/980925c1.html (the contract price was seen as pointing to the wide-neck packaging of bottles of fish oil, which was found to be more expensive than simple packaging bottles).

The notion of packaging is probably broad enough to include markings, instructions, as well as information concerning content and expiration dates,[96] if the circumstances so dictate, such as where the seller supplies the goods for an immediate sale in a reputable supermarket chain. Even if it is not possible to imply a requirement as to marking, labelling or the need to contain some other information, but the goods are nevertheless marked, labelled or contain information regarding content, expiration dates or use of the goods, it is submitted that 'the usual manner' should be interpreted to require that the goods comply with all this information. This interpretation can be justified on the basis that they give rise to legitimate expectations on the part of a buyer that the goods will correspond to any representations with regard to their packaging and/or on the basis of good faith as a principle of interpreting the Convention (Article 7(1)) or, more controversially,[97] as a general principle underlying the Convention (Article 7(2)) and leading to the imposition of a duty on the parties to act in good faith.[98] An underlying policy formulated in the context of the US Uniform Commercial Code (UCC) seems just as relevant here: 'a buyer should not be placed in the position of reselling or using goods delivered under false representations appearing on the package or container'.[99]

Different countries may have different rules, requirements or standards in respect of packaging of the goods destined for export or import. The question arises whether they should be taken into account in assessing what constitutes a 'usual manner' of packaging. It is sometimes argued that the 'usual manner' requirement should not be so interpreted,[100] which seems to imply that Article 35(2)(d) has a truly autonomous meaning determinable in abstract. However, as suggested above, it is hardly possible to define what is usual or customary without having regard to the surrounding factual context. The standards or requirements in a country with which the goods are connected are part of this context and so should be taken into account as a factor[101] which may help to define what constitutes 'usual packaging' in the circumstances. For the sake of promoting legal certainty, it is helpful to have a guideline as to which country's standards are likely to influence the content of the seller's obligations. The position that has been set out in the case of Article 35(1) and Article 35(2)(a) and (b) seems appropriate here: generally, the seller should not be responsible for compliance

[96] See Schwenzer (n 8) para 30. But see § 2-314(e) and (f) UCC, mentioning labelling separately alongside packaging.

[97] See Chapter 1.

[98] See § 2-314(f) UCC (n 2) (providing that merchantability includes conformity with 'the promise and affirmations of fact made on the container or label if any').

[99] Comment 12 on § 2-314(f) UCC (n 2).

[100] Schwenzer (n 8) para 30.

[101] See Art 8(3).

with public law regulations in the country where the goods will be used or sold; the seller should only be liable for such non-compliance if there was a good reason why the seller should have known about the regulations at destination. There is no reason why these guidelines should not be equally applicable to the rules as to packaging.[102]

To some extent, some of the existing cases on packaging resonate with this position. In an earlier mentioned case involving the sale of marble panels,[103] the court took the view that the standards in the seller's country were controlling.[104] However, the seller not being liable for non-compliance with regulations in the country of use or sale does not mean that it should necessarily be bound by the regulations in its own country. It is in this respect that the decision extends the seller's obligations too far. Whether or not the seller was intended to be responsible for non-compliance with the packaging requirements in its own country is a matter of interpreting the parties' intentions.[105] The most that can probably be said is that, on balance, the seller will be held liable for non-compliance with its country's regulations more frequently than it will be for non-compliance with the requirements in a country where the goods are used or sold. The recognition of special circumstances where the seller is expected to ensure compliance with the regulations in the importing country is evidenced by a case[106] involving the sale of parmesan cheese by an Italian seller to a French buyer. The buyer alleged that the seller was in breach of its conformity obligations because the delivered cheese was not labelled in accordance with French law on the composition and expiry date of food products. It was held that considering that the dealings between the parties had lasted for several months, the seller knew that the goods would be marketed in France and in the light of this knowledge, the seller should have interpreted the buyer's order as being conditional on the goods complying with the 'marketing regulations of the French market'.[107]

C. 'Adequate Manner'

No usual manner of packaging the goods may exist, such as in the case of goods newly introduced to the market.[108] Where so, the Convention

[102] See Chapters 2, 3 and 4.

[103] See Appellate Court Saarbrücken, 17 January 2007 (n 83).

[104] For the same view in academic writings, see Kröll (n 10) para 140; Bianca (n 3) 276.

[105] See Chapters 2, 3 and 4.

[106] Appellate Court Grenoble, 93/4126, 13 September 1995 (France), available at http://cisgw3.law.pace.edu/cases/950913f1.html.

[107] Ibid.

[108] In fact, it is the possibility of contract goods being of a new kind that triggered a member of the Australian delegation to introduce this rule in addition to the initial requirement as to the 'usual manner' (see Summary Records of Meetings of the First Committee, 15th meeting on 20 March 1980, available at www.cisg.law.pace.edu/cisg/firstcommittee/Meeting15.html).

requires the goods to be contained or packaged 'in a manner adequate to preserve and protect the goods'.[109] A manner is adequate if packaging protects or preserves the goods under the usual circumstances for the goods or transaction in question.[110] In other words, packaging needs to be capable of withstanding normal risks arising in comparable circumstances.[111] It follows that, in the absence of a special agreement, the inability of packaging to protect the goods against exceptional or extraordinary circumstances will not constitute a breach of Article 35(2)(d).[112] The adequacy of packaging cannot be determined without having regard to the circumstances of a sale and the performance of a sales contract. This means that the factors relevant in assessing the 'adequate manner' of packaging are the same as those set out with respect to the requirement as to the 'usual manner' and include: the nature and value of the goods;[113] type of transport, the duration of carriage and the particularities of the route of the journey;[114] the climatic conditions[115] and other types of environment to which the goods will be exposed;[116] trade usages[117] or industry standards,[118] as well as any relevant practices[119] or dealings the parties may have had between themselves.[120]

All these factors can be taken into account only if the seller was reasonably in the position to know about them because otherwise it cannot be expected to interpret the adequate manner requirement with reference to them. The relevant time for ascertaining whether the seller had such knowledge must,

[109] Art 35(2)(d).

[110] See, similarly, Kröll (n 10) para 141.

[111] See ibid.

[112] Ibid.

[113] Schwenzer (n 8) para 32; Kröll (n 10) para 141.

[114] 'A packaging is adequate if it is sufficient to protect the goods from damage during its foreseeable route to their destination' (Appellate Court Saarbrücken, 17 January 2007 (n 83)).

[115] Schwenzer (n 8) para 32.

[116] '[T]he seller of laminated glass panels delivered in France and destined for use in the hotel dome in Egypt is obligated to deliver the panels packaged so as to withstand damage from humidity and variations in temperature which result normally from sea transport and storing at the destination port or, at the very least, to inform the buyer of particular precautions to take to prevent such damages' (Supreme Court, 1312 FS-P; 01-16107 D, 24 September 2003 (France), available at http://cisgw3.law.pace.edu/cases/030924f1.html). This decision appears to suggest that informing the buyer of precautions that need to be taken could replace the need to comply with the requirements as to packaging. In principle, such a statement by the seller can indicate its unwillingness to be responsible for packaging and an intention to attempt to derogate from Art 35(2)(d). It is suggested, however, that for the reasons discussed above in the main text, such derogation should not be assumed lightly. The seller's statements and conduct will have to be assessed as part of the totality of the surrounding circumstances. See also Wuhan Economic and Technology Development Zone People's Court, Hubei Province, 30 June 2000 (China) (n 87).

[117] See Art 9.

[118] See Art 8(3).

[119] See Art 9(1).

[120] See Art 8(3).

in principle, be the time of the conclusion of the contract[121] because that is the time when duties are allocated and risks are divided between the parties. It is also arguable that the time of the contract is a practically convenient reference point from which the seller can proceed to performing the contract, including arranging for packaging, without worrying that new factors may emerge which could influence its obligations. However, considering that the seller is liable for any lack of conformity which exists at the time when the risk passes to the buyer,[122] it cannot be ruled out that even if the seller acquires knowledge after the contract, it may be expected to change or revise its performance or plans to perform in accordance with the information acquired subsequent to the conclusion of the contract, but before the risk passes to the buyer.

Such an interpretation seems undesirable because it will introduce uncertainty and insecurity into the seller's mind. The seller will not be able to fully rely on the information available to it at the time of the contract and to benefit from the finality that such time would otherwise produce. Suppose, for example, that at the time of the contract the buyer had told the seller that the goods would proceed directly to a particular destination, but then subsequently informed the seller that the goods would be redispatched or redirected to another destination, which would require more rigorous and expensive packaging. It is argued that, unless the seller agreed to provide this more expensive packaging, the need to ensure such packaging would run contrary to the risks the seller assumed at the time of the contract.[123] Therefore, the adequacy requirement, albeit being a term implied under the Convention as opposed to one emanating from the contract, should not be interpreted with the possibility of redispatch in mind.[124] It can be contended that the Convention requires that all factors, including those subsequent to the contract,[125] be taken into account in interpreting the parties' intentions. This point is relevant where the very meaning of the parties' intentions is unclear, and a factor arising subsequent to the contract is relied upon to help to determine or clarify such a meaning. Where, however, the parties' intention *is* clear, as was the premise of the example just given, such factors should not be used to change the allocation of responsibilities as they would reasonably be understood by the parties at the time of the contract.

[121] See Schwenzer (n 8) para 32.

[122] See Art 36(1).

[123] Using Art 38(3) by analogy would seem to support such an interpretation: 'If the goods are redirected in transit or redispatched by the buyer without a reasonable opportunity for examination by him and *at the time of the conclusion of the contract the seller knew or ought to have known* of the possibility of such redirection or redispatch, examination may be deferred until after the goods have arrived at the new destination' (emphasis added).

[124] See also Schwenzer (n 8) para 32.

[125] See Art 8(3) referring, amongst others, to 'subsequent conduct'.

D. Defective Packaging with Goods being Otherwise Conforming

One question relevant to both the 'usual' and 'adequate' manner requirements in Article 35(2)(d) that has arisen in several cases is whether the seller can be said to have committed a breach of its packaging obligations where the packaging was unusual or inadequate or has been damaged, but where the goods were otherwise conforming in all other respects. The first point to note is that whilst damaged packaging will often be evidence of it being 'unusual' or 'inadequate', in some cases this damage may be caused by some exceptional circumstances, going beyond what may be called normal or usual risks. If the latter is the case and if it is shown that packaging before being damaged was in conformity with Article 35(2)(d), the seller is not in breach of its obligations as to packaging. Therefore, in the context of this discussion, damaged packaging is taken to be an indication of it being unusual or inadequate. In such cases, some tribunals appear to have taken the view that the seller was not liable. In a case[126] involving the sale of chemical compound which was found to be conforming, except that the packing of the bags containing the compound 'was contaminated/defiled to various extent', the arbitrator held that no breach had been committed by the seller. In another case,[127] the tribunal accepted the experts' testimony that it was not usual to ship fully dried cow's liver fungus in refrigeration at –14°C. However, the buyer's failure to establish that the goods themselves were damaged as a result of such refrigeration simply led the tribunal to dismiss the buyer's claim without any mention of the possibility that the seller might be liable for breaching its obligations as to packaging.

These decisions fail to recognise Article 35(2)(d) as containing a standalone aspect of conformity. Being set out as a separate obligation of the seller, a breach of this provision in itself constitutes a basis for the seller's liability for a lack of conformity of the goods even if all other requirements of conformity are complied with. That said, it is understandable that where the sole purpose of packaging is to protect or preserve the goods from damage or deterioration, there is little to be gained from alleging a breach in respect of packaging. The buyer is unlikely to suffer any loss,[128] the value of the goods in such a case is unlikely to be affected[129] and the breach is certainly not serious enough to amount to a fundamental breach.[130] It may

[126] ICC Arbitration Case No 8247, June 1996, available at www.unilex.info/case.cfm?pid=1&do=case&id=458&step=FullText.

[127] *Cow's Liver Fungus*, CIETAC Arbitration, 30 March 1994, available at http://cisgw3.law.pace.edu/cases/940330c1.html.

[128] Which is a prerequisite for the right to claim damages (see Art 74).

[129] Which is essential for the buyer to be able to reduce the price under Art 50.

[130] Proving a fundamental breach is necessary in order for the buyer to avoid the contract, except in the case covered by Art 49(1)(b) (see Arts 49(1)(a) and 25), and to demand substitute goods (see Art 46(2)).

be possible for some such cases to be characterised as meeting the requirements of Article 35(2)(d). As explained earlier, both the usual and adequate manner requirements need to be interpreted in the light of the purpose of packaging. It can be argued that if the sole purpose of packaging is to protect or preserve the goods and the buyer does receive the goods undamaged, then in that case packaging is adequate or usual because, regardless of its flaws, it manages to preserve the goods. However, it is difficult to see how this interpretation can be adopted without violating the language of Article 35(2)(d) in cases where there is clear evidence that the packaging is, in fact, unusual (as seen from the case of refrigeration of cow's liver fungus at –14°C) or falls well below what can reasonably be expected (as was the case in the above 'chemical compound case'[131]). It is thus suggested that in such cases the seller is liable under Article 35(2)(d), even if such a finding is unlikely to have any beneficial remedial consequences for the buyer.[132]

Packaging may be used not only to protect or preserve the goods, but also where it is a part of the goods.[133] Liquids cannot be sold unless they are contained in bottles or containers.[134] The goods may be of a particular brand with a distinctive design, of which packaging is an integral part, and the same applies to luxury items or expensive goods.[135] Packaging may be permanent with the goods being intended for subsequent resale. In such cases, the question of whether the seller has complied with Article 35(2)(d) becomes more significant than in cases discussed in the previous two paragraphs. Here, non-conforming packaging is likely to produce more serious remedial consequences: the buyer may suffer very real losses;[136] the value of the goods is likely to be affected;[137] and the prospects of the seller committing a fundamental breach are more realistic.[138]

E. Proof

It is the buyer who will seek to invoke Article 35(2)(d) and under the 'rule and exception' principle,[139] it will bear the burden of proving the seller's

[131] See nn 126 and 127 above and the accompanying main text.

[132] For a different view, see Schwenzer (n 8) para 32; Kröll (n 10) para 144.

[133] See similarly Schwenzer (n 8) para 32.

[134] See *Geddling v Marsh* (n 75); *Morelli v Fitch and Gibbons* (n 75).

[135] See CIETAC Arbitration, 25 September 1998 (n 95).

[136] It is difficult to be exhaustive when it comes to losses the buyer may suffer, but some of the typical examples are the buyer's loss of profit on a sub-sale or loss in the value of the goods which can potentially be calculated, for example, by the difference in value formula or costs of curing the goods. See further Chapter 1.

[137] Possibly enabling the buyer to reduce the price under Art 50. See CIETAC Arbitration, 25 September 1998 (n 95), where the buyer was entitled to reduce the price due to non-conforming packaging.

[138] Increasing the probability of the buyer having the right to avoid the contract (see Art 49) or to demand replacement goods with conforming packaging (see Art 46(2)).

[139] See Chapter 3.

breach of this provision. The buyer must prove that the packaging was not usual or, if this standard is not applicable, that it was not adequate to preserve or protect the goods. That, in turn, will require, first of all, establishing what constitutes a usual or adequate manner in the circumstances. The fact that the buyer received damaged goods may often be an indication that packaging was non-conforming. This means that where the buyer receives damaged goods, its evidentiary position in respect of proving a breach of Article 35(2)(d) is likely to be quite strong. However, the buyer will still have to establish that damage to the goods arose as a result of non-conforming packaging.[140] In a case where the buyer received non-conforming laminated glass panels,[141] one essential factor which led to the decision that there was no breach of the seller's packaging obligations was the fact that 'the non-conformity of the panels could have had as its cause a defect in manufacturing, or it could have had as its exclusive cause transportation or stocking conditions under circumstances in which [the buyer] did not take the precautions recommended by [the seller]'.

A lack of conformity in packaging can be established by different types of evidence, including testimony by experts,[142] witnesses, photos,[143] bills of lading[144] and inspection certificates. The parties may present conflicting pieces of evidence and, subject to the rules on the admissibility of evidence, a court or tribunal will have to make a judgment based on the evaluation of all the available evidence. For example, in an earlier discussed case,[145] the parties disputed whether refrigeration at –14°C was usual when shipping cow's liver fungus. The seller's report, issued by an inspection company,[146] seeking to show that such refrigeration would not be detrimental to the goods was rejected on the ground that the evidence in the report was 'obviously cited from some paper'. The seller neither presented the original paper nor explained what that source of evidence was. The buyer provided a letter, issued by a company with experience in the import and

[140] '[The seller] fails to acknowledge that the defects of the bottles were actually not due to their miscarriage, but due to their improper packaging with a particular porous and unsuitable foil' (Appellate Court Koblenz, 14 December 2006 (n 87)).

[141] See Supreme Court, 24 September 2003 (France) (n 116), affirming the decision of the Appellate Court Paris.

[142] See, eg Appellate Court Saarbrücken, 17 January 2007 (n 83).

[143] See *Dingxi Longhai Dairy, Ltd v Becwood Technology Group, LLC*, F Supp 2d, 2008 WL 2690287 (D Minn) (the buyer submitted photographs of the alleged moulding on packaging and the eyewitness testimony, but they were deemed insufficient to prove the buyer's claim).

[144] See ibid ('Moreover, other evidence negates Becwood's assertion that the inulin was damaged at Tianjin. The ocean carrier that transported the inulin issued clean bills of lading for both shipments. See *Nat'l Transp., Inc. v. Inn Foods, Inc.*, 827 F.2d 351, 354 (8th Cir. 1997) (clean bill of lading is evidence of delivery in good condition as to goods carrier can visually observe or inspect)').

[145] See CIETAC Arbitration, 30 March 1994 (n 127).

[146] Namely, Chongqing Commodity Import and Export Inspection Bureau.

export of cow's liver fungus, which the tribunal chose to use as 'as a reference but not as evidence' because the company did not sign it. In the end, it was the testimony by two experts that was accepted as proof of the buyer's claim that such refrigeration was not usual.

III. EXEMPTIONS FROM LIABILITY

A. Buyer's Knowledge

(i) General

The Convention regards the buyer's knowledge of a lack of conformity as being relevant to the question of whether the seller should be liable for a lack of conformity. The issue of relevance of the buyer's knowledge in interpreting the contract was discussed earlier[147] and the focus is now on Article 35(3), which exempts the seller from its liability under *terms implied* under Article 35(2). Specifically, Article 35(3) states that the 'seller is not liable under subparagraphs (a) to (d) of the preceding paragraph for any lack of conformity of the goods if at the time of the conclusion of the contract the buyer knew or could not have been unaware of such lack of conformity'. To be clear, this provision does not negative the finding that the goods are non-conforming. As a matter of law, the goods remain non-conforming but the effect of Article 35(3) is to relieve the seller from liability for non-conforming goods.[148] Since it is the seller who will seek to invoke this provision, the burden of proving the preconditions for its applicability lies with the seller.

There are a number of ways in which this provision can be rationalised. One rather obvious explanation is based on good faith and fair dealing.[149] If the buyer knows or cannot be unaware of a lack of conformity at the time when the contract is made, it can hardly be fair or honest for this buyer to later claim that it was entitled to the goods free from that non-conformity. Another way of justifying this provision is to look at it from the angle of contract interpretation and allocation of risks between the parties. If the buyer knows or is in the position to know about the actual state and condition of the goods, it cannot reasonably and legitimately expect the seller to deliver better or even different goods.[150] This buyer, in other words, can be taken to have assumed the risk of, or to have consented to

[147] See Chapter 2.

[148] See *Castel Electronics Pty Ltd v Toshiba Singapore Pte Ltd* [2011] FCAFC 55, para 309.

[149] T Neumann, 'Features of Article 35 in the Vienna Convention: Equivalence, Burden of Proof and Awareness' (2007) 11 *Vindobona J Int'l Commercial L Arbitration* 81, para 52, also at www.cisg.law.pace.edu/cisg/biblio/neumann.html.

[150] See Kröll (n 10) para 149.

receiving, non-conforming goods,[151] having waived its right to demand the goods meeting the minimum standards fixed by the Convention. From this standpoint, Article 35(3) is simply a tool of, or a rule rooted in, contract interpretation, reflecting a presumed intention of the parties. If this is indeed how most parties would interpret the effect of the buyer's knowledge of a lack of conformity (whether actual or imputed) on their agreement, it is arguable that Article 35(3) may even be unnecessary. The same result can simply be achieved by using the Convention's rules on interpreting the parties' intentions,[152] with Article 6 and the opening words of Article 35(2)[153] enabling the agreement to be construed as derogating from the implied terms on conformity.

A rationalisation such as this, which regards Article 35(3) as no more than a tool of contract interpretation, may add some support to those who view the legal nature of the Convention's implied terms as emanating solely from the parties' presumed intentions, as opposed to any other policy external to the parties' contractual relationship. Thus, one commentator suggests that the purpose of Article 35(3) is 'to fine-tune the rules in Article 35(2) to ensure they operate as intended—as tools for determining the true agreement of the parties relating to the quality of the goods'.[154] However, as argued earlier,[155] whilst the purpose of Article 35(2) and (3) is largely to aid with interpreting the parties' intentions, the legal nature of these rules cannot be reduced to a contract since they are implied by law and not by inferring the parties' intentions in the particular case. The fact that Article 35(3) is only said to apply to the Convention's implied terms seems to support this view. There was a conscious decision by the drafters to restrict its applicability solely to rules implied in law, whereas in cases concerning 'pure' contract interpretation under Article 35(1) the buyer's knowledge is a *factor* in assessing the content of the seller's obligations,[156] rather than an automatic ground for exempting the seller from liability.

The rule in Article 35(3) also appears to be largely in line with economic considerations used to rationalise the rules on conformity. It will be remembered that the rules on conformity have been partly rationalised on the basis of the information asymmetry between the buyer and the seller, leading to the seller being treated as the better risk[157] bearer than the buyer. This means, in turn, that the rules perform the functions of signalling the quality

[151] Bianca (n 3) 277.
[152] See Arts 8 and 9.
[153] 'Except where the parties have agreed otherwise'.
[154] J Honnold (updated and revised by H Flechtner), *Uniform Law for International Sales under the 1980 United Nations Convention*, 4th edn (The Netherlands, Wolters Kluwer Law & Business, 2009) 338.
[155] See Chapter 3.
[156] See Chapter 2.
[157] Arising from a lack of conformity in the goods.

(and other aspects of conformity) that buyers can expect and induce sellers to invest in quality and insurance and to share information with buyers. Now, where the buyer is, or is in the position to be, aware of a lack of conformity, there is no need for quality (and other aspects of conformity) to be signalled to the buyer and that, it can be argued, justifies the departure from the Convention's implied terms in such cases. Similarly, the fact that the buyer can be said to assume the risks arising from non-conforming goods means that the reasons why the seller was initially thought to be the better risk bearer (that is to say, it is generally in a better position than the buyer to know about, control and influence the state and condition of the goods) are irrelevant. In addition, it has been suggested that where the buyer can inspect the goods before the sale without incurring any costs, putting itself in the position of learning about the state and condition of the goods, the seller's exemption from liability is a 'method of creating incentives for the *ex ante* information and reduction of *ex post* litigation'.[158] The point about encouraging the sharing of information seems correct because the seller, who is aware of Article 35(3) and who wishes to avoid or reduce the risk of liability for a lack of conformity, has an incentive to inform the buyer or at least to create opportunities for the buyer to inspect the goods prior to making the contract. Such an incentive is in keeping with an objective of rebalancing the information asymmetry between the parties and encouraging them to share information. The second point about reducing litigation is more debatable. Litigation is likely to be avoided or reduced where rules are clear and predictable, whereas establishing the buyer's actual or even imputed knowledge can be difficult since it requires the assessment of the individual circumstances. The rule may in fact invite litigation which can be complex and expensive.[159]

As the CISG makes clear, the buyer's knowledge is relevant at the time of the conclusion of the contract. Therefore, knowledge acquired by or imputed to the buyer subsequent to that time, even if before delivery, is irrelevant. Any after-acquired knowledge cannot change the risks assumed by the seller under the contract.[160] Put differently, the buyer cannot be said to have consented to non-conforming goods if it becomes aware of a lack of conformity subsequent to the contract since that was not the basis upon which the contract was made. Article 35(3) is mostly relevant to identified or specific goods,[161] but it may also apply to generic or unascertained

[158] F Parisi, 'The Harmonisation of Legal Warranties in European Sales Law: An Economic Analysis' (2004) 52 *AJCL* 403, 419.

[159] '[I]f courts must adjudicate what the buyer knew and when it knew it, warranty litigation will become much more complex' (CP Gillett and SD Walt, *Sales Law: Domestic and International*, 2nd edn (New York, Foundation Press/Thomson West, 2009) 326).

[160] See, similarly, Kröll (n 10) para 156.

[161] See Schwenzer (n 8) para 35; Honnold (n 154) 338.

goods[162] if, for example, the buyer has examined part of the bulk from which the goods will be delivered or is told that the goods will be exactly the same as those delivered under previous contracts.[163]

(ii) Actual Knowledge

The seller will, first of all, be exempt from liability if it is established that the buyer had *actual* knowledge of a lack of conformity. Such knowledge will be proved if the seller expressly points out a lack of conformity to the buyer,[164] or where the buyer examines or tests the goods or a sample or model thereof and notes a lack of conformity but raises no objection or approves the sample/model.[165] The contract itself may evidence the buyer's actual knowledge by specifying a lack of conformity and the buyer's consent to receiving the goods with that non-conformity.[166] There may be more difficult cases where the buyer argues that the seller should be liable despite the buyer's knowledge of a lack of conformity. Such an argument may be raised on the basis that having actual knowledge of a lack of conformity is not the same as giving consent to it. Suppose that the buyer requested that a lack of conformity be repaired or that there were some other circumstances evidencing the parties' reasonable expectation that the contract related to the goods free from a lack of conformity of which the buyer was aware before the contract was made.[167] Should this seller be liable or should the seller be allowed to rely on the exemption under Article 35(3)? The latter should not be allowed because the buyer cannot be said to have consented

[162] The Convention recognises the distinction between identified and unidentified goods (see Arts 31(2), 32(1), 67(2), 69(3)).

[163] See Kröll (n 10) para 150.

[164] See Appellate Court Valais, C1 97 167, 28 October 1997 (Switzerland), available at http://cisgw3.law.pace.edu/cases/971028s1.html. Such a statement can also be interpreted as being a term of the contract, in which case the seller's obligations can be defined with reference to the contract under Art 35(1). The reference in the decision to both Art 35(1) and (3) is therefore not surprising.

[165] See, eg Appellate Court Granada, 546/1999, 2 March 2000 (Spain), available at http://cisgw3.law.pace.edu/cases/000302s4.html, where the buyer examined and approved samples of frozen chicken.

[166] Again, such cases can equally be dealt with on the basis of Art 35(1). The so-called 'as is' clauses are normally included for the purpose of achieving the same effect as the clause mentioned in the main text. See, eg Arbitration Chamber of Paris Case No 9926, 2007, available at http://cisgw3.law.pace.edu/cases/079926f1.html ('the Contract provides that "the buyer (the Claimant) has inspected the quality of this cargo at the X warehouse and accepts it without any claims regarding the quality". Indeed, the Claimant hired an independent expert, company Y, who took samples and photographs of the cargo. Furthermore the Claimant has admitted that company Y performed the laboratory tests on non-representative samples. Company Y selected these samples alone with no intervention of the Respondent, [who] is therefore not liable for the selection of the samples').

[167] For a reverse scenario, see Appellate Court Valais, 28 October 1997 (n 164), where the seller was exempt from liability, with one of the factors in the decision being that '[e]xcept for the replacement of three specific parts, the parties had not agreed on repair of further defects before delivery'.

to or assumed the risk of receiving the goods with a lack of conformity of which it was aware. The question relates to a precise legal reasoning that needs to be adopted. The buyer is likely to prevail on the basis of Article 35(1) since the contract will be interpreted as prohibiting the presence of a lack of conformity which was known to the buyer. But if the buyer wishes to claim a breach of rule(s) in Article 35(2),[168] how can it counter the seller's reliance on Article 35(3)? It is suggested that the buyer cannot be said to know of a lack of conformity in the sense that would entitle the seller to be exempt from liability.[169] The buyer's knowledge under Article 35(3) needs to relate to the final state and condition of the goods to be sold. In this example, the buyer does not treat the state and condition of which it was aware as being final since there was a reasonable expectation that a lack of conformity would be removed. Put differently, the goods with a lack of conformity which is known to the buyer cannot be said to be the goods which the buyer agreed to buy under the contract.

(iii) Implied Knowledge

It is not easy to prove the buyer's actual knowledge since that would require evidence concerning the buyer's state of mind.[170] The Convention has eased the seller's burden of proof by providing that the exemption can also be invoked if the buyer 'could not have been unaware' of a lack of conformity. The natural meaning of these words does not indicate the required level of implied knowledge with absolute precision, which means that its exact meaning must be determined on the basis of the particular circumstances. Some guidelines have nevertheless emerged in literature, which seek to inject a degree of clarity into this provision. The prevailing view is that 'could not have been unaware' requires something more than the buyer's 'gross negligence'[171] and is intended to indicate a higher standard than 'ought to have known', which is also used in a number of the Convention's provisions.[172] 'Ought to have known' is usually interpreted as requiring

[168] Assuming Art 35(2) is not displaced by the parties' agreement.

[169] See Schwenzer, Hachem and Kee (n 72) para 31.159, stating in respect of this type of case that 'a simple clear cut rule on the exclusion of the seller's liability at the time of contract may prove inappropriate'.

[170] 'Mr Hew did not admit that there were serious defects in all such units; and the questions were focussed upon his knowledge of defects after receipt, and before on-sale, not upon the material time, which was when Castel and TSP contracted for the supply of any particular batch. It did not seek to elicit admissions that Mr Hew knew, or must have been aware of, defects in all the J35 units, the subject of each order, at the time the orders were placed by Castel. The cross-examination was not targeted with sufficient precision to engage the operation of Article 35(3). TSP failed to establish that the particular defects which gave rise to the lack of conformity in respect of which Castel sued TSP were known to Castel at the time each batch of goods was ordered by it' (*Castel Electronics Pty Ltd v Toshiba Singapore Pte Ltd* (n 148) para 313).

[171] Schwenzer (n 8) para 35; Neumann (n 149) para 48; Huber and Mullis (n 88).

[172] See Arts 2(a), 9(2), 38(3), 43(1), 49(2)(b)(i), 64(2)(b)(i), 68, 74, 79(4).

the buyer to examine the goods.[173] If that were the approach to interpreting Article 35(3), the question would be: Would a lack of conformity be discoverable upon an examination that the buyer (or a reasonable person in its position) is expected to undertake? However, this is not how 'could not have been unaware' is generally interpreted. The prevailing view is that Article 35(3) does not require the buyer to examine the goods prior to making the contract.[174] Knowledge will be implied where a lack of conformity would be 'obvious' to a reasonable person in the buyer's position.[175] In the words of one commentator, the standard of 'could not have been unaware' relates to 'the facts that are before the eyes of one who can see'.[176]

The very fact that the weight of international opinion is pointing towards a particular interpretation is, in this context, a strong argument in favour of supporting this opinion since any degree of certainty and uniformity in the interpretation of the CISG is so hard to achieve, especially when it comes to such generally formulated provisions. But this interpretation is also preferable on policy grounds. It appears to strike a relatively equal balance between the parties on the *caveat emptor* and *caveat venditor* spectrum. On the one hand, there are, as shown, good reasons why the seller should be exempt from liability in the case of the buyer's knowledge of a lack of conformity (actual or implied). On the other hand, because the Convention's implied terms provide the minimum level of protection to the buyer they must not be easily displaced. Interpreting Article 35(3) as being based on the expectation that the buyer has to pre-contractually examine the goods in every transaction would often deprive the buyer of legal protection. Such interpretation would place the buyer dangerously close to the *caveat emptor* end of the spectrum, which is contrary to the Convention's spirit of fairness and equal balance between the contracting parties.[177]

It must thus be asked whether a lack of conformity would be obvious to a reasonable person in the buyer's position. The relevant factors to be taken into account in answering this question include the nature of the goods and the buyer's expertise and experience.[178] As explained, under Article 35(3)

[173] See, eg Honnold (n 154) 339; Kröll (n 10) paras 159–60.

[174] Schwenzer (n 8) para 36; Schlechtriem and Butler (n 18) 120; Enderlein and Maskow (n 82) 147; J Lookofsky, 'The 1980 United Nations Convention on Contracts for the International Sale of Goods' in J Herbots and R Blanpain (eds), *International Encyclopaedia of Laws: Contracts* (Supplement 29, The Hague, Kluwer Law International, 2000) eds; S Kruisinga, *(Non-)conformity in the 1980 UN Convention on Contracts for the International Sale of Goods: A Uniform Concept?* (Antwerp/Oxford/New York, Intersentia, 2004) 53.

[175] See, similarly, Schwenzer (n 8) para 36.

[176] Honnold (n 154) 339.

[177] See, eg the Convention's preamble. The Convention's aspiration to treat the buyer and the seller equally is particularly evident in its remedial structure which, as far as possible, reflects symmetry of remedies available to the buyer and the seller. See Chapter 1; also I Schwenzer and P Hachem in Schwenzer (n 8) Art 7, para 34.

[178] See, eg Federal Supreme Court, 4C.296/2000/rnd, 22 December 2000 (Switzerland), available at http://cisgw3.law.pace.edu/cases/001222s1.html (in the context of Art 35(1)). See also the discussion of this case in Chapter 2.

the buyer does not have a duty to inspect the goods, but it may choose to do so and request the seller to be given an opportunity to examine. If then the buyer examines the goods, or their sample/model, and raises no objection in respect of a lack of conformity that the examination revealed or would have revealed, knowledge of a lack of conformity is likely to be imputed to the buyer.[179] The buyer should not be expected to carry out an unusually rigorous or costly examination. It is suggested that the idea of reasonableness, which stems both from the rules on the evaluation of the parties' conduct[180] and the Convention's general principle of reasonableness,[181] dictates that the buyer can only be expected to carry out an examination which is normal in the circumstances, having regard to common understandings in the relevant industry or trade sector.[182] One question arising here is whether the seller should be entitled to rely on the fact that the buyer actually went beyond what would be regarded as normal examination which led to the discovery of a lack of conformity, otherwise not discoverable by an ordinary examination.[183] It is submitted that it would be artificial and contrary to the rationale of Article 35(3) to ignore the actual examination carried out by the buyer.[184] That would also be contrary to the rules on interpreting the parties' conduct, which will inevitably come into play in assessing what the buyer was expected to do and which require *all* relevant circumstances to be taken into account.[185]

Another question arising from the position that the buyer is not required to carry out a pre-contractual examination of the goods concerns the situation where the seller offers an opportunity for an examination but the buyer fails to take it. If a lack of conformity would have been discovered if the goods had been examined, should the seller be exempt from liability

[179] See Appellate Court Granada, 2 March 2000 (n 165); Arbitration Chamber of Paris Case No 9926, 2007 (n 166); Foreign Trade Arbitration Court attached to the Yugoslav Chamber of Commerce in Belgrade, Serbia, 25 May 2001, available at http://cisgw3.law.pace.edu/cases/010525sb.html ('The [buyer] could not have been unaware of the situation with respect to admixtures at the time of conclusion of the contract, considering the fact that it was Mr X, the intermediary in this transaction, who, after having inspected the goods, informed the [buyer] that the goods were of good quality and that there was less than 1% of admixtures').

[180] See Art 8(2).

[181] See, eg A Kritzer (ed), 'General Principles of the CISG', http://cisgw3.law.pace.edu/cisg/text/principles7.html#reason (with further references).

[182] For a similar view, see Kröll (n 10) para 158; Bianca (n 3) 278.

[183] The question can arise both in the context of 'actual' and 'imputed' knowledge. All points made in this section are equally applicable to 'actual' knowledge.

[184] See Huber and Mullis (n 88) also stating that an actual, and not a hypothetical, examination by the buyer needs to be relied upon. See also Appellate Court Zweibrücken, 7 U 4/03, 2 February 2004 (Germany), available at http://cisgw3.law.pace.edu/cases/040202g1.html ('The [seller] itself did not submit that it was disclosed to the [buyer] that the equipment was available only as a foreign imitation. It cannot be discerned from its submission that this is an evident circumstance among experts, that it can be expected to be known also by a customer such as the [buyer]').

[185] See Art 8(3).

for this non-conformity? In contrast with some legal systems which give an affirmative answer,[186] the Convention is silent on this point. Bearing this in mind and considering that the threshold for imputing knowledge to the buyer depends on the circumstances, the matter will need to be resolved on a case-by-case basis. For example, it has been correctly suggested that if the seller offers an examination and mentions the possibility of a defect in the goods, it is reasonable to expect the buyer to examine the goods. This buyer, therefore, 'could not have been unaware' of a lack of conformity.[187] As a general matter, however, the seller should probably not be allowed to avoid its liability merely by offering the buyer an opportunity to examine.[188]

Prior dealings between the parties may also give rise to the question of whether the buyer could not have been unaware of a lack of conformity which was present in previous deliveries. In one case,[189] involving the sale and purchase of a hydraulic press, it was established that the parties had made a similar contract a year previously and that the press was of the same type and had the same problem (the breaking of the spring) as the press under the contract at hand. The tribunal held that the buyer 'knew that the machine had these defects when concluding the sales contract [and] did not put this forward in the contract for this machine, which indicated that [it] accepted these defects'.[190] Whilst every case needs to be resolved on the basis of its particular facts, this case shows the approach that courts and tribunals are likely to take where past transactions concerned the same goods and the same defect. The rationale is that because the buyer neither complained about a lack of conformity in the past nor sought to demand that the goods be free from it, the seller can reasonably expect that the buyer is content with the goods under the present contract being in all respects the same as they were in the past. In any case, the buyer 'could not have been unaware' of what it would be getting. This line of argument can only become stronger where there had been more than one transaction in the past involving the same goods with the same lack of conformity.[191]

Where the goods are not the same as they were in the previous contract(s), the seller can hardly have a reasonable expectation that the presence of a lack of conformity in those other goods put the buyer on notice that a lack of conformity would also be present in the future. In one case,[192] the

[186] See § 2-316(3)(b) UCC ('if the buyer before entering the contract ... has refused to examine the goods after a demand by the seller there is no implied warranty with regard to defects that an examination in the circumstances should have revealed to the buyer').

[187] Schwenzer (n 8) para 36.

[188] Ibid. For a different view, see Bianca (n 3) 277.

[189] *Hydraulic Press*, CIETAC Arbitration, 20 January 1994, available at http://cisgw3.law.pace.edu/cases/940120c1.html. See also Kröll (n 10) para 160.

[190] Ibid.

[191] See Bianca (n 3) 278.

[192] Appellate Court Saarbrücken, 17 January 2007 (n 83).

seller attempted to put forward such an argument, referring to past deliveries of marble stones where the same packaging was used. The court held that that was insufficient for the application of Article 35(3) on the basis that it had not been shown that the goods delivered in the past had been 'identical' to the goods at hand. It may, of course, be doubted whether the goods really need to be identical in order to justify the possibility of imputing the knowledge of a lack of conformity to the buyer. It can be argued that the differences may be irrelevant, for example, where they only concern the colour of marble stones, which is unlikely to have any impact on packaging. Nevertheless, the strict approach taken in this case is generally justifiable. It is worth stressing again that the implied terms on conformity provide the minimum legal protection to the buyer, and the seller must not be allowed to avoid liability for non-compliance with them too easily. As a general guideline, therefore, courts and tribunals should exercise caution before inferring the buyer's knowledge of a lack of conformity from previous dealings.

Other factors may lead to imputing knowledge of a lack of conformity. The price for the goods may be so low that it would be unreasonable for the buyer to expect goods that would comply with Article 35(2).[193] The same may be the case if the buyer is aware that the goods are second-hand and have been exposed to a considerable degree of wear and tear.[194] It has already been mentioned that one common way for the buyer to learn about the goods prior to the contract is to examine a sample or model. Considering that the seller is already required to ensure compliance with a sample/model, the question is whether Article 35(3) has any role to play in respect of the rule in Article 35(2)(c), discussed earlier.[195] If a sample/model has been 'held out' to the buyer and it raised no complaints in respect of qualities and characteristics in that sample/model, this already establishes the buyer's knowledge and acceptance, whether actual or implied, of the presence of any lack conformity pertaining to those qualities and characteristics. Article 35(3), therefore, has no relevance and application in such cases. This does not mean that Article 35(3) has no application at all where a sample/model is used. If the dispute relates to qualities and characteristics which are not present in (or not reasonably discoverable from the examination of) a sample/model, the seller can seek to rely on Article 35(3) to exempt itself from liability for a lack of conformity in respect of those qualities and characteristics.

[193] See Bianca (n 3) 278.

[194] Supreme Court, Recurso de Casación No 81/2001, 17 January 2008 (Spain), available at http://cisgw3.law.pace.edu/cases/080117s4.html, where both the price and the buyer's knowledge of the prior use of the goods were the reasons why it was held that a lack of conformity was to be expected.

[195] See I above.

Finally, it may be that the buyer was in a position in which it could not have been unaware of a lack of conformity, but the seller was aware of it and did not disclose it to the buyer. Should the seller be exempt from liability under Article 35(3)? This scenario arose in a case[196] where the seller was held liable because the licensing year and the mileage of a car indicated in the contract turned out to be untrue. The seller's conduct was characterised by the court as being 'fraudulent' due to concealment of the age of the car from the buyer.[197] Even though the buyer was thought to be in a position in which it could have detected the non-conformity, the court stated that Article 35(3) was not applicable in the case of a seller's fraudulent conduct. This was done on the basis of extrapolating the idea underlying Article 40 CISG, which provides that the seller cannot rely on the buyer's failure to give notice of a lack of conformity 'if the lack of conformity relates to facts of which he knew or could not have been unaware and which he did not disclose to the buyer'. The court took the position that the idea underlying Article 40 is that 'a seller is not entitled to rely on the conduct of the buyer if the seller is to blame more [than the buyer]', and that in accordance with Article 7(1) CISG if the seller's conduct is fraudulent, the seller has to 'accept responsibility even if the [buyer] could not be unaware of the non-conformity'.[198] The gist of this position was described thus: 'Even a grossly negligent unknowing buyer appears to be more protection-worthy than a seller acting fraudulently'.[199] This is clearly an example of judicial creativity since if the court had only focused on Article 35(3), the seller would have been exempt from liability. This approach reflects a moral stance, to be found in a number of legal systems,[200] where fraud is thought to be more blameworthy than a high degree of negligence on the buyer's part. This position has gained support in academic writings which now treat the stated idea underlying Article 40 as being a general principle of the CISG.[201] This approach seems in line with the need to interpret the CISG having regard to 'the observance of good faith in international trade'[202] and is based on a morally commendable objective of deterring fraudulent conduct. This solution is based on the Convention's own legal framework and underlying principles and ideas.

[196] Appellate Court Köln, 22 U 4/96, 21 May 1996 (Germany), available at http://cisgw3.law.pace.edu/cases/960521g1.html.

[197] 'The conduct of the [seller's] agent has to be attributed to the [seller] and regarded as [seller's] own fraudulent conduct' (ibid).

[198] Ibid.

[199] Ibid.

[200] See Schwenzer, Hachem and Kee (n 72) para 31.164.

[201] Schwenzer (n 8) para 38; Kröll (n 10) para 162; Kruisinga (n 174) 54.

[202] Art 7(1).

B. Article 39 CISG

Another exemption (with which this book does not propose to deal in any detail)[203] can be found in Article 39 CISG which requires the buyer to give the seller a notice 'specifying the nature of the lack of conformity'. A failure to give such a notice deprives the buyer of its right 'to rely on a lack of conformity'. In such a case, the seller will still be regarded as having committed a breach under Article 35, but the buyer will not be able to invoke any of its remedies for a lack of conformity against the seller. This notice serves a number of purposes.[204] It gives the seller an opportunity to cure a lack of conformity by repair or substitution (whichever is relevant or appropriate in the circumstances). The notice enables the seller to respond to or dispute the buyer's claims or to prepare for further negotiations with the buyer, securing relevant evidence where necessary. The notice will further help the seller to prepare a claim against the buyer or the seller's supplier. Finally, the notification requirement is intended to bring finality and certainty to the seller, who will know that after the passage of the time limit for giving a notice, it can close its books and have the peace of mind that no claim arising from a lack of conformity can be brought by the buyer.

The buyer must give notice within a reasonable time after it discovered or ought to have discovered a lack of conformity.[205] An absolute cut-off point after which no notice can be given is 'a period of two years from the date on which the goods were actually handed over to the buyer, unless this time-limit is inconsistent with a contractual period of guarantee'.[206] There are, however, several instances where the seller will not be able to raise Article 39 as a defence to the buyer's claim for a lack of conformity. First, the parties can of course derogate from or exclude the applicability of Article 39 in their contract. Secondly, the seller will not be able to rely on Article 39 'if the lack of conformity relates to facts of which he knew or could not have been unaware and which he did not disclose to the buyer'.[207] Finally, if the buyer has a 'reasonable excuse' for its failure to give a notice, it may still exercise the remedy of the reduction of the price or claim damages, except for loss of profit.[208]

[203] There is plethora of material and a large body of cases on Art 39. See, eg CISG Advisory Council Opinion No 2, 'Examination of the Goods and Notice of Non-conformity Articles 38 and 39', available at www.cisg.law.pace.edu/cisg/CISG-AC-op2.html; I Schwenzer in Schwenzer (n 8) Arts 38 and 39 at 607–42 (with further references).

[204] See, generally, I Schwenzer in Schwenzer (n 8) Art 38, para 4.

[205] Art 39(1).

[206] Art 39(2).

[207] Art 40.

[208] Art 44.

C. Disclaimers

Freedom of contract is a principle enshrined in the CISG, which allows the contracting parties to 'derogate from or vary the effect of any of its provisions'.[209] This principle manifests itself in the context of the Convention's implied rules on conformity which are applicable, '[e]xcept where the parties have agreed otherwise'.[210] Therefore, the seller can attempt to include a clause to limit or exclude the rules in Article 35(2) or its liability for breach of those rules.[211] However, domestic legal systems often police such clauses, pursuing a variety of policies,[212] and may lay claim to having control over their validity. Article 4(a) CISG states, in this respect, that 'except as otherwise expressly provided in this Convention, it is not concerned with the validity of the contract'. This provision may appear to clearly delimit the Convention's scope, by leaving it to domestic law to decide whether such a limitation or exclusion clause is valid and/or enforceable.[213] However, that would be an oversimplification as is evident from a lack of agreement on this matter. The main point which gave rise to a debate concerns the interpretation of Article 4(a), which assigns issues of validity of contract to domestic law only where 'otherwise is [not] expressly provided in this Convention'. One view is that 'the effectiveness of a disclaimer simply involves interpretation of the contract terms concerning quality'[214] and because the rules on quality are 'expressly provided' in Article 35, 'the validity of a disclaimer can be addressed as a question of interpretation of that Article and the enforceability of a clause in the contract'.[215] Bearing in mind that Article 35(2) is applicable 'unless the parties have agreed otherwise', the proponents of this view suggest that because a

[209] Art 6.

[210] Art 35(2).

[211] For example, the following has been suggested as a possible clause attempting to exclude the Convention's implied terms: 'Except for the Warranty set forth in Section 5(a) above, the BUYER acknowledges and agrees that the SELLER has made no other representations, promises or warranties concerning the quality and description of the Goods. THE SELLER AND THE BUYER EXPRESSLY DISCLAIM AND EXCLUDE THE APPLICATION OF ALL OTHER WARRANTIES, GUARANTEES, EXPRESS OR IMPLIED, ARISING BY OPERATION OF LAW, UNDER ARTICLE 9(2) CISG OR OTHERWISE, SPECIFICALLY EXCLUDING THE APPLICATION OF ARTICLE 35(2) OF THE CISG' (VS Cook, 'CISG: Taking the Leap into Drafting' in HM Flechtner, RA Brand and MS Walter (eds), *Drafting Contracts under the CISG* (New York, OUP, 2008) 14).

[212] The policies which are relevant in the case of limitation or exclusion of liability for non-conformity include those which seek to tackle gross disparity between the contracting parties or unconscionable conduct (see, generally, Schwenzer, Hachem and Kee (n 72) paras 21-01–21-39), or to prevent unexpected or unbargained for disclaimers becoming part of the contract (see the discussion of § 2-316(2) UCC in the main text below). For a broad statement of policies pursued by the rules on validity, see Schwenzer, Hachem and Kee (n 72) para 15-02.

[213] See Appellate Court Köln, 21 May 1996 (n 196).

[214] Gillett and Walt (n 159) 368.

[215] Ibid.

disclaimer is one way for parties to 'agree otherwise', disclaimers and their validity are expressly provided for in the Convention. There would thus be no need to resort to domestic law.[216] This position reflects the view that if the control over disclaimers were taken outside the Convention, it would lose its ability to promote uniformity.[217]

As noted, domestic rules on validity are there to implement a variety of policies and considerations, many of which are worthy of protection. The CISG will not be capable of doing so because, as Article 4(a) makes clear, it was not intended to deal with validity.[218] It is submitted therefore that, contrary to the above view, interpreting a contract using the Convention's rules is not and cannot be functionally equivalent to what rules on validity are intended to do.[219] Does this mean that every issue which domestic law may label as one of 'validity' is to be outside the Convention's scope, even where the CISG is functionally capable of dealing with it? A much discussed provision in § 2-316(2) Uniform Commercial Code (UCC) illustrates the problem. It provides that to exclude or modify the warranty of merchantability implied under the UCC, 'the language must mention merchantability and in case of a record must be conspicuous'. To exclude or modify the warranty of fitness also implied under the UCC, 'the exclusion must be in a record and be conspicuous'.[220] The requirements of the language being conspicuous and precise, clearly mentioning the warranty of merchantability, are there to protect the buyer from 'unexpected and unbargained language of disclaimer' and possibly from the seller taking advantage of the buyer with a weaker bargaining position.[221] In the eyes of the UCC, these

[216] Ibid. See also *Supermicro Computer Inc v Digitechnic, SA*, 145 F Supp 2d 1147, where the position of the court on the validity of disclaimers appears ambiguous. On the one hand, the decision stated that Art 35 did 'not discuss disclaimers'. On the other, it judged the validity of the clause on the basis of whether it was incorporated into the agreement, using the Convention's provisions on the formation of contracts.

[217] Gillett and Walt (n 159) 367.

[218] Some writers advocate the need for the 'lowest common denominator for all legal systems', whereby a total exclusion of liability would always be invalid and no liability could be excluded for fraudulent conduct (see Schwenzer (n 8) para 43). It is not entirely clear what this proposition seeks to achieve since the same commentator takes the view that the control of the content of a disclaimer is outside the Convention's scope. Perhaps the proposition is intended to provide some certainty as to the extent to which a disclaimer will be recognised regardless of which domestic law is applicable in a given case.

[219] See M Bridge, 'Choice of Law and the CISG: Opting In and Opting Out' in Flechtner, Brand and Walter (n 211)97 ('the exclusion of validity means that there is no material in the CISG to mine'). See also J Lookofsky, *Understanding the CISG*, 3rd (Worldwide) edn (The Netherlands, Kluwer Law International, 2008) 165, n 62.

[220] English law is similarly demanding in requiring that clear language be used in a contract to exclude the statutorily implied terms of quality and description (see, eg *Air Transworld Ltd v Bomardier Inc* [2012] EWHC 243 (Comm); *Dalmare SpA v Union Maritime Ltd, Valor Shipping Ltd (The Union Power)* [2012] EWHC 3537 (Comm)).

[221] See LE Longobardi, 'Disclaimers of Implied Warranties: The 1980 United Nations Convention on Contracts for the International Sale of Goods' (1985) 53 *Fordham L Rev* 863, 381–82.

requirements may be treated as issues of validity. In essence, though, they concern the methods or modes through which parties can effectively incorporate a clause into their agreement. The CISG does govern the issue of the formation of contracts,[222] but it has been argued that because under the applicable domestic law (in this case, the UCC) these are issues of validity, which are based on public policy, for a clause and/or contract to be valid, the clause must comply with the stated requirements of the UCC.[223]

This approach, if adopted, would produce results which have been rightly characterised as 'perverse'.[224] To introduce a valid disclaimer into a contract governed by the CISG, a drafter would have to refer to the exclusion of a warranty of 'merchantability', a UCC concept which does not exist in the CISG.[225] This would distort a true legal picture because such a clause would not reflect the real intention of the parties, which is to exclude the Convention's rules.[226] The better view is that rules such as those in § 2-316(2) UCC, even if they are treated as rules of 'validity' under domestic law, should not be seen as rules of 'validity' within the meaning of Article 4 CISG. There is increasing support for the view that whilst the CISG defers to domestic law in matters of validity, the latter, being the term used in the CISG, must have an autonomous meaning to be determined solely within the Convention's framework.[227] Uniformity is required in respect of the application of Article 4, just as it is required of all other provisions. If the meaning of validity were to be determined with reference to domestic law which happened to be applicable in a particular case, Article 4 would be incapable of being applied uniformly. With this view of validity in mind, it is submitted that matters which the Convention is intended to govern or which functionally fall within its scope, such as the formation of contracts, which includes the 'incorporation of terms', and the determination of the meaning of a disclaimer clause,[228] are not to be treated as matters of validity under Article 4.[229]

222 See Arts 4, 8–9, 14–24.

223 See Longobardi (n 221) 381–83. This approach has already been taken in some cases. See *Norfolk Southern Railway Co v Power Source Supply, Inc*, (WD Pa), 66 UCC Rep Serv 2d 680.

224 See HM Flechtner, 'Selected Issues relating to the CISG's Scope of Application' (2009) 13 *Vindobona J Int'l Commercial L Arbitration* 91, 95.

225 '[N]ational law is unlikely to speak directly to Article 35 CISG' (Bridge (n 219) 98).

226 See ibid.

227 M Bridge, *The International Sale of Goods*, 3rd edn (Oxford, OUP, 2013) 498–99; I Schwenzer and P Hachem in Schwenzer (n 8) Art 4, para 31.

228 See Supreme Court, U.2006.2210H, 3 May 2006 (Denmark), the abstract of the case is available at http://cisgw3.law.pace.edu/cases/060503d1.html ('The fact that the buyer had provided the seller with mould specifications could not relieve the seller of its obligation to deliver a machine and mould fit for these purposes, nor could the warranty disclaimer regarding the quality of the products manufactured reasonably be interpreted to have such an effect, article 8(2) CISG').

229 For a similar position, see Schwenzer (n 8) para 43; Kröll (n 10) para 165.

Since the meaning of potential disclaimer clauses is to be ascertained on the basis of the CISG, it may be helpful to look at some of the typical clauses seemingly purporting to exclude the Convention's rules in Article 35(2) or the seller's liability for their breach. If parties wish to do so, they must make their intentions clear to avoid any doubt as to the meaning of the clause, such as where a contract expressly excludes the applicability of Article 35(2). Where there is no such express stipulation in the contract, it is by no means easy to ascertain whether the parties can be taken to have intended to exclude Article 35(2). There are two conflicting considerations at play. On the one hand, if a contract contains detailed specifications of the goods, the parties may have intended to create their own contractual regime of conformity of the goods that would displace the more general terms implied under Article 35(2).[230] On the other hand, it must be remembered that Article 35(2) contains basic standards of conformity that a buyer can expect. Buyers should not be taken to have abandoned their valuable rights, implied in law, lightly.[231] Therefore, the mere fact that there are express contractual stipulations on conformity should not necessarily be taken to reflect an intention to exclude Article 35(2),[232] particularly where there is no apparent conflict between the contractual stipulations and the terms implied under Article 35(2).[233] On this view, the contractual provisions and the terms implied under Article 35(2) apply cumulatively. These two opposing considerations need to be balanced against one another every time the question of whether parties intended to exclude Article 35(2) is raised.

A clause which is frequently used in practice and is often seen as purporting to disclaim the implied terms of conformity is the so-called 'as is' clause. The clause normally means that the buyer agrees to buy the goods 'as they

[230] This approach appears to have been taken in the majority of cases. See Supreme Court, 32 Odo 725/2004, 29 March 2006 (Czech Republic), available at http://cisgw3.law.pace.edu/cases/060329cz.html; *Linseed Cake*, CIETAC Arbitration, 9 January 1993, available at http://cisgw3.law.pace.edu/cases/930109c1.html ('The Arbitration Tribunal concludes that [the buyer] should have described the corresponding stipulation about the quality of the goods ... Otherwise, the Arbitration Tribunal cannot support the assertion that the goods are not conforming to a standard which is not stipulated in the contract when the goods are in accordance with the specification of the contract'); *Hot-rolled Coils*, CIETAC Arbitration, 27 October 1997, available at http://cisgw3.law.pace.edu/cases/971027c1.html; ICAC 94/1996, 27 January 1997, available at http://cisgw3.law.pace.edu/cases/970127r1.html.

[231] In English law, see, similarly, *The Union Power* (n 220) para 71; *Air Transworld Ltd v Bomardier Inc* (n 220) para 26.

[232] See, similarly, HM Flechtner, 'Decisions on Conformity of Goods under Article 35 of the UN Sales Convention (CISG): The "*Mussels* Case", Evidentiary Standards for Lack of Conformity, and the "Default Rule" vs "Cumulative View of Implied Conformity Obligations"' in I Schwenzer, Y Atamer and P Butler (eds), *Current Issues in the CISG and Arbitration* (The Hague, Eleven International Publishing, 2014) 188–93.

[233] *International Housewares Ltd v SEB* (2003), High CourtofAuckland, CP 395 SD 01, paras 58–60; ICC Arbitration Case No 8213, March 1995, available at http://cisgw3.law.pace.edu/cases/958213i1.html ('[The seller] is fully bound by the express warranty, which effectively matches the statutory implied warranty under each legal system').

were' at the point in time specified in the contract. The seller's obligation does not extend to any aspect of conformity which was not present in those goods at the stipulated time. Should such a clause be regarded as sufficiently reflecting the parties' intention to exclude Article 35(2)? It may appear to point strongly to such an intention,[234] but it is submitted that there can be no general answer to this question. The meaning of this clause depends on the interpretation of the parties' intentions in each particular case. The conclusion that the rules in Article 35(2) were intended to be excluded should also not be drawn too readily because, as noted,[235] the buyer must not be taken to have abandoned the valuable rights given to it by the Convention too easily. Take, for example, a recent English case[236] which involved the sale of a second-hand vessel[237] under the Norwegian Saleform 1993. Clause 11 stated that the 'vessel shall be delivered and taken over as she was at the time of inspection' and the court held that the words 'as she was' were a necessary part of the sentence which was merely recording the obligation to deliver the vessel in the same condition as she was when inspected. The court explained that these words were part of a temporal obligation which arose because normally there would be a period of time of weeks or even months between inspection and delivery and they said nothing about what the seller's obligations were, either on inspection or delivery, as regards the quality of the goods. The court concluded that clause 11 could not be taken to exclude terms of quality implied in law[238] and was in fact consistent with them.[239] Although not decided under the CISG, the case illustrates the considerations that may lead to the decision that an 'as is' clause cannot exclude the implied terms of conformity. On the whole, however, the natural meaning of such a clause, which expressly refers to the particular state and condition of the goods at a fixed point in time, will often indicate an intention to displace the Convention's rules and the buyer will bear a heavy burden of proving otherwise.

[234] See, eg § 2-316(3)(a) UCC (n 2) ('unless the circumstances indicate otherwise, all implied warranties are excluded by expressions like "as is", "with all faults" or other language which in common understanding calls the buyer's attention to the exclusion of warranties and makes plain that there is no implied warranty').

[235] See n 231 above and the accompanying main text.

[236] *The Union Power* (n 220).

[237] The sale of vessels is excluded under the CISG (see Art 2(e)). The case is simply used to illustrate when and how an 'as is' clause in a particular context can be interpreted as not having been intended to exclude implied terms of conformity.

[238] That is, under Sale of Goods Act 1979, s 14 (UK).

[239] The court reached this conclusion on the basis that clause 11 was not a true 'as is' clause, first assuming that true 'as is' clauses had an effect of excluding statutory terms. After reaching this conclusion the court considered whether an 'as is' clause had, in principle, the effect of excluding implied terms. The decision states that an 'as is' clause is not a term of art and expresses a preference that such a clause should exclude the right to reject the goods (and, presumably, to terminate the contract) with the buyer's remedies confined to damages.

6

Third Parties' Rights or Claims in Respect of the Goods (Article 41 CISG)

I. GENERAL

A KEY FEATURE of a sales contract in most legal systems is that the seller is required to transfer property in the goods to the buyer.[1] Similarly, the Convention treats the seller's obligation to transfer property in the goods as its central duty, along with that of delivering the goods and handing over any documents relating to the goods.[2] A buyer's fundamental expectation, therefore, is that it will receive clean ownership and possession of the goods.[3] This expectation has translated itself into a further obligation of the seller, set out in Article 41 CISG, to 'deliver goods which are free from any right or claim of a third party, unless the buyer agreed to take the goods subject to that right or claim'. It is probably true that Article 41 correlates with the seller's obligation to transfer property in a way which is similar to the correlation between the seller's conformity obligations in Article 35 and its duty to deliver the goods. Despite a close link between this obligation and the seller's obligation to transfer property in Article 30,[4] the two are distinct duties, each governed by a separate regime[5] with breach of either of them constituting a

[1] See I Schwenzer, P Hachem and C Kee, *Global Sales and Contract Law* (Oxford, OUP, 2012) paras 8.01, 28.14–28.19.

[2] Art 30 CISG.

[3] See J Honnold (updated and revised by H Flechtner), *Uniform Law for International Sales under the 1980 United Nations Convention*, 4th edn (The Netherlands, Wolters Kluwer Law & Business, 2009) 389. See also *Rowland v Divall* [1923] 2 KB 500.

[4] J Lookofsky, *Understanding the CISG*, 3rd (Worldwide) edn (The Netherlands, Kluwer Law International BV, 2008) 92.

[5] If the buyer wishes to rely on the seller's breach of Art 41, it must give the seller notice 'specifying the nature of the right or claim of the third party within a reasonable time after he has become aware or ought to have become aware of the right or claim' (Art 43(1)). No such requirement exists if the buyer wishes to rely on the seller's breach of its duty to transfer property in the goods under Art 30.

separate basis for the buyer's exercise of remedies.[6] For the sake of conceptual clarity it is worth stating that whilst a breach of the seller's duty to transfer property under Article 30 may constitute a breach of Article 41,[7] the fact that the two obligations are distinct means that the seller commits in such a case the breaches of both Article 30 and Article 41.[8] The independent nature of the obligation to ensure that the goods are free from encumbrances corresponds to the experience of domestic legal systems. Whilst generally requiring the transfer of property and recognising the link between this requirement and the need for the goods to be free from the rights of third parties,[9] domestic legal systems differ when it comes to the ways in which the latter requirement is implemented.[10] The scope and the level of protection afforded to the buyer by the requirement that the goods be free from third parties' rights or claims are largely driven by policy choices made by a particular legal regime and by its legal structures.

Before gauging the breadth and strength of legal protection afforded to the buyer by the CISG, it is important first to articulate the ways in which Article 41 can be rationalised. The main rationale has already been noted above: the goods' freedom from third parties' rights or claims is rightly regarded as the buyer's basic expectation,[11] emanating from the seller's obligation to transfer property in the goods. A related justification of imposing this obligation on the seller is that the buyer buys the goods to own them, to enjoy possession of them, or to be able to use or dispose of them. The buyer should not be buying litigation or a risk of a lawsuit.[12] The buyer also normally expects to obtain a title to the goods which is marketable[13] whereas goods which are not free from third parties' rights or claims may damage the value of the goods and may restrict their ability to be freely sold or bought in a particular market.[14] Allowing traders to sell

[6] See Art 45 CISG; Appellate Court Dresden, 9 U 1218/06, 21 March 2007 (Germany), available at <http://cisgw3.law.pace.edu/cases/070321g1.html>.

[7] See also II and VI below.

[8] See S Kröll in S Kröll, L Mistelis and P Viscasillas (eds), *UN Convention on Contracts for the International Sale of Goods (CISG):—Commentary* (Munich, CH Beck/, Hart Publishing, 2011) Art 41, para. 11.

[9] Schwenzer, Hachem and Kee (n 1) para. 32.01.

[10] 'There are differences regarding the legal regime governing situations where encumbered goods have been delivered. The exact consequences of a breach by the seller vary among legal systems. Legal systems also differ as to whether only existing third-party property rights give rise to liability of the seller or whether (mere) claims by a third party already trigger liability' (Schwenzer, Hachem and Kee (n 1) para. 32.02).

[11] See, similarly, Honnold (n 3) 389; Kröll (n 8) para 2.

[12] Honnold (n 3) 385.

[13] See Official Comment 1 on § 2-312 UCC in *Uniform Commercial Code: 2009–2010 Edition* (West-Thomson Reuters, 2009).

[14] See *Jeanneret v Vichey* 693 F2d 259 (2d Cir 1982) (where the expert in art trade stated that if the painting lacked 'the necessary export documents from any country where it had been located', it would be impossible to sell the painting because '[n]o reputable auction house or dealer would be prepared to handle it'. The expert further stated that 'on the legitimate market its value is zero').

such goods without liability would contravene the Convention's objective of encouraging trade and stimulating a free flow of commerce.[15] Article 41 can be further rationalised in a way similar to the rules in Article 35(2), by looking at the balance between the parties so far as access to information is concerned. It can be argued that the obligation to ensure freedom from third parties' rights or claims is imposed on the seller because it is generally in a better position than the buyer to know or trace the origin of the goods,[16] particularly considering that such rights or claims will often be based on the law of the seller's country.[17] Consequently, the seller is also in a better position to avoid any damage or other adverse consequences flowing from such rights or claims, and to predict, earlier than the buyer, the likelihood of any claim being brought or right being asserted.[18] Imposing an obligation such as the one in Article 41 provides sellers with an incentive to avoid or minimise any future losses or costs, which are likely to result from proprietary and related claims of third parties, or to insure against them.[19] The avoidance or reduction of such losses and costs will, in turn, promote economic efficiency.

The goods, delivered by the seller, must be 'free from any right or claim of a third party'.[20] The notion of a 'right' in Article 41 refers to the existing and established right, whereas a 'claim' refers to a mere assertion of a right.[21] The obligation of the seller is not restricted to rights or claims arising under any particular law, such as the law of a country where the seller or the buyer has its place of business or of a country where the goods are intended to be used. The seller's knowledge of any such rights or claims or its fault are not preconditions for the seller's liability under Article 41.[22] The burden of proving that the goods are not free from a third party's rights or claims lies with the buyer.[23]

[15] See, eg the Convention's Preamble.

[16] See CP Gillett and SD Walt, *Sales Law: Domestic and International*, 2nd edn (New York, Foundation Press/Thomson West, 2009) 358–59. See District Court Freiburg, 8 O 75/02, 22 August 2002 (Germany), available at http://cisgw3.law.pace.edu/cases/020822g1.html ('it was the responsibility of the [seller] to inquire into the background of the car. If it did, the [seller] should have found out that the car had actually been stolen, and thus should have refrained from selling it').

[17] See P Schlechtriem, 'The Seller's Obligations Under the United Nations Convention' in NM Galston and H Smit (eds), *International Sales: The United Nations Convention on Contracts for the International Sale of Goods* (New York, Matthew Bender 1984) para 6–31; Honnold (n 3) 385.

[18] Ibid.

[19] Ibid.

[20] Art 41.

[21] See Kröll (n 8) para 9.

[22] See, similarly, ibid paras 7–8; Honnold (n 3) 385.

[23] I Schwenzer in I Schwenzer (ed), *Schlechtriem and Schwenzer, Commentary on the UN Convention on the International Sale of Goods (CISG)*, 3rd edn (Oxford, OUP, 2010) Art 41, para 28.

II. THIRD PARTIES' RIGHTS

Article 41 covers 'any' right of a third party, but this right is generally understood to be one which enables a third party to exert influence on the buyer's ownership, control over the goods or to restrict, disrupt or infringe upon the buyer's use, enjoyment[24] or disposal of them.[25] A common scenario falling within this provision is where, under the applicable law,[26] the seller[27] does not have the power or is not authorised to transfer property in the goods to the buyer and a third party remains their rightful owner. If the goods are stolen from a third party,[28] for example, property in them cannot be passed *bona fide* under the law of some countries with the third party having the right to reclaim the goods from the buyer.[29] It may also be that there is a reservation of title clause in a contract between the seller and its supplier, whereby the latter is to retain title in the goods until the seller makes full payment. If the seller fails to do so, the supplier may, in some legal systems, retain title to the goods. In both types of case, the seller will be in breach of its obligation to ensure freedom from third parties' rights as well as to transfer property under Article 30.

The goods may also be subject to security interests of third parties who can be the seller's creditors or other parties, such as warehouse owners or carriers. Legal effects flowing from having a security interest in movable goods vary considerably amongst legal systems and it is up to the applicable law to decide whether a third party has a valid security interest and, if so, what legal consequences follow from it. The existence of a security interest

[24] P Huber and A Mullis, *The CISG: A New Textbook for Students and Practitioners* (Munich, Sellier European Law Publishers, 2007) 170.

[25] Schwenzer (n 23) para 4; P Schlechtriem, *Uniform Sales Law: The UN Convention on Contracts for the International Sale of Goods* (Vienna, Manz, 1986) 72; Kröll (n 8) para 10; F Enderlein and D Maskow, *International Sales Law* (New York, Oceana Publications, 1992) 164.

[26] The question of whether property has passed is not governed by the CISG and must be resolved on the basis of the applicable law (see Art 4(b)).

[27] See Guangxi Beihai Maritime Court, (2001) Haishangchuzi No 119, 5 March 2002 (China), available at http://cisgw3.law.pace.edu/cases/020305c1.html, where the contract required payment to be made via a letter of credit for property to pass to the buyer. The seller was not able to perform the contract and the buyer did not pay the price, with property consequently not passing to the buyer. The court treated the seller as being in breach of Art 41, but the seller should primarily have been found to be in breach of its duty to pass property under Art 30 (see the discussion above in the main text). If the seller remained the owner of the goods, there was no breach of Art 41, which refers to a right of a third party.

[28] See, eg Federal Supreme Court, VIII ZR 268/0411, January 2006 (Germany), available at http://cisgw3.law.pace.edu/cases/060111g1.html; Appellate Court Dresden, 21 March 2007 (n 6); District Court Freiburg, 22 August 2002 (n 16).

[29] See Schwenzer (n 23) para 3; Kröll (n 8) para 11. Where the goods have been bought *bona fide*, the seller may still be liable under Art 41 if a third party makes a claim against the buyer, even if the claim is based on its previous rights (see Schwenzer (n 23) para 3 and the discussion below).

may depend on a third party's possession of the goods. Where this is the case, it is probably true that the relevance of such a security interest lies at the delivery stage. If the goods cannot be delivered due to a third party's possession of them, the seller is in breach of its duty to deliver the goods under Article 31, rather than Article 41, because Article 41 is premised on the goods being 'delivered'. It may also be the case, in legal systems where the existence of a security interest depends on possession, that a third party will lose security in the goods if they are delivered to the buyer and it obtains possession of them.[30] In such a case, the goods cannot be regarded as encumbered by a third party's right. It may be, however, that a third party's valid security interest will exist after the goods are delivered to the buyer and, where so, the seller will be in breach of Article 41. For instance, if a bank financed the seller's purchase of the goods, which the seller resold to the buyer and in respect of which a charge has been created, the bank's security interest may well continue to exist even after the goods are delivered to the buyer. If this is the case, the seller fails to ensure the goods' freedom from rights of a third party.

Liens are also a common type of security which may come into being after the delivery of the goods. Take a CIF[31] seller, who invoiced the buyer with a full contract price, having responsibility for pre-paying freight, and placed the goods on board the vessel, fulfilling its duty to deliver the goods.[32] Suppose also the seller tenders not a 'freight pre-paid' bill of lading, as sellers normally do where they have a duty to pay freight to the carrier,[33] but a bill of lading referring to 'freight payable as per charter-party'. In this case, there is a possibility that a carrier might not release the goods to the buyer without payment of freight, alleging its right of lien over the goods.[34] In such circumstances, the buyer seems entitled to claim that the delivered goods were encumbered by a carrier's right. This scenario is subject to one

[30] Schwenzer, Hachem and Kee (n 1) para 32.19.

[31] For the definition of a CIF term, see Chapter 2.

[32] In a CIF contract, the goods can also be delivered by procuring the goods in transit. A CIF seller will also be required to deliver documents to the buyer (see, generally, J Ramberg, *ICC Guide to Incoterms 2010* (Paris, ICC Services Publication, 2011) 183–91, 199–201).

[33] 'In the case of c.i.f. contracts, payment of the freight element in the price may be effected in two ways. The first way is for the sellers to prepay the freight and invoice the buyer for the full c.i.f. price, which is payable by the buyer against the shipping documents. The second way is for the seller to leave the buyer to pay the freight on the delivery of the goods, invoicing him only for the c.i.f. price less freight. When the first method is used the seller provides freight-prepaid bills of lading. When the second method is used he provides what have conveniently been called freight-collect bills of lading, that is to say, bills of lading under which freight is payable by the receiver (who may be the buyer himself or a sub-buyer from the buyer) to the ship at the port of discharge' (*Norsk Bjergningskompagni A/s v Owners of the Pantanassa (The Pantanassa)* [1970] 1 Lloyd's Rep 153, 163).

[34] '[A] bill of lading stating "freight payable as per charterparty" leaves wide open the possibility that the shipowners would demand freight at the discharge port' (*Soules CAF v PT Transcap of Indonesia* [1999] 1 Lloyd's Rep 917, 921).

important proviso. The fact that the buyer is attempting to obtain possession of the goods will usually mean that it has the bill of lading on hand,[35] having accepted and paid for it. This fact may lead to the finding that the buyer has waived the seller's duty to ensure the goods' freedom from the rights of third parties since it paid against the documents despite seeing the possibility, apparent on the face of the bill of lading, that the carrier might not release the goods. The legal basis for the buyer's loss of its right to invoke Article 41 can be a possible modification of the contract (flowing from accepting and paying against the documents)[36] or such principles as waiver or estoppel which may conceivably be developed under the CISG.[37]

The position should be different[38] where the *buyer* is responsible for paying freight (a 'freight collect' scenario)[39] and *its* failure to do so leads to the carrier's exercise of a lien over the goods. In this case, a third party's right in respect of the goods arises solely as a result of the buyer's failure to perform its own obligation. The seller's conduct and performance have no connection with the carrier's lien and even a bill's reference to 'freight payable as per charter-party' cannot change that fact. Such a bill may be found to be defective, leading to the seller's liability for a documentary breach,[40] but not to liability under Article 41. The prevention of the lien is within the buyer's sphere of control. An alternative way of making this argument is to contend that even if the seller is initially held to be in breach of Article 41, the buyer will not be able to rely on it because the buyer's 'act or omission' has caused that breach to occur.[41] This interpretation is in line with the rationale of Article 41 set out above.[42]

A contentious issue is whether public law encumbrances constitute 'rights of a third party' under Article 41. One view is that such issues fall outside Article 41 since they are fully covered by the rules on conformity in Article 35.[43] This view finds some support in the history of the provision. At UNCITRAL's third session, proposals to expressly include restrictions of

[35] Unless the buyer seeks to obtain the goods by presenting an indemnity.

[36] See Art 29(1) CISG: 'A contract may be modified or terminated by the mere agreement of the parties'.

[37] See M Bridge, 'A Law for International Sales' (2007) 37 *Hong Kong LJ* 17, 32. The buyer may attempt to 'reserve its rights' when accepting and paying for the documents, but the precise effect of this reservation will depend on interpreting the parties' intention.

[38] For a similar view, see Kröll (n 8) para 12.

[39] See *The Pantanassa* (n 33).

[40] See Chapter 8.

[41] Art 80 CISG: 'A party may not rely on a failure of the other party to perform, to the extent that such failure was caused by the first party's act or omission'.

[42] That is to say, the seller has an obligation under Art 41 because it is in a better position to control, avoid or reduce the adverse consequences flowing from a third party's right whereas in this example the exercise of lien was both triggered and preventable by the buyer.

[43] Huber and Mullis (n 24) 171; Secretariat Commentary on Article 39(1) of the 1978 Draft, para 5, available at www.cisg.law.pace.edu/cisg/text/secomm/secomm-41.html.

state authorities were rejected as being too complex.[44] Another view seeks to differentiate between the nature and character of, and reason for, public law regulations and/or restrictions or measures by state bodies. The proponents of this view[45] argue that those regulations and restrictions which concern physical characteristics of the goods are outside the scope of Article 41 because they target those features of conformity of the goods which are defined and covered by Article 35. Thus, the consequences for contracting parties of regulations and restrictions which address the goods' compliance with standards relating to health and safety, environment, protection of consumers or workers should under this view be determined under Article 35.[46] Such restrictions as export or import bans should only be relevant to the question of whether the seller failed to deliver the goods[47] or the buyer failed to take delivery.[48] The character of such a ban can only be relevant for deciding whether the breaching party should be exempt from its liability in damages under Article 79.[49] However, those encumbrances and measures which arise, say, from tax or customs duties liabilities, as well as measures taken in connection with those liabilities or as a result of some other circumstances, such as illegal export or import of cultural objects or theft, should constitute rights of a third party, putting the seller in breach of Article 41.

It is submitted that the second view is preferable. Whilst the buyer is in principle adequately protected by Articles 35 and 30 in the first two categories of public law measures and regulations, similar protection will be lacking, if the first view is adopted, should any of the measures or liabilities in the last category of cases arise. As explained, Article 41 seeks to protect the buyer from any disruptions or infringement on its ability to own, use or dispose of the goods. It also seeks to protect the buyer from the need (necessitating additional costs, time and effort) to contend or challenge any measures taken by a third party. This second view fills a considerable gap in the legal protection that Article 41 was intended to provide to the buyer. That protection would not be there if the first view were adopted. It is also worth mentioning that the language of Article 41 refers to 'any right of a third party', a language broad enough to include rights of state authorities to take measures arising from public law. Take a case[50] where the seller imported a bus into the buyer's country under the 'temporary' import

[44] Schwenzer (n 23) para 6 (with further reference); also Schlechtriem (n 25) 72, n 279.

[45] Schwenzer (n 23) paras 7–8.

[46] Different legal consequences follow depending on whether the seller is liable under Art 35 or under Art 41 (see Arts 39, 40, 43, 50 and the discussion throughout this chapter).

[47] See Arts 30 and 31.

[48] See Arts 53 and 60.

[49] See Chapter 1.

[50] ICAC 99/1997, 21 January 1998, available at http://cisgw3.law.pace.edu/cases/980121r1.html.

regime, whereby the bus could remain in that country's territory only for a limited period of time,[51] and the seller sold the bus to the buyer after the expiration of that time without changing its customs status, as required by customs legislation. The seller was rightly held liable for a failure to ensure the goods' freedom from rights of a third party after the bus had been confiscated. It is suggested, however, that actual confiscation may not be necessary to trigger a breach of Article 41 since a mere right of state authorities to do so already satisfies the wording of this provision. An actual seizure or confiscation of the goods by public bodies is powerful evidence of the existence of that right and of the extent to which the buyer's ability to own or use the goods is disrupted. The practical value of such measures also lies in the fact that it is usually as a result of these measures that the buyer becomes aware of the goods being encumbered.

III. THIRD PARTIES' CLAIMS

Article 41 requires the seller to deliver goods which are free not only from 'any rights', but also from 'claims' of third parties. As explained, a claim is understood to refer to a mere assertion of a right by a third party.[52] The Convention does not require a claim to be brought in any particular form as long as a claim manifests itself in some way. A mere communication of the existence of a third party's demand should be sufficient. There is no requirement for a third party to bring a legal action against the buyer.[53] Just like rights, claims can be grounded in various legal bases. They can be brought, for instance, by a party who regards itself as being the owner of the goods[54] or having some other proprietary interest in the goods (eg a charge or some other form of a security interest) or relying on a contractual right against the seller, which may be exercisable in respect of the buyer. An example of the latter situation is where the contract between the seller and its supplier prohibits the sale of the goods to certain countries or regions.[55] If then the goods are sold to the buyer who is located in such a country/region,

[51] '[T]he Tribunal referred to the Russian Federation Customs Code 1993. Art 68 of this Code says that temporary import of goods is a special customs status providing for temporary use of goods in the territory of Russia while the goods are partially or totally exempted from import taxes and customs duties, but the temporarily imported goods must be exported in a non-changed condition' (ibid).

[52] See n 21 above and the accompanying text.

[53] See Schwenzer (n 23) para 12.

[54] See Federal Supreme Court, January 2006 (Germany) (n 28), where an insurance company demanded the return of a stolen car from the buyer on the basis that the car belonged to the company because it had made the payment to the original owner.

[55] See Supreme Court, 10 Ob 518/95, 6 February 1996 (Austria), available at http://cisgw3.law.pace.edu/cases/960206a3.html, where the contract with the seller's supplier did not allow for the goods to be exported to Benelux countries.

or if the buyer sells the goods to a sub-buyer in such a country/region, the seller's supplier may bring a claim against the buyer.[56] The supplier may, for example, demand that the goods be transferred to or be used in some other country or seek an injunction against the sale to or use of the goods in a country which is subject to the prohibition in the contract with the seller. The question that arises is whether the seller's obligation to deliver the goods free from a third party's claims depends on whether such claims are legally justifiable. The answer given by most legal systems is that the seller cannot be expected to undertake an obligation that there will be no random or frivolous claims by third parties.[57] In a similar vein, a recently proposed regional harmonisation instrument, the Draft Common Frame of Reference (DCFR), requires the seller to ensure the goods' freedom from claims of a third party which are 'reasonably well founded'.[58]

Should Article 41 be interpreted in a similar way? It is true that no seller can warrant that no unfounded or spurious claims will be brought against the buyer. However, there are other important considerations that need to be borne in mind. First, it is by no means easy to draw a line between, say, a 'frivolous' claim, on the one hand, and (to use the standard in the DCFR) a 'reasonably well founded' claim, on the other.[59] The need to draw this distinction will generate considerable uncertainty in the application of the CISG, and disputes and litigation between the parties, with the seller arguing that a claim was frivolous whereas the buyer contends that a claim was well founded. These in turn give rise to the need for the parties to incur additional costs in terms of time, negotiations and dispute resolution, whereas no such costs will need to be incurred if the meaning of Article 41 is clear. Secondly, the very rationale of Article 41 is that by buying the goods the buyer should not be buying litigation or the need to deal with third party claims,[60] which are the prospects that the buyer may have to face if the seller is not responsible for unfounded claims by third parties.[61] Finally, the seller is, on balance, in a much better position than the buyer to identify, evaluate and deal with any third party's claims,[62] considering that the seller will usually have better knowledge than the buyer of the history of the goods and that claims will often arise under the law of the

[56] See Schwenzer (n 23) para 4.

[57] See Schwenzer, Hachem and Kee (n 1) para 32.32.

[58] See Art 2:305 DCFR.

[59] Huber and Mullis (n 24) 172.

[60] See Federal Supreme Court, January 2006 (Germany) (n 28) ('According to its meaning and purpose, Art 41 CISG is supposed to protect the buyer from the very outset from having to deal with any third party claims concerning the purchased item, the justification of which he cannot immediately check').

[61] See n 12 above and the accompanying text; also Schwenzer (n 23) paras 10 and 13.

[62] 'When the claim is frivolous, such as one based on an encumbrance of a debt that has been paid but not discharged in the public records, the seller could often immediately secure clarification of the record' (Honnold (n 3) 387).

seller's country.[63] This superior position will generally enable the seller to deal with such claims more effectively and, possibly, in a less costly manner. Therefore, there are strong arguments in favour of the view that it is reasonable, as well as more efficient, for the seller to be responsible for *any* claim by a third party, no matter how unfounded it may be. It is also clear that this position, favoured by the majority of writers,[64] is conducive to legal certainty. A concern for the seller being liable under Article 41 whenever a third party brings an unfounded claim is alleviated at the remedial stage. The buyer's losses, for example, are unlikely to be substantial. The seller is further protected by the rules on limiting damages, such as mitigation[65] and, particularly, foreseeability which will prevent the recovery of those losses which the seller was not in the position to foresee at the time of the contract.[66] Equally unlikely is a finding of a fundamental breach,[67] with the result that the buyer will not be able to avoid the contract[68] or to demand substitute goods. A mere assertion of a claim will, on this view, constitute a breach of Article 41 by the seller.

Yet another view which appears to strike the middle ground between the two positions is that the seller should initially be presumed to be responsible for *all* claims by third parties. The seller, however, has an opportunity to rebut this presumption if it shows that a claim was frivolous or unfounded.[69] This view has the advantage of taking the two conflicting sets of considerations into account. On the one hand, the starting point is that the buyer should not face the risks of litigation, handling a claim, incurring the necessary costs, or even being held liable to a third party. On the other hand, it takes account of a widely held view that the seller should not be responsible for random claims by third parties.[70] The seller can thus be exempt from liability if it can show that the claim was indeed frivolous. This allocation of burden of proof to the seller corresponds well to the rationale that the buyer should not have to deal with any obstacles, including exerting additional effort and/or incurring cost, to its ability to freely use or dispose of the goods.

Despite its attractions, this position, if adopted, would give rise to additional complexity and costs. The possibility of the seller challenging the initial presumption will still necessitate the need to differentiate between frivolous and well-founded claims. The second view is therefore preferable

[63] See, similarly, Schwenzer (n 23) para 10.

[64] Schwenzer (n 23) para 11; Kröll (n 8) para 19; Huber and Mullis (n 24) 172; Lookofksy (n 4) 92.

[65] See Art 77.

[66] See Art 74; see, similarly, Kröll (n 8) para 19.

[67] See, similarly, Huber and Mullis (n 24) 172; Kröll (n 8) para 19.

[68] See Arts 25 and 49 CISG.

[69] See Secretariat Commentary (n 43) para 4.

[70] See nn 57 and 58 above and the accompanying main text.

due to the simplicity and clarity it brings to interpreting the notion of 'claims' under Article 41, whilst still largely resting on sound principle and policy. This view must be subject to one exception. It is not beyond the realm of imagination that the buyer may collude with a third party, so that the latter will raise a claim just to put the seller in breach of Article 41, thereby creating the possibility that the buyer may be able to avoid the contract. In such a scenario, the seller should not be liable under Article 41.[71] A claim by a third party is solely within the sphere of the buyer's responsibility and the rationale of Article 41, substantially based on the seller being in a better position than the buyer to deal with or prevent third parties' claims, is not relevant here. Alternatively, on the basis of Article 80,[72] it can be argued that what seems to be a seller's breach under Article 41 cannot be relied upon because it was caused by the buyer's act (or omission).

IV. RELEVANT TIME

The next issue relates to the time with reference to which the existence of rights or claims of third parties must be established. Domestic legal systems take different approaches to this issue, with the relevant time ranging from the time of the conclusion of the contract to the transfer of property or risk.[73] The CISG takes its own distinctive stance and is more favourable to the buyer than, say, a regime using the time of the conclusion of the contract, as the wording of Article 41 is unanimously understood to mean that it is the time of delivery of the goods that is decisive.[74] The later in time the relevant point is, the greater the protection afforded to the buyer. Therefore, the seller will be in breach of Article 41 if third parties' rights or claims exist or arise before or at the time of delivery. The seller will not be in breach if such rights or claims arise after that point.[75]

Despite the time of delivery appearing as being favourable to the buyer, it has nevertheless been criticised as failing to protect the buyer sufficiently in cases involving the carriage of goods.[76] Where the carriage of goods is involved, it may be that the delivery has already occurred (for instance, if the goods are handed over to the first carrier)[77] but the seller's creditors

[71] See Schlechtriem (n ??) para 6-31; Schwenzer (n 23) para 11.

[72] See n 41 above.

[73] See Schwenzer, Hachem and Kee (n 1) para 32.35 (with specific references to numerous legal systems).

[74] 'The seller must *deliver* goods which are free from any right or claim of a third party' (Art 41; emphasis added). See Huber and Mullis (n 24) 173; Schwenzer (n 23) para 16; Kröll (n 8) para 29; Enderlein and Maskow (n 25) 164.

[75] See Huber and Mullis (n 24) 173.

[76] Schwenzer (n 23) para 16.

[77] See Art 31(a) CISG.

seize the goods in transit. Similarly, the carrier may exercise its right of lien over the goods after delivery if the seller fails to pay freight, thereby preventing the buyer from obtaining possession and custody of the goods. Some[78] have argued that the buyer is worthy of legal protection in such cases and the seller should be liable under Article 41.[79] In principle, the buyer suffers no injustice even if the seller is not found to be in breach in such cases. The time with reference to which the existence of rights and claims is assessed cannot be indeterminable and last indefinitely. Not only would that make the law too uncertain but would also turn the seller's obligation into a limitless one. A time-line has to be drawn somewhere. The buyer who is aware of the time of delivery being the relevant point and the risks associated with it can seek to derogate from this provision and/or bargain for additional protection in the contract.[80]

That said, it is understandable why there is concern for the buyer when delivery has occurred. The price may have already been paid, but the buyer may not be able to access the goods because of the exercise of rights by a seller's creditor or a carrier. The seller will have fulfilled its duty to deliver, which means that the only recourse against the seller under the Convention is Article 30, providing for the seller's obligation to transfer property, and/or Article 41. Whether the seller has complied with Article 30 will have to be determined by domestic law.[81] Until the applicable law and its content are determined, the strength of protection afforded to the buyer under Article 30 cannot be ascertained. This leaves the buyer with only one possible legal basis under the Convention: Article 41. It is probably for this reason that it has been suggested that Article 41 should cover the above scenarios, despite the possibility of these rights and claims arising after delivery. There are two ways of alleviating this concern and problem for the buyer. One is to bear in mind that it should not be necessary for such rights or claims to be actually exercised or raised prior to or at the time of delivery.[82] As long as the facts or grounds on which such rights or claims are based exist at the time of delivery, Article 41 can be triggered. The second, and an arguably more radical, approach is to turn to the primary rationale of Article 41, which is that the buyer should be able to enjoy possession and use of the goods without disruption. Since such disruption does take place (as the buyer is not able to access the goods), it can be argued that on such a broad interpretation the seller is in breach of Article 41.

[78] See Schwenzer (n 23) para 16, referring to the outcome produced by the time of delivery in Art 41 as an 'inappropriate result'.

[79] Kröll (n 8) para 30 (with further references).

[80] Such as specifying a different point in time or the scenarios in which the seller will be liable.

[81] See Art 4(b). See also District Court Freiburg, 22 August 2002 (n 16).

[82] Kröll (n 8) para 29.

However, this second approach basically dispenses with the need for any relevant time for determining the existence of rights and claims. If the seller has an obligation to ensure that the buyer enjoy quiet possession of the goods, such an obligation will look into the future[83] and will cease to have a definable duration.[84] Is this how the CISG should be interpreted? It can be argued that by referring to the seller's duty to 'deliver the goods' free from third parties' rights or claims, Article 41 alludes to the need to have a relevant time for assessing the existence of such rights or claims.[85] But in the absence of an express reference to such a time, this argument does not seem to be capable of preventing this broad interpretation. The question is, at its core, one of policy. How far should the buyer's legal protection from third party's rights or claims extend? Should there be a clear point where the seller's obligation under Article 41 must fully end or should it be a continuous obligation? It is certainly true that the buyer may be exposed to risks arising from a third party's rights or claims after delivery, which include those arising from the carriage of goods or other third party's claims, especially unfounded ones. Nonetheless, for the sake of maintaining a balance between both parties and preventing Article 41 from becoming a one-sided provision, there must be a point where risks have to be borne by the buyer. As one commentator has rightly noted, 'delivery marks the borderline between the seller's and the buyer's spheres of responsibility'.[86]

V. FREEDOM OF THE GOODS FROM A THIRD PARTY'S RIGHT OR CLAIM

The examples given so far concern cases where a third party's right or claim relates to the goods. There may, however, be cases where a third party's right or claim arises due to circumstances not connected with the goods, but which has a direct impact on the buyer's ability to access, possess or use the goods. For instance,[87] suppose that an FOB[88] buyer had chartered a vessel carrying the goods bought from the seller, which was detained by the authorities at the port of shipment on the ground that the port terminal

[83] See *Microbeads AG and Alfred Ehrismann AG v Vinhurst Road Markings Ltd* [1975] 1 Lloyd's Rep 375, 377; also M Bridge, *The Sale of* Goods, 3rd edn (Oxford, OUP, 2014) para 5.38.

[84] See Sale of Goods (SGA) Act 1979 (UK), s 12(2)(b) providing for an implied term that 'the buyer will enjoy quiet possession of the goods except so far as it may be disturbed by the owner or other person entitled to the benefit of any charge or encumbrance so disclosed or known'.

[85] See n 74 above.

[86] Schwenzer (n 23) para 16.

[87] The example is based on the English case *Great Elephant Corp v Trafigura Beheer BV* [2012] EWHC 1745 (Comm).

[88] For the definition of this trade term, see Chapter 2.

operator had not complied with the rules governing the terminal operations. Suppose also that the relevant ministry in the country of shipment issued an unlawful and abusive condition that a vessel would be released only upon the payment of a fine. If the shipowner brings a claim against this buyer for the costs the shipowner has incurred as a result of the detention of the vessel, the buyer may want to pass on its liability to the shipowner to the seller, contending that the goods were not delivered free from a right or claim of a third party.

The difficulty in this case is that the actions of the relevant authorities arise in connection with circumstances that had nothing to do with the goods. Should the buyer be able to rely on Article 41? If an overarching duty of the seller to ensure that the buyer enjoy possession of the goods could be inferred from this provision, the seller would be in breach of this duty because the buyer is not able to obtain possession of the goods.[89] However, as argued in the previous section, interpreting Article 41 in such a broad manner would introduce uncertainty into the Convention and disrupt a fair balance between the interests of the buyer and the seller, which the CISG seeks to maintain. The question therefore is whether the authorities' actions in the given example prevent the goods from being free 'from any right or claim of a third party'. It is submitted that the answer should be 'yes'. It is arguable that the goods were part of the subject matter of the measures (that is, a vessel with all its cargo) taken by the authorities, and if the subject matter is defined in this broad manner, such a definition might just hook on the wording of Article 41. More crucially, however, the effect of these measures—the buyer's inability to obtain possession of the goods—is the same as if the goods themselves were targeted. It is primarily for this reason that the buyer seems to need legal protection, for which Article 41 is the only appropriate basis since no other provision in the Convention is able to create a relevant obligation for the seller.

In addition, this example requires having another look at the meaning of a 'right' or 'claim' of a third party. The detention of a vessel can be interpreted as a 'right' of the authorities if they have the power to do so. If detention was not within their power, it could still be argued that the authorities had a 'claim' on having that power. In that case, the scenario would probably still fall within the wording of Article 41. The same can be said about the authorities' demand of the payment of a fine. Whilst the demand was

[89] In *Great Elephant Corp v Trafigura Beheer BV* (n 87), the seller was held liable for breach of the term of enjoyment of quite possession of the goods implied under SGA 1979, s 12(2)(b) caused by the detention of the vessel due to the actions of the authorities. No such breach was however found in respect of a further period of detention caused by an unlawful demand by the relevant Minister for the payment of a fine.

arbitrary, unlawful and abusive, in all likelihood such demands will specify some ground triggering such a demand,[90] which can be interpreted as raising a 'claim', accompanied by the detention of the vessel with all its cargo, including the contract goods.[91] In any case, such demands will expressly or implicitly purport to be based on the authorities claiming to have the power to detain. The wording of Article 41 is flexible enough to accommodate this scenario.

VI. SELLER'S RIGHTS OR CLAIMS

The seller may also have rights or raise claims similar to those of third parties. It may be, for example, that, in breach of contract, the seller retains its title to the goods.[92] The seller may also prevent the buyer from using the goods, such as where the goods are a computer system and the seller, as a result of a dispute with the buyer, activates a device (time lock) in the computer, which prevents the computer from being used by the buyer.[93] Yet another example is a demand by the seller that the goods ought not to be resold by the buyer to a particular country. The question arising in such cases is whether the buyer can claim that the seller is in breach of Article 41. This provision refers only to rights or claims of a third party which, if read literally, excludes the seller's rights or claims from its ambit. Despite this clear wording there are suggestions that the buyer should be protected, with Article 41 being applied 'by analogy' where other provisions of the CISG are not able to protect the buyer.[94] In the first example, where the seller wrongfully retains title to the goods, there is a legal basis in the Convention (Article 30 which requires the seller to transfer property in the goods) on which the buyer can rely. There is no specific provision to protect the buyer in the other two examples, although the applicable domestic rules on property may do so in the second example. In some other cases, where the seller wrongfully retains the goods, for instance, the buyer may be able to rely on the seller's failure to deliver the goods by

[90] '[T]he Ministry of Petroleum Resources wrote to Total advising it that the Minister had "approved the following measures" as a consequence of the vessel being loaded "without compliance with the statutory requirements for loading operations"' (*Great Elephant Corp v Trafigura Beheer BV* (n 87) para 18).

[91] In contrast with the approach of English law (see n 89 above), it has been argued that under the CISG the seller should be liable for any claim of a third party, no matter how frivolous or arbitrary it may be (see III above).

[92] Schwenzer (n 23) para 15; Kröll (n 8) para 21.

[93] See *Rubicon Computer Systems Ltd v United Paints Ltd* (2000) 2 TCLR 453.

[94] See Kröll (n 8) para 22.

invoking, once again, Article 30.[95] But the fact that there are cases[96] which involve the seller's rights or claims, but lack a specific legal basis in the Convention to establish a breach by the seller, can understandably give rise to an impulse to advocate the extension of the reach of Article 41. After all, if the buyer is protected in the case of a third party's rights or claims, why should it not be protected where similar rights or claims are asserted or raised by the seller?

This concern may be justifiable as a matter of policy, but the desirable result cannot be achieved at the cost of ignoring the language of the law and without a solid legal basis. The argument that Article 41 should be applied 'by analogy', with respect, lacks any such basis. For the ideas underlying Article 41 to extend to the seller, either a relevant general principle underlying the CISG needs to be found[97] or an expansive interpretation of Article 41 needs to be adopted. As mentioned, it is possible to draw on the rationale of Article 41, that the buyer must be able to enjoy possession and use of the goods, and to attempt to extrapolate a broader idea from it. This broad idea of the buyer having the right to enjoy possession and use of the goods without disruption can either form the basis for the Convention's general principle or be used as a platform for an expansive interpretation of Article 41. However, this work has argued against the latter approach. Constructing a legal basis with reference to a general principle may be a better solution since it does not violate the wording of any specific provision. The principle of reasonableness, with its emphasis on the protection of the parties' reasonable expectations, can provide an appropriate legal basis. A reasonable buyer will no doubt be surprised to discover that whilst its possession and use of the goods are protected in the case of a third party's rights or claims, no such protection is available when the rights or claims are those of the seller. Therefore, the buyer can reasonably and legitimately expect that the same legal regime applies to rights or claims of the seller.

[95] But see *Empresa Exportadora de Azucar v Industria Azucarera Nacional SA, (The Playa Larga and Marble Islands)* [1983] 2 Lloyd's Rep 171, involving a C&F contract with the delivery having been made since the goods were loaded on board the vessels and shipped by the seller, the Cuban sugar trading organisation, to the buyer, a Chilean company. After a coup d'etat in Chile on 11 September 1973, the Cuban authorities ordered some vessels not to discharge and to withdraw from a port in Chile whilst others were ordered to divert from their port of discharge and not to deliver goods to the buyer. The seller was held to be in breach of SGA 1979, s 12(2)(b).

[96] The facts of one Australian case may fall within that category. In *Healing (Sales) Pty Ltd v Inglis Electrix Pty* [1969] ALR 533, the seller wrongfully retook possession of the goods after they had been delivered to the buyer, and resold them to other persons. If these facts were governed by the CISG, it could be argued that this would not be a case of non-delivery (Art 30) because the goods had initially been delivered to the buyer.

[97] See Art 7(2).

VII. EXEMPTIONS

A. Buyer's Agreement

There are several circumstances where the seller may be exempt from its obligation under Article 41. The first is stipulated in the provision itself, which provides that the seller will have an obligation to deliver the goods which are free from any right or claim of a third party, 'unless the buyer agreed to take the goods subject to that right or claim'.[98] It is the seller who will want to raise this exception and therefore the burden of proving the preconditions for this exception lies with the seller.[99] Compared to Article 35(3), which exempts the seller from its obligations to provide conforming goods as defined in Article 35(2) 'if the buyer knew or could not have been unaware of such a lack of conformity', Article 41 establishes a higher threshold. The buyer's *agreement*, as opposed to mere *knowledge* (actual or implied), must be established. The need for the buyer's consent also means that the buyer must actually be aware of the existence of a third party's rights or claims, which excludes the possibility of implied knowledge.[100] The reason for the stricter requirement probably reveals the Convention's treatment of the goods' freedom from third party rights or claims as being the most basic and fundamental obligation of the seller,[101] particularly considering its close relationship with the seller's duty to pass property in the goods, which in turn is an essential feature of a sales contract.[102] It is, however, questionable whether there is in fact such a principled difference between the significance of the obligations under Article 35, on the one hand, and the obligation under Article 41, on the other. The former, as argued earlier,[103] are equally essential when it comes to defining not only the content of the seller's obligations but also the goods, the subject matter of the contract. It is notable, for example, that under the DCFR, the buyer's actual or presumed knowledge is an exemption applicable to both the seller's obligations as regards fitness for purpose, qualities, packaging *and* as regards the goods' freedom from a third party's right or claim.[104] The Comments explain the rationale for this common exemption as its aiming to 'maintain the equilibrium of the contract'.[105] Thus, the DCFR's

[98] Art 41.
[99] See Schwenzer (n 23) para 28.
[100] See Enderlein and Maskow (n 25) 164.
[101] See Honnold (n 3) 389.
[102] See I above.
[103] See Chapter 1.
[104] As well as the goods' freedom from a third party's rights or claims based on industrial or other intellectual property. See Art 2:307(1) DCFR.
[105] Comment A on Art 2:307(1) DCFR in C von Bar and E Clive (eds), *Principles, Definitions and Model Rules of European Private Law: Draft Common Frame of Reference (DCFR)* (Munich, Sellier European Law Publishers, 2009) vol II, 1306.

position is that the threshold of actual or presumed knowledge is what represents the equal balance between the parties. If this logic is followed, it can be argued that the Convention's position disrupts the 'equilibrium' by favouring the buyer.

That said, the possibility of an implicit agreement by the buyer, which the Convention's contextual rules of interpreting the parties' intention undoubtedly allow,[106] may give some consolation to the seller. The question of which circumstances can lead to a finding of an implicit agreement by the buyer is to be resolved on a case-by-case basis. A general guideline to be borne in mind, considering the rationale underlying a stringent test for the seller's exemption, is that the buyer's consent must not be inferred easily.[107] For this reason, contrary to some suggestions,[108] the buyer's mere knowledge of a third party's claim, such as a carrier's or a warehouseman's lien over the goods,[109] and failure to protest should not be assumed to amount to consent to take the goods subject to this claim. Unless accompanied by some additional circumstance, silence in itself should not be taken to indicate the buyer's consent.[110] Such an additional circumstance can be, for example, the seller's indication that it will transfer its rights under a retention of title clause to a bank as security for payment and instruction to the buyer to make a payment directly to the bank.[111] The buyer's unconditional acceptance of the goods in such a case is likely to indicate its consent to take the goods subject to the bank's rights in relation to the goods.[112] The seller may also inform the buyer, before or after the conclusion of the contract, that the goods are subject to a warehouse owner's lien and that the warehouse costs will not be paid by the seller. If, following this communication, the parties agree to reduce the originally negotiated price by the amount of a warehouse owner's lien, that will point strongly to the buyer's consent to take the goods subject to that right.[113] Another example is where the seller explicitly states that the goods are in the possession of a third party and that it expects the buyer to recover the goods from that third party. In such a case, the buyer's failure to protest and an attempt to recover the goods would most likely indicate the buyer's consent to take the goods subject to that third party's rights.[114] Yet another circumstance which may point to the buyer's consent where it has taken the goods without protest, is where a third party belongs to the same group of companies

[106] See Arts 8 and 9 CISG.
[107] See, similarly, Kröll (n 8) para 33.
[108] See Enderlein and Maskow (n 25) 164–65.
[109] See Schwenzer (n 23) para 20.
[110] *Cf* Art 18 CISG.
[111] Schlechtriem (n 17) para 6-30.
[112] Ibid; Schwenzer (n 23) para 20.
[113] See Kröll (n 8) para 34; Schwenzer (n 23) para 20.
[114] Kröll (n 8) para 34.

as the buyer and is either prevented from asserting its rights against the buyer or the latter is in the position to require that third party to give up its rights or claims.[115]

The Convention is silent as to the time when the buyer's consent must be given, but there is little doubt that it is the time of the conclusion of the contract that is primarily relevant. The buyer's *agreement*, to use the language of Article 41, to take the goods encumbered by a third party's rights or claims has to be part of the contract. The rights, obligations and risks under the contract are, of course, generally assumed at the time when the contract is entered into. However, in answering the question of whether there has been an agreement by the buyer, the focus may have to be on circumstances arising subsequent to the conclusion of the contract. First, the relevant time for defining the seller's obligation under Article 41 is the time of delivery, a later point in time in most cases. Secondly, the buyer's agreement can be inferred from the circumstances which arise after the contract is made.[116] In terms of legal analysis, one way of characterising the buyer's consent in such cases is to regard it as the modification of the contract.[117] In some cases, it may also be possible to view the subsequent circumstances as evidencing the buyer's original consent at the time of the contract.

B. Buyer's Notice

The second circumstance in which the seller may be exempt from liability under Article 41[118] is analogous to the Article 39 requirement of giving notice of a lack of conformity, as defined by Article 35. Article 43(1) provides that the buyer loses 'the right to rely on the provisions of Article 41 ... if he does not give notice to the seller specifying the nature of the right or claim of the third party within a reasonable time after he has become aware or ought to have become aware of the right or claim'. What constitutes a reasonable time for the purpose of this notice will depend on the circumstances of the case. The relevant factors[119] include the time the buyer requires to assess its legal position, the nature of a third party's right or claim and whether the third party has actually taken certain steps or measures to enforce its right

115 Ibid.

116 All circumstances in the examples given in the previous paragraph of the main text may arise after the conclusion of the contract.

117 Art 29 CISG. See Schlechtriem (n 25) 72, n 276. See also Enderlein and Maskow (n 25) 164 (referring to the buyer's consent as being 'retroactive', an arguably incorrect description from the standpoint of legal analysis). The modification of the contract may be subject to the requirement that any modification be made in writing, if a contracting party has its place of business in a state which made a reservation under Art 96 (see Arts 12 and 96), or if the contract made in writing requires the modification to be made in writing (see Art 29(2)).

118 The same applies to Art 42, discussed in Chapter 7.

119 See, generally, I Schwenzer in Schwenzer (n 23) Art 43, para 3 (with further references).

or claim, or whether the buyer is in possession of the goods.[120] However, the seller will not be able to rely on the buyer's failure to give notice in accordance with Article 43(1) if the seller 'knew of the right or claim of the third party and the nature of it'.[121] If the buyer has a 'reasonable excuse' for its failure to give this notice, the buyer can still rely on the seller's breach of Article 41,[122] but its remedies will be confined to the right to reduce the price and to claim damages, except for loss of profit.[123]

C. Exclusion Clause

Article 6 allows parties to exclude or derogate from any of the Convention's provisions[124] and, therefore, the parties have the right to exclude the seller's obligation under Article 41. Whether the parties had such an intention is to be determined in accordance with the Convention's rules on interpreting the parties' statements and conduct. It would be unusual for the buyer to agree to take and pay for the goods which are not free from third parties' rights or claims. This means that caution must be exercised before finding an intention to exclude or derogate from Article 41.[125] Because the validity of a contractual provision is outside the scope of the CISG,[126] it is for the applicable domestic law to decide whether a clause, which is based on and shows the parties' intention to derogate from or exclude Article 41, is valid. Whilst the division of roles between the CISG and domestic law may seem straightforward, there are still difficult questions as to whether a particular rule in domestic law is one of 'validity' or whether it relates to the sphere which the Convention is intended to govern. Take, for example, § 2-312 of the US Uniform Commercial Code (UCC) which provides that a warranty of title (and against infringement) 'will be excluded or modified only by specific language or by circumstances which give the buyer reason to know that the person selling does not claim title in himself or that he is purporting to sell only such right or title as he or a third person may have'. If a clause in a contract, governed by the CISG and intended to exclude Article 41, is found by a court in the United States not to meet the requirements

[120] If not, the buyer, it has been argued, may be required to give notice more quickly to prevent a lengthy delay, which may jeopardise the seller's ability to assert any rights against a third party (see ibid para 3).

[121] Art 43(2).

[122] The same applies to Art 42, discussed in Chapter 7.

[123] Art 44.

[124] Except Art 12. See also Art 96.

[125] See, similarly, Honnold (n 3) 390. But see Appellate Court Dresden, 21 March 2007 (Germany) (n 6), where the stipulation that the car was sold 'without warranty' was interpreted as excluding the seller's obligations under Art 41 (but not its obligations to transfer property under Art 30).

[126] See Art 4(a).

of § 2-312 UCC, will such a clause become invalid? There is certainly a possibility that a court might take this approach. As a matter of principle, however, the meaning of 'validity' should be determined by and within the CISG.[127] What this means, at least in part, is that the issues that are functionally dealt with in the CISG, which include the incorporation of terms and the determination of the meaning of a clause, should not be regarded as matters of validity. § 2-312 UCC appears to aim to ensure the clarity of the meaning of the clause, thereby verifying the genuine intention of the parties to exclude 'a warranty of title'.[128] The rules performing this function[129] are contained in the Convention, and therefore the rules such as those in § 2-312 UCC should not be viewed as rules of validity.[130]

VIII. DOMESTIC RULES ON VALIDITY

Another point at which an inquiry into the meaning of 'validity' needs to be made concerns the case where domestic law, which applies to the issues not covered by the CISG, provides that a contract is void in some cases falling within the scope of Article 41. For example, the French Civil Code provides that the 'sale of a thing belonging to another is void'.[131] If this is the case, should the buyer be able to invalidate the contract governed by the CISG by relying on the French Civil Code on the basis that issues of 'validity' are outside the Convention's scope? As a practical matter, the possibility of such an interpretation cannot be ruled out. However, the majority of writers rightly argue that, as a matter of principle, such rules should not displace the Convention's rules.[132] The purpose of such domestic rules is the same as that pursued by the Convention, that is, to provide the buyer with an adequate remedy.[133] The Convention has a special regime, specifically designed for the needs of international trade, to deal with cases where the goods are not free from third parties' rights or claims and the functionally equivalent rules of domestic law must not be allowed to interfere.[134]

[127] See Chapters 1 and 5.

[128] 'The rules on disclaiming the warranty of title in UCC § 2-312(2) … expresses a general principle—the expectation that the buyer will receive unencumbered ownership of sold goods is so basic that the seller's obligation in that regard can only be excluded by a particularly specific and clear agreement' (Honnold (n 3) 390–91).

[129] See Arts 8 and 9 CISG.

[130] See Honnold (n 3) 391, seemingly taking a similar position.

[131] French Civil Code, art 1599, available at www.legifrance.gouv.fr/content/download/1950/13681/.../Code_22.pdf.

[132] Schlechtriem (n 25) 72; Honnold (n 3) 388–89; Kröll (n 8) para 45; Schwenzer (n 23) para 26.

[133] Honnold (n 3) 388; Kröll (n 8) para 45.

[134] Honnold (n 3) 388 ('The purpose of Article 4(a) is to prevent the Convention from *authorizing* transactions and contract provisions that domestic law *prohibits*').

In respect of matters governed by it, the Convention is an autonomous and a self-contained instrument;[135] moreover, this interpretation promotes uniformity in the Convention's application.[136] Where, however, the rules of domestic law making the contract void or voidable seek to *counter the seller's conduct*, such as fraud, deceit or intentional harm to the buyer's economic interests, they arguably go beyond the Convention's purpose of providing protection to the buyer.[137] Such rules should therefore be treated as issues of 'validity'[138] and should be applied to a contract governed by the CISG.

[135] See Art 7(1) and (2).

[136] See Art 7(1); Honnold (n 3) 388–89; Kröll (n 8) para 45. See also Art 53 ULIS which specifically provides that the buyer's rights under this provision, equivalent to Art 41 CISG, exclude all other remedies which could otherwise be available for the seller's breach. See A Tunc, 'Commentary on the Hague Conventions of the 1st of July 1964 on International Sale of Goods and the Formation of the Contract of Sale', www.cisg.law.pace.edu/cisg/biblio/tunc.html, explaining the rationale of Art 53 ULIS in terms of it being 'necessary to exclude the possibility, which Article 8 would otherwise have preserved for the buyer, of relying on municipal rules providing that a sale of another person's goods should be null and void'.

[137] See P Schlechtriem, 'The Borderland of Tort and Contract: Opening a New Frontier?' (1988) 21 *Cornell Int'l LJ* 467, also available at www.cisg.law.pace.edu/cisg/biblio/sclechtriem.html ('The duty not to defraud or intentionally harm other people exists independently of an agreement of the parties, and the respective interests are not only created by contract'); Kröll (n 8) para 45.

[138] See Art 4(a) CISG.

7

Third Parties' Rights or Claims Arising from Intellectual Property (Article 42 CISG)

I. GENERAL

RIGHTS OR CLAIMS of third parties may stem from intellectual property. A vast majority of legal systems would subsume such rights or claims within the same regime as that governing any other third parties' rights or claims.[1] The CISG, in contrast, distinguishes between the rights or claims under Article 41, discussed in the previous chapter, and those based on intellectual property. The latter are subject to the special regime in Article 42, which requires the seller to 'deliver goods which are free from any right or claim of a third party based on industrial property or other intellectual property'.[2] The reason for a separate rule[3] lies in the territorial nature of intellectual property rights, which have not received the same level of universal recognition amongst national legal systems as property rights.[4] In other words, the fact that copyright, patents, trademarks and other intellectual property rights are recognised and protected in one legal

[1] See, eg Sale of Goods Act (SGA) 1979, s 12(1) and (2)(b) and *Niblett v Confectioners' Materials Co Ltd* [1921] 3 KB 387; Art 52 ULIS; see also Note 2 on Art 2:306 DCFR in C von Bar and E Clive (eds), *Principles, Definitions and Model Rules of European Private Law: Draft Common Frame of Reference (DCFR)* (Munich, Sellier European Law Publishers, 2009) vol II, 1305; I Schwenzer in I Schwenzer (ed), *Schlechtriem and Schwenzer, Commentary on the UN Convention on the International Sale of Goods (CISG)*, 3rd edn (Oxford, OUP, 2010) Art 42, para 1 (with further references). Amongst European legal systems, only sales laws in the Czech Republic and Slovakia have a special provision dealing with this issue (see Note 2 on Art 2:306 DCFR in von Bar and Clive (above) 1305). See also § 2-312(3) UCC providing that the seller 'warrants that the goods shall be delivered free of the rightful claim of any third person by way of infringement or the like.'

[2] Art 42(1).

[3] The proposal to merge the provision on defects in title with the provision dealing with rights or claims arising from intellectual property was rejected at the Vienna Conference (see P Schlechtriem, *Uniform Sales Law: The UN Convention on Contracts for the International Sale of Goods* (Vienna, Manz, 1986) n 283).

[4] See I Schwenzer, P Hachem and C Kee, *Global Sales and Contract Law* (Oxford, OUP, 2012) para 33.01.

system does not necessarily mean that they are so recognised and protected in another.[5] If the seller and the buyer are both based and operate in one country, the seller can reasonably be expected to know whether the goods are subject of a third party's intellectual property right because the seller is generally in the position to be aware of the relevant legislation and related matters[6] in its own country. In contrast, the seller, trading internationally, cannot be expected to know the intricacies of intellectual property protection (if any) in all countries and it is not justifiable to impose a general obligation on the seller to warrant that the goods will be free from any right or claim based on intellectual property worldwide.[7] Therefore, the rationale underlying Article 42 is twofold. On the one hand, it protects the buyer's basic expectation that it will be able to enjoy the use of the goods without any disruption from third parties[8] and without the additional cost and time of negotiating or litigating with third parties, warding off their claims. On the other hand, for the reasons just described the seller's obligation cannot be absolute and must be duly limited in international transactions.[9] Article 42 seeks to strike a balance between these two considerations.[10]

The seller's obligation under Article 42 is limited in two ways. First, the seller is only liable for those intellectual property rights or claims of third parties 'of which at the time of the conclusion of the contract the seller knew or could not have been unaware'.[11] In contrast with Article 41, the seller's liability here is fault based.[12] Secondly, the seller is only liable for a failure to ensure freedom from rights or claims based on intellectual property in a particular country, if both parties contemplated at the time of concluding the contract that 'the goods would be resold or otherwise used' in that country.[13] Otherwise, it is the law of the buyer's country that will need to be relied upon. Both limitations reflect the idea that the seller can only be held liable for third parties' intellectual property rights or claims that it is in the position to foresee. This recognition of the need to limit the seller's liability in the case of intellectual property rights or claims in international transactions represents an instance where the CISG takes account of the peculiarities of international trade.

[5] SK Date-Bah in M Bianca and J Bonell, *Commentary on the International Sales Law* (Milan, Giuffrè, 1987) 319; F Enderlein and D Maskow, *International Sales Law* (New York, Oceana Publications, 1992) 166–67.

[6] Such as the possibility of searching for the existence of a patent, trademark or copyright.

[7] Schwenzer (n 1); Date-Bah (n 5).

[8] J Honnold (updated and revised by H Flechtner), *Uniform Law for International Sales under the 1980 United Nations Convention*, 4th edn (The Netherlands, Wolters Kluwer Law & Business, 2009) 394.

[9] See Secretariat Commentary on Article 40 of the 1978 Draft, para 4.

[10] S Kröll in S Kröll, L Mistelis and P Viscasillas (eds), *UN Convention on Contracts for the International Sale of Goods (CISG): Commentary* (Munich, CH Beck/Hart Publishing, 2011) Art 42, para 1.

[11] Art 42(1).

[12] See, similarly, Schwenzer (n 1) para 2.

[13] See Art 42(1)(a).

II. INDUSTRIAL OR OTHER INTELLECTUAL PROPERTY

The notion of 'industrial property' is a sub-category of 'intellectual property' and was expressly mentioned in Article 42 solely for the purpose of clarifying that such claims as those based on an infringement of a patent are covered.[14] Therefore, it is the meaning of the term 'intellectual property', which is a general term encompassing 'intangible property rights',[15] that is key to identifying what rights or claims fall within Article 42. With the CISG not providing the definition of intellectual property, its meaning has to be ascertained bearing in mind the Convention's international character and the need to promote uniformity in its application.[16] There has been much support for the view that it is a broad definition of intellectual property, inferred from the relevant international conventions, that is in line with the Convention's international character. Thus, the Convention Establishing the World Intellectual Property Organization (WIPO)[17] defines intellectual property rights as rights 'resulting from intellectual activity in the industrial, scientific, literary or artistic fields'.[18] More specifically, the WIPO Convention provides that such rights include: 'literary, artistic and scientific works, performances of performing artists, phonograms, and broadcasts, inventions in all fields of human endeavor, scientific discoveries, industrial designs, trademarks, service marks, and commercial names and designations, protection against unfair competition'.[19] With respect to industrial property specifically, another international convention stipulates that '[t]he protection of industrial property has as its object patents, utility models, industrial designs, trademarks, service marks, trade names, indications of source or appellations of origin, and the repression of unfair competition'.[20] It is probably true that whilst numerous

[14] Secretariat Commentary on Article 40 (n 9) n 1.

[15] Schwenzer (n 1) para 4.

[16] Art 7(1); also Kröll (n 10) para 12. See C Rauda and G Etier, 'Warranty for Intellectual Property Rights in the International Sale of Goods' (2000) 4 *Vindobona J Int'l Commercial L Arbitration* 30, 31–32, suggesting possible tension between the Convention's international character and Art 42 because intellectually property rights are of national origin (subject to the existence of various international treaties) (see nn 17 and 20 below)).

[17] Signed in 1967 and amended in 1979, available at www.wipo.int/treaties/en/convention/trtdocs_wo029.html#P50_1504.

[18] WIPO Convention, art 2.

[19] Ibid.

[20] Paris Convention for the Protection of Industrial Property, art 1(2) (in force from 1970; *available at* www.wipo.int/treaties/en/ip/paris/trtdocs_wo020.html#P19_137). See also Paris Convention, art 1(3): 'Industrial property shall be understood in the broadest sense and shall apply not only to industry and commerce proper, but likewise to agricultural and extractive industries and to all manufactured or natural products, for example, wines, grain, tobacco leaf, fruit, cattle, minerals, mineral waters, beer, flowers, and flour'. For other relevant international treaties, see, eg the WTO Agreement on Trade-related Aspects of Intellectual Property Rights (TRIPS), Berne Convention for the Protection of Literary and Artistic Works, Universal Copyright Convention, Treaty on Intellectual Property in respect of Integrated Circuits. For the list of various legal instruments within the European Union, see Schwenzer (n 1) para 4, n 14.

types of intellectual property may potentially be infringed, in practice it is patents, trademarks, designs and copyright that are likely to be primarily relevant in the context of sale of goods.[21]

It has been rightly argued that the meaning of intellectual property within the Convention cannot depend on the requirements that different legal systems use in relation to registrability, the degree of inventiveness[22] or mode of protection of intellectual property rights.[23] For one thing, it is only the meaning that reflects the international consensus as to what constitutes intellectual property that can be relied upon in the light of the Convention's international character and the need to promote uniformity in its application. This position also flows from the rationale, which partly underlies Article 42, of protecting the buyer's expectation of free and undisturbed use of the goods. It is not the peculiar features of the intellectual property protection in a given country that are decisive, but whether a third party's right or claim is capable of disturbing or impairing the buyer's ability to use the goods.[24] It is for this reason also that whether or not a legal system uses a special body of the law, such as tort, restitution or competition law, to protect intangible property rights should be irrelevant in defining intellectual property under Article 42.[25] In respect of the competitive practices specifically, the rights against unfair competition are expressly included in the definition of intellectual property rights under the WIPO Convention.[26] If intellectual property rights were not defined in this way, there would be cases where no breach of intellectual property rights would occur if, for example, the goods bore the characteristics which, whilst not identical to those protected by intellectual property, led to confusion between the goods at hand and those which were subject of intellectual property due to similarities between them. The effect of a third party's assertion of rights or claims flowing from such practices on buyers is the same as that resulting from other types of intellectual property infringement.[27] That, together with the international acceptance of such practices as being part of intellectual property, points to the conclusion that rights or claims, based on the allegation of unfair competitive practices, fall within Article 42.[28] That is so regardless of which body of law (unfair competition laws or, say, the tort of passing off in the common law) is relied upon by a third party in the context of the applicable law.[29]

[21] See AM Shinn, 'Liabilities Under Artcle 42 of the U.N. Convention on the International Sale of Goods' (1993) 2 *Minnesota J Global Trade* 115, 121–22.
[22] A patent specific notion.
[23] Schwenzer (n 1) para 4; Kröll (n 10) para 12.
[24] Schwenzer (n 1) para 4; Kröll (n 10) para 13.
[25] Schwenzer (n 1) para 4; Kröll (n 10) para 13.
[26] See above.
[27] See Schwenzer, Hachem and Kee (n 4) para 33.08.
[28] See Rauda and Etier (n 16) 35.
[29] Ibid.

There is no agreement as to whether the rights arising from one's personality fall within the scope of Article 42. These rights, which are recognised in many jurisdictions and include, for example, a person's voice, image, name or 'general identity',[30] may impair or disrupt the use of the goods by the buyer. For example, the personality right of a well-known person may preclude the use of the goods bearing his/her image or name.[31] No one argues that such rights constitute 'intellectual property' since they cannot be regarded as the 'product of human endeavour'.[32] Nevertheless, there is a view that they should fall within Article 42 because their function is similar to that of intellectual property rights[33] or because they are 'most closely analogous to intellectual property rights because of the manner in which they can affect the goods'.[34] This proposition is based on several reasons. First, personality rights as well as intellectual property rights are attached to the goods in a way which 'cannot be simply lifted as an encumbrance might'.[35] Secondly, whilst property rights vest in the particular goods, personality rights, just like intellectual property, affect a great number of goods.[36] Thirdly, a holder of personality rights can license the use of aspects of his/her personality just as a holder of intellectual property rights can.[37] Finally, because protection of personality rights varies from state to state, the seller's liability must be limited in the same way as its liability for intellectual property based rights or claims. Based on these points, it has been suggested that Article 42 should apply by analogy to personality rights.[38]

There are also powerful, albeit obvious and simple, arguments that personality rights should fall outside Article 42. One is that even if the nature of personality rights lies closer to intellectual property than it does in respect of property and related rights covered by Article 41, the legal basis within the Convention for applying Article 42 'by analogy' is far from clear.[39] The wording of Article 42, in contrast, could not be clearer in that it is confined to industrial and other intellectual property rights. The drafters were no doubt aware of personality rights and a lack of a specific reference to them in

[30] See Schwenzer, Hachem and Kee (n 4) para 33.10.

[31] For an example of a case decided under German law, see ibid 416, n 13. For a different approach in English law, see *Robyn Rihanna Fenty and others v Arcadia Group Brands Ltd (t/a Topshop) and others* [2013] EWHC 2310 (Ch), para 2 ('Whatever may be the position elsewhere in the world, and however much various celebrities may wish there were, there is today in England no such thing as a free standing general right by a famous person (or anyone else) to control the reproduction of their image').

[32] Schwenzer, Hachem and Kee (n 4) para 33.11.

[33] Schwenzer (n 1) para 5.

[34] Schwenzer, Hachem and Kee (n 4) para 33.11.

[35] Ibid.

[36] Schwenzer (n 1) para 5.

[37] Schwenzer, Hachem and Kee (n 4) para 33.11.

[38] Schwenzer (n 1) para 5; Schwenzer, Hachem and Kee (n 4) para 33.11; Kröll (n 10) para 13.

[39] The only potential basis for doing so could, in theory, be constructed through the Convention's general principles mechanism in Art 7(2).

Article 42 can be read as an intention not to subsume them under this provision. In contrast, the language of an earlier discussed Article 41 is broad and flexible and easily captures the assertion of one's personality rights as being 'a right or claim by a third party'. It can also be contended that some accepted general principles of interpretation, such as *singularia non sunt extendenda* (exceptions must be interpreted narrowly), point to the need for Article 42 to be interpreted restrictively, that is, without the possibility of being extended to cases not expressly covered by it.[40] Most of these reasons are driven by the concern for certainty in the Convention's application, which demands strict adherence to its text and not creating an 'unwritten legal basis' for promoting certain solutions, unless there are exceptionally strong reasons for doing so. Despite the incisive nature of the arguments set out in the previous paragraph, the reasons do not appear to be so exceptionally strong as to justify a departure from what appears to be a clear structural division of spheres of application between Articles 41 and 42, probably reflecting policy choices made by the drafters. Although not without hesitation, it is nonetheless submitted that personality rights fall within Article 41, and not Article 42.

III. RIGHTS OR CLAIMS

A. General

Like Article 41, Article 42 refers to third parties' 'rights or claims'. Considering a variety of types of intellectual property, the scenarios where such rights or claims can arise are many. A third party may, for example, assert its rights, such as its copyright in the designs of sweaters that the buyer bought from the seller[41] or trademark rights, resulting in the buyer removing the labels, infringing the trademark, and selling the goods at a loss.[42] More drastically, a third party may commence a legal action against the buyer for the infringement of the former's trademark rights, resulting in the buyer paying damages to the third party,[43] in the prohibition of the buyer's distribution of the goods supplied by the seller[44] or confiscation of

[40] 'As Art 42 CISG is the more specific rule, an analogy is not possible because the seller's liability for names and personality rights is already contained in the general rule of Art 41' (Rauda and Etier (n 16) 34).

[41] Appellate Court Arnhem, 95/246 AL, 21 May 1996 (Netherlands), available at http://cisgw3.law.pace.edu/cases/960521n1.html.

[42] *Niblett v Confectioners' Materials Co Ltd* (n 1).

[43] District Court Versailles, 01/08276, 23 November 2004 (France), available at http://cisgw3.law.pace.edu/cases/041123f1.html (counterfeit furniture).

[44] Supreme Court, T 00-14.414, Arrêt no 526 F-P, 19 March 2002 (France), available at http://cisgw3.law.pace.edu/cases/020319f1.html, affirming the decision of Appellate Court Rouen, 1998/710, 17 February 2000 (France), available at http://cisgw3.law.pace.edu/cases/000217f1.html (the sale of shoes with counterfeit ribbons).

the goods.[45] Similarly, a third party may obtain an injunction restraining the buyer's use of road marking apparatus, in respect of which a third party has been granted a patent.[46] In all these examples, a third party invokes its rights or brings a claim against the buyer. But is it necessary for a third party to do so for the buyer to be able to claim that the seller is in breach of Article 42? Suppose that a buyer bought blank CDs from the seller who had bought them from its supplier to whom, in turn, a licence had been granted by a person (licensor) holding a processing patent in respect of blank CD media. If the buyer suddenly learns that the licensee and the licensor have been involved in a legal dispute regarding the terms of the licence, does this mean that the buyer can now claim that the seller is in breach of Article 42 on the ground that there is a danger that the licence may be terminated and that the licensor may bring a claim against the buyer because of the latter's use and distribution of unlicensed CDs?[47]

Some have argued that as long as it is clear that an intellectual property right is *in existence*,[48] such as where there is a patent protection clearly in place, there is no need for a third party actually to invoke it, with the mere existence of the right being sufficient for the buyer to rely on Article 42. This position seems uncontroversial because Article 42 simply requires that the goods be free from third parties' 'rights' which, as suggested earlier in the context of Article 41,[49] implies their mere existence with no additional requirement that they must be invoked. However, there will often be uncertainty as to the very existence of that right. In the example in the previous paragraph, all that the buyer relies upon is a *suspicion* that a valid claim may be brought against it, whereas the natural meaning of the word 'claim' implies some positive action, such as an assertion or a statement. It follows that a mere suspicion that a claim, whether justifiable or not, will be brought should not trigger Article 42. However, it has been contended that where the buyer has 'legitimate expectations' that a claim will be brought by a third party, Article 42 should be applicable.[50] The reason is that the buyer cannot be expected to wait until the third party has threatened or

[45] District Court Köln, 85 O 200/05, 5 December 2006 (Germany), available at http://cisgw3.law.pace.edu/cases/061205g1.html (faceplates for mobile phones); Supreme Court, 3912/90, 22 August 1993 (Israel), available at http://cisgw3.law.pace.edu/cases/930822i5.html (Levi's trademark on jeans; decided on the basis of ULIS).

[46] *Microbeads AG and another v Vinhurst Road Markings Ltd* [1975] 1 WLR 218.

[47] For a case, based on these facts, see Supreme Court, 10 Ob 122/05x, 12 September 2006 (Austria), available at http://cisgw3.law.pace.edu/cases/060912a3.html, where the Austrian Supreme Court reversed the decision of the Court of Appeal, treating the buyer's claim as justifiable, and remanded the case for further hearing.

[48] Rauda and Etier (n 16) 36.

[49] See Chapter 6.

[50] Kröll (n 10) para 10.

commenced such proceedings before invoking its remedies for a breach of Article 42:

> Even if the third party has not yet approached the buyer about an alleged violation of its intellectual property rights, the threat of such claims being brought is so imminent, that in itself it already prevents the unfettered use of the goods.[51]

This concern for the buyer facing uncertainty is understandable, but is it sufficiently weighty to justify the extension of the natural meaning of the provision? This, in turn, raises the question of whether this position strikes the balance that Article 42 was intended to create between the buyer and the seller. 'No' seems to be the right answer.[52] First, Article 42 is, to a considerable degree, based on the need to limit the seller's liability, whereas accepting this argument would lead to a considerable extension of this liability. Secondly, affording the buyer protection for even an unjustifiable or a frivolous claim, as is advocated by the majority of commentators,[53] already adds much weight to the buyer on the scales of balancing the parties' interests. The concern for the buyer's state of uncertainty should also be alleviated by the existence of remedies for an anticipatory non-performance, such as suspension of its obligations where it is 'apparent' that the seller 'will not perform a substantial part of his obligations'[54] and avoidance of contract where 'it is clear' that the seller will commit a 'fundamental breach of contract'.[55]

Further, suppose that the goods themselves do not infringe any third party's right, but the buyer uses the goods in a process or within a device which is patented by a third party. If the patent holder brings a claim against the buyer, can the latter claim that the seller is in breach of Article 42?[56] At first sight, the answer is 'no', because the infringement

[51] Ibid.

[52] Schwenzer (n 1) para 6, appears to take a similar position.

[53] See ibid; Rauda and Etier (n 16) 37–38; Kröll (n 10) para 9; R Janal, 'The Seller's Responsibility for Third Party Intellectual Property Rights under the Vienna Sales Convention' in CB Andersen and UG Schroeter (eds), *Sharing International Commercial Law across National Boundaries, Festschrift for Albert H Kritzer on the Occasion of his Eightieth Birthday* (London, Wildy, Simmonds & Hill Publishing, 2008) 209.

[54] Art 71(1). This non-performance must result from: (a) a serious deficiency in [the seller's] ability to perform or in his creditworthiness; or (b) his conduct in preparing to perform or in performing the contract. The requirements of Art 42 constituting an essential part of the seller's obligations, the goods' not being free from third parties' intellectual property based rights or claims can certainly be characterised as a seller's 'serious deficiency' in its ability to perform or even as 'his conduct in preparing to perform or in performing the contract'.

[55] Art 72(1).

[56] For the discussion of this issue in the context of US law, see JJ Schwerha, 'Warranties Against Infringement in the Sale of Goods: A Comparison of UCC 2-312(3) and Article 42 of the UN Convention on Contracts for the International Sale of Goods' (1995) *Michigan J Int'l L* 441, also available at www.cisg.law.pace.edu/cisg/biblio/schwerha.html.

appears to have been caused by the buyer's choice as to the use of the goods.[57] However, should the answer be different if the goods supplied were such that they could *only* be used in a process which was patented by a third party? It is submitted that whether such a scenario can trigger the seller's liability will depend on further requirements of Article 42, discussed below, relating to the seller's and the buyer's knowledge of a possible infringement.[58]

The next question is whether Article 42 covers cases where the goods are subject to the seller's intellectual property rights or claims. Despite the absence of any support for the affirmative answer in the wording of Article 42, which concerns exclusively 'a third party', there is a view that the seller's rights and claims should be within the scope of this provision.[59] What matters is that the buyer's use of the goods is impaired and whether the rights or claims are those of a third party or of the seller is of no significance.[60] The correctness of this argument is almost self-evident, but there is a difficulty concerning the basis in the CISG for this expansive reading of Article 42. The suggested way forward in relation to the same problem in the context of Article 41 is equally applicable here.[61]

B. Frivolous Claims

It has just been stated that the majority view regards the claims which are not well founded as falling within Article 42.[62] This issue now needs to be examined more closely. To a considerable degree, the rationale for this view mirrors that presented in the context of Article 41.[63] The seller is deemed to be in a better position than the buyer to identify whether or not the goods are subject to a third party's intellectual property rights, to assess and to defend against any such rights or claims. Secondly, it is also recognised that the buyer's basic expectation is that by purchasing the goods it will not face

[57] See, similarly, Schwenzer (n 1) para 4. If, however, the buyer, who had an option of a non-infringing use, purchases the goods with a view to using them in a process patented by a third party, the question of whether the seller is liable depends on whether the seller was in the position to know about the intended purpose at the time the contract was made. This follows from the requirement, discussed below, that the seller is only liable under Art 42 if it knew or could not have been unaware of a third party's right or claim. For a similar view, see Rauda and Etier (n 16) 39.

[58] See III D below where this situation is addressed further.

[59] Schwenzer (n 1) para 7; Kröll (n 10) para 11.

[60] Schwenzer (n 1) para 7.

[61] See Chapter 6.

[62] See n 53 above. A third party may, for example, wrongfully claim that it is the owner of a patent in respect of the goods or that the mark on the goods bears resemblance to a trademark which is protected (see Rauda and Etier (n 16) 36–37; Schwenzer (n 1) para 6).

[63] See Chapter 6.

any claims from third parties, especially considering that that will involve additional costs, time and effort. Finally, this approach is conducive to legal certainty, considering that it is difficult for the buyer to determine whether or not a claim is frivolous.

Not everyone[64] finds this reasoning sufficiently persuasive and one main argument to the contrary is that the seller's liability is extended too far because no seller can reasonably warrant that no unjustifiable claim will be brought. For this reason, it has been argued that only well founded claims or those made in good faith should fall within Article 42.[65] However, as argued earlier,[66] in international transactions evaluating whether or not a claim is frivolous or whether it has been made in good faith, a notoriously obscure criterion, is too complex. A simpler and more clear-cut solution is preferable.

Another argument challenges the idea that the seller is necessarily in a better position than the buyer to identify and to defend against intellectual property rights or claims. For example, if the seller is an expert in manufacturing certain equipment, in respect of which it holds a patent, whereas the buyer has no comparable expertise, the seller will usually be in a better position than the buyer to identify the claims that may potentially arise.[67] In contrast, it has been suggested that if the trademark on the seller's goods happens to be the same or very similar to a trademark of a third party in the buyer's country, the buyer may be in a better position than the seller to identify potential claims or rights of third parties. This is particularly so if the seller has never had any dealings in the buyer's country and the third party's business is wholly unrelated to that of the seller's products[68] (which are, say, shoes, whilst the third party's business is trading in fruits and vegetables). That may well be true, but the considerations of certainty once again seem much too valuable to be given up for the sake of differentiating between different scenarios, particularly considering that the seller is already sufficiently protected by the provision in Article 42, discussed below, which makes the seller liable only for those rights or claims of which it 'knew or could not have been unaware'.[69] Many of the frivolous claims will simply be unforeseeable to the seller and, consequently, the prospect of its liability for such claims is not as disturbing as it may appear at first.

[64] See Schwerha (n 56).
[65] Ibid.
[66] See the discussion in the context of Art 41 in Chapter 6.
[67] JA VanDuzer,'A Seller's Responsibility for Third Party Intellectual Property Claims: Are the UN Sales Convention Rules Better? (2001) 4 *Canadian International Lawyer* 187, also available at www.cisg.law.pace.edu/cisg/biblio/vanduzer1.html.
[68] Ibid.
[69] Art 42(1).

C. Relevant Time

The seller having an obligation under Article 42 to *deliver* the goods which are free from intellectual property rights or claims suggests that the question of when such rights or claims must exist is to be answered with reference to the time of delivery. The rationale for this position is that even if a right or claim exists at the time of the conclusion of the contract, the seller should not be liable, because by the time of delivery the seller has an opportunity to discharge such rights or to resolve claims by acquiring a licence, for example.[70] This position works somewhat in the seller's favour since a third party's assertion of a right or raising a claim prior to the time of delivery does not constitute a breach of Article 42. One question that may arise in this regard relates to a case where a right had been invoked prior to delivery, which the seller has not resolved and which for some reason has not been pursued by the third party since then. Can the buyer claim that the seller is in breach of Article 42? It is suggested that the seller should be in breach if it is clear that the seller has not taken an adequate action to discharge such a right. The third party's earlier assertion of its right will most probably *evidence* that there is some factual basis for such a right which, in the absence of an adequate resolution by the seller, presumably continues to exist up to the time of delivery and further in time.

Another related issue is that in reality any claims or rights will be raised or asserted after delivery because, generally, for a third party to be concerned about any possible infringement, the goods must at least enter the territory of a state where the goods will be used and/or the buyer must at least take delivery,[71] or even start using the goods. It may also be that an intellectual property right only entered into force after the time of delivery.[72] It is suggested that the seller can and should be in breach of Article 42 in such circumstances provided that the factual basis for such rights or claims existed at the time of delivery,[73] such as where a third party had already applied for a registered right by the time of delivery without any obstacle to the application being successful.[74] Otherwise, the seller would hardly ever be in breach of Article 42, making it a virtually useless provision.

D. Seller's Knowledge

An important caveat to the above discussion of the relevant point in time for identifying and assessing a third party's rights or claims is that the seller's

[70] See Schwenzer (n 1) para 8.
[71] See Janal (n 53) 209.
[72] Ibid 209.
[73] See, similarly, ibid; Kröll (n 10) para 24.
[74] See Janal (n 53).

liability is limited to those rights or claims of which the seller 'knew or could not have been unaware' at the time of the conclusion of the contract.[75] It is this requirement that ultimately determines whether the seller is in principle liable for a particular right or claim. Put differently, the significance of the time of delivery is considerably undercut by the need to prove the seller's knowledge (actual or implied) at an earlier point of concluding the contract. Much, therefore, turns on the meaning of this provision.

Its underlying purpose seems largely based on the idea of the assumption of risk. If the seller is in the position to know about its potential liability, it can take action to prevent it or to protect itself from it. Entering into a contract without taking any such action is taken as implicit consent of the seller to assume the risk of this liability.[76] Such a limitation provides sellers with security and certainty, thereby promoting trade.[77] The precise meaning of the provision, however, is much less clear. Establishing actual knowledge is possible where there is clear evidence to that effect, such as where a third party has contacted the seller directly or possibly where a third party has asserted its rights or raised claims against other buyers who had purchased the same goods from the seller.[78] Proving actual knowledge, as is well known, is no easy task and therefore it is the implied knowledge that is likely to be invoked more frequently.

As explained earlier,[79] in contrast with 'ought to have known' the formulation referring to a party who 'could not have been unaware' is often taken not to require this party to undertake investigation or research.[80] That would mean that the seller does not have a duty to investigate the existence of intellectual property rights or the possibility of the infringement claims being raised. However, there is a view that this provision should not be so interpreted in the context of Article 42. First, the seller, the argument runs, is often in a better position than the buyer to know the individual components making up the goods, and to identify possible infringements; and, secondly, if there is no such duty imposed on the seller, its liability for a third party's intellectual property rights will be considerably reduced, so much so that it would wholly lose its practical significance.[81] Following this reasoning, the suggestion is that the seller should a have a duty to research, at least in the case of registered intellectual property rights.[82]

These propositions are contentious, as regards both the broad stance that a duty to research should be imposed and the specific arguments in

[75] Art 42(1).
[76] *Cf* Arts 25 and 74 CISG.
[77] For another rationale, see the discussion of Art 42 above.
[78] See Kröll (n 10) para 26.
[79] See Chapter 5 with further references.
[80] See Kröll (n 10) para 28.
[81] See Schwenzer (n 1) para 15.
[82] See Schwenzer (n 1) para 15; Rauda and Etier (n 16) 46.

support of this stance. To begin with the objections to the imposition of a duty to investigate, one objection is that not imposing such a duty promotes consistency in the Convention's application as a whole since this is how the very same wording is interpreted by the majority of commentators in the context of Article 35(3).[83] Attributing the same clear meaning to each of the standards of implied knowledge injects precision and certainty and this approach must be encouraged. This is a serious objection and it must not be dismissed lightly. That said, whilst there is considerable support in favour of not interpreting the words 'could not have been unaware' as imposing a duty to investigate under Article 35(3), this view is by no means a settled one. For example, the same wording is used in Article 40[84] and there is certainly no consensus there regarding the precise meaning of this phrase, with the views ranging between conduct which amounts to something more than gross negligence,[85] gross negligence[86] or a mere failure to exercise ordinary care.[87] In contrast with some other provisions where this phrase is used in order to *exempt* parties from liability (Article 42(2)(a)) or from the adverse consequences of failing to give the required notice[88] (Article 40), Article 42(1) seeks to *define a seller's obligation* under the contract, an important part of which is to ensure that the buyer's use of the goods will not be disturbed. Therefore, it seems justifiable to expect that in some circumstances the seller may have to investigate whether there are third parties' rights or claims which can interfere with the buyer's use of the goods.[89]

It can be contended that extending the seller's potential liability by imposing a duty to investigate may result, paradoxically, in the elimination of its liability if attention is briefly turned to another provision of Article 42, according to which the seller has no obligation under Article 42 if 'at the time of the conclusion of the contract the buyer knew or could not

[83] See Chapter 5.

[84] See Chapter 5 for a brief discussion of this provision.

[85] See Appellate Court Ghent, 2006/AR/477, 16 April 2007 (Belgium), available at http://cisgw3.law.pace.edu/cases/070416b1.html ('severe negligence'); Appellate Court Ghent, 4 October 2004 (Belgium), available at http://cisgw3.law.pace.edu/cases/041004b1.html ('fraud'); Appellate Court Schleswig, 22 August 2002 (Germany), available at http://cisgw3.law.pace.edu/cases/020822g2.html ('bad faith'); Commercial Court Bern, 17 January 2002 (Switzerland), available at http://cisgw3.law.pace.edu/cases/020117s1.html ('bad faith or fraud').

[86] See Federal Supreme Court, VIII ZR 123/88, 5 July 1989 (Germany), available at http://cisgw3.law.pace.edu/cases/890705g1.html (ULIS); Appellate Court Düsseldorf, 17 U 110/02, 23 January 2004 (Germany), available at http://cisgw3.law.pace.edu/cases/040123g1.html; Appellate Court Celle, 10 March 2004 (Germany), available at http://cisgw3.law.pace.edu/cases/040310g1.html; ICAC 53/2006, 19 October 2006, available at http://cisgw3.law.pace.edu/cases/061019r1.html; Schlechtriem (n 3) 69.

[87] Enderlein and Maskow (n 5) 163.

[88] See Art 39.

[89] The need to investigate may even be in the seller's own long-term interest as information thus obtained may be important for its future trading activities and development of products (see Kröll (n 10) para 31).

have been unaware of the right or claim'.[90] As can be seen, the standard of knowledge imputed to the buyer is identical to the one which is to be imputed to the seller and the obvious argument is that the buyer should also have a duty to investigate. If the seller has a duty to research in the country of use and if the research would reveal a third party's intellectual property right, the buyer is expected to discover the same, thereby preventing the seller's liability[91] in many cases.[92] Such an interpretation would undermine the strength of protection that Article 42 was intended to afford to the buyer. It is therefore suggested that despite the identical wording, the duty to investigate should not be imposed on the buyer whilst it *may* be imposed on the seller.

Turning now to specific points underpinning the view that the seller has a duty to investigate, it will be recalled that the first argument is that the seller is in a better position than the buyer to identify and deal with intellectual property rights or claims. The seller will not always be in such a superior position. For example, in the case of trademarks, the buyer, who knows the trademark on the goods, will often be in just as good a position, if not better, to foresee possible infringements because it will normally have better knowledge of the market where the goods will be used than the seller.[93] Similarly, a seller who is an intermediary, as opposed to a manufacturer who is well aware of the patented parts or features of the goods, cannot generally be expected to be in any superior position to identify possible patent infringements.[94] In such cases, there is little doubt that no knowledge of an intellectual property right can be imputed to the seller. However, doubts as to the absence of the requisite knowledge will arise if such a right is easily discoverable through the relevant registers[95] and/or there are other circumstances pointing to the need to imply this knowledge, such as where the seller sold the goods to this market before, has a branch in the country of use and was aware of or had to deal with a third party's rights or claims.[96] The size of the seller and its expertise in the aspects of intellectual property in question are also highly relevant. The seller being a large company with substantial expertise and resources, legal and otherwise, is a factor in favour of expecting the seller to have carried out the relevant investigation.[97]

[90] Art 42(2)(a).
[91] See Shinn (n 21) 124.
[92] But not in all cases because it cannot be assumed that the seller and the buyer will always be expected to discover the same information (because of the differences in their individual circumstances).
[93] See Janal (n 53) 213–14; VanDuzer (n 67).
[94] See Janal (n 53) 214.
[95] See Kröll (n 10) para 33.
[96] See Federal Supreme Court, VIII ZR 159/94, 8 March 1995 (Germany), available at http://cisgw3.law.pace.edu/cases/950308g3.html and the respective discussions in Chapters 3 and 4.
[97] See Kröll (n 10) para 33.

Does the fact that the relevant rights are registered constitute a dividing line between where the seller has, and where it does not have, a duty to investigate? The reason why some give an affirmative answer is that where a right is registered the seller is in a position to discover it. For example, patents usually come into existence when issued by a relevant authority and are listed in the register.[98] In this case, a seller who is a manufacturer and knows its technology will be able to search for a patent in the public registers.[99] It has been contended, however, that this view is too crude because the level of difficulty of identifying an intellectual property right is not always linked to whether it is registered.[100] For instance, the existence of copyright does not depend on registration,[101] but the relevant research may be relatively easy if the state in question has ratified a relevant international convention.[102] It is tentatively suggested, therefore, that whilst registration is a strong factor relevant in assessing whether the seller 'could not have been unaware' of a right, it cannot be regarded as an immutable line dividing cases where the knowledge can be imputed to the seller from those where it cannot.

The final question relates to what it is that the seller needs to know or be aware of. It has rightly been suggested that the seller should not be expected necessarily to know or to be in the position to be aware of a precise nature of a right or claim.[103] It is the seller's awareness (actual or implied) of the facts which can give rise to a right or claim that is critical because once this knowledge is established the seller can reasonably foresee that the buyer's use of the goods will be affected.[104] This approach resonates with the rationale, partly underlying Article 42, of ensuring that the buyer's use of the goods is not disrupted. For example, if the seller knows that the goods, whilst non-infringing in themselves, can *only* be used in a process which is patented by a third party, the seller is in a position to know that the buyer's use of the goods will lead to an infringement and should be liable.

IV. TERRITORIAL RESTRICTIONS

The sphere of the seller's liability is limited not only by the knowledge requirement, addressed in the previous section, but also by the categories of countries whose laws are relevant in assessing the existence of third parties' rights or claims. The starting point is that it is the law of the state where 'the

[98] See VanDuzer (n 67).
[99] Ibid.
[100] Janal (n 53) 214.
[101] Ibid.
[102] See Janal (n 53) 214.
[103] Ibid 216.
[104] See ibid.

goods will be resold or otherwise used' that is relevant, but that is so only 'if it was contemplated by the parties at the time of the conclusion of the contract that the goods would be resold or otherwise used in that State'.[105] The policy behind this provision lies once again in the Convention seeking both to be fair to the seller and to enable the parties to effectively manage the risks. As explained earlier, the seller cannot be expected to know intellectual property laws worldwide and can only be held liable for rights or claims under the law of a country in which, as the seller could foresee, the goods will be used. Once the seller knows the laws of which country are controlling, it is in the position to protect itself if it does not want to undertake this liability, by negotiating an exclusion or a limitation of liability clause, procuring insurance against that liability, or even refusing to enter into the contract altogether. A failure to do so can be taken as the seller's assumption of the risk of this liability. This means that no change in the destination of the goods subsequent to the conclusion of the contract is relevant to assessing the seller's obligation.[106]

The parties' 'contemplation' does not require an express agreement.[107] It should be sufficient to infer the seller's awareness of a relevant country from the circumstances. Such an inference could be easily drawn if the buyer unequivocally informed the seller about a relevant country. The buyer's request to deliver to a country other than the country where it has its place of business may be an example where knowledge can be imputed to the seller. The buyer's request for manuals or documents in a language which is not that used in the buyer's country may also be a factor pointing to the communication of an intention to use the goods in another country. However, where one and the same language is used in several countries, this request may be of little help in identifying the destination of the goods. If the parties have had a long-standing business relationship and the seller had always exported the goods to a particular state, other than that where the buyer has its place of business, a 'practice' may be established to this effect,[108] meeting the 'contemplation' requirement. Even if these dealings do not amount to a 'practice', they are still relevant factors in assessing whether that importing country was within the parties' contemplation.[109] The reference to the country where the goods will be 'sold or otherwise used' most probably means that the laws of more than one state may be controlling, in which case the seller's obligation will be expanded.[110] The buyer may, for example, inform the seller that it will *use* one part of the goods in one country and *sell* the other part to its sub-buyers in another

105 Art 42(1)(a).
106 See Schwenzer (n 1) para 11.
107 See ibid; Kröll (n 10) para 16.
108 See Arts 9(1) and 8(3).
109 See Art 8(3).
110 See Schwenzer (n 1) para 11; Kröll (n 10) para 16.

country. The seller in this case will have to be responsible for any rights or claims in both these countries.

Where the parties did not contemplate a country where the goods would be used or sold, it is up to the law of the country where the buyer has its place of business to determine whether there are intellectual property rights or claims of third parties.[111] This provision can be explained on the basis that in the absence of any circumstances to the contrary, it is reasonable to assume that the buyer will use or deal with the goods in the country where it has its place of business.[112] The reference to the need to rely on the law of the buyer's country 'in any other case'[113] makes clear that this provision is alternative to, and not cumulative with, the provision which relies on the law of the country where the goods will be used or sold.[114] With the conclusion of the contract being the relevant time, any change in the buyer's place of business after that point is to be disregarded.[115]

Can the laws of countries, other than those mentioned thus far, be relevant for the purpose of defining the seller's obligation under Article 42? It may be the case that the third parties' rights in the country of use or sale or in the buyer's place of business arise because these countries recognise, under the relevant international treaties, the existence of an intellectual property right in another country as if it were conferred or granted in them.[116] In such a case, the countries of use or sale or where the buyer has its place of business may, for example, protect a third party's right originating from the seller's country in the same way as they would protect a right granted on their own territory. There is no reason why such a case should not be covered because it is ultimately under the laws of the countries specified in Article 42 that the existence of a third party's right is recognised. This fact holds true despite it resulting from an international treaty mechanism.

A more difficult case is where, due to the existence of such treaties, a third party is able to enforce its rights, originating under the laws of the country of use or sale or the buyer's country, and that results in the goods being seized, say, whilst they were in the seller's country or in a transit country. The question is whether the buyer can claim a breach of Article 42 in such

[111] See Art 42(1)(b).
[112] See Kröll (n 10) para 18.
[113] See ibid.
[114] See, similarly, Schwenzer (n 1) para 12.
[115] See ibid.
[116] See Madrid Agreement Concerning the International Registration of Marks, Art 4(1), available at www.wipo.int/export/sites/www/madrid/en/legal_texts/pdf/madrid_agreement.pdf ('the protection of the mark in each of the contracting countries concerned shall be the same as if the mark had been filed therein direct'); see European Patent Convention, Art 64(1), available at http://documents.epo.org/projects/babylon/eponet.nsf/0/00E0CD7FD461C0D5C1257C060050C376/$File/EPC_15th_edition_2013.pdf ('A European patent shall, subject to the provisions of paragraph 2, confer on its proprietor ... in each Contracting State in respect of which it is granted, the same rights as would be conferred by a national patent granted in that State').

circumstances. If seizure takes place before the goods are delivered,[117] the buyer will be adequately protected as it will be able to invoke its remedies for non-delivery. The question is then significant where seizure occurs after delivery. It is submitted that the buyer should be able to invoke Article 42. Where the right originates from a country of use or sale and the parties contemplated the use or sale in that country, the right of a third party does exist so far as Article 42 is concerned.[118] The seizure of the goods before their arrival in that country is merely a consequence of the existence of that right.[119] In addition, if Article 42 were not applicable, there would be a gap in the legal protection afforded to the buyer because, with the goods having been delivered, no other breach by the seller (which could provide a legal basis for the exercise of remedies) would exist.[120]

V. EXEMPTIONS FROM LIABILITY

A. Buyer's Knowledge

The seller will not be liable under Article 42 if 'at the time of the conclusion of the contract the buyer knew or could not have been unaware of the right or claim' of a third party.[121] The provision corresponds to that in Article 35(3) and the rationale underlying the latter is generally relevant in the present context, with the exception that it targets not the aspects of conformity covered by Article 35(2), but the freedom from intellectual property right or claims.[122] Establishing the buyer's actual knowledge is often difficult, but there will be circumstances where there is little doubt of its awareness of a right or claim, such as where there is evidence that before the contract was made the buyer had been informed by a well-informed expert in the goods[123] or by its legal advisors that the goods were not free

[117] For the definition of delivery, see Art 31 CISG.

[118] See, similarly, Kröll (n 10) para 22.

[119] *Cf* Schwenzer (n 1) para 14, stating that in such circumstance the seller is liable 'for a seizure in the State of transit'.

[120] Outside the context of EU regulations (on which, see detailed references and explanations in ibid), seizure in transit is unlikely to occur frequently (see Paris Convention (n 20) Art 9(4); TRIPS (n 20) Art 51, n 13). See further Schwenzer (n 1) para 14, suggesting that if the goods are processed, packaged or finished in the transit country, that will constitute putting them into circulation and an infringement of an intellectual property right of a third party. That, in turn, means that seizure in transit will occur more frequently. This commentator also rightly notes that if these actions were performed at the request of the buyer, the seller should not be liable because any breach that would have otherwise existed would be caused by the buyer's actions (see Art 80 CISG).

[121] Art 42(2)(a).

[122] See Chapter 5.

[123] See District Court Versailles, 01/08276, 23 November 2004 (France), available at http://cisgw3.law.pace.edu/cases/041123f1.html, where the buyer of furniture consulted with specialists in the field of interior decoration.

from third parties' rights or claims. If the buyer is aware of the existence of a claim in relation to the goods, it is of no significance whether or not the buyer considers a claim to be justified.[124] Since the seller can be held liable for frivolous claims, so should it be exempt from liability if a claim, of which the buyer is aware, turns out to be unjustifiable.

As seen earlier,[125] the meaning of 'could not have been unaware' is far from clear. This standard of the buyer's implied knowledge is identically phrased to the standard of the seller's implied knowledge which is necessary for a seller to be liable under Article 42. It has been contended here[126] that despite the identical wording there are good reasons why a duty to investigate the existence of a right or claim can be imposed on the seller, whereas no such duty should be imposed on the buyer. However, if the parties agreed that the buyer would be responsible for investigating the existence of intellectual property rights in the country of use or distribution of the goods and that investigation would have revealed their existence, knowledge of these rights should be imputed to the buyer.[127] Ultimately, the meaning of 'could not have been unaware' is to be derived from the circumstances. Where the buyer knows, for example, that the goods purport to represent a well-known brand, but also knows that the manufacturer is not the owner of the brand and is not in any way authorised to manufacture the goods using that brand, the buyer certainly 'could not have been unaware' that the goods were counterfeit.[128] A more difficult question of whether such knowledge could be implied was raised in an earlier discussed case where the buyer was aware that there was a dispute between the licensee (the seller's supplier) and the licensor of CDs and merely suspected that a claim might be brought against it if it used or distributed these CDs bought from the seller.[129] It has been argued above that this scenario should not even trigger the seller's liability, let alone the seller's exemption from it on the ground of the buyer's knowledge. However, even if the seller's obligation under Article 42 is held to exist, it is unlikely that the high threshold of the buyer's implied knowledge has been crossed.[130] That said, much will depend on whether the dispute, of which the buyer is aware, manifests the existence of a right which can be asserted against the buyer. If, for instance, as a result of the dispute the licensor terminated the licence agreement with

[124] See, similarly, Kröll (n 10) para 37.
[125] See Chapter 5 for the discussion of Art 35(3) and III D below.
[126] See III D below.
[127] See Schwenzer (n 1) para 18.
[128] See District Court Versailles, 23 November 2004 (n 123).
[129] See Supreme Court, 12 September 2006 (n 47 and the accompanying main text).
[130] The court of first instance in this case took the view that no knowledge could be imputed to the buyer: '[Buyer]'s awareness concerning the licence fee dispute between [proprietary company] and [licensor] cannot be put on a par with [buyer] being aware of any existing property right on the side of [licensor]. The mere dispute over licence fees would not at all affect the validity of the licence contract concluded between [proprietary company] and [licensor]' (see ibid).

the licensee, that would be a factor pointing strongly in favour of imputing knowledge to the buyer that the goods bought after the termination of the licence agreement were not free from an intellectual property right.[131]

The bar as to the buyer's implied knowledge seems to have been unjustifiably lowered where courts have exempted the seller from liability merely on the basis that the buyer was itself a 'professional' or an expert in the relevant trade.[132] For instance, in a case involving the sale of footwear with ribbons, infringing a third party's trademark, it was held that '[the] buyer, as an informed professional, could not ignore the infringemental nature of the ribbons which he presented and sold in France'.[133]

This approach is based on two assumptions. First, the decision assumes that the very fact that the goods are intended to be used in France means that the buyer, who is based in France, cannot be unaware of the existence of intellectual property rights. It has been rightly pointed out that even an 'experienced buyer cannot be assumed to know of all relevant intellectual property rights in their home country'.[134] This assumption cannot therefore constitute a fixed position to be adopted in all cases. Secondly, decisions such as these are also premised on the expectation that the buyer should investigate the existence of intellectual property rights and, as explained, this is not a desirable way forward.

Where a trademark is one which is truly well known internationally, it will be difficult for the buyer to argue that it was not in the position to know about the existence of a third party's intellectual property right.[135] This will be particularly so where the buyer itself requests the seller to attach the trademark to the goods. In one case involving the sale of jean boots,[136] the buyer who, as contemplated by the parties, intended to distribute them in the United States requested the seller to attach the symbol 'Levi's Jeans'. Noting that the trademark was registered by the American company 'Levi's', the court stated that it was 'not a small, unknown company' and that its goods were 'marketed around the world'. The buyer,

[131] See, again, the following statement by the court of first instance in this case: 'The burden of proving the awareness or culpable unawareness of the buyer in terms of Art 42(2)(a) CISG was on the seller. [Liquidator of seller's assets] did not sufficiently substantiate that, before December 2000, [buyer] had been already aware of the termination of the licence contract by [licensor] and, therefore, of the existence of its industrial property rights regarding the CD media delivered in May and from September to November 2000 and those produced after the termination' (ibid).

[132] See Schwenzer (n 1) para 18, who is similarly critical of these decisions.

[133] Appellate Court Rouen, 1998/710, 17 February 2000 (France), available at http://cisgw3.law.pace.edu/cases/000217f1.html, the decision affirmed by Supreme Court, T 00-14.414, Arrêt no 526 F-P, 19 March 2002 (France), available at http://cisgw3.law.pace.edu/cases/020319f1.html. The same approach was taken in Appellate Court Colmar, 1B 98/01776, 13 November 2002 (France), available at http://cisgw3.law.pace.edu/cases/021113f1.html.

[134] See Kröll (n 10) para 38.

[135] For a similar view, see Schwenzer (n 1) para 18.

[136] Supreme Court, 22 August 1993 (Israel) (n 45).

therefore, could not have been unaware of a third party's right since 'any sensible person ought to have assumed that such a company would register a trade mark for its products, at least in its country of origin, which is the United States'.[137] However, the fact that the trademark was so well known also, in the end, worked against the seller. The court reasoned that, just like the buyer, it would have been aware of a third party's right and the parties' decision to proceed with the transaction despite knowing of a trademark infringement reflected 'bad faith' on their part. On this basis, each party was held to bear 50 per cent of the liability and the resulting damages.

The decision was based on the Convention relating to a Uniform Law on the International Sale of Goods (ULIS), but Article 42 CISG was invoked and engaged with by analogy and reflected the court's views on how the CISG should be interpreted. The case will, therefore, be considered since it highlights issues which are of direct relevance to the CISG. The decision is innovative and driven by moral considerations. Liability was imposed on both parties on the basis of the principle of good faith. The decision has rightly been criticised as flawed since it relied on the domestic law and doctrine to divide liability between the two parties.[138] But despite that fault in the reasoning, the decision still gives rise to the question of whether it is justifiable for the seller's exemption of liability to be overridden by the notion of good faith, particularly if good faith is regarded as a general principle underlying the CISG. It is submitted that this approach contravenes a carefully crafted balance between the parties, which is clearly expressed in Article 42. The relevance of the seller's knowledge is already factored into the distribution of liability under Article 42 as it is a precondition of the seller's liability. Where, however, the buyer also could not have been unaware of an infringement, Article 42 is uncompromising in that the seller should be fully exempt from liability without any possibility of liability being shared between the parties. The decision to split liability, therefore, lacks any legal basis.

B. Compliance with the Buyer's Specifications

The seller will also be exempt from liability if 'the right or claim results from the seller's compliance with technical drawings, designs, formulae or other such specifications furnished by the buyer'.[139] The main reason for this exemption can be explained with reference to causal considerations, reflected in Article 80, according to which '[a] party may not rely on a failure of the other party to perform, to the extent that such failure was caused

[137] Ibid.

[138] See A Reich, 'Editorial Remarks', available at http://cisgw3.law.pace.edu/cases/930822i5.html.

[139] Art 42(2)(b) CISG.

by the first party's act or omission'. Simply put, what would otherwise be a seller's breach will not be regarded as such because the buyer itself has caused it by having the seller comply with the buyer's specifications.[140] Another possible rationale for this provision is that the fact that the buyer provides specifications means that it has sufficient expertise to identify any rights or claims of third parties.[141] The rationale for this provision[142] together with its wording, which refers to 'specifications', seem to require that for the exemption to be triggered, the buyer's drawings, designs or formulae need to be sufficiently specific and detailed. There may be a potentially difficult question of the amount of detail or the degree of specificity that is required. However, the general guideline, which will dispense with the need to answer this question in most cases, is that if the seller has discretion over those aspects of the manufacture or production of the goods which are capable of infringement, the seller should be liable under Article 42. This is particularly so where the seller has an alternative *non-infringing* means of manufacture or production. The fact that the buyer expresses a 'preference' or a 'wish' that the goods comply with a design or specifications is likely to be indicative of where the seller has discretion or a choice as to methods of production or manufacture.[143] No knowledge of the buyer that the goods, manufactured or produced in accordance with the specifications, infringe an intellectual property right is required for this exemption to be triggered.

The next issue concerns the case where the seller, who has to comply with the specifications, knows that the goods produced in accordance with such specifications will or may infringe a third party's right. There is much support for the view that the principle of good faith requires the seller to warn the buyer about a possible infringement.[144] The imposition of such a duty to warn is desirable since it is only fair and reasonable to expect the seller to warn the buyer so that any possible claims or infringements and any waste resulting therefrom[145] do not arise in the first place. Any

140 See also Schwenzer (n 1) para 18; Kröll (n 10) para 38 (treating the idea in Art 80 as the Convention's general principle).

141 See Rauda and Etier (n 16) 57.

142 The more detailed and comprehensive the specifications, the more forceful are the arguments that the buyer has caused the infringement or that it has the relevant knowledge to identify possible infringement.

143 See P Schlechtriem, 'The Seller's Obligations under the United Nations Convention on Contracts for the International Sale of Goods' in N Galston and H Smit (eds), *International Sales: The United Nations Convention on Contracts for the International Sale of Goods* (New York, NY, Matthew Bender 1984) para 6–33, rightly stating that for this exemption to arise 'the buyer must have required the seller to comply with these specifications'.

144 See Secretariat Commentary on Article 40 (n 9) para 10; Schwenzer (n 1) para 22; Kröll (n 10) para 43; Enderlein and Maskow (n 5) 169; Rauda and Etier (n 16) 58; Schwerha (n 56).

145 Possible waste includes not only time, effort and cost invested into dealing with a third party's right or claim, but also both parties' costs and time of manufacture if the goods are, say, confiscated. In this case, the transaction turns out to be a valueless exercise creating a loss of opportunity to pursue a more valuable alternative, which in itself is a cost and an example of the occurrence of waste.

controversy surrounding good faith being a Convention's general principle may be avoided if reliance is placed on reasonableness, from which the duty to warn may also be developed and which undoubtedly is a general principle of the CISG.[146]

The question also arises as to whether the seller has any remedies against the buyer if the seller suffers harm, financial or otherwise (such as damage to its reputation), as a consequence of infringing a third party's right which, in turn, was caused by compliance with the buyer's specifications. Those favouring an affirmative answer reason that the provision of specifications is a buyer's 'ancillary' duty, and once it is recognised as such, there must be a corresponding duty to provide such instructions which do not entail an infringement of third parties' rights and do not pose legal risks to the seller.[147] The first part of this proposition is uncontroversial because, whether referred to as 'ancillary' or otherwise, the provision of specifications will be an obligation arising from the *contract*.[148] Otherwise, neither the seller's exemption nor the issues discussed in this section will arise. The next proposition in favour of the buyer's duty to provide non-infringing instructions is very sound in principle and policy. When the seller supplies goods it has a duty to ensure that the buyer is not exposed to third parties' rights and claims. At least as a matter of symmetry and equal treatment, the same should apply to those duties of the buyer which potentially expose the seller to third parties' rights or claims. But what is unclear is the legal nature of such a duty. Should such a duty be inferred from a contract in each and every case (implication in fact) or should it be a duty implied under the Convention (implication in law)? As a practical matter, implication in fact should be possible in the vast majority of cases. Nevertheless, to ensure that the policy underlying this duty is implemented consistently it is worth implying such a duty under the Convention. Again, such general principles as good faith[149] (if recognised as such), reasonableness[150] or equality of

[146] See, eg A Kritzer, 'Overview Comments' www.cisg.law.pace.edu/cisg/text/reason.html (with further references).

[147] See Schwenzer (n 1) para 24; Kröll (n 10) para 45.

[148] See, eg Art 65 CISG.

[149] Such ideas as fair dealing and acting with the other party's interests in mind, which arguably underpin the notion of good faith, clearly point to the need for the instructions not to harm the seller.

[150] It is only reasonable to expect the buyer to provide non-infringing instructions. If there is no such duty, sellers are likely to become wary of entering into contracts requiring them to produce goods in accordance with the buyer's instructions. That, in turn, would make the negotiation of such contracts more difficult and costly. In addition, the reasoning in the context of good faith may also be applicable here (see, eg the definition of reasonableness in Art 1:302 of the Principles of European Contract Law (PECL): 'Under these Principles reasonableness is to be judged by what persons acting *in good faith* and in the same situation as the parties would consider to be reasonable' (emphasis added)).

the parties[151] can serve as an appropriate legal basis within the CISG from which this duty can be implied.

C. Other Exemptions

There are two other situations where the seller may be exempt from its liability under Article 42. One is the buyer's failure to give notice specifying the nature of a right or claim of a third party, as required by Article 43, within a reasonable time after the buyer 'has become aware or ought to have become aware of the right or claim'. The other is where the parties exclude this obligation of the seller, as they are permitted to do under Article 6. Both these situations have already been addressed in the context of Article 41, discussed in the previous chapter, and the issues raised there are equally applicable to Article 42. The only point that is specific to Article 42 stems from the precondition, absent in Article 41, that the seller can only be held liable if it has the requisite knowledge of a third party's right or claim. This precondition is likely to limit the parties' ability to exclude Article 42 because most legal systems do not allow a party to exempt itself from consequences flowing from its deceit or gross negligence.[152]

VI. BURDEN OF PROOF

It follows from the 'rule and exception' principle[153] that if the buyer wishes to rely on a seller's breach under Article 42, it will bear the burden of proving the existence of an intellectual property right or a claim of a third party and the fact that the seller knew or could not have been unaware of such a right or claim.[154] It has been suggested that whilst this allocation of burden of proof is the correct starting point, it may be 'equitable'[155] or 'reasonable' to shift the burden of proving the existence of a right or claim to the seller if the buyer does not have the required expertise to identify the possibility of an infringement and/or the relevant evidence is 'within the seller's sphere'.[156] This approach will generate complexity and uncertainty, arising

[151] The Convention's premise is that the development of international trade is based on 'equality' (see the Preamble to the CISG), which is evidenced, for example, in a general symmetry of remedies available to both parties.

[152] For detailed references, see Schwenzer (n 1) para 26.

[153] For the discussion of this principle, see Chapter 3.

[154] Schwenzer (n 1) para 31; Kröll (n 10) para 54.

[155] Supreme Court, 12 September 2006 (Austria) (n 47), making the following statement with reference to scholarly writings: 'the burden to prove the breach of contract is on [buyer]. In exceptional circumstances, considerations of equity can lead to a shifting of the burden of proof, eg ... closeness to evidence or unacceptable difficulties for one party to furnish evidence'. See also Schwenzer (n 1) para 31; Janal (n 53) 210–11.

[156] Janal (n 53) 210–11.

from the need to determine whether the buyer has the required expertise and the inquiry into within whose 'sphere' the evidence lies. There is much to be said for clarity and simplicity in the allocation of burden of proof, which, it is submitted, will make the regime of Article 42 more robust and predictable. It is also of concern that the shifting of the burden of proof is advocated purely with reference to 'equity' and 'reasonableness' without rooting them in any legal basis. Even if such a basis can be developed,[157] it needs to be borne in mind that bringing the matter of burden of proof into the Convention's scope is already a rather creative and not uncontroversial exercise.[158] A further proposal to introduce exceptions to the basic principle of allocating burden of proof, which themselves lack precision, marks a point where legal creativity is undesirable, since in the absence of any express wording in the CISG, its uniform application becomes hardly achievable. The concern for the buyer not having the relevant expertise and information is much alleviated considering that mere proof of a claim, even if frivolous, is sufficient to trigger the seller's liability.

The buyer who alleges the existence of a third party's right or claim under the laws in a particular state,[159] will also need to prove that the parties contemplated that the goods would be used or sold in that state. If, however, the buyer relies on a third party's right or claim under the laws in a country where it has its place of business[160] and the seller wishes to disprove the buyer's allegation, the seller will need to prove that the parties contemplated that the goods would be used or sold in a different state. Finally, if the seller seeks to invoke an exemption under Article 42, it will bear the burden of proving the preconditions for these exemptions; that is, that the buyer knew or could not have been unaware of the alleged right or claim[161] and/or that a third party's right or claim resulted from the seller's compliance with the buyer's specifications.[162]

VII. CONCLUDING OBSERVATIONS

The above discussion gives rise to some general observations largely concerning the robustness of the regime created by Article 42. From the standpoint of the importance of intellectual property in our age of dramatic technological advancement and innovation, Article 42 has been seen

157 Say, from the relevant general principles of the CISG, such as reasonableness or good faith (if recognised as such).

158 See, eg Honnold (n 8) 86–92.

159 See Art 42(1)(a).

160 See Art 42(1)(b).

161 See Art 42(2)(a).

162 See Art 42(2)(b). See Schwenzer (n 1) para 31 and Kröll (n 10) para 54, making the same propositions.

as 'rudimentary'[163] by some writers, who advise that parties should design their own contractual regime rather than rely solely on the CISG.[164] This proposition is put forward on the basis that the CISG was drafted long before the major developments in information technology,[165] but with no real explanation as to what precisely is rudimentary about the Convention's approach. There may be some truth in this proposition, although no other sales law appears to offer a more 'advanced' solution.[166] In fact, as explained, most sales laws treat third parties' intellectual claims and rights in the same way as other rights or claims. Therefore, it may even be possible to go as far as to suggest that the CISG represents some of the latest legal thinking on this issue, even if an imperfect one. It is also arguable that Article 42 approaches the problem of third parties' rights or claims in a similar fashion to how the CISG tackles all other problems: in a 'minimalist' fashion by relying on broad rules encompassing a wide range of scenarios and sending only a basic signal as to how the risks between the parties should be allocated. If that is what underlies the criticism, it is the criticism not just of Article 42, but of the CISG as a whole. A related criticism is that there are too many uncertainties built into this provision. The discussion above attests that this criticism is justified.

However, for those wanting the CISG to be a success story, a desirable way forward is not to advocate the means of avoiding the CISG but to offer constructive solutions conducive to developing a fair, coherent and predictable regime within the CISG. This stance gives rise to a number of related challenges. One is to determine how exactly risks should be allocated between the parties. This difficulty has been seen in relation to such questions as whether the seller and the buyer should have a duty to investigate the existence of intellectual property rights. Another challenge concerns the question of how far legal creativity should be pursued. The answer should depend on the nature of a specific problem, but a general point is that creativity is not desirable where it disrupts a fair balance between the parties and/or undermines legal certainty. It has been suggested here that whilst there are good reasons for implying a duty to warn on the part of both the buyer and the seller in the context of Article 42(2)(a), some other instances of creativity, such as the view that the burden of proof should shift where it is 'equitable' to do so, are undesirable.

The story of Article 42 is so far one of attempts to carefully craft a delicate and equal balance between the parties, so that it is not just a 'seller

163 Kröll (n 10) para 5.

164 See, generally, TM Beline, 'Legal Defect Protected by Article 42 of the CISG: A Wolf in Sheep's Clothing' (2007) 7 *University Pittsburgh J Technology* L 6.

165 Honnold (n 8) 392; Kröll (n 10) para 5.

166 See § 2-312(3) UCC (n 1); Commercial Code of the Czech Republic, art 433(2), available at www.justiniano.com/codigos_juridicos/cheka/codigo_comercial.pdf.

friendly' provision, as it is sometimes perceived to be.[167] Unfortunately, there are very few cases testing this regime. For all the apparent importance of intellectual property and its implications for sales law, it is striking how few cases have been generated by Article 42 in comparison with those under Article 35.[168] This cannot but raise doubts about the alleged practical importance of these issues in sales law, even in such a technologically innovative age.

VIII. FREEDOM FROM THIRD PARTIES' RIGHTS OR CLAIMS: AN ASPECT OF 'CONFORMITY'?

A question that arises in relation to both Article 41, discussed in the previous chapter, and Article 42 is whether the seller's obligation to deliver goods which are free from third parties' rights or claims, including those arising from intellectual property, is one of 'conformity' analogous to the obligations under Article 35. This question is not merely one of the characterisation of the legal nature of these obligations, but one which also entails differences in remedial consequences. Several provisions on remedies explicitly refer to their applicability only in the case where the goods 'do not conform with the contract'. These provisions concern the buyer's right to require delivery of substitute goods,[169] repair of the goods[170] and to reduce the price.[171] It follows that if Articles 41 and 42 are about 'conformity of the goods', the buyer will be able to exercise these remedies and vice versa. At first sight, the answer to the question seems readily apparent if formal, textual criteria emanating from the Convention's structure and wording are relied upon. First, the very title of Section II (where Articles 35, 41 and 42 are placed), distinguishes between 'conformity of the goods' and 'third party claims'. Secondly, there are two analogous but separate notification requirements, one being applicable to a 'lack of conformity' (Article 39)[172] whilst the other (Article 43)[173] is applicable to Articles 41 and 42. Thirdly, the

[167] The Swedish legislators decided not to adopt the rule in Art 42 precisely for that reason (see Notes on Art 2:306 in von Bar and Clive (n 1) 1305). For the opposite view which regards Art 42 as offering the buyer a 'quite modest' protection, see H Flechtner, *Conformity of Goods, Third Party Claim, and Buyer's Notice of Breach under the United Nations Sales Convention (CISG), with Comments on the 'Mussels Case', the 'Stolen Automobile Case' and the 'Ugandan Used Shoes Case'*, University of Pittsburgh School of Law Working Paper Series (2007), available at http://law.bepress.com/pittlwps/papers/art64.

[168] As of 8 December 2014, the list of annotated cases on the Pace website listed 488 cases decided under Art 35 and only 16 decided under Art 42 (see www.cisg.law.pace.edu).

[169] Art 46(2).

[170] Art 46(3).

[171] Art 50.

[172] See Chapter 5.

[173] See Chapter 6.

provisions providing for the buyer's remedies of demanding substitute goods and repair of the goods contain, as a precondition for their application, the need for the buyer to give notice requesting a chosen remedy and one way in which this notice can be made is 'in conjunction with notice given under Article 39'.[174] Since no reference is made to Article 43, there is a strong argument that the remedies of demanding substitute goods and repair of the goods are not applicable in the case of the seller's breach of Articles 41 and 42. Finally, the time with reference to which conformity is to be assessed is the time of the passage of risk,[175] whereas the time for evaluating whether the goods are free from third parties' rights or claims is that of delivery.[176]

In the light of these provisions, the argument that the obligations under Articles 41 and 42 are those relating to conformity may seem untenable. Nonetheless, in the context of Article 42 this argument has been advanced and has received a degree of support in literature.[177] It is based on two sets of considerations. One relates to the alleged parallel between Articles 42 and 35. It has been contended that the limitation of the seller's liability with reference to territorial restrictions perform the same function as the fitness for the 'particular purpose' and the 'ordinary purposes' tests in Article 35(2). Establishing the seller's liability with reference to the laws of a country of use or resale of goods *if* the parties contemplated the use or resale of the goods in that country (Article 42(1)(a)) has been seen as having 'the same function and underlying rationale' as Article 35(2)(b); under Article 35(2)(b), the seller is liable for the goods not being fit for a particular purpose *if* that purpose was made known to the seller.[178] Presumably, the underlying rationale that is being referred to is that of the 'assumption of risk' by the seller. If the seller contemplates the relevance of the laws of the country of use or resale under Article 42(1)(a) *or* knows the particular purpose for which the goods are being bought (Article 35(2)(b)), and does not raise any objections, the seller can be taken to have assumed the risk of the goods' non-compliance under these provisions.[179] The parallel is also said to exist between the fall-back provision of Article 42(1)(b), according to which the law of the buyer's state is controlling, and the fall-back rule in Article 35(2)(a) requiring the goods to be fit for their ordinary purposes. The argument goes that insofar as the resale or use of the goods in the buyer's place of business constitutes the ordinary use of the goods, 'Art 42(1)(b) can be considered to be the intellectual property equivalent to Art 35(2)(a)'.[180] The second line of the argument, flowing from this

174 See nn 169 and 170 above.
175 See Art 36(1). See further Chapters 3 and 4.
176 See Arts 41 and 42 and III C above.
177 See nn 178, 180 and 181 below.
178 See Kröll (n 10) para 15.
179 See ibid.
180 Ibid para 18; see Schlechtriem (n 143) paras 6-32–6-33.

similarity in the structure and principles of liability between Article 42(1)(a) and (b), on the one hand, and Articles 35(2)(a) and (b), on the other, is that it is only the application of the same remedies that 'accomplishes an appropriate balance of interest of the parties'.[181]

Whilst the alleged parallels may well exist, their strength must not be exaggerated. Fundamentally, Article 35 is concerned with physical features and characteristics to be found *in* the goods, whereas Articles 41 and 42 concern the existence of rights or claims of third parties in respect of the goods. Despite possible parallels between Articles 35 and 42, Article 42 is still part of the Convention's legal regime dealing with third parties' rights or claims in the particular case of intellectual property. Thus, even conceptually the alleged parallels are by no means 'indisputable', as they are sometimes perceived to be.[182] The second argument, that the same remedies are needed to maintain an appropriate balance, weakens accordingly. The next point relates to the need to respect the structure and wording of the CISG. Whilst it may be criticised as being formalistic, it must be remembered that certainty, which is unachievable if a clear wording is not adhered to,[183] is part of justice. Without certainty, the idea of the rule of law can hardly have any meaning. The Convention recognises these considerations by requiring that it should be applied having regard to uniformity in its application.[184] Therefore, it is submitted that the seller's obligations under Articles 41 and 42 are not those of conformity,[185] with the consequence that the above stated remedies, applicable in the case of a lack of conformity, should not be available to the buyer if the seller is in breach of Articles 41 or 42.

[181] Janal (n 53) 225.

[182] Schwenzer (n 1) para 12.

[183] *Cf* Janal (n 53) 225, stating that 'there is no guarantee that all courts will prefer a formalistic interpretation'. This may be true, but it is undeniable that certainty is much less likely to be achievable under the approach which bends the language than if a clear language is adhered to.

[184] See Art 7(1). See further Chapter 1.

[185] See Schwenzer (n 1) para 28, who ultimately takes the same view.

8

Conformity of Documents

I. INTRODUCTION

DOCUMENTS PLAY A variety of commercial and legal functions in international trade. They make it possible for the seller to part with the goods before getting the price and for the buyer to pay the price before receiving the goods. They are at the heart of the letter of credit, one of the most widely used payment mechanisms (largely for the reason stated in the previous sentence). Documents enable the buyer to resell the goods while they are in transit, making it possible for chains of speculating traders to be formed. The buyer can raise finance by pledging documents to a bank, and banks use documents as security to guard themselves against the buyer's failure to pay off a loan.[1] Some documents are used by the parties as proof of the goods' compliance with the requirements as to quality, quantity and description and can help them avoid disputes and litigation in relation to these matters and promote early settlement of claims. In essence, all these functions aim to provide the parties with a necessary level of security, comfort and practical convenience enabling and, to an extent, encouraging them to trade internationally. Documents thus play a vitally important role in supporting and facilitating trade. Certain documents may also be required by the legislation of exporting or importing countries which, in turn, implement a variety of political, economic, social and other policies.

The multiplicity of documents and functions they perform can give rise to numerous legal questions, only some of which can be answered by sales law regimes. Some of the most obvious legal questions are: what documents, if any, must the seller tender to the buyer? What is a non-conforming document, and with reference to what standards must the issue of conformity of documents be assessed?[2] Considering the practical and legal significance of documents, it is probably unfortunate that the CISG gives little guidance on how these questions are to be answered. There is also a noticeable gap

[1] The significance and role of documents in international trade has been explained and illustrated on numerous occasions. See, eg E McKendrick (ed), *Goode on Commercial Law*, 4th edn (London, Penguin, 2010) 959–60 and further references.

[2] As explained in Chapter 1, this work will not address the buyer's remedies under the CISG, including those for documentary breaches.

in respect of these issues in the legal literature on the CISG,[3] despite the emergence of a body of cases dealing with various aspects of documentary performance. This chapter aims to contribute to the existing scholarship not only by evaluating the Convention's experience in the light of the above questions but also, more importantly, by developing a framework which would advance our understanding of the complex and multifaceted nature of legal issues arising from documentary performance and the use of documents in international sales contracts, and would help courts, tribunals and scholars in tackling them.

II. TYPICAL DOCUMENTS: AN OVERVIEW

A. Transport Documents

The great variety of documents used in international trade makes it almost impossible to provide an exhaustive list of them and of the purposes they serve.[4] It is this variety and, possibly, the need to define the documents and to explain diverse procedures associated with them that probably led the drafters simply to provide for the obvious proposition,[5] in defining the seller's documentary duties, that '[i]f the seller is bound to hand over documents relating to the goods, he must hand them over at the time and place and in the form required by the contract'.[6] But even if the Convention leaves it to the contract, which is to be interpreted against the surrounding trading context, including usages and practices,[7] to set out the documentary duties of the seller, it is clearly vital to understand the essence, functions and purposes of the main documents. Otherwise, the nature of the seller's duties, the issue of conformity of documents and the legal consequences of the breach of documentary obligations cannot be exhaustively evaluated.

[3] For the existing relevant sources, see references throughout this chapter.

[4] 'By various estimates there are between 10,000 and 100,000 documents used in all facets of international trade for all nations on earth' (EG Hinkelman, *A Short Course in International Trade Documentation: The Documents of Exporting, Importing, Shipping and Banking* (Petaluma, World Trade Press, 2009) 1).

[5] 'In view of the diversity of procedures involving such documents—direct handing-over, consignment, delivery by the carrier, deposit with a bank and so on—the drafters of the Convention had to confine themselves to pronouncing the self-evident rule that the seller is bound to deliver the documents at the time and place in the form required by the contract' (P Schlechtriem, 'The Seller's Obligations under the United Nations Convention' in NM Galston and H Smit (eds), *International Sales: The United Nations Convention on Contracts for the International Sale of Goods* (New York, Matthew Bender, 1984) para 6-16). For the view that no sales law statute should list documents that the seller needs to deliver, see M Bridge, 'Do We Need a New Sale of Goods Act?' in J Lowry and L Mistelis (eds), *Commercial Law: Perspectives and Practice* (London, Butterworths/LexisNexis, 2006) 30.

[6] Art 34 CISG.

[7] Arts 8(3) and 9.

With this in mind, it may be helpful to present a brief overview of some of the main types of document.

To be able to part with the price before receiving the goods, the buyer needs an assurance that goods of the agreed quality and description have been shipped to the agreed destination within the agreed period; that it will be able to gain possession of the goods upon arrival at that destination; or if the buyer wishes to resell the goods, that it can do so even while the goods are in transit. The buyer also needs rights of suit against the carrier, in the event of damage to or loss of the goods during the journey. A transport document known as a (negotiable)[8] *bill of lading* is capable of performing all these functions.[9] First, a bill of lading always performs a receipt function in which a carrier acknowledges receipt of the goods, confirming or qualifying their apparent good order and condition,[10] and states the quantity and date of shipment. This information not only provides the buyer with prima facie and, in some cases, conclusive evidence of the extent to which the seller complied with its obligations as to delivery and conformity of the goods, but also enables the buyer to hold the carrier to its representations in the bill if a claim is brought against the carrier.[11]

Secondly, a bill of lading provides evidence of the contract of carriage. Where the seller is responsible for arranging a carriage contract, the buyer has a clear interest in knowing that the seller has arranged for carriage in accordance with the sales contract or, if the latter is silent, with the requirements of the relevant sales law. A bill of lading is evidence of the terms of the carriage contract and, in some legal systems, is said to provide the best evidence as to the terms of the carriage contract between the buyer and carrier.[12] Equally important, transfer of the bill of lading to the buyer generally amounts to the transfer of rights of action against the carrier.[13]

Thirdly, a bill of lading, if issued in the correct form, functions as a document of title: a status which enables legal rights to be attached to the physical possession of a paper document. The person holding a document of title is, in principle, entitled to receive, hold and dispose of the goods, with the possession of this document amounting to constructive possession

[8] See n 30 below.

[9] See, generally, C Debattista, *Bills of Lading in Export Trade*, 3rd edn (London, Tottel Publishing, 2009) 123–25.

[10] See, eg *Chicago Prime Packers, Inc v Northam Food Trading Co*, 2005 US App LEXIS 9355.

[11] Debattista (n 9) 123–25.

[12] See, eg *SS Ardennes (Cargo Owners) v SS Ardennes (Owners)* [1951] 1 QB 55, 59–60; *Sewell v Burdick* (1884) 10 App Cas 74, 105; *Crooks v Allen* (1879) 5 QBD 38, 40 (CA).

[13] In English law, for instance, this is achieved by a form of statutory assignment under the Carriage of Goods by Sea Act (COGSA) 1992. In civil law, this is said to occur by virtue of the transfer of the document itself. See, generally, C Pejovic, 'Documents of Title in Carriage of Goods by Sea: Present Status and Possible Future Directions' [2001] *JBL* 461, 474–75.

of the goods[14] and the 'exclusive right to delivery of the goods [being] "locked up" in the document'.[15] This means that the buyer, as holder of the bill of lading, is entitled to receive the goods from the carrier by presenting the bill of lading[16] and/or, provided the bill is in an appropriate form, to sell the goods by endorsing and delivering the bill to a sub-buyer (transferability or negotiability). The question of whether the transfer of a bill of lading can transfer property in the goods is answered in different ways by legal systems. For instance, in English law the intention of the parties is decisive.[17] Relevant factors in determining this intent are the transfer of a bill of lading and the way it is issued (ie whether it is made to the seller's or buyer's order). Some legal systems, such as the German or Dutch, confer greater status on a bill of lading, with its delivery having the same effect as delivery of the goods, which is the second necessary condition for transfer of property in the goods.[18] Notwithstanding such differences, in all these systems it is often the case in practice that property passes with the transfer of a bill of lading.[19]

These functions can lead to specific requirements which a bill of lading must meet. To take the most widely used shipment contract, the CIF contract,[20] as an example, the receipt function can bring about the requirement that the bill of lading must state the contract goods and quantity; be dated within the shipment period;[21] be a 'shipped', rather than a 'received for shipment' bill;[22] be issued on shipment; be genuine

[14] Pejovic (n 13) 463; *Enichem Anic SpA v Ampelos Shipping Co Ltd (The Delfini)* [1990] 1 Lloyd's Rep 252, 268.

[15] UNCTAD Secretariat, *The Use of Transport Documents in International Trade,* UNCTAD/SDTE/TLB/2003/3 (26 November 2003) 14, available at www.unctad.org/en/docs// sdtetlb20033_en.pdf ('UNCTAD Report'); also Barber v Meyerstein (1870) LR 4 HL 317.

[16] See, eg *Trafigura Beheer BV v Mediterranean Shipping Co SA (The MSC Amsterdam)* [2007] EWCA Civ 794, para 29; The Stettin (1889) LR 14 PD 142, 147; Glyn Mills Currie & Co v East & West India Dock Co (1882) 7 App Cas 591, 610; Erichsen v Barkworth (1858) 3 H & N 601, 616; 157 ER 608, 615. See also United Nations Convention on Contracts for the International Carriage of Goods Wholly or Partly by Sea 2009 (Rotterdam Rules), Art 47(a)(i), which also adds the requirement that the holder of a negotiable transport document must 'properly' identify itself if it is 'the shipper or the consignee, or ... the person to which the document is duly endorsed' (Art 1(10)(a)(ii)).

[17] See *Sanders Bros v Maclean & Co* (1883) 11 QBD 327, 341.

[18] The first condition is the agreement of the parties (for a more detailed discussion see, eg Pejovic (n 13) 472; J Dalhuisen, *Dalhuisen on Transnational Comparative, Commercial, Financial and Trade Law: Contract and Movable Property Law*, 4th edn (Oxford/Portland, Hart Publishing, 2010) vol II, 570.

[19] See, eg Pejovic (n 13) 471.

[20] For definition, see Chapter 2.

[21] See A8 CIF, INCOTERMS 2010 in *INCOTERMS 2010: ICC Rules for the Use of Domestic and International Trade Terms* (ICC Publication No 715E, 2010).

[22] See J Ramberg, *ICC Guide to Incoterms 2010: Understanding and Practical Use* (Paris, ICC Services Publication, 2011) 188.

and clean.[23] The contract of carriage function will usually require the bill to evidence that the carriage has been made in accordance with the terms agreed between the buyer and seller. In the absence of such an agreement, the bill of lading will need to evidence the contract of carriage having been made on usual terms and shipment by the usual route[24] to the destination agreed in the sales contract.[25] A bill of lading may also be required to provide continuous documentary cover from the place of shipment to destination.[26] A number of further issues and corresponding requirements may arise, such as whether the bill of lading needs to be a freight pre-paid[27] or freight collect bill, or what statements the bill of lading should contain regarding transhipment and deck stowage.[28] Finally, the document of title function normally enables the buyer to claim the goods from the carrier upon the presentation of the bill, and to sell them whilst in transit by transferring the bill to its sub-buyer.[29] To do the latter, the bill of lading must be negotiable (transferable),[30] and negotiability normally results merely from the wording on the bill itself.[31] In English law, for instance, if the bill of lading contains the words 'to order', it is transferable by the shipper's endorsement and delivery. Where the bill indicates the named consignee 'or order', it is transferable by endorsement of the consignee.[32] A 'bearer' bill, where the consignee is indicated

[23] See, eg *Benjamin's Sale of Goods*, 9th edn (London, Sweet & Maxwell-Thomson Reuters, 2014) paras 19-026–19-041 (discussing the requirements under English law for CIF contracts); see also *M Golodetz & Co Inc v Czarnikow-Rionda Co Inc (The Galatia)* [1980] 1 WLR 495 (leading case on the meaning of a 'clean' bill of lading); see also Art 27 of the Uniform Customs and Practice for Documentary Credits (UCP) 600 ('[a] clean transport document is one bearing no clause or notation expressly declaring a defective condition of the goods or their packaging').

[24] A3 CIF, INCOTERMS 2010 (n 21).

[25] A8 CIF, INCOTERMS 2010 (n 21).

[26] See *Hansson v Hamel & Horley* [1922] 2 AC 36.

[27] See, eg *Federal Commerce & Navigacion Co Ltd v Molena Alpha Inc (The Nanfri, The Benfri, The Lorfri)* [1979] AC 757, 777.

[28] See Debattista (n 9) 164–75 (giving a detailed analysis of these issues in English law); see also Art 26(1) UCP 600 ('[a] transport document must not indicate that the goods are or will be loaded on deck. A clause on a transport document stating that the goods may be loaded on deck is acceptable').

[29] A8 CIF, INCOTERMS 2010 (n 21).

[30] In English law, it is understood that negotiability in the context of the bill of lading means transferability of the existing rights in the sense that the transferee cannot acquire better rights than those of the transferor. See Lickbarrow v Mason (1787) 2 TR 64, 71; *Heskell v Continental Express Ltd* (1950) 83 Lloyd's List LR 438, 453; *Kum v Wah Tat Bank* [1971] 1 Lloyd's Rep 439, 446; *The Future Express* [1993] 2 Lloyd's Rep 542, 547.

[31] Dalhuisen (n 18) 567.

[32] In fact, such bills of lading need not be endorsed (delivery is normally sufficient), but in practice sometimes are. See *East West Corp v DKBS 1912 and AKTS Svendborg* [2002] 2 Lloyd's Rep 182, 185.

as 'bearer', is simply negotiated by delivery.[33] However, considering that the bill of lading owes its origins and development to mercantile customs, these ways of transferring rights may well flow from their unique status rather than from domestic law.[34] If so, to this extent, perhaps, the bill of lading can 'claim a transnational status'.[35]

Other transport documents include *sea or air waybills* which constitute a receipt of the goods by the carrier, evidence of the terms of the carriage contract, and which identify a person to whom delivery is to be made.[36] In contrast with the bill of lading, they are not documents of title with the consequence that they cannot transfer possession and property.[37] The consignee does not need to present them to claim the goods from the carrier.[38] To do so, it merely needs to prove its identity.[39] Not being a document of title makes the waybill unsuitable where the buyer wishes to resell the goods in transit or to raise finance.[40] That said, it has a potential advantage over a bill of lading in that, while the latter often arrives later than the goods, creating a difficulty in claiming the goods from the carrier, no such difficulty arises where the waybill is used because the consignee merely has to supply evidence of its identity. Waybills are thus often used where the buyer has no intention of reselling the goods.[41] An equivalent document in road[42] and rail[43] transport

[33] See, eg McKendrick (n 1) 981.

[34] Dalhuisen (n 18) 568.

[35] Ibid 569; see also UNCTAD Report (n 15) 6 ('Although no uniform international law exists to define the characteristics and effects of different transport documents, the relevant rules, having been established by the custom of merchant, appear to be remarkably similar in most jurisdictions').

[36] The tender of this document was recognised as appropriate in CIF/CFR contracts under INCOTERMS 2000; see Ramberg (n 22) 111 (discussing A8 CFR). A non-negotiable sea waybill can also be tendered under the UCP 600 (see Art 21).

[37] But see CISG Advisory Council (CISG AC) Opinion No 11, 'Issues Raised by Documents under the CISG Focusing on the Buyer's Payment Duty', available at www.cisg.law.pace.edu/cisg/CISG-AC-op11.html, noting, in para 5, that under the Convention for the Unification of Certain Rules for International Carriage by Air 1999 ('Montreal Convention') the 'consignor may stop the cargo in transit or may require the carrier to deliver it to a consignee other than the one originally designated ... upon presentation of the consignor's copy of the air waybill' (with reference to Arts 12.1–12.3 of the Montreal Convention). This has the consequence that although 'the buyer/consignee does not need to get the seller/consignor's copy of the waybill to take delivery from the carrier, the buyer/consignee cannot be sure that the seller/consignor will not exercise its right to redirect the cargo to another consignee unless and until it receives the consignor's copy' (CISG AC, para 6.5).

[38] See COGSA 1992, s 2(1)(b) (giving the holder of a sea waybill rights of suit).

[39] See, eg Debattista (n 9) 43–44; Pejovic (n 13) 481.

[40] See, eg UNCTAD Report (n 15) 24.

[41] These and other features of this document are discussed in many sources. See Pejovic (n 13) 481–83; Debattista (n 9) 43–44; UNCTAD Report (n 15) 8–9.

[42] See, generally, Convention on the Contract for the International Carriage of Goods by Road (CMR), (1956) 399 UNTS 189, available at www.jus.uio.no/lm/un.cmr.road.carriage.contract.convention.1956/doc.html.

[43] See, generally, Uniform Rules Concerning the Contract for International Carriage of Goods by Rail (CIM), available at www.jus.uio.no/lm/cim.rail.carriage.contract.uniform.rules.19xx/.

is a *consignment note*—a non-negotiable document naming the consignee. It provides evidence of the receipt of the goods, their condition and the carriage contract.[44] A consignee can demand the goods from the carrier without presentation of this document.[45]

The so-called *straight bills of lading*, which are issued to a named consignee but are not issued 'to order' and are therefore non-negotiable, are also commonly used. Legal systems appear to agree on this document being non-negotiable, that is, that the named consignee cannot transfer rights by tendering this document. Therefore, similar to a waybill, a straight bill of lading is not well suited to cases where the goods are intended to be resold along the chain.[46] This document usually needs to be presented for the consignee to obtain delivery from the carrier (to this extent, being a document of title), although this position does not appear to be universal across legal systems.[47]

Sometimes, where the seller ships the goods in bulk under one bill of lading, a contract may allow the seller to tender a *delivery order*, a document entitling the buyer to delivery of part of the bulk. A ship's delivery order[48] contains an undertaking by the carrier to deliver the specified quantity to the person named within it.[49] Some legal systems treat it as conferring on

[44] See M Davies, 'Documents that Satisfy the Requirements of CISG Art 58', presented at the conference *Uniform Sales Law: The CISG at its 30th Anniversary*, University of Belgrade, Faculty of Law, Belgrade, 12–13 November 2010 (providing a more detailed review of this document and further references).

[45] But see CISG AC Opinion No 11 (n 37) para 6.12 ('Both CIM and CMR give the consignor the right to modify the contract of carriage by giving subsequent orders to the carrier including, in particular, the right to deliver the goods to a consignee different from the one entered on the consignment note ... In order to exercise the right of disposal, the consignor or consignee must produce to the carrier the duplicate consignment note (in the case of CIM) or the first copy of the consignment note (in the case of CMR). Thus, the consignor is no longer entitled to redirect the goods if it has sent the duplicate or first copy to the consignee. Conversely, the consignee cannot exercise the right of disposal until it has received the duplicate or first copy from the consignor').

[46] See UNCTAD Report (n 15) 9–11.

[47] US law is said not to require its presentation while the opposite is the case in some other common law systems, such as England and Singapore, as well as in some civil law systems. See S Girvin, 'Bills of Lading and Straight Bills of Lading: Principles and Practice' [2006] *JBL* 86, 98–116; H Tiberg, 'Transfer of Documents' [2002] *LMCLQ* 539. See also Rotterdam Rules, art 51.2(b).

[48] In English law, a ship's delivery order may be contrasted with a merchant's or trader's delivery order, which, in contrast with the former, contains an instruction by the shipper to the person in possession of the goods to deliver the goods to the buyer. See *Colin & Shields v Weddel & Co Ltd* [1952] 1 Lloyd's Rep 9; *Comptoir d'Achat et de Vented u Boerenbond Belge SA v Luis de Ridder Lta (The Julia)* [1949] AC 293; *Cremer and others v General Carriers SA* [1974] 1 WLR 341.

[49] Debattista (n 9) 48 ('Typically a single-sided document, a ship's delivery order will normally refer to the bill of lading originally issued for the goods shipped in bulk and will also incorporate its terms. The document also sometimes states that the goods had been shipped in apparent good order and condition').

its holder the rights to claim delivery, to possess and dispose of the goods,[50] while others, such as English law, regard it only as entitling the person named in the delivery order to delivery and to rights of suit against the carrier,[51] without allowing the holder to dispose of the goods by a mere transfer of the document.[52] However, in English law, if a delivery order is issued 'to order' of a named party, that person will acquire the rights of suit against the carrier upon transfer of the document.[53]

Finally, brief mention needs to be made of *multimodal transport*[54] *(MT) documents* which are increasingly used to meet the needs arising from carriage by more than one means of transportation. A multimodal operator (MTO) who assumes responsibility for transportation performed by several carriers issues an MT document to cover the entire journey.[55] MT documents can have various forms and characteristics. While sometimes they expressly state that they are negotiable, there may be some uncertainty as to whether they constitute documents of title in a given legal system.[56] In English law, for instance, the fact that the date of issue on MT documents refers to the date when the goods were received rather than when they were shipped has traditionally led to the position that MT documents could not be regarded as documents of title.[57]

B. Other Documents

Where goods are delivered to a warehouse, a warehouse keeper may issue a *warehouse receipt* or a *delivery warrant* which, similar to a bill of lading, may or may not be negotiable.[58] If it is, the buyer is able to sell or pledge the goods while they are still in the warehouse.[59] If the goods are delivered to a port, dock or terminal operator, a carrier may issue documents known as *dock receipts/warrants* or *quay receipts* acknowledging receipt at the port for later shipment. A carrier may also issue a *mate's receipt* which also acknowledges receipt, as well as the goods' quantity[60] and apparent condition. This

[50] See Pejovic (n 13) 477, n 31.
[51] See COGSA 1992, s 2(1)(c).
[52] See Pejovic (n 13) 477 (criticising this position).
[53] See COGSA 1992, s 5(3); see also Debattista (n 9) 4–75.
[54] See 1980 UN Convention on International Multimodal Transport of Goods, TD/MT/CONF/16 (1980) (not yet in force), available at www.jus.uio.no/lm/un.multimodal.transport.1980/doc.html; UNCTAD/ICC, 1990 Rules for Multimodal Transport Documents, UNCTAD/SDTE/TLB/2003/1 (13 January 2003).
[55] See McKendrick (n 1) 1000–2.
[56] See, generally, Pejovic (n 13) 477–81.
[57] See Debattista (n 9) 50–54, 72–74 (detailed discussion and critique).
[58] See Davies (n 44) 165–66; CISG AC Opinion No 11 (n 37) para 7.1.
[59] Davies (n 44) 166.
[60] See ICAC 56/2003, 2 February 2004, available at http://cisgw3.law.pace.edu/cases/040202r1.html, where the goods' conformity with contractual requirements as quantity was established on the basis of a mate's receipt.

document is often required in order to obtain a bill of lading, and if it is 'claused',[61] any qualifications in it should be incorporated in the bill of lading.[62] Dock receipts/warrants, quay and mate's receipts perform an evidentiary receipt function. They neither evidence the carriage contract nor enable the holder to claim against the carrier or to obtain possession of the goods.[63]

A contract will almost invariably require the seller to hand over a *commercial invoice*,[64] a document which sets out the details of the parties, quantity and description of the goods, the price and its structure, the buyer's order or contract number, time and mode of delivery and payment.[65] The precise content will eventually depend on the contract.[66] If the latter is silent, the relevant trade usages, practices between the parties, and/or the surrounding commercial context can often help to develop specific requirements as to the content of an invoice.[67] It has been suggested that in bulk trade, where separation within the bulk occurs only on discharge (as opposed to a commercial invoice which is commonly issued on shipment)[68] it 'is common enough for the invoice not to have to identify the very goods appropriated to the contract'.[69] An invoice is used by the buyer to ascertain the breakdown of the price.[70] An invoice is also often necessary in order for the goods to be cleared through customs and identified for the purposes of an import licence or foreign exchange regulations. It is the commercial invoice alone,[71] rather than any other document, which is relied upon to determine whether the description of the goods corresponds with that in the letter of credit.[72]

[61] That is, if it is qualified, as opposed to being clean where it 'does not contain adverse observations' (see C Murray, D Holloway and D Timson-Hunt, *Schmitthoff: The Law and Practice of International Trade*, 12th edn (London, Sweet & Maxwell-Thomson Reuters, 2012) 293.

[62] But see *Cremer and others v General Carriers SA* (n 48) (where this was not done).

[63] See Davies (n 44) 166–68. Nevertheless, in some legal systems the issue of a mate's receipt is said to have important consequences not only in terms of acknowledging receipt and that the goods are in the ship-owner's possession but also of providing prima facie evidence of ownership of the goods (see Murray, Holloway and Timson-Hunt (n 61) 294).

[64] A commercial invoice needs to be distinguished from a *pro forma invoice*, which is merely a price quotation in the form of an invoice usually made out either before the conclusion of a sales contract or before shipment at the buyer's request. A pro forma invoice may be needed so that the buyer could ascertain the cost of purchase, obtain an import licence, foreign exchange approval or apply for a letter of credit. See, eg Hinkelman (n 4) 32; McKendrick (n 1) 993–94.

[65] See Hinkelman (n 4) 36–37; McKendrick (n 1) 993–94.

[66] See, eg *John Martin of London Ltd v AE Taylor & Co Ltd* [1953] 2 Lloyd's Rep 589 (explaining that the contract required the invoice to contain a customs lodgement number and the location of a certificate of origin); see Art 18 UCP 600 (describing the requirements in relation to a commercial invoice for letter of credit purposes).

[67] See Arts 8–9 CISG.

[68] McKendrick (n 1) 993.

[69] M Bridge, *The Sale of Goods*, 3rd edn (Oxford, OUP, 2014) para 6.57.

[70] Ibid.

[71] McKendrick (n 1) 997 (stating that a contract may also call for a *certified invoice* which is simply a commercial invoice certified either by an exporter or an independent third party. A *consular invoice* is 'an invoice on an official consulate form which gives details of the goods, the price, the shipment etc, and is signed by a consular official of the country to which the goods are being consigned after verification against the shipping documents').

[72] See Art 18(c) UCP 600.

Where a contract requires the seller to procure insurance, as is the case in CIF contracts, the buyer needs an insurance document which evidences that the terms of insurance comply with the sales contract and enables the buyer to claim directly against the insurer.[73] While an *insurance policy* is such a document,[74] a sales contract may allow the seller to tender an *insurance certificate*[75] or even an *indemnity*.[76] This is so particularly where the goods are shipped in bulk, with goods to be delivered to several buyers, under one insurance policy.[77] INCOTERMS set out in some detail insurance obligations of a CIF seller such as those to procure minimum cover (contract price plus 10 per cent) in the contract currency for specified types of risk and duration, and from 'the point of delivery ... to at least the named port of destination'.[78]

As evidence of the seller's compliance with the requirements as to quality, quantity and description of the goods, the parties can agree that the seller should provide certificates and inspection reports to this effect. Parties usually entrust a recognised independent expert to carry out an inspection. *Certificates of quality, quantity, weight, grade, origin or phyto-sanitary health* are thus often required to be tendered by the seller as part of the set of documents against which payment is to be made.[79] In shipment contracts, where the seller's delivery obligation lies in placing the goods on board the vessel or procuring goods already in transit, with the risk of loss of or damage to the goods passing to the buyer on shipment, these documents acquire special importance. Because under such contracts the buyer may not have the right to examine the goods before payment,[80] or

[73] See CIF A3, INCOTERMS 2010 (n 21).

[74] See CIF A3, INCOTERMS 2010 (n 21).

[75] See *Benjamin's Sale of Goods* (n 23) para 19-047 (stating that this document merely certifies that the goods have been insured under a policy to which the certificate refers).

[76] See *John Martin of London Ltd v AE Taylor & Co Ltd* (n 66) 593.

[77] Art 28 UCP 600 (also allowing for the tender of an insurance certificate or declaration). Art 28 further contains the requirements that insurance documents must meet under the letter of credit.

[78] See CIF A3, INCOTERMS 2010 (n 21).

[79] Either under a 'cash against documents' clause or under a letter of credit.

[80] This is how CIF contracts are interpreted in English law: see *E Clemens Horst Co v Biddell Bros* [1912] AC 18. Even outside English law, a normal expectation is that, in CIF contracts, payment will be made against the documents and the documents may well arrive before the goods, with the payment having to be made before the arrival of the goods. If the buyer were allowed not to pay before examining the goods in CIF/CFR contracts, the examination would usually have to be carried out at destination. In this case, the seller would either have to provide inspection facilities at destination or allow the buyer to have the documents to obtain possession of the goods, thereby depriving the seller of documentary security before payment. Both scenarios run counter to the nature of a CIF contract where the seller has no obligation to ensure the arrival of the goods at destination and can expect to get paid after delivering the goods/purchasing them afloat and upon tendering the required documents. See *Benjamin's Sale of Goods* (n 23) para 19-077; A Mullis, 'Termination for Breach of Contract in CIF Contracts under the Vienna Convention and English Law: Is There a Substantial Difference?' in E Lomnicka and R Morse (eds), *Contemporary Issues in Commercial Law: Essays in Honor of Prof AG Guest* (London, Sweet & Maxwell, 1997) 137 (taking a similar view in the context of Art 58(3) CISG).

examination may be impracticable,[81] the inspection certificates provide the buyer with a reasonable degree of assurance as to the conformity of the goods. The assurances are essential regardless of whether the buyer intends to use or resell the goods, and are also essential to sub-buyers and to banks which may be lending money on the strength of these assurances.[82] In view of the significance of such certificates, the relevant contractual clauses are often carefully drafted by specifying an expert in charge of an inspection, a method and time-frames for inspection, and by indicating whether the certificates are to be 'final' or 'conclusive'. The latter provisions aim to promote certainty and reliability of the certificates, as well as to avoid legal disputes and encourage settlement between the parties. These provisions potentially give rise to various legal issues, including whether the finality of certificates can be challenged, their status, and the parties' legal positions if some or all procedures provided therein are not complied with.[83]

Another document which a contract may require the seller to deliver is *a packing list*, also known as *a bill of parcels*,[84] which gives details of the consignee, vessel and place of departure and destination; terms of delivery and payment; the type, contents and weight of each package, with shipping marks but no prices indicated. A packing list may be required by the export/import legislation of some countries, as well as by some buyers. This document is used for freight calculations, meeting customs requirements and assisting in checking which content is in which packages.[85] Finally, the seller may also have an obligation to procure and tender *export or import licences*.

III. CONFORMITY OF DOCUMENTS

A. Documentary and 'Physical' Obligations

By making separate mention[86] and allocating a separate provision[87] to the seller's obligation to hand over any documents relating to the goods, the CISG[88] makes it sufficiently clear that this obligation is separate from

[81] Such as where the goods are sold in transit.

[82] See *Alfred C Toepfer v Continental Grain Co* [1974] 1 Lloyd's Rep 11, 13 (quoting the award of the Board of Appeal).

[83] For a detailed discussion, see IV C below.

[84] See Hinkelman (n 4) 53.

[85] See ibid; McKendrick (n 1) 997.

[86] Art 30 CISG ('The seller must deliver the goods, hand over any documents relating to them and transfer the property in the goods, as required by the contract and this Convention').

[87] Art 34.

[88] For discussion of the issues of the time and place of the handing over of documents under the CISG, see D Saidov, 'Documentary Performance and the CISG' in I Schwenzer and L Spagnolo (eds), *State of Play: The 3rd Annual MAA Schelchtriem CISG Conference* (The Hague, Eleven International Publishing, 2012) 49.

the duty to deliver the goods.[89] Non-performance of a documentary obligation will therefore constitute a breach under the CISG, independent of any breach in relation to the goods ('physical' obligations), which in turn can trigger a separate set of remedies.[90] Thus, while there is an inherent link between documentary and 'physical' obligations, a distinction needs to be drawn between them for the purpose of legal analysis.[91]

B. What Documents Must the Seller Deliver?

Because in most cases it is the contract that expressly sets out a list of documents that the seller is to hand over, the above question should not pose any particular problems. Nevertheless, this question may arise in an acute form where, for example, the contract is silent (or says very little) on the seller's documentary obligations, or where the buyer alleges that despite the contract containing a list of documents, the seller ought to hand over an additional document. This question also becomes difficult to answer where a letter of credit, provided for in the contract, contains a list of documents different to that in the contract. Dealing with this situation makes it necessary to explore the relationship between the sales contract and the letter of credit.

To begin with an extreme scenario where the contract is silent on which documents the seller must hand over, the immediate general answer is that it is a matter of contract interpretation. Under the CISG, the parties' intentions ought to be ascertained in the light of all relevant circumstances, including any previous practices or applicable trade usages.[92] If the contract provides for a particular term, such as CIF[93] or FOB[94] with an express reference to INCOTERMS, it will usually be safe to conclude that INCOTERMS were intended to be the source from which the details of the seller's documentary duties should be derived. Thus, a CIF seller must provide a 'usual transport document',[95]

[89] See Secretariat Commentary on Art 32 of the 1978 Draft ('[Art 34] deals with the second obligation of the seller'); P Huber and A Mullis, *The CISG: A New Textbook for Students and Practitioners* (Munich, Sellier European Law Publishers, 2007) 126–27.

[90] But see D Maskow in CM Bianca and MJ Bonell (eds), *Commentary on the International Sales Law: The 1980 Vienna Sales Convention* (Giuffrè, Milan, 1987) 428 (taking a seemingly different view).

[91] See, however, Supreme Court, 4A_617/2012, 26 March 2013 (Switzerland), available at http://cisgw3.law.pace.edu/cases/130326s1.html, where the seller's failure to provide certificates as required by the contract was merely deemed to be a breach in relation to the goods under Art 35(1).

[92] See Arts 8 and 9 CISG; also Commercial Court St Gallen, HG.2010.421-HGK, 14 June 2012 (Switzerland), available at http://cisgw3.law.pace.edu/cases/120614s1.html.

[93] For the definition of this trade term, see Chapter 2.

[94] For the definition of this trade term, see Chapter 2.

[95] See A8 CIF, INCOTERMS 2010 (n 21) (the following are treated as such by the comments on the 2000 version of INCOTERMS: a negotiable bill of lading, a non-negotiable sea waybill or an inland waterway document); see also Ramberg (n 22) 188 (CFR A8).

a commercial invoice,[96] and the insurance policy 'or other evidence of insurance cover'.[97] Comments on the 2000 version of INCOTERMS also state that where the buyer intends to sell the goods in transit, under CFR/CIF terms, it can demand that the seller deliver a negotiable bill of lading.[98] Therefore, where the contract expressly refers to INCOTERMS, it becomes possible, by virtue of the Convention's rules of interpretation and consequently relying on INCOTERMS, to answer the question of what documents the seller ought to deliver.

The issue becomes more complicated if a contract refers to a trade term, but does not make it clear that it was the parties' intention to determine the content of these terms on the basis of INCOTERMS. While it may be possible to infer an intention to apply INCOTERMS from, say, the parties' previous practice, more often than not there will be no evidence pointing specifically to INCOTERMS. Where so, the question is: From what source is the meaning of the stipulated trade term to be derived? There is some support for the view that INCOTERMS constitute a trade usage under the CISG,[99] with the result that INCOTERMS would be applicable to such a contract even without an express reference to them and would define a contractually stipulated term.[100] There is a more cautious view which holds that while INCOTERMS are indeed widely known to and regularly applied by international traders, it cannot be assumed that this is the case in all trade sectors.[101] The proponents of this view also rightly note that an argument that INCOTERMS are widely known can work against treating INCOTERMS as a trade usage; if they are so widely known, a lack of reference to them can be regarded as an intention not to apply them.[102] If this position is taken, mere reference to a trade term cannot lead to the

[96] A1 CIF, INCOTERMS 2010 (n 21) (its 'equivalent electronic record or procedure if agreed between the parties or customary'). The same applies to any document referred to in A1–A10, INCOTERMS 2010.

[97] A3 CIF, INCOTERMS 2010 (n 21). *Cf Raincoat*, CIETAC, 10 August 1999, available at http://cisgw3.law.pace.edu/cases/990810c1.html (interpreting CIF under INCOTERMS as *requiring* the seller to deliver an inspection certificate).

[98] J Ramberg, *ICC Guide to Incoterms 2000: Understanding and Practical Use* (ICC Publishing SA, Paris, 1999) 112 (commenting on A8 CFR).

[99] See, eg *BP Oil Int'l v Empresa Estatal Petroleos de Ecuador*, 332 F 3d 333, 335 (5th Cir 2003) (US); *St Paul Guardian Insurance Co v Neuromed Medical Systems and Support, GmbH*, 2002 US Dist LEXIS 5096 (SDNY).

[100] See *PVC Suspension Resin*, CIETAC Arbitration, 7 April 1999, available at http://cisgw3.law.pace.edu/cases/990407c1.html; *China North Chemical Industries Corp v Beston Chemical Corp*, F Supp 2d, 2006 WL 295395.

[101] See Bridge (n 69) 546–47 (giving an example of dry commodities trade, as opposed to oil trade where INCOTERMS are often used). But see Supreme Court, 2 Ob 191/98x, 15 October 1998 (Austria), available at http://cisgw3.law.pace.edu/cases/981015a3.html (holding that to be regarded as a trade usage, it needs to be known to and regularly observed by a majority of (not by all) traders); Supreme Court, 10 Ob 344/99g, 21 March 2000 (Austria), available at http://cisgw3.law.pace.edu/cases/000321a3.html.

[102] M Bridge, *TheInternational Sale of Goods*, 3rd edn (Oxford, OUP, 2013) 526.

application of INCOTERMS.[103] If so, with reference to what source should a trade term be defined?

It may be the case that there is an internationally settled meaning of at least such terms as CIF or FOB.[104] But even in this (unlikely) case, the question of what documents the seller must deliver will probably not be answered very differently from INCOTERMS. Apart from the fact that tribunals will usually look at INCOTERMS for guidance anyway,[105] it is clear, for example, that in a CIF contract, a commercial invoice will have to be delivered since it is a document expected under most sales contracts. Most traders would undoubtedly recognise that 'I' in CIF stands for insurance, implying the seller's duty to provide an insurance document. Considering that risk passes on shipment and the goods may be damaged in transit, a transport document will be expected to enable the buyer to have the rights of suit against the carrier. If both parties are traders, the seller would be expected to tender a transport document which not only enables the buyer to obtain the delivery of the goods but also to dispose of them while they are in transit (negotiable/transferable bill of lading).[106] Such an interpretation can be based on Article 9(2) CISG, if there is indeed an internationally settled meaning of CIF which meets the requirement of this article, and/or on Article 8(2).[107] Thus, if there is an internationally understood meaning of a trade term, the CISG will largely operate as a channel for importing this meaning into the contract.

[103] See ibid.

[104] See *Old Paper*, CIETAC Arbitration, 11 April 1994, available at http://cisgw3.law.pace.edu/cases/940411c1.html (where CIF is interpreted without reference to INCOTERMS); *Linseed Cake*, CIETAC Arbitration, 9 January 1993, available at http://cisgw3.law.pace.edu/cases/930109c1.html (where FOB is explained without reference to INCOTERMS); Commercial Appellate Court, 31 October 1995 (Argentina), available at http://cisgw3.law.pace.edu/cases/951031a1.html; also Bridge (n 102) 527 ('to the extent [English decisions on CIF and FOB] espouse rules akin to those of other jurisdictions, and indeed may have been influential in instilling those rules in other jurisdictions ... they can be brought in on the terms allowed for by Article 9(2)'); ICC Arbitration No 7645, March 1995, available at http://cisgw3.law.pace.edu/cases/957645i1.html#cxii ('Even though in the present case the contract was not a CIF but rather a CFR contract, and although the applicable law is not the English law but rather the CISG respectively Austrian law, the opinion in the mentioned English case may be taken as an expression of an internationally recognized understanding of the CIF clause').

[105] Dalhuisen (n 18) 226 ('one may expect the courts and commercial arbitrators to look to Incoterms for lack of any better guide when the relevant sales terms are used in a contract without definition or reference to the Incoterms, even if they are not considered customary').

[106] This function of a bill of lading is well recognised in international cases. See, eg Wuhan Maritime Court, Hubei, (2000) Wu Hai Fa Shang Zi Di No 91, 10 September 2002 (China), available at http://cisgw3.law.pace.edu/cases/020910c1.html ('A bill of lading represents the goods; sale of the bill of lading equals sale of the goods, which is a normal business transaction ... under the term CFR, the delivery of goods is a symbolic delivery, which means that delivery of bill of lading, letter of credit, certificate of origin, etc equals delivery of goods'); *Wool*, CIETAC Arbitration, 27 February 1996, available at http://cisgw3.law.pace.edu/cases/960227c1.html; see also ICC Arbitration No 7645 (n 104).

[107] In the sense that this is how a reasonable person would understand a CIF term.

The CISG could potentially take on a greater role in what must be a rare case where a *shipment* contract is silent on what documents the seller is to deliver, and which does not refer to any trade term. In this case, the buyer who wishes to allege that the seller breached the contract by failing to deliver a document(s) could construct an argument implying a term into the contract to that effect. The buyer could argue that since the risk under the CISG passes when the goods are handed over to the first carrier,[108] a reasonable person in the buyer's position[109] would expect, for such a passage of risk to be justifiable,[110] the seller to deliver a document conferring on the buyer a right of suit against the carrier.[111] A reasonable person would also expect: a document enabling the buyer to claim the goods from the carrier;[112] and the seller to deliver a negotiable document if the seller is in the position to know[113] that the buyer's intention is to resell the goods. It is also a normal expectation that a commercial invoice will be delivered.

This set of arguments can either find its legal basis in contract interpretation (that is, what a reasonable person in the buyer's position would expect the seller's documentary duties to be in the light of relevant provisions of the applicable sales law (CISG) (implication in fact)) or, even more controversially, it can be presented as a term implied under the Convention as a logical inference from its various provisions (implication in law).[114] The latter probably stretches the CISG too far since the Convention was clearly intended to defer entirely to the contract in documentary matters.[115] However, there seems to be room for the former argument, rooted in contract interpretation. If so, it is submitted that, in the absence of any relevant contract clause/mechanism (eg cash against documents) indicating that the seller was intended to deliver documents or a particular document, or other relevant evidence (eg trading context, practices or usages), courts

[108] This rule applies if the contract involves carriage of the goods (see Art 67(1) CISG).

[109] Art 8(2).

[110] See Debattista (n 9) 98 (providing a similar argument in the context of English law).

[111] Documents that will satisfy these requirements are bills of lading (negotiable and straight), delivery orders and waybills. Although waybills do not in themselves confer the rights of suit to the buyer, the buyer nevertheless has those rights by virtue of being named as consignee in a waybill. Mate's, dock or quay receipts will not meet this requirement.

[112] This follows from the nature and purpose of a sales contract and from the seller's basic duty to deliver the goods (Art 30), all of which imply that ultimately the buyer needs to obtain possession of the goods. But see *Arnold Karberg & Co v Blythe, Green Jourdain & Co* [1915] 2 KB 379 (taking the view that CIF contracts are about the sale of documents, rather than goods).

[113] The CISG requires symmetry of the parties' knowledge in numerous provisions. See, eg Arts 1(2), 2(a), 8(1), 9(2), 10(a), 25, 31(b), 38(3), 42(1), 74 CISG. On the relevance of Art 58, see below.

[114] In this case, there is little difference between implying a term in law and interpreting the contract (implying a term in fact).

[115] See Secretariat Commentary on Art 32 of the 1978 Draft; C Widmer in I Schwenzer (ed), *Schlechtriem and Schwenzer, Commentary on the UN Convention on the International Sale of Goods (CISG)*, 3rd (English) edn (Oxford, OUP, 2010) Art 30, para 6; see also Art 34 CISG.

and tribunals ought to exercise great caution in order not to infer too much from contractual silence.[116] Had the buyer wanted a certain level of documentary security/performance, it could have bargained for it and articulated it in the contract. With party autonomy being a fundamental principle, courts and tribunals ought not to interfere with that autonomy by (re-)writing a contract and possibly disturbing the balance of commercial risks and burdens created by it.

Where, on the other hand, there is an indication of the parties' intention that the seller was expected to deliver some documents, such as the 'cash against documents' clause, the search for a detailed elaboration of the documents to be delivered from within the CISG by means of contract interpretation seems more justifiable. The court or tribunal is not in such circumstances (re-)writing the contract, but rather enforcing the parties' intention. Article 58 CISG is relevant here. Where 'the buyer is not bound to pay the price at any other specific time', Article 58(1) requires the buyer to pay only when the seller places 'the goods or *documents controlling the disposition* of the goods at the buyer's disposal'.[117] Where the contract involves carriage, Article 58(2) provides that the seller 'may dispatch the goods on terms whereby the goods, or *documents controlling their disposition*, will not be handed over to the buyer except against payment of the price'.[118] Article 58 thus signals that where the payment is to be made against the documents, the seller is expected to hand over 'documents controlling the disposition of the goods'. Much turns on the meaning of this phrase because not only does it potentially help to ascertain the documents that must be tendered, but additionally it authorises the buyer to withhold payment, without liability, if such documents are not handed over.

There is no agreement on what documents 'control the disposition of the goods' under Article 58. One view is that it can only be a transferable ('negotiable') document, such as a 'negotiable' bill of lading (or a warehouse receipt), which enables the holder not only to obtain possession, but also to transfer possession and rights of suit against the carrier.[119] Another view[120] is that it should be a document enabling the holder to obtain possession, such as a 'negotiable' (and possibly a straight) bill of lading, a warehouse receipt and a delivery order.[121] Yet another, broader, view is

[116] *Cf* Art 18(1) CISG (providing a similar approach in the context of contract formation).

[117] Emphasis added.

[118] Emphasis added.

[119] There was support for this view amongst some drafters (see CISG AC No 11 (n 37) para 4.5).

[120] See generally Davies (n 44); CISG AC (n 37) rule 5.

[121] According to this view, Art 58 also covers a document which 'once in the hands of the buyer, establishes that the seller no longer has the right to control disposition of the goods' (CISG AC (n 37) rule 5, paras 6.5–6.6 and 6.12 of the Comments; see also nn 37 and 45 above). This means that such documents as straight bills of lading, the consignor's copy of an air waybill, the consignor's duplicate copy of a rail consignment note, the consignor's duplicate or first copy of a road consignment note and road bills of lading in North America will also be covered by Art 58 (see CISG AC (n 37) rule 6, paras 6.5–6.6, 6.12 and 6.14 of the Comments).

that any document confirming receipt of the goods and the carrier's undertaking to deliver the goods at destination[122] also satisfies Article 58.[123] The proponents of this view go so far as to suggest including other documents *if* the importing country's legislation requires their presentation for the goods to be imported.[124] Even an insurance policy or certificate has been included, with an admission that strictly speaking such documents never control the disposition of the goods. This broad view is justified on the ground that the buyer should not be allowed to refuse to pay for the goods which were lost or destroyed after the risk had passed to the buyer, simply because the seller did not hand over, say, a negotiable bill of lading. The buyer is sufficiently protected because it can sue the carrier and/or claim against the insurer.[125] It could also be argued that Article 58 should not be interpreted too rigorously because, had the buyer wanted a negotiable or transferable document, it could have bargained for it.

It is submitted that the second view is preferable. The first view raises the threshold too high as the buyer is only able to withhold payment in very limited circumstances where the seller fails to provide a negotiable/transferrable document. The seller's non-delivery of a document which is not negotiable/transferrable but which enables the buyer to obtain possession, deprives the buyer of access to the goods, the very subject matter of a sales contract. If the buyer could not withhold payment in such cases, there would be a fundamental flaw in the level of security and legal protection that the CISG afforded to the buyer. Conversely, the third view gives the buyer a right to withhold payment in too wide a range of circumstances. A failure to deliver a document other than that enabling possession of the goods, such as a certificate, will not always have a drastic impact on the buyer's ability to access the goods and/or to resell or use them. Allowing Article 58 to be invoked in this case would make the CISG favour the buyer over the seller, whereas the Convention was intended to treat both parties equally.[126] It is thus the second view that achieves the most optimum balance between the parties' interests.

If a contract provides for payment by means of a letter of credit, the terms of credit can evidence either the parties' original intention regarding the seller's documentary duties,[127] or their subsequent agreement to

[122] That would include bills of lading (whether transferable or straight), warehouse receipts, ship's delivery orders, waybills, and consignment notes.

[123] See Maskow (n 90) 426; Davies (n 44).

[124] But see Federal Supreme Court, VIII ZR 51/95, 3 April 1996 (Germany), available at www.cisg.law.pace.edu/cisg/wais/db/cases2/960403g1.html ('Documents [under Art 58] are mainly the so-called true transfer documents ... Among these are in particular the Warehouse Receipt, but not the Certificate of Origin or of Quality: their tender is normally neither necessary nor sufficient to found the maturity of the purchase price').

[125] See Davies (n 44) 172.

[126] See, eg the Preamble to the CISG. See also Chapter 1.

[127] See CISG AC Opinion No 11 (n 37) para 5.1, taking a similar, but a more assertive position.

supplement or change their initial (silent) position, thereby effectively filling this gap in their contract.[128] That said, courts and tribunals must be satisfied that the terms of credit genuinely reflect the parties' mutual intention and that the buyer, when opening a credit with a list of documents to be presented by the seller, is not attempting to effectively change their initial agreement.

Treating the question of what (if any) documents the seller is to deliver as a matter falling exclusively within the realm of contract interpretation should, in principle, counter a possible argument that this question should be dealt with by domestic law, rather than the Convention, because some domestic legal systems are better equipped to deal with such issues.[129] Being a matter of contract interpretation, it is not a question of whether there is a gap in the Convention's substantive coverage.[130] The Convention's rules of contract interpretation are adequate and self-contained, which excludes any recourse to domestic law.[131] Although this position assumes that contract interpretation will always be able to provide answers, it seems that the approach to contract interpretation suggested here, which draws on trade terms, payment mechanisms, the trading environment and the internal logic of documents, should be able to deal with the question of the seller's documentary duties in the vast majority of cases.

As regards some other implications of letters of credit for the seller's duty to hand over a particular document(s), mention needs to be made of a situation where the contract provides for a list of documents to be handed over by the seller, but documentary requirements in the letter of credit differ from the contractual list. For example, a CIF contract may require a minimum set of documents (a bill of lading, a commercial invoice and an insurance policy) whereas a letter of credit may, in addition to these documents, require the seller to deliver certificates of quality and origin. Did the buyer breach the contract by opening a non-conforming letter of credit, or did the parties change the contract[132] by extending the seller's documentary obligation? The answer depends on the interpretation of the parties' intentions.[133] If the buyer sought pre-advice from the seller regarding this, and/or negotiated different terms departing from the contract with the seller, before opening the credit, and the seller approved the proposed terms, it is

[128] See, generally, *Ficom SA v Sociedad Cadex Lda* [1980] 2 Lloyd's Rep 118.

[129] For instance, English law with its long experience of dealing with CIF and FOB contracts would have a default position clarifying the seller's duties if a contract referring to such a term does not specify the documents to be tendered by the seller.

[130] Art 7(2) CISG.

[131] Art 7.

[132] Art 29; see also *WJ Alan & Co Ltd v El Nasr Export and Import Co* [1972] 1 Lloyd's Rep 313.

[133] Art 8.

clear the parties intended to vary the contract.[134] If the seller was unaware of or was not in a position to know about the buyer opening the credit on different terms, it is likely that the buyer simply failed to open a conforming credit, and the seller is under no obligation to tender documents in addition to those initially agreed upon in the contract. The absence of evidence on pre-advice or negotiation with the seller prior to the opening of a credit may not necessarily be fatal to an argument that the parties varied the contract in the light of their subsequent conduct.[135] If, after opening the credit, the buyer proposes an amendment to the credit and the seller does not reject the proposal or rejects it only in part, this response can be taken to mean that the seller was aware of the terms on which the credit was opened and implicitly agreed to the change of the contract to the extent to which no objection was raised.[136] To conclude, it is clear that while the terms on which a credit is opened can be far-reaching for the seller's documentary obligations, care must be taken to ensure that no presumptions are drawn, as was done in one CISG case,[137] about the relationship between a sales contract and the terms on which a letter of credit is opened. This issue ultimately rests on construction of the parties' intentions in the particular circumstances.

C. Conformity of Documents

(i) Transport Documents: Contractual Requirements

A sales contract will often define requirements with reference to which conformity of documents will be assessed. The contract may, for example,

[134] This is likely to be so regardless of whether the contract, in addition to setting out the seller's documentary duties, also sets out the corresponding requirements for a letter of credit.

[135] Art 8(3).

[136] See *Ficom SA v Sociedad Cadex Lda* (n 128) 132.

[137] ICC Arbitration No 7645 (n 104) ('if the goods ... [are] frequently traded on the international markets, a seller must be aware ... that the purchaser may possibly not be interested so much in actually receiving and using the goods purchased for its own purposes but might rather be interested to trade them on. Since the documents become extremely relevant in such circumstance it would appear that the specification of documents to be submitted under [a letter of credit (L/C)] to obtain payment usually is meant to also constitute a contractual obligation of the seller to deliver the documents as specified, and *all* such documents, to the purchaser. The arbitral tribunal is of the opinion that there is a presumption to such effect in international sales transactions and that a contractual agreement to the contrary, namely to the effect that the documents specified need to be submitted only if the seller chooses to make use of the L/C, would have to be set out *specifically* in the contract. If in a written contract with extended wording no distinction is being made between the documents to be submitted under the L/C provided for in the contract, it must therefore be taken that the documents mentioned under the L/C clause are meant to have to be submitted to the purchaser in any event, irrespective of whether the seller wants to take advantage of the L/C or not').

provide for an on-board[138] clean[139] order bill of lading.[140] In a CIF/CFR contract where the seller is responsible for arranging carriage, the seller may also be required to prepay freight and to deliver a freight pre-paid bill of lading,[141] as well as to ensure carriage of goods to the contractual destination as evidenced by a bill of lading. The contract may specify a route, such as shipment directly to the destination[142] and, again, a bill of lading needs to evidence that a CIF seller made a carriage contract on these terms. If shipment to a particular destination is expressly prohibited,[143] the seller commits a documentary breach by delivering a bill specifying that destination. A sales contract may contain provisions on whether carriage on deck is allowed, and a bill of lading must evidence compliance of the carriage contract with such a term.[144] A contract may require delivery of an original bill, or of all the original bills.[145] In one CISG case,[146] where the contract required the seller to deliver an air waybill, the tribunal stated that what the seller had tendered was not an air waybill, since it was merely its digital copy 'without the seal of the carrier' and 'not an official document issued by the carrier'.[147]

If the contract does not contain express requirements of documentary compliance, such requirements can often be derived from the nature of a trade term and from INCOTERMS if they are referred to in the contract.[148]

[138] See Art 20(ii) UCP 600.

[139] See Ramberg (n 21) 196 ('the buyer is not obliged to accept a document which does not provide adequate proof of delivery, for example, one which has notations on it showing that the goods are defective or that they have been provided in less than the agreed quantity. In these cases, the document is termed "unclean"'); see also Art 27 UCP 600.

[140] See, eg Dalian Maritime Court, 29 June 2005 (China), available at http://cisgw3.law.pace.edu/cases/050629c1.html (order clean bill lading); *Fluorite*, CIETAC Arbitration, February 2006 (shipped clean bill of lading).

[141] See CIETAC Arbitration, 11 April 1994 (n 104); *Spare Parts*, CIETAC Arbitration, September 2006, available at www.cisg.law.pace.edu/cisg/wais/db/cases2/060900c4.html (freight pre-paid airway bill).

[142] See CIETAC Arbitration, 23 February 1995, available at http://cisgw3.law.pace.edu/cases/950223c1.html.

[143] See, eg Appellate Court Genova, 211, 24 March 1995 (Italy), available at www.cisg.law.pace.edu/cisg/wais/db/cases2/950324i3.html.

[144] See Wuhan Maritime Court, 10 September 2002 (n 106) (an appendix to the contract stating that 'a bill of lading marked with goods on deck is acceptable'); also Art 26(1) UCP 600; Debattista (n 9) 164–67 (for the discussion of the position under English law).

[145] Typically, bills of lading are issued in sets, often of three. See *Glyn, Mills & Cov East & West India Dock Co* (n 16) 605; *Sandersv Maclean* (1883) 11 QBD 327, 342; also A8 CFR/CIF, INCOTERMS 2010 (n 21) ('when ... a transport document is issued in negotiable form and in several originals, a full set of originals must be presented to the buyer'); Arts 20(a)(iv), 21(a)(iv), 22(a)(iv) UCP 600.

[146] See CIETAC Arbitration, September 2006 (n 141).

[147] *Cf* Art 23 UCP 600.

[148] See *Gloves*, CIETAC Arbitration, 28 September 1996, available at http://cisgw3.law.pace.edu/cases/960928c1.html (clean bill of lading, as defined in INCOTERMS 1990, determinative as to apparent condition of the goods on shipment).

If not, and if they are not regarded as a trade usage, they will, as noted above,[149] usually be used as guidance for defining a given trade term. If payment is to be made by means of a letter of credit with reference to the UCP, this provision may evidence the parties' intention, ascertained under the CISG,[150] to be governed by the UCP as regards standards of documentary compliance (strict compliance),[151] in terms of the type, form, content and time of documents/documentary tender.[152] Even if the UCP are not expressly referred to, it has been argued that it is a trade usage within the meaning of Article 9 CISG[153] and hence should be used notwithstanding absence of any specific reference to it. Whatever the true position may be, courts and tribunals must ensure that the terms of the letter of credit truly reflect the parties' intentions and the buyer is not using its opening of the credit to create documentary obligations to which the seller cannot be taken to have agreed.[154]

(ii) Transport Documents: Contractual Silence

A difficult and often overlooked question is how to determine whether documents are conforming where the contract is silent on standards of conformity, there are no relevant trade usages or practices, and neither INCOTERMS nor UCP are applicable. For example, if all that the contract says as regards transport documents is that the seller must tender a bill of lading, on what legal basis should a decision be made regarding whether a proper transport document was delivered?

An attempt could be made to develop specific requirements by construing the contract with reference to the relevant provisions of the Convention, the internal logic of a document such as a bill of lading, its functions in practice and the surrounding trading environment. Thus, as regards its receipt function, the buyer can argue that the bill of lading needs to accurately record the date of shipment, and for the bill of lading to comply with the contract, that date must conform to the delivery date/period stipulated

[149] For the discussion of these issues, see III B above.

[150] Arts 8 and 9 CISG.

[151] See Arts 2, 14, and 15 UCP 600; see also *Benjamin's Sale of Goods* (n 23) para 23-101.

[152] See *Pork*, CIETAC Arbitration, 24 February 2005, available at http://cisgw3.law.pace.edu/cases/050224c1.html (documents rejected under documentary credit because the bill of lading date did not comply with a stipulation in the letter of credit).

[153] See, eg ICC Arbitration No 7645 (n 104); CISG Advisory Council, CISG AC Opinion No 5 'The Buyer's Right to Avoid the Contract in case of Non-Conforming Goods or Documents', available at www.cisg.law.pace.edu/cisg/CISG-AC-op5.html; L Singh and B Leisinger, 'A Law for International Sale of Goods: A Reply to Michael Bridge' (2008) 20 *Pace Int'l L Rev* 161, 183.

[154] For the discussion of the relationship between a sales contract and letter of credit, see III B above.

in the contract.[155] The date of shipment is particularly important in commodities trade as the value of the goods may depend on it,[156] and it is the transport document such as a bill of lading which usually provides evidence of that date.[157] This may appear not to have been recognised in one CISG case where the seller seems not to have been found to be in breach where an incorrect year (1999 instead of 1998) was indicated on a bill of lading:

> Under the usual circumstances, the documents must strictly comply with the L/C, but not every non-compliance constitutes a breach ... The Contract in this case was signed and performed in 1998, and [the seller] presented the documents to the bank for negotiation in 1998, so it is easy for [the seller], [the buyer] or any person with international trade knowledge to know that this was obviously a typing error.[158]

It needs to be borne in mind that even English law which, in order to be conducive to documentary trade, pursues legal certainty and rigour in compliance with documentary obligations, views a clerical error[159] or, possibly, an extremely minor discrepancy[160] as insufficient to hold the seller in breach of contract. In this case, the fact that the documents were presented in 1998 left no doubt that a reference to '1999' was a typing error. Nevertheless, a reference to an incorrect shipment date, strictly speaking, should constitute a breach, and if so, the tribunal's analysis is probably not entirely accurate.[161] That said, the tribunal's willingness not to penalise the

[155] If the contract does not stipulate a date of delivery, the CISG requires the seller to deliver the goods within a reasonable time and, presumably, a bill of lading would then need to be dated within what is determined to be a reasonable time. See Art 33(c) CISG; see also *Novorossisk Shipping Co v Neopetro Co Ltd (The Ulyanovsk)* [1990] 1 Lloyd's Rep 425 (where a difference of a few days in the bill of lading date involved an enormous fluctuation in the commodity price and saw the shipowners liable for damages of US$865,591.42 for disobeying the charterer's voyage instructions).

[156] See, eg *Esteve Trading Corp v Agropec International (The Golden Rio)* [1990] 2 Lloyd's Rep 273, 276.

[157] See ICC Arbitration No 7645 (n 104) (expressly recognising this). *Cf Fishmeal*, CIETAC Arbitration, 1 April 1997, available at http://cisgw3.law.pace.edu/cases/970401c1.html (where, on the one hand, the tribunal stated that the bill accurately recorded the date of shipment and, on the other, found that 'the fact of anti-dating the B/L existed between the shipping agent and master'. The tribunal further held that since the seller committed no fraud, the seller committed no breach as it had performed its duty, as a CIF seller, of loading the goods. With respect, this reasoning fails to distinguish between physical and documentary duties of a CIF seller, since not only must the seller load the goods but also tender documents, including an accurately dated bill of lading).

[158] *Industrial Raw Material*, CIETAC Arbitration, 4 June 1999, available at http://cisgw3.law.pace.edu/cases/990604c1.html.

[159] *SIAT di del Ferro v Tradax Overseas SA* [1980] 1 Lloyd's Rep 53, 64.

[160] This is known as the *de minimis* rule. See *Arcos Ltd v EA Ronaasen & Son* [1933] AC 470; *Moralice (London) v ED & F Man* [1954] 2 Lloyd's Rep 526; see Debattista (n 9) 212–19 (advocating strict documentary compliance in English sales law).

[161] In contrast with English law, there is no doctrine of *de minimis* in the CISG which means that any departure from the applicable requirements will constitute a breach (see Arts 30 and 34 CISG).

seller for a trivial discrepancy is to be welcomed, but it is submitted that the trivial nature of the discrepancy should have been recognised not by holding that there was no breach, but by taking it into account in assessing the remedial consequences of this breach (for example, by not finding a fundamental breach).[162]

Documentary and commodities trading raise a similar but distinct problem of whether the seller is in breach of contract where it delivers a falsely dated bill of lading which, nonetheless on its face conforms to the contract. High price fluctuations and string trading mean that time and speed are important considerations. Together with the fact that documents often have to be handled by banks which are not in a position to make detailed factual inquiries, this leads to the situation where documents 'have to be taken up or rejected promptly'.[163] Certainty is highly prized and the position is sometimes taken that the seller duly performs its documentary obligations where documents are conforming on their face, fraud being an exception.[164] However, this position does not appear to have gained wide support, and the prevailing view seems to be that a bill of lading needs to be genuine,[165] that is, its content must be 'true in all material respects'.[166] This view is even more relevant in CISG waters, since the Convention favours pursuit of truth, usually requiring a legal analysis on the basis of the *actual* state of affairs.[167] Good faith, if regarded as a general principle,[168] can strengthen this position. The same reasoning can also provide the basis from which another requirement, that a bill of lading must not be procured through fraud, can be developed, with a consequence that a bill procured by fraud will be regarded as non-conforming. Fraud will be relevant to the question of what constitutes a conforming document, with a bill procured by fraud constituting a breach of contract triggering remedies available under the CISG. There is an agreement that the applicable domestic law on fraud will still be applicable, affording the buyer (additional) legal protection.[169]

The receipt function is further understood as containing evidence of the quantity, apparent condition of the goods and of their actual receipt by

[162] See Arts 25 and 49.

[163] *Hansson v Hamel and Horley* (n 26) 45.

[164] See *Berger & Co Inc v Gill & Duffus SA* [1984] 1 AC 382.

[165] *James Finlay & Co Ltd v NV Kwik Hoo Tong HM* [1929] 1 KB 400, 408; *Hindley & Co v East Indian Produce Co* [1973] 2 Lloyd's Rep 515; *Procter & Gamble Philippine Mfg Corp v Becher* [1988] 2 Lloyd's Rep 21, 29; *PT Putrabali Adyamulia v Société Est Epices (The Intan 6 v.360a SN); Same v Enrico Webb James SNC* [2003] 2 Lloyd's Rep 700, 709.

[166] *Procter & Gamble Philippine Mfg Corp v Becher* (n 165) 29.

[167] Art 8(3) CISG; see also the damages provisions (Arts 74–77) which appear to prioritise the 'concrete' calculation over the 'abstract' calculation.

[168] Art 7.

[169] See, generally, UG Schroeter in Schwenzer (n 115), Introduction to Arts 14–24, para 59 (with further references).

the carrier.[170] As to the latter, a question may arise whether a 'received for shipment', rather than a 'shipped' bill is good tender. In some systems, it is not, at least in CIF contracts, because such bills do not state the date of shipment, are not documents of title, do not provide the buyer with adequate security given the risk of damage before goods are loaded,[171] and because banks do not usually lend on the security of such documents. Notwithstanding these considerations, and in the absence of a reference to any trade term, a reasonable person in the buyer's position may interpret contracts governed by the CISG[172] differently, since under the Convention if the carriage of goods is involved, delivery and the passing of risk both occur once goods are handed over to the first carrier.[173] In this surrounding legal framework, a reasonable person may well conclude that the seller is entitled to tender a 'received for shipment' bill.

A bill of lading is typically relied upon as evidence of the delivered quantity.[174] At least in the case of a shipment contract where the buyer intends to resell the goods in transit, and the seller is in a position to know of the intended resale, a bill of lading can be expected to refer to contract quantity. Otherwise, it would be very difficult for the buyer to resell them in transit.[175] Whether the statement in a bill of lading is conclusive on whether the seller delivered the contractual quantity depends on the agreement. Where no intention can be inferred from the contract, the evidentiary value of the bill will probably need to be determined on the basis of the applicable law. This appears to be the position implied in one CISG case[176] where the quantity was misstated on an air waybill and the court held, with references to US cases, that waybills and bills of lading constituted only prima facie evidence of delivery, with the presumption being rebuttable.

Whether the seller commits a breach of contract by tendering an 'unclean' bill of lading where the contract is silent on this matter, and where a standard cannot be implied into the contract from INCOTERMS or UCP is a difficult question. While the notion of a clean bill of lading appears well

170 See Appellate Court Köln, 2 U 175/95, 9 July 1997 (Germany), available at http://cisgw3.law.pace.edu/cases/970709g3.html, where the seller tendered a bill of lading indicating that a container, which was 'said to contain' contract goods, had been delivered to a freight forwarder, as opposed to the first carrier as required for the delivery to occur under the CISG (see Art 31(a)). The bill also did not indicate the buyer as the recipient of the goods. In these circumstances, the court held that the seller had failed to prove that the goods were handed over to the first carrier.

171 See Bridge (n 102) 157–58.

172 Art 8(2) CISG.

173 Arts 31 and 67.

174 See CIETAC Arbitration, 28 September 1996 (n 148).

175 Debattista (n 9) 137.

176 *SV Braun, Inc v Alitalia-Linee Aeree Italiane, SpA* F Supp 1994 WL 121680.

known in international trade,[177] it is questionable whether this fact can lead to an inference that bills of lading must always be clean. Perhaps, the most that can be said is that if a trading environment is such that the seller expects the buyer to resell the goods, and if it is generally understood that an unclean bill of lading will prevent the buyer from reselling, it may be arguable that a term as to the cleanliness of a bill of lading must be implied.

Where the seller is responsible for carriage, the Convention contains a general provision which may have implications for contract interpretation in relation to the bill of lading. The CISG requires the seller to 'make such contracts as are necessary for carriage to the place fixed by means of transportation appropriate in the circumstances and according to the usual terms for such transportation'.[178] An examination of the 'means of transportation appropriate in the circumstances' and of 'usual terms' may reveal specific expectations[179] regarding the route, and relating to transhipment or deck stowage, which, in turn, can lead to implication of a relevant term into the contract. Arguably, the bill of lading must then evidence a carriage contract in compliance with such implied terms. Because the risk passes to the buyer when the goods are handed over to the first carrier,[180] the buyer, it seems, can reasonably argue that it is entitled to a transport document enabling it to have the rights of suit against a carrier.

If the seller is in a position to know that the buyer wishes to resell in transit, the buyer can argue that by tendering, for example, a straight bill of lading, the seller commits a breach of contract because this document is not capable of being negotiated to anyone other than the named consignee. A term that a 'negotiable' bill of lading is to be delivered cannot, however, be implied lightly since a reasonable person is no doubt aware[181] that the CISG defers to contract when it comes to documentary obligations and, on a balanced interpretation, it should generally be up to the buyer to negotiate a term to this effect and to bear the consequences of not doing so.[182]

177 To some extent, the references to this standard in UCP 600 (see n 23) and (most likely) in INCOTERMS 2010 (see B8 CIF/CFR, INCOTERMS 2010 (n 21) and, particularly, comments in Ramberg (n 98) 117 on the INCOTERMS 2000 with a similar provision to that in the 2010 version) evidence international recognition of this standard. SeeDalian Maritime Court, 29 June 2005 (n 140) (providing references to cases on the CISG); New Pudong District People's Court of Shanghai, (2004) Pu Min Er (Shang) Chu Zi Di No 3221, 23 September 2005 (China), available at http://cisgw3.law.pace.edu/cases/050923c1.html; *China North Chem Ind Corp v Beston Chem Corp* (n 100); *The David Agmashenebeli* [2003] 1 Lloyd's Rep 92, 94; *Sea Success Maritime Inc v African Maritime Carriers Ltd* [2005] 2 Lloyd's Rep 692.

178 Art 32(2) CISG.

179 Art 8(2) and (3).

180 Art 67.

181 Art 8(2).

182 *Cf* Widmer (n 115) 563 ('Whether the seller is actually obliged to procure a document in negotiable form for the buyer must be decided on the basis of the contract and trade usage. There is no general rule').

Whether a bill of lading is negotiable must be determined by the applicable law.[183]

(iii) Other Documents

The contract may contain specific requirements in relation to non-transport documents. In relation to a commercial invoice, the seller can be held liable if an incomplete set of invoices is tendered, and where invoices refer to a price lower in amount than the contract price,[184] or to a different trade term and destination than those required by the contract.[185] As regards an insurance document, the contract will often specify the amount and type of risk to be covered by, as well as the type of, insurance document. In one case,[186] for example, the tribunal dismissed the buyer's claim that the CIF seller did not procure an insurance policy covering all risks, including war risk, as well as two types of special risks (Salmonella and Shigella) relating specifically to the nature of the goods, because there was evidence that the buyer had already successfully brought an insurance claim for those risks. Contracts may call for certificates confirming the origin of the goods[187] and specify procedures to be followed in carrying out an inspection, such as the use of a particular inspection agency[188] and/or methods of inspection, and the requirement for all these to be evidenced by inspection certificates.[189] Once the contractual standards of conformity are ascertained, the question of whether the seller delivered conforming documents can be answered. A breach can be committed not only where an individual document is non-conforming, but also where there is discrepancy within the documentary

[183] See ibid, taking a similar view; see also Dalhuisen (n 18) 568–69, 580 (although a transfer mechanism in a bill of lading is said to be based 'on their own status ... independent from domestic law', this issue is now increasingly nationalised and it will have to be the applicable law that will ultimately be decisive on this point).

[184] Mexican Commission for the Protection of Foreign Trade, 30 November 1998, available at www.cisg.law.pace.edu/cisg/wais/db/cases2/981130m1.html; see also AM Garro, 'The UN Sales Convention in the Americas: Recent Developments' (1998) 17 *J L and Commerce* 219, available at www.cisg.law.pace.edu/cisg/biblio/garro2.html.

[185] *Canned Asparagus*, CIETAC Arbitration, 8 November 2002, available at www.cisg.law.pace.edu/cases/021108c1.html (invoice rejected by a bank under a letter of credit).

[186] See CIETAC Arbitration, 1 April 1997 (n 157).

[187] Supreme Court, 3 April 1996 (Germany) (n 124) (certificate of origin wrongly referring to the European Union as a place of origin (United Kingdom being required by the contract) whereas the goods originated from South Africa); *Isobutanol*, CIETAC Arbitration, 7 July 1997, available at http://cisgw3.law.pace.edu/cases/970707c1.html (Russia or Korea contractually required to be the place of origin while the certificate of origin was issued by an organisation in the United States).

[188] See, eg *Flexo Label Printing Machine*, CIETAC Arbitration, 24 July 2007, available at http://cisgw3.law.pace.edu/cases/070724c1.html.

[189] Federal Supreme Court, 3 April 1996 (Germany) (n 124) ('As far as the Certificates of Analysis to be presented by the [seller] are concerned, it has to be concluded that none of the four documents presented was in accordance with the contractual requirements').

bundle,[190] such as where different contract numbers appear on the bill of lading and on a commercial invoice.[191]

IV. QUALITY, QUANTITY, ORIGIN AND OTHER CERTIFICATES: CONFORMITY AND BEYOND

A. General

Considering that certificates are widely used in practice and that much of the CISG body of cases on documents concerns them, they warrant separate treatment. These certificates serve the important purpose of evidencing the results of an assessment of the goods' quantity, quality, description and origin, and as such inform the buyer about these matters.[192] This, in turn, either provides the buyer with a sense of security and facilitates a resale, particularly where the sub-sale is on the same terms as the original sale contract, or evidences a breach of contract by the seller. From whatever standpoint certificates are looked at—security or evidence of breach—it is helpful for the parties to be able to rely on them to finalise legal positions and prevent disputes. This is why contracts often provide that certificates of quality or quantity are 'conclusive' or 'final'. In some cases, finality clauses may be unnecessary where, for example, certificates are the only way of determining quality, quantity, origin and/or description. In one case[193] where the seller was to deliver organic barley, it was held that in the relevant wholesale business and under the EC Regulation to which the contract referred, organic origin could only be proved by 'certificates accompanying the goods, issued by companies admitted for certification'.

[190] See Art 14(d) UCP 600 (for a provision to this effect).

[191] See ICC Arbitration No 7645 (n 104); see also *Art Paper*, CIETAC Arbitration, 25 June 1997, available at http://cisgw3.law.pace.edu/cases/970625c1.html.

[192] See Appellate Court Madrid, Recurso No 683/2006, 20 February 2007 (Spain), available at www.cisg.law.pace.edu/cases/070220s4.html (SGS certificate proving the humidity level in olive stones exceeding that specified in the contract); CIETAC Arbitration, 28 September 1996 (n 148) ('the Inspection report sufficiently proves that the goods were wet before or during the loading process').

[193] Appellate Court Munich, 27 U 346/02, 13 November 2002 (Germany), available at http://cisgw3.law.pace.edu/cases/021113g1.html ('The fundamental principle is to ensure an inseparable and unique link between goods and documents that prove the organic origin … Organic barley cannot be distinguished from other barley, at least not by usual methods and with proportional expenditure'). A failure to deliver such certificates would constitute both a documentary breach (non-delivery of the contractually required document) and a breach in relation to the goods (failure to deliver organic goods). Similarly, see Foreign Trade Court of Arbitration, Serbian Chamber of Commerce, 23 January 2008, available at http://cisgw3.law.pace.edu/cases/080123sb.html (only EUR-1 certificate could prove origin of sugar); Commercial Court St Gallen, 14 June 2012 (n 92) (the goods had to be certified by Bio Suisse and the absence of the relevant certificates rendered the goods non-conforming). See also Supreme Court, 26 March 2013 (Switzerland) (n 91).

B. Conformity

The question of whether the seller has breached its obligation in relation to a certificate is to be answered by interpreting the contract.[194] Where a contract states that the seller must deliver a certificate evidencing the goods' compliance with the contract, an intention can be inferred that a certificate showing the goods not corresponding to the contract would be a non-conforming document. The situation is less clear where the contract does not specify the role of the certificate, but merely states that one must be delivered. If then a certificate states that the goods do not correspond to the contract, does it make a certificate defective? Has the seller, in addition to a physical breach committed a documentary breach? English law, for example, appears to give a negative answer because the certificate does what it is intended to do,[195] that is, it verifies accurately the goods' state, condition, quality, quantity or description.[196] This is to be contrasted with the position as regards transport documents, especially bills of lading, which, as explained, are normally expected to be clean. The reason for this difference in treatment can be that a 'negotiable' bill of lading is often used to resell the goods in transit, whereas certificates are generally not, to use the Convention's language, 'documents controlling the disposition of the goods'.[197] However, it seems that a situation where the particular trading context demonstrates that such certificates will affect resale (not just in evidencing non-conformity, but also leading to an unacceptable documentary tender) and cannot be transferred as part of a sub-sale cannot be ruled out.[198] If so, the surrounding environment may ultimately be decisive on the question of whether such certificates are conforming.[199]

Courts and arbitration tribunals should be able to rule on the status of a delivered certificate, its (non-)conformity, evidentiary value and its implications for the seller's documentary and physical duties. However, because the CISG does not specifically deal with these matters, and merely provides a framework for contract interpretation, it is difficult to state definitively how they should be dealt with. One situation is where it is proved that the certificate does not relate to contract goods. In such a case, it is clear that the certificate is flawed at its core, and some tribunals have correctly set it aside

[194] Arts 8 and 9 CISG.

[195] See *Tradax Int'l SA v Goldschmidt SA* [1977] 2 Lloyd's Rep 604, 612.

[196] This is by no means uncontroversial. For a different view in literature, see Debattista (n 9) 219 ('A "good" document is not one which simply does what it is intended to do, but one which also does it in the manner stipulated in the contract').

[197] Art 58; see also Maskow (n 90) 426–27 (referring to cases where certificates may meet the requirements of Art 58); Davies (n 44) 169 (agreeing with this proposition).

[198] *Tradax Int'l SA v Goldschmidt SA* (n 195) 612 ('[the certificate] is a valid document capable ... of being transferred as part of a subsequent sale').

[199] In which case, the view referred to in n 196 above is probably preferable.

and treated the seller as committing a documentary breach.[200] If the contract does not provide for the finality of the certificate, it may, in some cases, be right to regard the certificate as defective if it is proved to be incorrect simply because it does not state the truth.[201] However, it must be borne in mind that where the contract requires delivery of a certificate, particularly where it sets out the procedure for inspection and issuance of a certificate,[202] that can, in principle, evidence the parties' implicit intention to treat the certificate as conclusive. Even if not, contractual stipulations as to the certificate and related procedures should not be dismissed lightly: the very fact of their inclusion indicates that the parties intended to create a contractual mechanism for ascertaining conformity of the goods, and were serious about the ability of the certificate to verify conformity (or lack of it). Only strong evidence unequivocally showing that the certificate was incorrect should lead to a finding that the certificate is defective.[203] Courts and tribunals should be particularly careful about making such findings where the procedure for inspection and issuance of the certificate has been complied with, since the procedure is there precisely to ensure the accuracy, rigour and quality of the inspection. As to cases where a certificate was procured by fraud, it may be that, as argued above, a requirement can be inferred from the contract that documents procured by fraud are to be viewed as non-conforming.[204] In any event, the applicable law on fraud is likely to afford legal protection.

[200] See *Steel Cylinders*, CIETAC Arbitration, 19 January 2000, available at http://cisgw3.law.pace.edu/cases/000119c1.html.

[201] See Federal Supreme Court, 3 April 1996 (Germany) (n 124) (although the seller was not expressly stated to have committed a documentary breach, the decision implies that the certificate was not a good certificate).

[202] Such as the appointment of an inspector, methods of and time-frames for the inspection. See also *Old Boxboard Corrugated Cartons*, CIETAC Arbitration, 8 March 1996, available at http://cisgw3.law.pace.edu/cases/960308c1.html ('The Arbitration Tribunal concludes that China Anhui Import and Export Commodity Inspection Bureau inspected the goods in accordance with the requirements of the Contract, and the inspection results demonstrates that the content level of OCC in the goods is not in conformity with the specifications of the Contract, so the Buyer can use this Inspection Certificate issued by China Anhui Import and Export Commodity Inspection Bureau as proof for the quality of goods').

[203] See CIETAC Arbitration, 24 July 2007 (n 188), which did not involve the issue of conformity of a certificate presented by the *seller*, but is nevertheless reflective of the approach advocated here in respect of conformity of certificates to be delivered by the seller. In this case, a contract required the buyer to present a certificate to raise quality claims and referred to the previously used, rather than the current, title of an inspection body. The buyer presented a certificate issued by a specialised organisation which was 'vertically administered' by the inspection body incorrectly stated in the contract. The tribunal stated that '[t]he parties in an international trade are not always sure about the changes of the titles of the Chinese state organs' and held that the incorrect formulation did not affect either the clause itself or the buyer's ability to present a certificate under that clause. The decision seems correct since there was little uncertainty about the parties' true intentions.

[204] See Dalian Maritime Court, 29 June 2005 (n 140), where the court appears to have accepted that the inspection results were subject to the fraud exception. Unfortunately, the basis for introducing this exception was not made clear.

In one case,[205] the contract required a pre-shipment certificate by a neutral body confirming the goods' readiness for shipment and it was proved that all that the certificate did was to restate the conformity of other documentation with the contractual safety and sanitary standards. The seller was held to have committed a documentary breach. The certificate was rightly not regarded as evidence of the readiness for shipment because the certificate did not even attempt to fulfil its objective. Another CISG case,[206] although being silent on whether there was a documentary breach, is an illustration of where even greater reliance was placed on the circumstances surrounding the issuance of the certificate. In this case, a CIF contract required the seller to deliver a quality and weight certificate. Although the certificate verified the goods' compliance with the contract, upon arrival they were found to be non-conforming. The court could not definitively determine their condition on loading, but held that it was highly likely that the non-conformity had been caused by circumstances prior to loading, and that the certificate issued 'more than twenty days before loading [was] certainly not sufficient to challenge such likelihood'.[207]

Courts are in a difficult position in this type of case. On the one hand, there is a contractually agreed mechanism for determining quality and weight. On the other hand, the circumstances (in this case, a substantial time gap between inspection and loading) indicate a high likelihood that the certificate may be incorrect. There was no allegation that the contract procedure relating to inspection, including the time for inspection, was not followed. If it *was* followed, was it imperfect pursuit of truth, on the one hand, or certainty and respect for party autonomy, on the other, that should have prevailed? While it is not an easy choice to make, on balance, the buyer should probably have borne the risk on the basis of its failure to restrict the conditions under which the certificate was to be issued. The buyer agreed to the use of a certificate as the method of determining quality and weight. Decisions such as this also arguably encourage a degree of irresponsibility in buyers, since they will be more relaxed about inserting safeguards into the contract.

The date of issuance of the inspection certificate was also an issue in another case[208] where there was a contractual provision regarding, this time, the buyer's duty to present a certificate to bring a quality claim. The seller argued that because the contract provided that the goods were to be inspected at their destination (Shanghai), a certificate issued two weeks

[205] See ICAC 226/1999, 11 February 2000, available at http://cisgw3.law.pace.edu/cases/000211r1.html.

[206] Appellate Court Lugano, 12.97.00193, 15 January 1998 (Switzerland), available at www.cisg.law.pace.edu/cases/980115s1.html.

[207] Ibid.

[208] *Beech Log*, CIETAC Arbitration, 4 November 2002, available at www.cisg.law.pace.edu/cases/021104c1.html.

after they had been unloaded in Shanghai could not be used as evidence. The goods were in fact inspected at the place where the sub-buyer was based (Huzhou). The tribunal stated that the inspection was within the contractual period allowed for examination. The tribunal also noted that it was right to inspect the goods in Huzhou because, in order to be examined in Shanghai, the goods would have had to be removed from the containers, inspected, then repacked into containers and transported to Huzhou. 'This would have wasted time and money, and was impracticable.'[209] While the decision is open to criticism,[210] it shows the potential relevance of Article 38 CISG, which provides for the buyer's duty to examine the goods,[211] to the question of what requirements the certificate has to meet. If all that the contract requires is that the buyer must provide an inspection certificate, the CISG should be used to fill the gap by helping to determine the time and place[212] for the inspection,[213] thereby generating additional requirements which the inspection certificate will have to meet.[214]

It has been suggested that the buyer should not bear the consequences of an incorrect inspection[215] 'if parties agreed upon a neutral third party, or if the seller himself insisted upon examination by a particular third party'.[216] It follows from this proposition that the evidentiary value of certificates issued by such third parties is diminished. But the statement was surely not intended to apply to cases where the contract itself provides for

[209] Ibid. In this case, the seller also challenged the certificate on the ground that it did not refer to contract goods. The tribunal dismissed this challenge, having taken into consideration some other evidence presented by the buyer, including a letter and inspection record from inspectors, as well as photos attached to the certificate.

[210] Why did the tribunal disregard the contractual provision requiring the buyer to inspect the goods at destination, which appears to have been clearly specified as Shanghai?

[211] Art 38: '(1) The buyer must examine the goods, or cause them to be examined, within as short a period as is practicable in the circumstances. (2) If the contract involves carriage of the goods, examination may be deferred until after the goods have arrived at their destination. (3) If the goods are redirected in transit or redispatched by the buyer without a reasonable opportunity for examination by him and at the time of the conclusion of the contract the seller knew or ought to have known of the possibility of such redirection or redispatch, examination may be deferred until after the goods have arrived at the new destination'.

[212] See *Polypropylene*, CIETAC Arbitration, 23 July 1997, available at http://cisgw3.law.pace.edu/cases/970723c1.html, where on the basis of Art 38(3) CISG the tribunal held that the goods could be examined at their final destination. This probably meant that the certificate, which was required by the contract to be the basis for the buyer's claim of a lack of conformity and was issued at destination, complied with the contract and was able to prove a lack of conformity.

[213] The question may arise as to whether such a provision should be construed as derogation from Art 38. However, in the absence of any evidence to the contrary, such a provision is unlikely to evidence an intention to derogate since the certificate does what Art 38 itself provides for—the buyer's examination of the goods, even if done by a third party.

[214] See CIETAC Arbitration, 28 September 1996 (n 148), where the tribunal ruled on the certificate's ability to prove a lack of conformity in the goods depending on whether the examination was within the period prescribed in Art 38 CISG.

[215] Which, presumably, shows (incorrectly) that the goods are conforming.

[216] See I Schwenzer in Schwenzer (n 115) Art 38, para 10.

an inspection by a neutral third party or for a third party to be selected by the seller. It is understandable that, particularly in the latter situation, there is room for abuse, but if that is the procedure to which the buyer agreed, it becomes part of the parties' bargain and party autonomy must be respected.[217] Cases of fraud, as noted, should be taken care of by the applicable domestic law and/or by inferring, where possible, a requirement against fraud from the contract.

C. Finality Clause

Where the contract treats the certificate as final, the above argument in defence of party autonomy and certainty applies with a greater force. The parties unequivocally express their intention to be bound by the results in a certificate to avoid disputes and to bring finality.[218] To be able to advance these objectives, certificates must not be questioned unless in exceptional circumstances. Fraud or a certificate not referring to contract goods are sometimes regarded as such.[219] The Convention's role of providing rules of contract interpretation is important because it is these rules that will usually decide the standing and function of a finality clause. Therefore, the question as to whether the application of these rules leads to satisfactory results should be examined.

In a case where a certificate inaccurately stated the quality of the goods, the buyer was held not to be bound by its results because the certificate was based on the inspection by a third party who was mutually agreed by the parties, as was required by the contract, and not by a third party suggested by the buyer alone.[220] This decision was based on the above-mentioned

[217] See Huber and Mullis (n 89) 150 (providing a similar view).

[218] See, eg *Cedar Petrochemicals, Inc v Dongbu Hannong Chemical Co Ltd*, F Supp 2d, 2011 WL 4494602, where the contract required phenol to be inspected '[b]y a mutually acceptable independent surveyor whose finding as to quantity/quality as per shoretank figures at load port are final and binding on both parties'. See also Appellate Court Linz, 1 R 206/11m, 8 February 2012 (Austria), available at http://cisgw3.law.pace.edu/cases/120208a3.html, where the certificate appears to have been treated as final by virtue of a practice between the parties. The buyer's argument that the goods were non-conforming because they did not comply with the applicable safety regulations was precluded by the certificate showing that the goods complied with the regulations.

[219] See *Benjamin's Sale of Goods* (n 23) para 19-165; see, eg *Bominflot Bunkergesellschaft fur Mineralole mbH & Co v Petroplus Marketing AG* [2012] EWHC 3009 (Comm) 1145 (where, according to the contract, the certificate was to be conclusive in the absence of fraud or manifest error).

[220] See ICC Award No 9187, June 1999, available at www.unilex.info/case.cfm?pid=1&do=case&id=466&step=FullText ('The Contract is silent to the applicability of its Art 9 in case of incorrect certification through the appointed inspection body and, as a consequence it has to be referred to the CISG in order to answer this question. In principle, the buyer has to bear the consequences of an incorrect examination in the sense of Art 38 CISG performed by third parties; it is bound by the examination and has approved the (non-contractual) delivery ... However,

view[221] that a buyer is not bound by inspection results agreed by both parties. With respect, this decision is untenable. Apart from the questionable rationale on which the tribunal relied, the tribunal ignored the parties' intention as to finality of the certificate and effectively rewrote the contract. Unfortunately, there are other cases where tribunals refused to give full recognition to finality clauses. One decision did not treat the finality clause as having 'the legal effect of the exclusion of the proof to the contrary by the buyer' but only as shifting the burden of proving the incorrectness of the certificate to the buyer.[222] It must be stressed that there is nothing in the Convention that leads to such results. Although the CISG requires all relevant circumstances to be taken into account,[223] the goal of contract interpretation is, after all, to determine the parties' true intentions, as far as reasonably possible. Where the contractual risk allocation is such that the buyer is prepared to accept the risk of the results in a certificate as final and conclusive, there are no grounds, as far as the CISG is concerned, not to respect this bargain in the absence of strong evidence outside the written contract showing that the parties' intention as regards the role of a certificate was different from that formulated in the contract.[224] There is hardly a stronger and clearer way of expressing an intention to be bound by a certificate than saying that a certificate is to be final and binding. If the approach taken in these cases is followed, it will become virtually impossible for parties to ensure that their agreement on the finality of certificates will be upheld. This would mark a bold invasion into freedom of contract and party autonomy and would erode certainty.

Another decision,[225] although less objectionable than the ones just discussed, also shows that some tribunals have no qualms in depriving finality clauses of their intended effect. In that case, the contract appears to have been interpreted as treating a certificate by the China Entry-Exit Inspection and Quarantine Bureau (CIQ) to be issued on loading as final. After the seller had disputed the results in the certificate and referred instead to the results of its own examination, the buyer said that it would inspect the

this finding does not apply if the parties have jointly appointed the neutral inspection body or if the seller alone has insisted on the third party; the quality determination, if wrong, renders it non-binding to the parties ... Because the inspection of the coke through a third party was mutually agreed by the parties in Art 9 of the Contract, and not suggested by Claimant alone ... Claimant is not bound by [A]'s quality determination') (citations omitted).

221 See nn 215 and 216 above and the accompanying main text.

222 See Vienna Agricultural Exchange Arbitration Tribunal, 10 December 1997, available at www.cisg.law.pace.edu/cisg/wais/db/cases2/971210a3.html.

223 Arts 8(3) and 9 CISG.

224 See *MCC-Marble Ceramic Center v Ceramica Nuova D'Agostino*,144 F 3d 1384 (11th Cir 1998), where evidence regarding intentions overrode the express terms of the contract; see also Federal Supreme Court, 4C.296/2000/rnd, 22 December 2000 (Switzerland), available at http://cisgw3.law.pace.edu/cases/001222s1.html, discussed in Chapter 2.

225 CIETAC Arbitration, February 2006 (n 140).

goods upon discharge and that the inspection would be done by SGS.[226] There was no objection by the seller, which led the tribunal to conclude that the parties changed the contract by introducing the SGS certificate on discharge and treating it as final. Should the tribunal have reached this conclusion with such ease, particularly considering that the buyer had said that the results in the SGS certificate would 'be an additional basis for discussion'[227] about the quality of the goods?[228] The answer should be 'no', for much stronger and less equivocal evidence ought to be expected in order to infer an intention to depart from an express contractual term.

The situation is different where the contractual preconditions for the issuance of a certificate, which is to be final, are not met. In this case, it seems correct not to regard such a certificate as final.[229] It does not mean, however, that its evidentiary value is altogether lost, since although having lost its status as a contractual mechanism, it may still be used as evidence (outside the contract) relevant to proving the issues at hand.

D. Certificate as Extra-contractual Documentary Evidence

Even where the contract does not contain a 'certificate' clause, certificates are often relied upon as documentary evidence of the goods' quality, quantity, weight, description, including origin and other matters.[230] The issues of both the admissibility of certificates as evidence and their validity is governed by the applicable law and therefore some certificates may be held inadmissible or invalid due to their non-compliance with the relevant rules

[226] See Société Generale de Surveillance, www.sgs.com.

[227] CIETAC Arbitration, February 2006 (n 140).

[228] If further attention is paid to the way the tribunal interpreted the contract, its reasoning becomes even more questionable. Apart from the certificate clause, the contract provided that any quality/quantity objections could be raised by the buyer within 15 days after the goods' arrival at destination. In the light of the parties' conduct, the tribunal stated that this latter clause ought to be interpreted as meaning the following: 'the buyer shall raise objections to quality or quantity problems based on the inspection result within 15 days since the date of goods arriving at the destination port, and the inspection institution shall be SGS'. The tribunal added that even 'if the two parties used to determine the quality of goods by CIQ Quality Certification, the potency of their written contract provision is stronger'. The tribunal converted a provision designed to deal with the procedure for raising claims into a provision on the finality of an SGS certificate. That, together with a reference to the 'potency of a written agreement' which the tribunal itself created made an original provision on CIQ certificates meaningless.

[229] See CIETAC, 10 August 1999 (n 97) (the buyer used a certifier different from that specified in the finality clause and the tribunal held that a certificate issued by that certifier could not be conclusive).

[230] See *Shirt*, CIETAC Arbitration, 15 December 1998, available at http://cisgw3.law.pace.edu/cases/981215c1.html ('The contract does not stipulate the quality of the goods ... However, one of the necessary documents stipulated in the L/C is the copy of the inspection certificate ... Thus, the Arbitration Tribunal holds that the inspection certificate shall be important evidence of the quality of the goods').

of domestic law.[231] However, even outside the scope of the admissibility or validity rules, parties often seek to undermine the evidentiary value of a certificate. Thus, sellers have successfully argued that certificates were incapable of proving a lack of conformity because their content was in need of verification and they did not cover the entire goods[232] or because they referred to parties who were neither the seller nor the buyer, and indicated the quantity which did not correspond to the contract quantity.[233] In contrast, in another case,[234] the tribunal dismissed the seller's challenge to the evidentiary value of an inspection certificate based on the certificate's alleged incapability of proving that the inspected goods were in fact the contract goods because the certificate had 'no shipping marks, contract numbers, container numbers, or indications of the quantity of the goods inspected'. The tribunal reasoned that the certificate still referred to several relevant item numbers corresponding to the packaging of the goods and that it had taken the seller more than a year to raise an objection that the certificate did not relate to contract goods. This latter reason shows that the circumstances external to a certificate, such as the parties' conduct, may be relevant to assessing its evidentiary value.

Where both parties present certificates to prove their arguments, the tribunals may have to resolve a 'battle of certificates' by taking into account any relevant factors affecting the strength of the evidence. In one case,[235] the seller presented a quality certificate issued by the manufacturer, while the buyer presented two certificates issued by different inspection organisations. Not accepting one of the buyer's certificates due to doubts about whether it truly related to contract goods,[236] the tribunal had to decide on the quality of the goods by choosing between the two remaining and

[231] '[T]he inspection memorandum was not issued according to the Import and Export Commodity Inspection Law of the People's Republic of China; therefore, it has no legal effect' (see *Engines*, CIETAC Arbitration, 6 September 1996, available at http://cisgw3.law.pace.edu/cases/960906c1.html). See also *Hydraulic Pressure Geologic Equipment*, CIETAC Arbitration, 12 September 2005, available at http://cisgw3.law.pace.edu/cases/050912c1.html, where the tribunal dismissed the seller's argument that the certificate was 'ineffective'. The legal basis for the tribunal's reasoning is, however, unclear.

[232] See ibid.

[233] See CIETAC Arbitration, 9 January 1993 (n 104).

[234] *Cotton Bath Towel*, CIETAC Arbitration, 26 October 1996, available at http://cisgw3.law.pace.edu/cases/961026c1.html.

[235] *Cysteine*, CIETAC Arbitration, 7 January 2000, available at http://cisgw3.law.pace.edu/cases/000107c1.html.

[236] Ibid ('The trademark had a substantial discrepancy with that of the goods involved in the present case. Although the possibility that the specimens were taken from the goods involved in the present case still existed, the Tribunal cannot be convinced that the specimens were taken from the goods involved in the present case based on the aforesaid evidence. Therefore, the Tribunal holds that the inspection report of the F & M Lab does not have the effect to prove the quality of the goods').

conflicting certificates. The tribunal accepted the buyer's (SGS) certificate, stating that although it would normally not have a higher probative value than a certificate issued by another organisation, the tribunal chose to rely on it because of a potential 'self-serving interest on the part of the manufacturer of the goods'.[237] The parties' conduct in relation to a certificate can also influence the decision as to which of the certificates should be taken as the proof of quality. Thus, the evidence that the seller did not object to the inspection report presented by the buyer when quality complaints had been raised may be decisive in the tribunal relying on that report.[238]

V. EMERGING THEMES

A. Is the CISG a Construction Site for Documentary Duties?

Several broad but interrelated themes emerge from this analysis and it is suggested that they not only describe the Convention's experience in documentary matters to date, but should also be used as signposts with reference to which legal issues relating to documentary performance need to be dealt with in the future. The CISG is still a 'construction site'.[239] But how far should we exercise our creativity in producing thicker layers of flesh of detailed rules to address various legal and practical questions that demand resolution? Nowhere is this question more topical than in discussing the seller's documentary obligations. Although the Convention was intended to defer to contract in documentary matters, it has been shown that difficult questions regarding the seller's documentary obligations will still arise, because contracts are neither complete nor perfect. How and with reference to what legal source(s) are these questions to be answered? As

[237] Ibid.

[238] *Heliotropin*, CIETAC Arbitration, 10 July 1993, available at http://cisgw3.law.pace.edu/cases/930710c1.html ('because [the buyer] sent the inspection report to [the seller], and [the seller] did not make any objection within a reasonable time, [the seller] accepted and admitted [the buyer]'s inspection report'). That was not the only reason why the tribunal chose to rely on the buyer's report. The tribunal also examined the seller's certificate and concluded that it did not fully reflect all quality characteristics such as colour and flavour. See also *PTA Powder*, CIETAC Arbitration, 18 April 2008, available at http://cisgw3.law.pace.edu/cases/080418c1.html, where both the buyer and the seller appear to have provided quality certificates, with the seller's certificate showing the goods being 'on-specification'. The decision simply held that the goods were non-conforming without any explanation as to why the content of the seller's certificate was ignored. Nor does the decision explain whether the certificate was required to be provided by the contract or whether the certificates were presented by the parties as part of their extra-contractual evidence in support of their respective claims.

[239] P Schlechtriem, 'Interpretation, Gap-Filling and Further Development of the UN Sales Convention' (2004) 16 *Pace Int'l L Rev* 279, 306.

demonstrated, in the case of transport documents such as a bill of lading, there may be some room for developing the rules of conformity within the CISG. However, it is argued that the questions are potentially too numerous, detailed and multifaceted to be left to the Convention, which was probably never designed to be a source from which the rules of conformity of documents could be developed. That should not mean that domestic legal systems, generally, have a role to play here, because the CISG treats the issue of what documents are to be delivered and of conformity of documents as falling within the ambit of contract. There is a need therefore to be creative in interpreting the contract, and the Convention's primary role is to provide rules of contract interpretation. Its role, however, does not end there because, as demonstrated, a number of its provisions can help a reasonable person to develop an understanding of the seller's documentary duties. Under this approach, the Convention, albeit falling short of providing the relevant implied term, provides a framework from which a reasonable person can draw inferences in those rare cases where neither the contract itself nor the surrounding circumstances shed light on documentary duties. In any case, one point is hardly debatable: to avoid disputes and uncertainty relating to the legal treatment of documentary duties, parties will be well advised to set out the seller's documentary obligations in their contract.

B. Assessing Conformity: Face of Documents versus Extrinsic Factual Inquiry

Is conformity to be assessed purely on the face of the documents or should a tribunal have regard to external circumstances surrounding a document? While the former promotes certainty, even legal systems committed to legal certainty have some regard for external circumstances in deciding whether the seller has provided a conforming document.[240] How this question is to be answered in a case governed by the CISG will largely depend on the contract and/or whether other instruments, such as INCOTERMS and UCP, are applicable. In an extreme case of contractual silence, it is preferable to judge the conformity of transport documents on their face except for fraud and where the requirement of a document being 'genuine' (if such a requirement is adopted) is at issue, which involves a factual inquiry. This should be so because a major transport document, a 'negotiable' bill of lading, is

[240] For example, the requirements that a bill of lading must be genuine or not procured by fraud, adhered to in English law, necessitate an inquiry into extrinsic circumstances (see cases in n 165 above).

used for on-sale purposes, which seem to require that the bill of lading not only be clean, but also that the buyer be able to rely on statements in the bill, such as those relating to the shipment date.[241]

C. Attack on Party Autonomy and Legal Certainty

This approach advocating certainty is particularly important in cases governed by the Convention because, as cases involving certificates demonstrate, courts and tribunals not only tend to look at circumstances surrounding the issuance of a certificate, but also give little or no effect to the express terms of the contract, thereby rewriting and reallocating the risks inherent in the bargain struck by the parties. This is disturbing because doing so violates party autonomy and undermines certainty. There is also a danger that trust in the Convention's ability to uphold the parties' bargain and to be a credible and a reliable sales law regime may be undermined. The truth is that the problem is not with the Convention, but with how the tribunals chose to interpret the contract. While the CISG allows all relevant circumstances to be taken into account in contractual interpretation, the goal of interpretation is to determine (and not to override) the parties' true intentions where reasonably possible. In the decisions in question, tribunals neither referred to the Convention's rules, nor did anything to show why and how its rules led to a failure to give full effect to the parties' intention.

D. Documentary Performance and the Future of the CISG

The Convention's experience in documentary matters is in need of improvement. On the one hand, this cannot come as a surprise because the CISG shifts the responsibility for defining the seller's documentary duties to the parties. On the other hand, considering that delivery of documents constitutes a separate set of the seller's obligations, and given the practical significance of documents, it is reasonable to expect courts and tribunals to be more rigorous in analysing the issue of the content and conformity of documents in the light of the Convention's rules of contract interpretation. Ideally, the hope is to see a body of cases where the rules of contract interpretation result in factual scenarios being subjected to a clear and rigorous analysis and consistent legal treatment. When it comes

[241] See nn 23, 139 and 177 above.

to details, the law of international sales often ends up being one of construction of contracts.[242] There also appears to be a degree of reluctance amongst some courts and tribunals to afford separate treatment to the seller's documentary duties,[243] and to raise (and answer) the question of whether there was a documentary breach. Instead, their focus tends to be on a breach in relation to the goods. If this is correct, such a state of affairs only weakens the position of those who advocate the Convention's suitability to govern documentary and commodities trade. As time marches on, cases decided under the CISG will be increasingly perceived as reflecting its identity.

[242] See, eg Bridge (n 102) 40.

[243] See, eg Appellate Court Lugano, 15 January 1998 (n 206), where a certificate which the seller was required to deliver, was suspected of incorrectly stating the quality and weight of the goods; this only led to the certificate being rejected as evidence of the conformity of the goods, with the question of whether the seller thereby committed a documentary breach not even having been raised; also Supreme Court, 26 March 2013 (Switzerland) (n 91).

Index

References such as '178–9' indicate (not necessarily continuous) discussion of a topic across a range of pages. Wherever possible in the case of topics with many references, these have either been divided into sub-topics or only the most significant discussions of the topic are listed.

acceptance 5, 30–1, 84, 104, 132, 134, 160
actual knowledge 75, 93, 173–4, 176, 219, 225
actual reliance 96
actual state 3, 39, 62, 118, 170, 259
adequate manner 164–8
admissibility of evidence 24, 146, 169, 270–1
  fitness for a particular purpose 105–9
admixtures 46, 52, 176
advertisements 35–7, 75, 100, 122
after-acquired knowledge 58, 141, 172
agreement 3, 31, 71, 148, 161, 171, 181–3
  express 148, 223
  implicit 42, 148, 203
  licence 226–7
air waybills 242, 252, 256, 260
allocation
  of burden of proof, *see* burden of proof
  of responsibilities 144, 166
  of risks 29, 37, 39, 55, 58, 128, 131
animals 44, 74, 78, 80, 124, 128
apparent condition 244, 256, 259
appearance 49, 111, 131–4
applicability 3, 27, 156, 159, 170–1, 180, 184
applicable domestic law 23–5, 27, 183, 200, 205, 259, 268
applicable standards 52, 86, 139
application, uniformity of 4, 17–18, 21–2, 103–4, 107, 182–3, 210–11
arbitration tribunals 7, 18, 84, 113, 184, 264–5, 270
arbitrators 4, 18, 21, 46, 167
Argentina 63, 106–8, 127, 250
assembly diagrams 98, 129
assumption of risk 71, 75, 91–3, 95, 219, 235
asymmetry, information 83, 134–9, 171–2
Australia 82, 86, 100
Austria 81, 84, 92, 94, 134–6, 151–2, 249
autonomy, party 2, 4, 9, 29, 266, 268–9, 274
average quality tests 113–14, 116, 118
awareness 18, 72, 170, 222–3, 225–7

bad faith 33, 220, 228
banks 37, 190, 203, 237–8, 247, 258–60, 262
basic expectations 187, 209, 216
Belgium 11, 79, 131, 140, 145, 154, 220
bills of lading 65, 146, 190–1, 239–45, 250–4, 256–64, 273–4
  clean 169, 256, 260
  date 257–8
  dated 258–9
  negotiable 248–9, 253
  unclean 260–1
boundaries of Convention 22–8
burden of proof 61, 78
  allocation 23, 102–3, 195, 231–2
  fitness for a particular purpose 102–3
  intellectual property 231–2
buyers 56–68, 78–106, 121–32, 144–55, 157–207, 223–37, 239–63
  claims 154, 159, 167, 169–70, 180, 262, 267
  consent 173, 202–4
  expertise 40, 129, 175
  knowledge 38–41, 170–5, 178, 216, 225–8
  reliance 37, 39, 70–1, 76, 86, 92, 101
  remedies 14–16, 185, 235, 237
  responsibilities 54, 196
  specifications 29, 70, 93–4, 98, 101, 105, 228–32

carriage 6, 161–2, 196, 239, 241, 256, 260–1
  contracts 60, 239, 241–3, 245, 256, 261
carriers 59, 189–91, 196–7, 238–45, 250–3, 256, 260–1
cash against documents clauses 246, 252
catalogues 37, 94, 133–4
caveat emptor 10–11, 13, 69
caveat venditor 10, 69, 84, 118, 132, 134, 175
certainty, legal 13, 19, 103, 135, 142, 153, 273–4

certificate clauses 45, 270
certificates 48, 62–3, 85, 156, 246–7, 262–72, 274–5
  conformity 264–8
  as extra-contractual documentary evidence 270–2
  finality 247, 268–70
  of origin 41, 245, 250, 262
  quality 62–3, 146, 246, 254, 263, 271–2
  weight 65, 266
C&F contracts 63, 127, 201
CFR contracts 62–3, 127, 242, 246, 248–50, 256, 261
characteristics
  advertised 36
  contractual 60, 64
  essential 43–5
CIF 61, 240–1, 248–50, 256
  contracts 240, 242, 246, 250–1, 254, 256, 260
  sellers 190, 246, 248, 256, 258, 262
circumstances, special 83–4, 135–9, 164
claims
  buyers 154, 159, 167, 169–70, 180, 262, 267
  frivolous 140, 194, 215–17, 226
  unfounded 194–5
clean bills of lading 169, 256, 260
climatic conditions 76, 81, 89, 97, 99, 165
codes of conduct 86–7
collateral contracts 12, 32
colour 38, 46, 50, 62, 79, 154, 178
commercial invoices 245, 249–51, 254, 262–3
commercial risks 13, 252
common intention 56, 137
communication, implicit 71, 75, 93, 153
competition, unfair 210–11
complexity 8, 45, 84, 103, 108, 195, 231
compliance 48, 63, 73–5, 81–2, 85–7, 138, 156
  documentary 256–8
  obligation 149–50
  presumption 63
  sellers 98, 228, 232, 246
composition 43, 46, 50, 52, 54, 164
conditions
  apparent 244, 256, 259
  climatic 76, 81, 89, 97, 99, 165
conduct 2–3, 30–1, 41, 86–7, 176, 179, 270–2
  codes of 86–7
  sellers 55, 105, 179, 191, 207
  subsequent 3, 166, 255
conforming goods 9, 14, 16, 29–30, 45, 202
conformity 42–6, 56–66, 68–71, 140–3, 184–5, 234–6, 262–7
  assessment 273–4
  certificates 264–8
  documents 237–75
    documentary and 'physical' obligations 247–8
    documents to be delivered by seller 248–55
    face of documents v extrinsic factual inquiry 273–4
    quality, quantity, origin and other certificates 263–72
    transport documents 255–62
    typical documents 238–47
  goods 11, 13–14, 17–20, 22, 29–67, 69, 81
  guarantee and durability 59–64
  implied terms 184–5
  lack of 11, 15, 81, 180, 184, 234
  legislative changes and/or knowledge acquired subsequent to contract 57–9
  obligations 10, 13, 30–1, 39, 50, 58, 88
    sellers 12, 42, 87, 142, 156, 186
  quantity and packaging 64–7
  rules 10–14
  with sample or model 147–60
    how far is sample or model allowed to 'speak' 153–5
    proof 159–60
    public law regulations 158–9
    relationship with contractual provisions and other terms implied under CISG 155–8
  standards 46, 58, 257
  tests 90–1
consent 71, 203–4
  buyers 173, 202–4
  implicit 43, 219
  implied 72
consignees 240–3, 247, 251
  named 241, 243, 261
consignment 6, 238
  notes 243, 252–3
consignors 242–3, 252
consistency 17–18, 35, 50, 87, 220
construction 53, 55, 84, 155–6, 255, 275
consumption 120–1
  direct 121–2
  human 54–5
containers 60, 120, 163, 168, 260, 267
contamination 129, 140–1, 145
contract goods 43, 59, 90, 92, 264, 267–8, 271
contract interpretation 29–30, 56, 170–1, 251–2, 254, 268–9, 273–4
contract law 8, 12, 26, 29, 37, 84, 93
contract prices 16, 65, 113, 117, 123, 132–3, 162
contract quantity 260, 271
contracts 1–7, 21–34, 36–74, 88–99, 146–53, 170–85, 245–70

C&F 63, 127, 201
CFR 62–3, 127, 242, 246, 248–50, 256, 261
CIF 240, 242, 246, 250–1, 254, 256, 260
collateral 12, 32
DDP 58
FOB 62–3, 198, 248, 250, 254
licence 226–7
sales 1–2, 11–13, 239, 241, 245–6, 250–1, 255–7
shipment 61, 63–4, 240, 246, 251, 260
contractual description 43, 79, 117
contractual expectations 69–70
contractual provisions 47–8, 53, 68, 74, 152, 155–6, 266–7
contractual silence 66, 95, 252, 273
transport documents 257–62
contractual term 32, 34, 37, 57, 72, 74, 139
control 23, 60, 172, 181–2, 189, 191, 252–3
quality 11, 95, 119
cost, insurance and freight, *see* CIF
costs 1, 11, 30, 61–2, 188, 194–5, 229
transaction 1, 11, 69, 83
country of destination 85, 136, 138
creativity 233, 272
legal 20, 232–3
credit 253–5, 257
letters of 37, 42, 245–6, 248, 250, 253–5, 257
customers 38, 43, 79, 95–6, 114, 121, 130

damaged goods 169
damaged packaging 167
damages 5, 7, 16, 28, 104, 165, 258–9
provisions 71, 259
dangerous goods 128, 141
date of shipment 239, 257–8, 260, 274
dated bills of lading 258–9
DDP contracts 58
defective packaging 162
with goods otherwise conforming 167–8
defects 53, 121, 123–5, 133, 145–6, 173–4, 177
hidden 60, 114, 158
latent 101, 158
minor 111, 119, 131–3
delivered descriptions 48
delivered goods 30, 37, 46, 57, 118, 140, 161
delivery 6–7, 59, 64–5, 196–8, 218–19, 238–47, 250; *see also* non-delivery
orders 243–4, 251–3
substitute goods 15, 124, 234
symbolic 250
time 59, 196–7, 204, 218–19
delivery of substitute goods 15, 124, 234
description 42–50, 79, 125–6, 150–2, 155–6, 245–6, 263–4
contractual 43, 79, 117
delivered 48
detailed 115, 130
and fitness for ordinary use 125–6
designs 29, 48, 98, 133–4, 211, 213, 228–9
faulty 133
destination 58, 60–2, 83–4, 136–8, 164–6, 246–7, 266–7
country of 85, 136, 138
destination port 165, 270
detailed description 115, 130
detention 199–200
deterioration 66, 92, 127, 167
dioxin 124–5, 128–9, 140
direct communications between parties 37–8
direct consumption 121–2
disclaimers 181–5
discretion 78, 229
disputes 65, 77, 126, 130, 178, 180, 226
documentary compliance 256–8
documentary duties/obligations 238, 248, 257–9, 261, 273
CISG as construction site for 272–3
sellers 10, 63, 238, 248, 251, 253–5, 272–5
documentary performance 21–2, 238, 247, 272
and future of CISG 274–5
documents 5–6, 8–10, 14–15, 19–23, 190–1, 237–66, 272–4
to be delivered by seller 248–55
cash against documents clauses 246, 252
conformity, *see* conformity, documents
insurance 246, 250, 262
non-conforming 237, 264
shipping 190, 245
of title 239, 242–4, 260
transport 238–44, 248, 250, 255–8, 261, 264, 273
domestic law 24–8, 32, 103–4, 108, 181–3, 205–7, 254
remedies 25–8
domestic legal systems 4, 17, 45, 104, 110–11, 116, 187
domestic rules 23–5, 28–9, 107–8, 146, 182, 200
on validity of third party rights/claims 206–7
durability 49, 59–62, 64, 75, 111, 130
and fitness for a particular purpose 90–2
and fitness for ordinary use 126–7

economic considerations 36, 115, 171
Ecuador 89–90, 249
English law 11–12, 26–7, 44–5, 239–41, 243–4, 246, 258

equality 1–2, 11, 55, 69, 132, 230–1
equilibrium 202–3
equity 103, 231–2
essential characteristics 43–5
evaluation 96–7, 105, 132, 139, 141, 169, 176
evidence 41–3, 102–9, 169–70, 241–3, 255–63, 265–7, 269–72
  admissibility, *see* admissibility of evidence
  expert 66, 160
  relevant 102, 107, 180, 231, 251
  strong 64, 131, 143, 265, 269
evidentiary value 260, 264, 267, 270–1
examination 65, 100, 166, 175–8, 246–7, 261, 267–9
  normal 155, 176
  pre-contractual 39, 176
  reasonable 154–5, 158
exclusion 2, 71, 158, 174, 181–3, 185, 223
  clauses 181, 205–6
exemptions from liability 170–85
  intellectual property 225–31
  third party rights/claims 202–6, 225–31
expectations 34, 36, 64–6, 115, 117–19, 122–3, 132
  basic 187, 209, 216
  legitimate 163, 214
  normal 121, 246, 251
  reasonable 26, 29, 39, 143, 150, 173–4, 177
expert arbitration 106
expert evidence 66, 160
expertise 21, 33–4, 95–100, 108, 130–1, 217, 221
  buyers 40, 129, 175
  relevant 95, 97–8, 232
  sellers 101
experts 54, 56, 94, 97, 167, 169–70, 187
export 58, 73, 81, 138, 163, 170, 192
express agreement 148, 223
express terms 269, 274

fault 28, 49, 133–4, 188, 209, 228
  minor 133
finality 45, 166, 180, 265, 268–70
  certificates 247, 269
  clauses 63, 263, 268–70
Finland 38, 41, 56, 62, 93, 122
fitness
  for ordinary use 110–46
    Art 35(2)(b) v Art 35(2)(a) 144
    case-by-case analysis 138–9
    changes to public law regulations and other related changes subsequent conformity assessment 140–2
    definition of ordinary use 119–25
    and description 125–6
    and durability 126–7
    health and safety 128–9
    informational asymmetry and guidelines in *New Zealand Mussels* 134–8
    and inquiry into notion of quality 111–12
    instructions, manuals and labels 129–32
    legal nature of public law regulations and reality of enforcement 142–3
    minor defects, appearance and finish 132–4
    proof 145–6
    public law regulations 134–44
    and quality level 111–19
    and quality tests 112–19
    servicing and spare parts 132
  for a particular purpose 53, 68–111, 139, 144, 153, 157, 235
    admissibility of evidence 105–9
    burden of proof 102–3
    climatic and other conditions 89–90
    conditions in a specific place 80–90
    definition of particular purpose 74–80
    and durability 90–2
    general considerations 70–2
    industry standards and standards adopted by private entities and trade associations 86–9
    legal nature of implied rules on conformity 68–70
    making particular purpose known 92–6
    proof 102–9
    public law regulations 80–6
    relationship with Art 35(1) CISG 72–4
    reliance on seller's skill and judgement 96–102
    standard of proof 103–5
FOB contracts 62–3, 198, 248, 250, 254
food products 38, 57, 65, 120, 123, 164
foodstuffs 51–2, 74–5, 78, 80, 95, 101, 120
formalistic interpretation 236
France 92–3, 121, 164–5, 169, 213, 225, 227
fraud 26–8, 179, 220, 258–9, 265, 268, 273
fraudulent misrepresentation 27
frivolous claims 140, 194, 215–17, 226
functionality 76, 133

general principles 4–5, 98, 103–4, 107, 160, 201, 228–30
Germany 37, 71–3, 88–90, 119–24, 187–9, 220–1, 262–3
good condition 40, 169
good faith 4, 32–3, 54–5, 66–7, 163, 179, 228–30

goods
conforming 9, 14, 16, 29–30, 45, 202
conformity 11, 13–14, 17–20, 22, 29, 49, 69; *see also* conformity
contract 43, 59, 90, 92, 264, 267–8, 271
damaged 169
dangerous 128, 141
delivered 30, 37, 46, 57, 118, 140, 161
high quality 12, 14, 50, 116, 139
manufactured 118–19, 134
non-conforming 14–16, 170–2, 257
substitute 124, 167, 195, 234–5
unidentified 6, 43, 173
guarantees 59–61, 90, 180–1, 236
implicit 61, 91
guidelines 20, 30, 32–3, 84–5, 134–5, 138, 163–4
general 87, 135, 159, 178, 203, 229

health 49, 69, 121, 128–9, 141, 192
hidden defects 60, 114, 158
high quality 34, 38, 50, 54, 57, 116, 119
goods/products 12, 14, 50, 116, 139
honesty 28, 32–3
human consumption 54–5
human health 55, 123
human life 128–9, 141
humidity 52, 165, 263

identification 43, 45
identity 45, 93, 95–6, 138, 242, 275
imperfect knowledge 63
implication 69, 72–3, 156, 158, 230, 251, 261
implicit agreement 42, 148, 203
implicit communication 71, 75, 93, 153
implicit consent 43, 219
implicit guarantees 61, 91
implicit intention 61, 66, 127, 265
implied consent 72
implied knowledge 3, 26, 174–9, 202, 219–20, 226–7
implied rules 68, 70–1, 95, 111, 135, 181
implied terms 72, 74, 132, 135, 171–2, 175, 181–2
implied warranties 177, 182, 184–5
import 37, 54–5, 58, 143, 163, 169, 192
licences 54–5, 245, 247
temporary 192–3
importing country 82–3, 85, 99, 134–6, 138, 143, 164
improper packaging 162, 169
incentives 12, 70, 95, 115, 159, 172, 188
INCOTERMS 240–2, 246, 248–50, 256–7, 260–1, 273
industrial property 9, 208, 210; *see also* intellectual property
industry standards 49, 81, 122, 138, 159
fitness for a particular purpose 86–9
information asymmetry 83, 134–9, 171–2
innocent misrepresentation 26
instruction manuals 90
instructions 101, 105, 129, 131, 163, 203, 230
insurance 11, 60–1, 172, 249–50
documents 246, 250, 262
policies 75, 246, 249, 253–4, 262
intangible property rights 210–11
intellectual property 6, 9, 20–1, 82, 136, 202
burden of proof 231–2
and buyer's knowledge 225–8
and compliance with buyer's specifications 228–31
exemptions from liability 225–31
industrial property as sub-category 210–13
rights/claims 213–22
frivolous claims 216–17
seller's knowledge 218–22
third party rights/claims arising from 208–36
intentions 2–3, 37–9, 56–8, 63–5, 148–52, 156–9, 267–70
common 56, 137
implicit 61, 66, 127, 265
mutual 67, 254
presumed 69, 171
international character 4, 18, 29, 113, 115–16, 210–11
international standards 54–5, 57, 143
interpretation 18, 166, 175, 181, 197–8, 206–7, 249–50
contracts 29–30, 56, 170–1, 251–2, 254, 268–9, 273–4
formalistic 236
invoices 190, 245, 262
commercial 245, 249–51, 254, 262–3
pro forma 245
'as is' clauses 173, 184–5
Italy 4, 86, 122–3, 146, 256

judicial creativity 179

knowledge 27, 91–4, 99–100, 164–6, 172–6, 221–3, 226
actual 75, 93, 173–4, 176, 219, 225
after-acquired 58, 141, 172
buyers 38–41, 170–5, 178, 216, 225–8
of destination 82, 136
implied 3, 26, 174–9, 202, 219–20, 226–7
imputed 172, 176–8, 227
presumed 202–3
sellers 27, 30, 73, 76, 82, 84–6, 218–19

labels 66, 129, 131, 156, 163, 182, 213
lack of conformity 11, 15, 81, 180, 184, 234
lading, bills of, *see* bills of lading
latent defects 101, 158
legal analysis 131, 143, 204, 248, 259
legal bases 45, 191, 193, 197, 200–1, 212–13, 231–2
legal certainty 13, 19, 103, 135, 142, 153, 273–4
legal consequences 27, 42, 44–5, 50, 189, 192, 238
legal creativity 20, 232–3
legal risks 142, 230
legal systems 23–4, 28–9, 160, 186–7, 189–90, 239–40, 243
legitimate expectations 163, 214
letters of credit 37, 42, 245–6, 248, 250, 253–5, 257
level of quality 111, 113, 115, 117
liability 9–12, 77–8, 170–9, 181–3, 191–2, 219–20, 225–9
  and Art 39 CISG 180
  and buyer's knowledge 170–9
  and disclaimers 181–5
  exemptions from 170–85
  potential 79, 83, 219–20
  sellers 13–16, 127, 209, 212–13, 215–17, 226, 235
licence agreements 226–7
licence contracts 226–7
licences, import 54–5, 245, 247
licensees 214, 226–7
licensors 214, 226–7
liens 190–1, 197

machines/machinery 40, 112, 119–20, 125–6, 128, 133, 177
manuals 42, 129–31, 223
  instruction 90
  product 42
  service 129
manufactured goods 118–19, 134
manufacturers 98, 101, 129–30, 153, 155, 221–2, 271–2
market prices 36, 115, 117–18, 123
markets 12, 14, 36, 80, 113–18, 123, 221
mate's receipts 65, 146, 244–5
merchantability 114, 117–18, 163, 182–3
  test 113–15, 118
minimalist structure 19–20
minor defects 111, 119, 131–3
misrepresentation 26–7, 32
  innocent 26
  negligent 26
mobile units 53–4, 73, 81, 84–5
models 5, 7, 9, 94, 100, 173, 178
  conformity with, *see* conformity, with sample or model
Mozambique 54–7, 143
mutual intention 67, 254

named consignees 241, 243, 261
named ports 61–2, 246
natural meaning 174, 185, 214–15
necessary specifications 94, 105
negative reliance 157
negligent misrepresentation 26
negotiability 240–1
negotiable bills of lading 248–9, 253
Netherlands, the 53–5, 69, 73–4, 78–9, 135, 143, 186
neutral third party 267–8
non-compliance 83, 87–9, 98–100, 135–7, 144, 153–5, 164; *see also* compliance
non-conforming documents 237, 264
non-conforming goods 14–16, 170–2, 257
non-conforming packaging 168–9
non-conformity 12–13, 61–3, 103–4, 119, 127, 169–70, 179; *see also* conformity; lack of conformity
  post-risk 60
  risk of 13, 83
non-delivery 44–5, 201, 225, 253, 263; *see also* delivery
normal expectations 121, 246, 251
normal purposes 76, 80, 111, 122
Norway 78
notification requirements 180, 234

opinions and puffery 31–5
orders, delivery 243–4, 251–3
ordinary purposes 79–80, 111–12, 116–17, 119–25, 128, 131–2, 157–8; *see also* ordinary use
  test 90, 114, 119, 235
ordinary use 235
  definition 119–25
  fitness for, *see* fitness, for ordinary use
origin 41–2, 49–50, 253–4, 262–3, 265, 267, 269–71
    certificates of 41, 245, 250, 262
    place of 46, 49, 262
ought to have known standard 174, 219
owners 189, 193, 198, 216, 226

packaging 45–6, 64–7, 147–8, 150, 152, 154, 160–70
  adequate manner 164–8
  defective 162, 167–8
  improper 162, 169
  non-conforming 168–9

obligations/requirements 60, 65, 67, 161, 164, 167, 169
proof 168–70
purpose 66, 162, 167–8
usual manner 162–5
particular purpose
definition 74–80
fitness for a, *see* fitness, for a particular purpose
making known 92–6
party autonomy 2, 4, 9, 29, 266, 268–9, 274
passage of risk 7, 43, 59–60, 62, 127, 140–2, 145
past transactions 88–9, 94, 177
patents 100, 208–11, 214, 216–17, 222
payment 189–90, 199, 203, 245–7, 252–3, 255, 257
withholding of 252–3
perfection 40, 118–19
performance 5, 7, 9–10, 67, 69–70, 112, 165–6
documentary 21–2, 238, 247, 272, 274
personality rights 212–13
physical obligations 247–8
phyto-sanitary health 246
place of origin 46, 49, 262
policies, insurance 75, 246, 249, 253–4, 262
ports 190, 198, 201, 244
destination 165, 270
named 61–2, 246
possession 186–7, 190–1, 199, 201, 239, 245–6, 251–3
quiet 198
post-contractual conduct 41
post-contractual representations 32–3
post-contractual statements and conduct 30, 41–3
potassium bromate 54–7, 143
pre-contractual examination 39, 176
pre-contractual representations and conduct 27, 31–41
buyer's knowledge 38–41
direct communications between parties 37–8
public statements 35–7
puffery and opinions 31–5
pre-shipment approval 55
preconditions 23, 72–3, 102, 104, 228, 231–2, 235
presumed knowledge 202–3
prices 5–7, 16, 36, 113–15, 117–18, 189–90, 245
contract 16, 65, 113, 117, 123, 132–3, 162
market 36, 115, 117–18, 123
reduced 16, 113–14
pro forma invoices 245
product manuals 42
promises 13–14, 29, 32, 100, 163, 181
proof 22–3, 102–7, 109, 145, 148, 170, 231–3
burden of, *see* burden of proof
conformity with sample or model 159–60
fitness for a particular purpose 102–9
fitness for ordinary use 145–6
packaging 168–70
standard of, *see* standard of proof
property 2, 6, 186–7, 189, 196, 240, 242
industrial, *see* industrial property
intellectual, *see* intellectual property
rights 21, 208, 210
intangible 210–11
transfer of 186–7, 189, 196–7, 200, 205, 240
public law regulations 74, 86–9, 99, 164, 192
Art 35(2)(b) v Art 35(2)(a) 144
conformity with sample or model 158–9
fitness for a particular purpose 80–6
fitness for ordinary use 134–44
public representations 35, 37, 122
public statements, pre-contractual 35–7
puffery and opinions 31–5

quality 8–10, 12–14, 49–69, 122–3, 171–3, 181–5, 263–72
certificates 62–3, 146, 246, 254, 263, 271–2
control 11, 95, 119
definition 49–50
and fitness for ordinary use 111–19
formulations of quality standards 50–2
guarantee and durability 59–64
industry or public law standards 52–7
inquiry into notion of 111–12
legislative changes and/or knowledge acquired subsequent to contract 57–9
low 12, 116–17
minimum benchmark 11, 151
quantity and packaging 64–6
reasonable 113–14, 116, 118–19, 122, 133
standards 50–2, 55, 57, 59, 69, 117, 139
tests 112–19, 142
quantity 5, 64–5, 239–40, 244–6, 259–60, 263–5, 269–71
contract 260, 271
quay receipts 251
quiet possession 198

reasonable examination 154–5, 158
reasonable expectations 26, 29, 39, 143, 150, 173–4, 177
reasonable person 3, 35–6, 138–9, 175, 250–1, 260–1, 273
reasonable quality 113–14, 116, 118–19, 122, 133
reasonable reliance 5, 72, 99–102, 144
reasonable time 16, 44, 64, 180, 186, 204, 258
reasonableness 5, 64, 96, 113, 176, 230, 232
receipt function 239–40, 245, 257, 259
receipts 40, 174, 239, 242–5
  mate's 65, 146, 244–5
  quay 251
  warehouse 244, 252–3
redirection 166, 242–3, 267
redispatch 166, 267
reduced prices 16, 113–14
refrigeration 167–70
registration 100, 222, 224
relevant evidence 102, 107, 180, 231, 251
relevant expertise 95, 97–8, 232
relevant time 89, 91, 141, 145, 165, 204, 224
  intellectual property 218
  third party rights/claims 196–8, 218
reliance 29, 36–7, 49, 72, 82, 88–9, 96–102
  actual 96
  buyers 37, 39, 70–1, 76, 86, 92, 101
  defence 73, 97
  negative 157
  partial 101
  presumption of 82, 98
  reasonable 5, 72, 99–102, 144
  on seller's skill and judgement 96–102
remedies 6–7, 13–14, 25–8, 215, 225, 230–1, 234–6
  buyers 14–15, 185, 235, 237
  domestic law 25–8
repair 7, 15, 104, 132, 173, 180, 235
replacement 7, 129, 173
representations 26–7, 31–7, 39, 42, 149, 156, 163
  post-contractual 32–3
  pre-contractual 27, 31–3
  public 35, 37, 122
  sellers 26, 34–5, 38–40
resale 113–15, 117–18, 120, 123, 235, 260–1, 263–4
resaleability 120, 123, 140
responsibilities 138, 141–2, 144, 179, 188, 190, 198
  allocation 144, 166
  allocation of 144, 166
  buyers 54, 196
restrictions, territorial 222–5, 235
risk 57–64, 126–7, 136–7, 140–2, 161–2, 195–8, 260–2
  allocation of 29, 37, 55, 128, 131, 150, 170
  assumption of 71, 75, 95, 219, 235
  commercial 13, 252
  legal 142, 230
  passage of 7, 43, 59–60, 62, 127, 140–2, 145
rule and exception principle 102–3, 168

safety 49, 52, 55, 69, 76, 123, 128
  measures 128–9
  regulations 72, 75
sale 97, 121–3, 151–3, 163–5, 206–7, 224–5, 250–1
  contracts of, *see* sales contracts
  by sample 151
saleability 114, 120
sales contracts 1–2, 6, 11–13, 161, 245–6, 250–1, 255–7
samples 42, 48, 79, 162, 172–4, 176, 178
  conformity with, *see* conformity, with sample or model
satisfactory quality 117, 125, 142
sea waybills 242, 248
security 62, 70, 190, 237, 253, 260, 263
security interests 189–90, 193
sellers 29–48, 53–68, 70–105, 120–33, 159–84, 186–205, 213–33
  CIF 190, 246, 248, 256, 258, 262
  compliance 98, 228, 232, 246
  conduct 55, 105, 179, 191, 207
  country 56–7, 81, 83, 134–5, 137, 139–40, 224
  documentary duties/obligations 10, 63, 238, 248, 251, 253–5, 272–5
  knowledge 27, 30, 73, 76, 82, 84–6, 219
    intellectual property 218–22
  liability 13–16, 127, 209, 212–13, 215–17, 226, 235
  representations 26, 34–5, 38–40
  rights/claims 200–1
  skill and judgement 70, 82, 84, 96–9, 101, 104, 157
  statements 33–4, 54, 165
  suppliers 78, 180, 193–4, 226
service manuals 129
servicing 132
shipment 62–4, 198–9, 240–1, 244–6, 250, 256, 266
  contracts 61, 63–4, 240, 246, 251, 260
shipping documents 190, 245

silence, contractual 66, 95, 252, 257–62, 273
skill and judgement, sellers 70, 82, 84, 96–9, 101, 104, 157
software 119–20, 133
Spain 37, 40, 73–4, 94–5, 98, 173, 178
spare parts 132, 256
special circumstances 83–4, 135–9, 164
special risks 262
special standards 53–4
specifications 20, 41–3, 51, 80, 94, 101, 228–9
buyers 29, 70, 93–4, 98, 101, 105, 228–32
necessary 94, 105
technical 35, 40, 74, 147
standard of proof 23, 104–6
fitness for a particular purpose 103–5
standards 52–3, 86–9, 117, 132, 134, 159, 162–4
applicable 52, 86, 139
conformity 46, 58, 257
industry 49, 81, 86, 88, 122, 138, 159
international 54–5, 57, 143
quality 50, 50–2, 55, 57, 59, 69, 117
special 53–4
state, actual 3, 39, 62, 118, 170, 259
statements
post-contractual 30, 41
pre-contractual 31
public 35–7
sellers 33–4, 54, 165
strong evidence 64, 131, 143, 265, 269
sub-sales 16, 168, 263–4
subject matter 12–13, 33, 48, 156, 161, 199, 202
subsequent conduct 3, 166, 255
substantive law 23–4, 105–6, 108
substitute goods 124, 167, 195, 234–5
delivery 15, 124, 234
suppliers 35, 43, 78, 119, 122, 189, 193–4
sellers 78, 180, 193–4, 226
Switzerland 15, 55, 75–6, 90, 133–4, 152, 248
symbolic delivery 250

technical specifications 35, 40, 74, 147
temporary import 192–3
terms
contractual 32, 34, 37, 57, 72, 74, 139
express 269, 274
implied 72, 74, 132, 135, 171–2, 175, 181–2
trade 61–2, 198, 248–51, 254, 256–7, 260, 262
territorial restrictions 235
intellectual property 222–5
third parties 6, 9, 19–22, 82, 99, 136, 267–9
neutral 267–8
rights/claims 9, 186–236
arising from intellectual property, *see* intellectual property
burden of proof 231–2
and buyer's agreement 202–4
and buyer's knowledge 225–8
and buyer's notice 204–5
claims 193–6
domestic rules on validity 206–7
and exclusion clauses 205–6
exemptions 202–6, 225–31
freedom from as aspect of conformity 234–6
freedom of goods from 198–200
and relevant time 196–8, 218
rights 189–93
and seller's knowledge 218–22
and seller's rights/claims 200–1
time
of contract 91, 174
of delivery 59, 196–7, 204, 218–19
relevant 89, 91, 141, 145, 196–8, 204, 218
time-frames 75, 117, 247, 265
title 125–6, 187, 189, 200, 205, 208, 265
documents of 239, 242–4, 260
warranty of 205–6
tort 12, 27–8, 207, 211
trade terms 61–2, 198, 248–51, 254, 256–7, 260, 262
trade usages 88, 94, 144, 151, 249, 257, 261
tradeability 140–1
trademarks 100, 208–11, 213, 216–17, 221, 227–8, 271
traders 17, 35, 40, 99, 122–3, 143, 249–50
transaction costs 1, 11, 69, 83
transactions, past 88–9, 94, 177
transfer of property 186–7, 189, 196–7, 200, 205, 240
transhipment 241, 261
transit 59–60, 225, 237, 241–2, 246–7, 249–50, 260–1
countries 224–5
transport 58, 62, 65, 91–2, 123, 161–2, 261
documents 65, 238–44, 248, 250, 264, 273
contractual requirements 255–7
contractual silence 257–62
typing errors 258

unclean bills of lading 260–1
unfair competition 210–11

unfounded claims 194–5
unidentified goods 6, 43, 173
uniformity of application 4, 17–18, 21–2,
  103–4, 107, 182–3, 210–11
usual manner 162–5

validity 2, 22, 25, 181–3, 205–7, 226, 270–1
value 16, 36, 61, 133–5, 165, 167–8, 187
  ethical 49, 87
  evidentiary 260, 264, 267, 270–1

warehouse receipts 244, 252–3
warranties 12–13, 32, 37, 112, 115,
  181–3, 185
  implied 177, 182, 184–5
  of title 205–6
waybills 242–3, 251, 253, 260
  air 242, 252, 256, 260
  sea 242, 248
weight certificates 65, 266
workmanship 53, 121

www.ingramcontent.com/pod-product-compliance
Ingram Content Group UK Ltd.
Pitfield, Milton Keynes, MK11 3LW, UK
UKHW020241290926
15470UKWH00002B/668

9 781849 461559